Cold War Deceptions

David H. Price

COLD WAR DECEPTIONS

The Asia Foundation and the CIA

University of Washington Press / Seattle

Cold War Deceptions was made possible in part by a grant
from the Donald R. Ellegood International Publications Endowment.

Copyright © 2024 by the University of Washington Press
Design by Mindy Basinger Hill
Composed in Minion Pro

All rights reserved. No part of this publication may be
reproduced or transmitted in any form or by any means,
electronic or mechanical, including photocopy, recording,
or any information storage or retrieval system, without
permission in writing from the publisher.

UNIVERSITY OF WASHINGTON PRESS   uwapress.uw.edu

LIBRARY OF CONGRESS CATALOGING-IN-PUBLICATION DATA

Names: Price, David H., 1960– author.

Title: Cold war deceptions : the Asia Foundation and the CIA / David H. Price.

Description: Seattle : University of Washington Press, [2024] | Includes bibliographical references and index.

Identifiers: LCCN 2023037535 | ISBN 9780295752235 (hardcover) | ISBN 9780295752242 (paperback) | ISBN 9780295752259 (ebook)

Subjects: LCSH: United States. Central Intelligence Agency | Asia Foundation. | Espionage, American—Asia. | Anti-communist movements—United States. | Anti-communist movements—Asia. | Propaganda, American—Asia. | United States—Foreign relations—Asia. | Asia—Foreign relations—United States. | Cold War.

Classification: LCC JK468.I6.P7445 2024 | DDC 372.5073009—dc23/eng/20231107

LC record available at https://lccn.loc.gov/2023037535

∞ This paper meets the requirements of ANSI/NISO Z39.48-1992 (Permanence of Paper).

FOR ALL THE PEOPLE FUNDED BY THE CIA'S DTPILLAR PROGRAM WHO WOULD NOT HAVE ACCEPTED THE MONEY HAD THEY KNOWN THE SOURCE OF THESE FUNDS

Contents

Preface *ix*
Acknowledgments *xv*
List of Abbreviations *xvii*

1   Funding Fronts and the Roots of the Committee for Free Asia   *1*
2   The Birth of the Asia Foundation   *24*
3   Sponsored Exchanges, Cultural Programs, Conferences, and Scholarships   *46*
4   How the CIA Tried to Make Friends and Influence People   *66*
5   Collecting Intelligence   *86*
6   Foundation Anticommunism and Counterinsurgency Programs   *108*
7   Interactions with Other Organizations and Foundations   *126*
8   Books and Movies as CIA-Funded Propaganda   *147*
9   Asia Foundation Reports as Active and Passive Intelligence   *167*
10 Suspicions   *191*
11 Exposed CIA Fronts and the Fate of CIA Orphans   *212*
12 The CIA's 1967 Termination and Liquidation of DTPILLAR   *232*
13 Conclusions, Implications, and Continuities during the Remaining Cold War Years   *255*

Notes   *275*
Bibliography   *319*
Index   *327*

Preface

> We can see the Cold War as the global circumstances under which the vast majority of the world's countries moved from direct colonial rule to something else, to a new place in a new global system.
> **VINCENT BEVINS** / *The Jakarta Method*

This book examines how a foundation, secretly founded and funded by the CIA, tried to shape Asian political, economic, intellectual, and cultural developments during the early Cold War. Fragmented awareness and memories of these events exist in small academic corners, and some of these events have been documented and explored by scholars and journalists. Mostly, however, this story was inadequately explored when these CIA links were first disclosed and then these connections were largely forgotten before anyone outside the foundation and CIA understood what had happened. The important parts of this story can't be remembered because the CIA never wanted anyone to know what happened. The Asia Foundation's long-ago receipt of CIA funds has been known for over half a century, yet there remains little serious exploration of how deep the CIA's ties to the foundation were, from its founding until 1967, when some CIA connections were revealed. There has been even less consideration of what these connections tell us about things like the development of postcolonial Asian states and the foundation's curation of knowledge production. This book unpacks details of this forgotten and unknown history as it considers these and other questions.

What was first publicly revealed about some of the Asia Foundation's CIA links is easily summarized. In March 1967, following a month of press revelations about the CIA's secret funding of various organizations and foundations, the *New York Times* ran a story under the headline "Asia Foundation Got CIA Funds: Trustees Deny Influence—Bar Future Hidden Aid." The story had no information on the size or duration of these CIA funds, although the wording of the foundation board's statement of response suggested that, like other recently exposed organizations, it had only received a small amount of CIA funding.[1]

This story broke in a period when investigative journalists were starting to publish dozens of stories revealing that labor unions, judicial organizations, publishers, and various educational and cultural organizations had wittingly or unwittingly received CIA funds passed through a labyrinth of front organizations that hid the source of these funds. This bonanza of revelations about CIA fronts grew from the publication of a story in the February 1967 issue of *Ramparts* magazine, a story that revealed the CIA as the primary (and secret) funder of the National Student Association for over a decade. These revelations disturbed many Americans in ways that are difficult to appreciate today. Although the CIA tried to stop the publication of this *Ramparts* article, its publication spawned an avalanche of stories exposing secret CIA funding projects targeting both Americans and people in other countries.

Surprisingly, there was no substantial journalistic follow-up to the *New York Times* story revealing the Asia Foundation's receipt of CIA funds. Without answers to simple questions about how much money the CIA had given the foundation or for how long, the public was left to assume that the foundation had received only a small amount of CIA funds for a few projects that overlapped with agency goals. But had any journalists done something as simple as demanding a list of foundation donors or an overview of its budget and tax records, or dug just a little beneath the lies of the foundation board's press release, they would have learned that the foundation was not a private one that only occasionally received CIA funds: it was actually (to quote a 1966 government document) "a Central Intelligence Agency proprietary" that existed only because of its "total dependence upon covert funding support from this Agency."[2] Until late 1967, the Asia Foundation operated under the CIA codename DTPILLAR. Its March 1967 exposure by the *New York Times* led the CIA to sever ties with the foundation—after providing it with several million dollars in untraceable "surge funding" to help it survive one more year as it became what was privately referred to in Washington circles, as a "CIA orphan."

During the 1960s and 1970s, investigative journalists and congressional inquiries exposed dozens of CIA funding fronts, conduits, and pass-throughs. While scholarly research on CIA infiltration of academic, artistic, and intellectual domains during the 1950s and 1960s has produced important work by authors such as Frances Stoner Saunders, Hugh Wilford, Karen M. Paget, and Joel Whitney, most of these studies focus more on the projects funded than on the workings of the individual CIA fronts sponsoring this work.[3] This focus has in part been due to the scarcity of surviving records from known CIA fronts. While published research on CIA fronts reveals how the agency influenced the production of knowledge, art, and critique, focusing primarily on those receiving these funds leaves gaps in our understanding of how CIA fronts functioned on a day-to-day basis.

When I began researching this project in 2013, I had no idea where these inquiries would lead me, though the basics of these relationships were clear to me after reading the CIA's released DTPILLAR documents in 2015.[4] During the last decade, a body of important scholarly and journalistic work emerged and began exploring elements of the Committee for Free Asia and the Asia Foundation's CIA ties. These include works on committee- and foundation-backed movies, publishing, Buddhist movements, democracy programs, and journalistic coverage of important CIA documents released under the Freedom of Information Act.[5]

This book's focus on the surviving released records of a one-time funding front, created by the CIA, provides a rare view into the bureaucratic functioning of a Cold War covert operation in which more than half the US employees knew they were working for the CIA. This study relies on a wealth of archival sources and documents released under the Freedom of Information Act (FOIA) to explain how these operations worked. These documents reveal a foundation at once unique in its secret relationship with the CIA yet remarkably similar to the functioning of mainstream non-CIA linked foundations, a finding perhaps more disturbing than reassuring for what it indicates about how closely aligned to CIA desires were the activities of completely independent foundations.

I am not a scholar of Asia. I came to write this book through a series of accidents—none of which would have occurred if I had not spent two decades researching CIA and FBI interactions with anthropologists and other scholars, an effort that familiarized me with many of the names of individuals and foundations that would later catch my eye when looking through Asia Foundation records. I inadvertently came to undertake this project in the winter of 2013, when, after presenting an invited talk at Yale University, I spent a couple of days working on some of Yale's archival collections, including deposited papers of Asia Foundation president Robert Blum. Blum's papers included several boxes of foundation documents.

What I found in Blum's archived papers, during that trip and subsequent ones, was remarkable. These papers included Blum's confidential reports to the foundation's board reporting on his extensive travels in Asia and his meetings with Asian academics and political leaders (see chapter 9). Some reports contained detailed political analysis of the sort the CIA would have been institutionally negligent not to include in agency intelligence reports—information from closed-door meetings with national leaders, dissidents, members of the local news media, intellectuals, informed expats, or members of foreign embassy staff commenting on important political developments. I found folders with glossy eight-by-ten black-and-white photographs from embassy parties, sometimes carefully labeled to mark the names of those in the photographs. These confidential board reports frequently contained remarkable insights of political analysis mixed with the mundane bureaucratic business of running the foundation.

Like any archival collection, the papers in Blum's manuscript holdings did not contain all his correspondence and reports, but for a relatively small collection of papers (2.25 linear feet), I found a significant number of reports and correspondence from Blum's years as Asia Foundation president.[6] Blum's Yale papers contain an invaluable collection of his confidential board reports—reports that are mostly missing from the foundation's papers deposited at the Hoover Institution.

The second source of documents I examined to understand how the foundation interfaced with the CIA was a limited collection of over a thousand pages of CIA documents released under FOIA. These documents confirm the CIA's code name for the Asia Foundation was DTPILLAR and provide a paper trail documenting the mundane bureaucracy of ongoing CIA involvement in the foundation's operations and the high value the agency placed on those operations.

The third source of documents on the foundation's CIA years is a large collection of records that the foundation deposited at the Hoover Institution on the campus of Stanford University. This collection now totals over 512 linear feet and represents the largest publicly available assemblage of documents on any known CIA front.[7] These documents provide invaluable information on the internal workings of the foundation and reveal crucial internal dialogues occurring as dual-use policies were developed and implemented. Even with this large collection of official foundation documents from the 1951–67 CIA-linked period, significant items are missing—documents that were either destroyed, never filed with the foundation's main records, or remain with the foundation. Between the summer of 2016 and the closing of the archive (as a new building to house the archive was being constructed, followed by restrictions due to the COVID pandemic) in December 2018, I made six visits to the archive to work through relevant portions of this large collection. With generous financial assistance from the Hoover Institution, during a year-long sabbatical in 2017–18 provided by my university, I worked through and photographed significant portions of this collection, gaining understanding of the programs and the operations of the foundation during the period from its founding until 1967, when its CIA connections ended.

This book draws heavily on over a hundred thousand pages of documents I consulted at the Hoover Institution, thousands of pages of declassified CIA documents, a wealth of documents from other archival holdings, and the knowledge of CIA academic operations I had acquired since the early 1990s by studying interactions between academics and the CIA. The bulk of the materials in the foundation's archival holdings are records showing its normal day-to-day work. These records confirm that much of that work mirrored the efforts of other nongovernmental foundations supporting international education, economic development, democracy, and cultural projects. The records stored at Hoover frequently show mundane activities undertaken by office workers: working out the details of a foreign student seeking to study rural sociology at an American college, reconciling budget needs, requesting office supplies, tracking book-buying records for Asian libraries, reconciling invoices, and so on, but these records also document sub-rosa political projects seeking to shape specific Asian political theaters. And whether mundane or not, these records raise serious questions about the CIA-directed hegemonic outcomes the foundation was charged to support. And as I argue in this book, these efforts to shape Asian political developments must be seen as not just some kindly attempt at gentle persuasion but as part of the CIA's larger political project during this era, with goals that included violent interventions that undermined local Asian political movements not to the CIA's liking.

While most of the foundation's CIA-funded programs occurred abroad, prior to March 1967 the foundation also relied on its public image as a benevolent, politically neutral organization to undertake various domestic political functions. These functions included things like hosting visiting Asian political leaders, an activity providing foundation personnel with access to these leaders. One example of such activities occurred in June 1965, when, in cooperation with the World Affairs Council, the foundation cohosted a San Francisco speech by Indonesia's President Sukarno in which he claimed to support democracy and equality while calling for support of rapid economic development.[8]

It is an axiom of political life that the documents people need to hold accountable the powerful forces governing or suppressing them are usually hidden from public view during the period this information could be used to confront powerful actors. There are notable exceptions to these arrangements, usually involving leaks or bungling incompetence. Such episodes include Daniel Ellsberg's leaking of the Pentagon Papers, Seymour Hersh's revelations about the CIA's Family Jewels report and other programs, such as Operation CHAOS, or Christopher Pyle's 1970 disclosures of military spying on US antiwar protesters—leaks that spawned public outrage and fed movements resulting in demonstrable political change. Such timely revelations of powerful elite covert activities are rare historical anomalies. If such documents ever become available for public inspection, it is most often decades later, when those whose actions are revealed have long left the scene and the passage of time has provided institutional alibis for collective identities and allowed academic apologists to shrug dismissively and say "so what?" But I argue it is vital that we, the later-day recipients of these documents, do not simply consign the political significance of historical revelations to the dustbins of history. The analysis of these records over half a century later reveals links connecting this past to the present, and if we analyze recurrent power relations—focusing on how foundations and governmental agencies recurrently organize and focus academic inquiries and propagations—then this half-century-old news has political uses in our political present.

Finally, while this book focuses on the CIA's directive roles in the operation of the Committee for Free Asia and the Asia Foundation between 1951 and late 1967, the Asia Foundation continues to exist. Everything I know indicates the foundation stopped receiving funding from, ended all direct contact with, and being directed by, the CIA in late 1967. When it severed these CIA relationships, the foundation agreed to continue its original "soft-power" US-boosting mission, and during the remaining Cold War years it continued to run cultural and educational programs strengthening US relationships with Asia, while ending covert activities and switching funding streams from a reliance on the CIA to the State Department and other sources.

This book's focus on inevitable links between foundations and governmental agendas has lessons for us today, in an era presumably without covert CIA funding of foundations and international educational programs. As the final chapter argues, perhaps the most significant lesson to be learned from the Asia Foundation's history is that without CIA funding or contacts after 1967, much of the foundation's Cold War mission remained on the same trajectory of its earlier years but with different funding. The meaning of this observation remains as contested as the CIA's role in democracy itself.

Acknowledgments

Because of the inevitable difficulties in securing foundation funds for a project critiquing funding foundations, it is important to acknowledge that significant segments of this research were accomplished by adding archival visits to speaking engagements and by accepting the generosity of many individuals. Erik Harms and Hal Conklin kindly invited me in 2013 to give a talk at Yale's Council on Southeast Asia Studies Seminar Series, a trip that led me to discover the rich cache of Asia Foundation documents in the Robert Blum Papers in Yale's archives. Chris Hebdon's assistance with housing helped make a follow-up research trip to Yale possible. Work in the archives of both the Ford Foundation and Rockefeller Foundation in March 2017 was made possible by funds received for a public talk I gave at Hartwick College, at Michael Woost's kind invitation. In early 2017 I presented a talk to the New York Academy of Sciences on my preliminary findings on DTPILLAR documents, which helped me formulate this critique, and I also used this trip for archival research. A 2018 trip to present a campus talk sponsored by the faculty union at CUNY's Baruch College, where concerned members were trying to get CIA recruiters kicked off campus, allowed further archival work and was made possible by anthropologist Glenn Petersen welcoming me into his home. A 2019 talk to the Smithsonian's Department of Anthropology, at the invitation of Joshua Bell, allowed for some significant archival research. Much of the archival work for this project was completed in 2017–18, during a sabbatical in part granted by university administrators hoping to get rid of me and a few other scholars after a lengthy labor union battle on campus was quashed by conservative anti-union forces. My dear friends David Patton and Cathy Wilson hosted me in their home during several archival trips to Washington, DC. As with many of my past projects, this one would not have been possible without their kindness, friendship, and listening.

Archivists at the Hoover Institution Library and Archives helped direct me toward key archival resources, and Hoover provided generous funds to help support several research trips. Eric Wakin, deputy director of the Hoover Institution and director of the institution's library and archives, as well as archive staff Sarah Patton and David H. Sun, provided significant assistance to me. I gratefully acknowledge the Hoover Institution Library and Archives as an essential resource in the development of these materials. Obviously, the views expressed here are entirely my own and do not reflect the views of the fellows, staff, or Board of Overseers of the Hoover Institution.

During the early part of the COVID-19 pandemic, the ruminations for this book were far more internal than for past books. Exceptions to this were backyard fireside sessions over beer with Steve Niva, who patiently listened to me ramble about loose ends and dangling analysis, and ongoing conversations with Aaron Goings, who read and commented on an early draft of the manuscript. Correspondence with Mike Seltzer aided me with my analytical focus. Sylvia Martin helped me broaden my understanding and critique of the foundation's Hong Kong media ventures, and three anonymous peer reviews offered valuable critiques of an early version of the manuscript. Among the many others who helped me with elements of thinking about what became this project were Thomas Anson, Jeff Birkenstein, Dale Depweg, Kerim Friedman, Irina Gendelman, Roberto González, Gustaaf Houtman, Stephen X. Mead, Laura Nader, the National Writers Union, Bill Peace, Jack Price, Lisa Queen, Eric Ross, and Jeff St. Clair. As always, my wife, Midge, patiently listened to my ever-changing ongoing reports of this research, from its earliest sketches to the final manuscript, and helped me piece this complicated picture together. I left another fine academic press after it refused to recognize its workers' unionization efforts and am happy to publish this work at the University of Washington Press, where employees are represented by SEIU 925. I am grateful for the support and thoughtful advice I have received there from my editor, Lorri Hagman, and would like to acknowledge Maureen Bemko's excellent copyediting, as well as the assistance of Joeth Zucco, Marcella Landri, David Schlangen, Molly Woolbright, and Benny Sisson.

Abbreviations

AAA	American Anthropological Association
AID	Agency for International Development
AFL	American Federation of Labor
AFME	American Friends of the Middle East
AFV	American Friends of Vietnam
ARPA	Advanced Research Projects Agency
ASA	Associated Students of Afghanistan
CA	Covert Action (CIA abbreviation for Covert Action staff)
CARE	Cooperative for American Remittances to Europe/Cooperative for American Relief Everywhere
CFA	Committee for Free Asia (1951–53)
CIA	Central Intelligence Agency
CIG	Central Intelligence Group
CIO	Congress of Industrial Organizations
COS	chief of station (CIA)
CS	Clandestine Services (CIA)
CU	Bureau of Educational and Cultural Relations, State Department
DOP	Directorate of Plans (CIA's Clandestine Service, 1951–73)
DTPILLAR	CIA code name for Committee for Free Asia and Asia Foundation operations (1951–67)
ESA	Economic Stabilization Agency
EWA	Education and World Affairs
FBI	Federal Bureau of Investigation
FFA	Fund for Asia
FOA	Foreign Operations Administration (1953–55)
HRAF	Human Relations Area Files
ICA	International Cooperation Agency (1951–61)
ICFTU	International Confederation of Free Trade Unions
ILO	International Labor Organization
IIA	International Information Administration
IIE	Institute of International Education
IO	International Organizations Division, CIA

IVS	International Voluntary Service (UK)
MSA	Mutual Security Agency (1951–53; became Mutual Security Administration in 1953)
NATC	New Asia Trading Company
NCFEP	National Committee for a Free Europe
NLF	National Liberation Front (Vietnamese; sometimes referred to in Western media by the pejorative term "Viet Cong")
NRC	National Research Council
NSA	National Student Association
ONE	Office of National Estimates (1950–73)
OO	operations officer (CIA)
OPC	Office of Policy Coordination
OSO	Office of Special Operations (CIA, 1946–52, then under Directorate of Plans)
OWI	Office of War Information
PPB	Plans, Programming, and Budget (CIA)
PKI	Communist Party of Indonesia
TAF	The Asia Foundation
TCA	Technical Cooperation Administration (1950–54)
USIA	United States Information Agency
USIS	United States Information Service
VOA	Voice of America
WFB	World Fellowship of Buddhists
WFDY	World Federation of Democratic Youth

Cold War Deceptions

1 Funding Fronts and the Roots of the Committee for Free Asia

CFA [Committee for Free Asia] is, of course, the creature of OPC [Office of Policy Coordination]/CIA and its missions, objectives and operations must be in consonance with the mission and objectives of OPC.

CIA DTPILLAR 1, 40 / September 28, 1951

With the passing of time, the people of the United States decreasingly appear to know much about the history of the Central Intelligence Agency. This loss of shared critical memory brings collective gaps in understanding why so many intellectuals came to distrust the agency during the late twentieth century. As the academics who came of age during the 1960s, 1970s, and 1980s fade from academia and a new generation of scholars socialized during the sprawling post-9/11 growth of intelligence agencies ascends, this lack of knowledge has increasingly serious consequences. This now forgotten institutional history includes episodes of US- and corporate-backed neocolonial military coups overthrowing democratically elected leaders in Iran (1953), Guatemala (1954), Congo (1960), the Dominican Republic (1961), South Vietnam (1963), Brazil (1964), and Chile (1973), as well as CIA assassination programs, kidnappings, drug running, systematic torture, drug experiments on unwitting civilians, and interference in foreign elections, press operations, and economies.[1] When documents establishing these CIA activities became public in the 1960s and 1970s, public outrage surged, leading to press investigations, presidential commissions, congressional hearings, and short-lived agency restrictions and congressional oversight. Among the CIA's secret activities that came to light during this period was the existence of American foundations that appeared to be private organizations but were secretly funded and directed by the CIA. While it might be tempting to view these front organizations as separate from the CIA's more violent efforts to maintain US global hegemony, such a compartmentalization of different CIA Cold War operations distorts understandings of how violent and nonviolent covert operations worked together as part of the agency's strategy to maintain US global dominance.

From the early 1950s to late 1960s, the CIA secretly used dozens of foundations to fund projects of interest to the agency. There were several variations on how these CIA-linked programs operated. Sometimes the CIA used organizations known as pass-throughs or conduits to channel CIA funds to frequently unwitting foundations or individual recipients undertaking projects of interest to the CIA. Most commonly, these pass-throughs were essentially paper entities with mailing addresses located in law offices, but sometimes they were legitimate foundations with knowledge of these CIA links. Funding fronts were foundations or businesses that appeared to be privately independent operations but were secretly financed and established or managed by the CIA.

The CIA used fronts to covertly fund projects for several reasons. In most instances the funding recipients, as well as those in communities impacted by these funds, were unaware of the funds' source, but other groups were also deceived. Among these were foreign intelligence organizations such as the KGB, political or intelligence entities in host nations, or US politicians, because the CIA, under orders by the executive branch, sometimes ran operations that the US Congress would likely not have willingly funded. The CIA's motivation to establish the Committee for Free Asia (code-named DTPILLAR) as a funding front was in part designed to deceive members of Congress who opposed such forms of international aid. DTPILLAR funded the types of foreign aid liberal anticommunist programs that conservative anticommunist members of the US House and Senate criticized and frequently refused to fund. Presidents from Harry Truman to Lyndon Johnson approved using this trickery to bypass congressional oversight, and such maneuvers are one of the ways that American presidents have historically pursued policy directives without congressional or public oversight.

The CIA used fronts to finance a range of activities. These included research projects, scholarships, cultural programs, literary magazines, book-buying programs, agricultural assistance programs, art commissions, and other soft-power programs designed to spread pro-American views in emerging economies and to undermine communist enemies—all while hiding US government funding. Favored projects advanced what the CIA understood to be the United States' global interests.[2]

With little notice, the first public disclosure that the CIA had secretly funded private foundations occurred during 1964 congressional hearings led by Representative Wright Patman (D-TX). His committee was investigating whether communists were using US nonprofit foundations to influence Americans.

While examining Internal Revenue Service (IRS) documents, his staff discovered reporting irregularities in the filings of several foundations. Patman's public inquiries into the Kaplan Fund's financial records forced Mitchell Rogovin, assistant to the IRS commissioner, to testify in an open session that the Kaplan Fund was a CIA front financing projects of interest to the agency. After the CIA refused to provide Patman's committee with further information on the CIA's use of front foundations, Patman publicly identified eight nonprofits that had secretly received CIA funds from the Kaplan Fund: the Gotham Foundation, the Michigan Fund, the Andrew Hamilton Fund, the Borden Trust, the Price Fund, the Edsel Fund, the Beacon Fund, and the Kentfield Fund.[3]

At the time, newspapers and the *Congressional Record* reported Patman's discovery, yet public interest and journalists' examination of the extent of the CIA's use of foundations was limited.[4] A 1964 *New York Times* editorial demanded that the CIA's use of foundations cease, arguing that the practice made it easy for "the Communists and the cynical everywhere to charge that American scholars, scientists, and writers going abroad on grants from foundations are cover agents or spies for C.I.A. All scholars—especially those involved in East-West exchanges—will suffer if the integrity of their research is thus made suspect."[5] Patman had revealed the basic structures of the CIA's use of pass-throughs and fronts, and while he identified several CIA-funded organizations, he failed to further investigate the extent of these activities. These fronts were not further examined until three years later, when investigative reporter Sol Stern published an exposé in *Ramparts* magazine.[6]

The *Ramparts* investigation began after National Student Association (NSA) insiders confided to Stern that the CIA was secretly funding the NSA. *Ramparts* discovered CIA money flowed through fronts to finance a range of cultural and academic enterprises. When the NSA had experienced financial difficulties in the past, the president of a "prominent New England foundation" had facilitated contact between NSA leaders and the CIA. This led to a secret agreement to channel "CIA money into the foundation without it ever being traced back to the CIA."[7] Later research established even deeper historical ties between the NSA and the CIA.[8] *Ramparts* revealed that the CIA had continued using many of the foundations identified by Representative Patman years earlier. Investigations of the IRS produced records showing that "two foundations were funneling money to 100 organizations. Much of the money moved through law firms that had one thing in common: a partner with connections to the OSS, the CIA's precursor."[9]

Stern's *Ramparts* article not only established how the CIA used third-party foundations to channel funds to the NSA but also identified several intermediary foundations receiving agency funds. When the CIA learned of the magazine's plan to publish the exposé, the agency attempted to preempt the *Ramparts* scoop by staging an NSA press conference in which staff would admit the connection and publicize claims that the NSA had severed all ties with the CIA. But NSA insiders alerted *Ramparts* of this plan, and the magazine immediately ran a full-page ad in the *New York Times* (on February 14, 1967) announcing that the NSA-CIA story would run in the next issue of *Ramparts*. This ad had the desired effect, stirring public outrage and congressional protests over this secret arrangement and neutralizing the CIA's damage control plan.

Stern's *Ramparts* article unleashed a flood of investigative exposés, as magazines and newspapers soon identified other CIA fronts and funded groups. The suddenness and scope of these articles raises questions about whether some reporters previously knew of or suspected these CIA connections but had been unwilling to publish their findings. Newspapers across the country ran articles listing dozens of groups receiving CIA funds.[10] The *New York Times*'s March 1967 report revealing that the Asia Foundation received CIA funds was one of these derivative articles following Stern's *Ramparts* article on the NSA.

These journalistic revelations about CIA funding fronts disturbed many Americans. The reports revealed CIA lies betraying basic public trust in, for example, the independence of foundations, the academic integrity of those funded by fronts, and the US government's favoring select democratic institutions at home and abroad. These journalistic investigations were the beginning of the end for most of these fronts, though a second wave of investigations provided greater depth of detail. Post-Watergate congressional inquiries brought even greater understanding of the fronts. Before examining how and why the CIA established the Committee for Free Asia, which later became the Asia Foundation, it is important to consider the institutional roots of the organizations within and outside of the CIA that conceived of using the foundation as an anticommunist Cold War weapon.

THE OFFICE OF POLICY COORDINATION (OPC) AND THE DIRECTORATE OF PLANS (DOP)

Although primarily a creature of the Cold War, the CIA grew directly out of the institutions, models, and experiences of the Second World War's Office of Strategic Services (OSS). As the final days of World War II approached, President

Truman planned the dismantlement of the OSS, the nation's most powerful international intelligence agency. During the war, the OSS had grown in power and importance in the Asian, European, and African theaters, and despite its impressive record of intelligence analysis and covert operations, Truman feared the growth and reach, in the international arena, of another powerful intelligence agency, one that might rival the FBI's control over national affairs. Less than two months after the war's end, Truman quickly dismantled the OSS, issuing Executive Order 9621 on October 1, 1945. This order discharged approximately 57 percent of the OSS's employees and relocated the remaining ones from the OSS Operations staff to the War Department's Strategic Services Unit. The remaining analysts from the OSS's Research and Analysis Branch relocated to the Department of State's Interim Research and Intelligence Service. Most of the OSS personnel relocated to the State Department or War Department came from OSS operations, with 9,028 individuals moving to the War Department and only 1,362 relocating to State.[11] Under this arrangement, State acquired OSS analysts while the War Department absorbed the OSS's field operatives.

Truman dismantled the OSS after the war because he recognized a danger to democracy created by an international intelligence agency that could become a law unto itself, but the Cold War's rapid development soon buried these concerns. Fear of communism, new global realignments, and rapid postwar developments supported arguments that the United States needed something like the OSS to collect and analyze intelligence, as well as to engage in the sort of covert operations that had helped the allies win the war. On July 26, 1947, President Truman signed the National Security Act, creating the CIA.

On June 18, 1948, eleven months after the CIA's creation, Truman signed National Security Council Directive 10/2, authorizing an unnamed governmental agency to undertake paramilitary actions, propaganda and guerrilla campaigns, and other covert activities under the executive branch's command. The new organization created on August 1, 1948, by NSC 10/2 became the Office of Policy Coordination (OPC), which, though staffed by CIA personnel, was bureaucratically under the Departments of State and Defense but directed by CIA personnel. This odd arrangement meant OPC had little oversight by State, Defense, or CIA. A declassified internal memo, "CIA Organizational History in Brief," explains that at its initial creation, the OPC

> had an anomalous relationship with the rest of the Agency, since the NSC ordered it to remain as independent of the remainder of CIA as

possible and placed it under the policy direction of the Departments of State and Defense. For OPC's first two years, policy guidance came directly from State and Defense, although the chain of command was through the Director of Central Intelligence. It was during this period, under OPC, that such activities as Radio Free Europe, the Committee for Free Asia, Radio Liberty, the Asia Foundation, and the youth, student, and labor programs of the Agency began.[12]

The CIA's Frank Wisner directed the OPC, and his exploits there made him a legendary figure in the agency's early years. A former New York lawyer, during the war Wisner was chief of OSS operations in southeastern Europe, where he first spied on the Soviet Union. When Truman shuttered the OSS, Wisner went to State, where "he and other OSS members tried to preserve OSS records and assets and they looked forward to a time when their services and talents might again be better used."[13]

This betwixt and between bureaucratic structure provided Wisner with the perfect environment in which to develop secret CIA operations with little oversight or accountability, and the OPC was where many early Cold War off-the-books CIA operations came to life. Under Wisner, the OPC became the CIA's "dirty tricks division," and "policy guidance thus completely bypassed the director of Central Intelligence."[14] The OPC was the agency's covert action arm, and its operations included assassination, economic warfare, sabotage, subversion of foreign states, establishing and assisting foreign underground resistance groups, smuggling, and assorted quasi-legal and illegal activities aimed at undermining global communism. Yet the implementation of these anticommunist goals frequently meant interfering with democratic movements abroad. During the early 1950s, the OPC received a significant portion of the CIA's operating budget, and Wisner's reliance on unconventional means and covert operations increased.[15]

In 1950, Wisner convinced Richard Bissell, a future CIA officer then at the Economic Cooperation Administration, to secretly channel Marshall Plan funds to his OPC covert operations in Europe.[16] This arrangement was characteristic of OPC's cavalier approach to acquiring covert funding lines for operations that had little external oversight. The OPC's initial operations were in Europe, staying out of Asia because General Douglas MacArthur, as Supreme Commander, kept tight control over US-Asian intelligence operations, generally not cooperating with civilian intelligence agencies. After Truman fired MacArthur in 1951, the OPC expanded into Asian operations.

After four years, the OPC's odd bureaucratic status—operating under the State Department but with CIA personnel undertaking off-the-books cloak-and-dagger operations—raised enough concerns within the CIA that the agency recommended that the OPC and Office of Special Operations be restructured, ending overlapping duties and bringing OPC operations directly under CIA control.[17] In August 1952, Director of Central Intelligence (DCI) Walter Bedell Smith officially moved the OPC under CIA command, merging the OPC with the CIA's Office of Special Operations (OSO).[18] Although this reorganization occurred in 1952, some overseas stations continued to report directly to the DCI through overseas senior representatives until 1954. Under the new and equally misleading name of the CIA's Directorate of Plans (aka the CIA's "Clandestine Service"), Wisner remained in charge of these operations, with Richard Helms (previously OSO's chief of operations) as his deputy director of plans. The Directorate of Plans oversaw the CIA's covert operations from 1951 to 1973, when it became known as the Directorate of Operations. This covert division of the CIA birthed and directed the Committee for Free Asia.

DTPILLAR AND ROOTS OF THE ASIA FOUNDATION

In early 1951, the CIA secretly authorized a program code-named DTPILLAR, which sought to "promote, aid and assist the cause of individual and national freedom in Asia, as opposed to Communist and other totalitarian doctrines."[19] DTPILLAR used CIA funds to create what appeared to be a nongovernmental organization to disseminate anticommunist propaganda in Asia. Early DTPILLAR documents described the new entity as designed to undertake radio broadcasting, publishing, as well as assisting noncommunists and nontotalitarian elements within communist countries and aiding anticommunist and nontotalitarian travelers, refugees, and exiles. To implement DTPILLAR operations, in 1951 the CIA established an organization known as the Committee for Free Asia (CFA).[20] In September 1954 it would be renamed (with a pompously capitalized definite article) The Asia Foundation (TAF). While the names "Committee for Free Asia" and "The Asia Foundation" publicly appeared to show two different organizations, the CIA referred to both the committee and the foundation with the code name DTPILLAR.

During DTPILLAR's sixteen years of operation, the CIA oversaw the hiring of seven different committee/foundation presidents. One measure of how chaotic CFA's years were is that four of these presidents served abbreviated terms during DTPILLAR's first three years. The CFA's first president was George H. Greene Jr. (March 1951–December 31, 1951), whose previous work as a CIA officer facilitated agency oversight of committee activities. Greene's presidency lasted only a few months, and he was replaced by Allen Valentine (January 1, 1952–September 1952). Valentine had previously worked at the State Department's Economic Stabilization Agency (ESA), and at CFA he planned to launch radio broadcasts throughout Asia. These plans were never realized during Valentine's nine months as CFA president.[21] He was replaced by an acting president, General Ray Maddocks, whose experience in China stretched back to the Second World War. Maddocks primarily worked to keep committee operations functioning until 1953, when Brayton Wilbur became committee president (1953–54). Wilbur was the cofounder of an Asian import-export brokerage and agricultural supply company. As committee president, he was a placeholder keeping the doors open while the board searched for a president who would bring needed, fundamental changes.

The most dramatic changes came to the Committee for Free Asia during its final months, after Robert Blum became president during the summer of 1954. Blum was hired to transform the operations of the shady Committee for Free Asia into the more respectable-appearing Asia Foundation. As president (1954–62), Blum shifted DTPILLAR operations away from funding bluntly obvious anticommunist propaganda campaigns to funding what appeared to be the sort of academic scholarship programs that *normal* foundations funded. Blum reinvented DTPILLAR as the less obviously suspicious Asia Foundation, a transformation that improved DTPILLAR's chances of achieving the CIA's anticommunist goals.

In 1962 Robert Blum retired, and former Bank of America vice president Russell G. Smith became president for two years (1962–64). Smith continued to build programs claiming to support democracy, education, and scientific programs throughout Asia. In 1964 Smith stepped down as president and chaired the foundation's board. The last foundation president during the foundation's CIA DTPILLAR years was Franklin Haydn Williams, who began his presidency in January 1964. Although he was president when the foundation's receipt of CIA funds was publicly exposed in 1967, Williams remained president for another quarter century (1964–89)—a remarkable feat and one measure of how successful the foundation was at avoiding public scrutiny of the extent of its pre-1968 CIA ties. Williams was a Washington insider who used his connections to keep the foundation afloat after its CIA links were exposed. Prior to assuming the foundation's presidency, he had been the US deputy assistant secretary of defense for national and international security.[22]

As in any organization, the workers more so than the chief administrators shaped DTPILLAR's accomplishments. It appears all committee/foundation country representatives knew about CIA links, and declassified CIA records establish that most but not all US committee/foundation employees were aware of CIA connections.[23] The country representatives were the local face of the organization. Most had served in military or intelligence roles during the Second World War or Korean Conflict. Most had studied Asian cultures, history, or languages at top universities or had worked as journalists or in government service abroad. Some staff, like James L. Stewart, had deep roots in Asia—having been born to Methodist missionaries in Kobe, Japan, and grown up in Hiroshima. He studied journalism at Duke University before the war. He then served as a CBS war correspondent in China and Burma from 1939 to 1944, later working in Korea for the US Army and the US embassy in Seoul. He joined CFA staff in 1951, remaining with the Asia Foundation until 1985.[24] Similarly, staff member Robert Sheeks grew up in Shanghai and studied at Harvard until the war, when he became a Marine combat Japanese interpreter, work for which he was awarded the Bronze Star. He later worked in committee and foundation offices in Kuala Lumpur and San Francisco.

Some staff members, like Noel Busch, came from journalism or public relations backgrounds with degrees from elite American universities where postwar CIA recruiting networks flourished. Educated at Yale and Cambridge, Lou Connick had landed with the Marines on Iwo Jima, and after the war he taught English in Burma on a Fulbright fellowship. Some staff had studied in fields like anthropology, history, political science, religious studies, and Asian languages and were hired to establish DTPILLAR programs in Asia. Richard "Dick" Heggie was a navy officer during World War II, then studied international relations while serving as vice president of the National Student Association; while at the Asia Foundation he worked in India, Japan, Pakistan, the Philippines, and Sri Lanka. Edgar Pike survived his landing craft sinking on Omaha Beach on D-Day and later studied at the Sorbonne, worked as a journalist and on the Marshall Plan, and then between 1956 and 1970 was with the Asia Foundation, with assignments in San Francisco, Vietnam, Taiwan, and Hong Kong. David

Steinberg, foundation representative in New York, Japan, and Korea during the 1950s and 1960s, was educated at Dartmouth, Harvard, and the School of Oriental and African Studies, University of London, and he later settled into a Georgetown University professorship.

The backstories of committee and foundation staff show trajectories of bright, young, liberal, mostly WASP men (women played valuable secondary staff roles) coming from strong educational backgrounds, many with military or intelligence experience, often showing knowledgeable respect for Asian societies. All appear to have been drawn to trying to reshape Asia during the height of the "American Century."

THE CIA'S CREATION OF THE COMMITTEE FOR FREE ASIA

A decade and a half after the Committee for Free Asia's creation, one CIA memo explained that it was formed "shortly after the Korean War in response to a demonstrated need for an ostensibly private organizational asset through which the United States Government could counter communist initiatives and cope with rising nationalism and economic insufficiency, in ways *not open to US official attentions*."[25] The committee's commitment to not being accountable to US official attentions was highly valued by the CIA.

The CFA established its headquarters in San Francisco and was incorporated under California state law on March 12, 1951. The committee started as a "sister organization to the National Committee for a Free Europe founded two years earlier and which operated Radio Free Europe."[26] Under President George Greene, the committee positioned itself as a nongovernmental, San Francisco–based organization making anticommunist "Radio Free Asia" broadcasts, printing pamphlets, and mobilizing "church groups and garden clubs behind a 'Seeds for Democracy' campaign in the Philippines."[27] Greene was a banker with intelligence contacts rooted in his OSS service, with later work connecting him to individuals from intelligence agencies working on the US aid mission in China. He was yet another example of CFA staff and board members having backgrounds that mixed military and intelligence connections with networks of elite corporate leaders.[28]

The committee's articles of incorporation list its first sponsors as civic leaders and businessmen, including Crown Zellerbach president James D. Zellerbach and director Charles R. Blyth; and Brayton Wilbur, president of Wilbur-Ellis Company and chairman of the North California World Affairs Council; *San*

Francisco Chronicle editor Paul Smith; and J. Leighton Stuart, a former US ambassador to China.[29] Only select members of the CFA's initial leadership knew of the committee's links to the CIA; one 1951 CIA memo identifies "three principal ('witting') members of the Committee": Brayton Wilbur, Charles Blyth, and J. D. Zellerbach.[30] Ten out of the original sixteen charter CFA members knew from the very beginning of CIA sponsorship.[31]

Some of the committee's earliest programs shared similarities with the cultural exchanges later funded by the Asia Foundation. Internal CIA memos referred to the funding for these programs as "weapons," observing that "the available weapons are many. They are all of the varied media for the exchange of ideas and information—books, pamphlets, newspapers, leaflets, plays, puppet shows, kamishibai [a form of Japanese street theater], ballad singers, pictures, sound recordings, the radio and cinema."[32] In 1951 the OPC directed "general policy guidance" for CFA's activities, and it oversaw the "maintenance of cover and achievement of the aims of security unity in the fight against communism."[33]

The CIA recognized two categories of committee employees. One group had security clearances and knowledge that CFA was a CIA operation, while the second group had no knowledge of CIA links. The committee developed protocols for dual filing systems and for the delivery of "overt and covert" mail. Under this dual mail system, the San Francisco office's overt mail was "delivered to the office by the mailman and left at the desk of the receptionist," while the covert mail was "received through an appropriate mail box which is attended by a fully cleared employee."[34]

The committee was organized into twelve branches: Foreign Organizations, Overseas Chinese Contacts, Asian Residents Contacts, Student Contacts, Editorial, Lecture Bureau, Publications, Visual Aids, Historical Research, Radio Free Asia, Activities, and Programs and Planning.[35] The Historical Research branch, which provided grants for basic academic research and served as a means of connecting with independent academics at universities, served "as a vehicle for the assistance through employment of needy Asian scholars."[36] The Overseas Chinese Contacts branch was led by L. K. Little, who worked in Chinese maritime customs to establish contacts with ethnic Chinese in other Asian nations.[37] The committee aspired to sponsor academic seminars with Chinese intellectuals, with hopes of "implanting the idea [of installing 'a truly national government of all non-communist parties' in China] in the minds of the leaders of various non-political groups."[38] US propaganda pioneer Paul Linebarger assisted in some early CFA Radio Free Asia activities.[39]

During the summer of 1951, the CIA "covertly financed a foreign students project for Western Europeans at Harvard." The agency reported that this program had positive impacts on these young Europeans exposed to American anticommunist values. These students were "under the constant supervision of a cleared sponsor consultant, who was able through the close association with the group to form a considered judgment as to the ability and future utility to the [CIA] sponsor of each individual."[40] This established an important model for US governmental interactions with young international scholars, and the CIA increasingly sought to establish similar conferences for young scholars—while Harvard personnel expressed interest in establishing conferences that would include Asian participants. The CIA proposed a summer 1952 conference with "twenty Asians, including countries in both the Far East and Near East, and twenty Europeans." There were enough CIA-linked individuals already at Harvard that CFA understood it would not need to provide additional personnel for the CIA to "have a voice in the selection of candidates and the agenda of the seminar."[41]

Other US-financed intellectual forums, like the Salzburg Seminars, were significant American Cold War fixtures connecting American intellectuals with the next generation of European leaders.[42] These seminars established ongoing relationships and frequently led to future fellowship or grant opportunities, which sometimes helped establish ongoing patron-client relationships. These seminars involved reading works advocating the virtues of American forms of free-market capitalism and political movements, though whatever intellectual shifts occurred among participants may have been secondary to the human networking ties established.

The CIA's covert sponsorship of these types of academic events circumscribed what might have been freer academic exchanges, and it shaped trajectories of postwar academic thought. By limiting participation to scholars whose ideologies aligned with desired political positions, the CIA regulated what American policy pretended was a free marketplace of ideas. Internal CFA correspondence from this first proposed Harvard seminar featuring Asian participants expressed worries about what it called "the matter of the Fairbanks complication"; the CIA had concerns that its efforts to exclude one of Harvard's top Asian scholars, John King Fairbanks, from these activities could create problems. The CIA hoped to exclude Fairbanks, because although he was one of the country's most prominent scholars of China, he publicly urged the US government to recognize Mao Zedong's government. The CFA told the CIA they could limit Fairbanks's impact on the group, writing that their "consultants are fully aware of the problem and have agreed to insure [sic] his non-participation in this seminar in any way."[43]

A late 1951 CIA memo describing the committee's relationship to the Office of Policy Coordination clarified CFA's limited ability to engage in "clandestine or unconventional warfare without prior specific headquarters approval." It stressed the lack of restrictions on CFA's ability to gather intelligence, clarifying that "OPC does not take the position that CFA cannot tap covert resources and in fact assumes that both the covert mission and CFA must largely utilize the same assets within certain areas. Any approach by CFA to a covert contact or group must, however, be coordinated in advance at the field or Washington level."[44]

Also in late 1951, the CIA used the US embassy pouch to send a letter to the Dalai Lama in Taktser. The missive "declared in effect that the time had arrived for the Dalai Lama to indicate whether or not he intended to flee Tibet, and further stated that his intentions must be made known immediately."[45] While the CIA trained Tibetan rebels or freedom fighters, the CFA funded Robert Ekvall to act as translator and culture broker for the Dalai Lama's eldest brother, Thubten Jigme Norbu, during his visit to the United States.[46]

A series of early CFA press releases reveal the public image the committee first cultivated.[47] One release had a series of questions and answers about the committee, which among other things claimed that the National Committee for a Free Europe underwrote the Committee for Free Asia's expenses, that the Crusade for Freedom donated a half million dollars to the committee in 1952, and that several other private foundations contributed funds.[48] The committee claimed its articles of incorporation prohibited engaging in propaganda "or otherwise attempting to influence legislation of our Government" and that the committee was "not otherwise prohibited from engaging in informational activities directed toward the countries of the Far East."[49]

An October 1951 newsreel showed committee leaders standing before a CFA banner with employees stapling goodwill messages onto seed packets. A US postal carrier delivered donated seeds to be processed, while workers lifted seeds and messages into a shipping crate; a final newsreel scene showed dignitaries receiving seed packets in the Philippines. Newsreel narrator Ed Herlihy proclaimed, "These seeds for democracy carry a goodwill message from Americans who have donated them to overcome a critical inadequacy in Philippine food production," which was all part of "a down to earth method of helping Philippine farmers fight communism."[50] Through such messaging the CIA hoped to plant seeds of influence abroad, while this newsreel cast seeds of domestic propaganda by ignoring the United States' historical record in the Philippines and the ways DTPILLAR would try and shape democratic movements there in ways aligned with US interests.

RADIO DAYS

On January 1, 1952, Allen Valentine replaced George H. Greene Jr. as CFA president. Greene's removal was engineered by a CIA faction pushing for more aggressive anticommunist messaging. After his purge, Greene wrote an eight-page letter venting anger over his sudden removal, complaining that Brayton Wilbur had undermined his authority at the committee and within the CIA.[51] For his severance, the CIA provided Greene with money passed through a CIA/CFA-funded "traveling fellowship for surveying the overseas Chinese communities for possible exploitation."[52] The CIA wanted committee propaganda materials to be distinct from those produced by the US Information Service. It instructed the committee to use more slang and strident language and thus carve out a niche as USIS's naughty cousin.[53] At OPC, Frank Wisner favored these types of blunt propaganda operations.

As the new CFA president, Valentine oversaw a range of programs, including Seeds for Democracy, funding for the *Young China Daily News*, the Harvard Summer Seminar program, a study of brainwashing in China, a YMCA tour of Japan by Asian American students, a student newsletter, a tour of US colleges by a "Father Liang," translation of the Boy Scout manual, a Chinese communism research project, a Hong Kong bookstore, Radio Free Asia, and the China House.[54] Valentine prioritized the committee's focus on ten countries: China, Korea, Burma, Thailand, Indo-China, Malaya, Indonesia, Japan, the Philippines, and India.[55]

While the CIA made headway with European radio propaganda operations, similar plans for Asia faced significant obstacles. The CIA initially planned to use existing radio stations for CFA broadcasts.[56] However, a 1952 study estimated that Asians only owned about fourteen million radio sets, and less than two million of them were shortwave radios. Consequently, the CIA provided $13 million for radio transmitters and other equipment, and CFA installed seven new transmitters, in Bangkok, Manila, and Taiwan.[57]

Hoping to copy Radio Free Europe's successful broadcasting campaigns, CFA launched its anticommunist broadcasting operations in 1951. Those efforts were doomed to fail. Broadcasting in English, Cantonese, and Mandarin, Radio Free

Asia signed on the air on September 4, 1951, by playing a theme song, soon followed by the sound of a gong and the announcer's voice declaring, "Radio Free Asia is a part of Committee for a Free Asia, supported by the money contributed voluntarily by men, women and children who know and appreciate the value of freedom. Radio Free Asia is not controlled or censored by any government. It has no political affiliations. It seeks no gain. It asks only your attention and confidence."[58] The announcer read news stories highlighting the dangers of communism and the promises of Western democracy and capitalism. Radio Free Asia broadcast that it was financed by voluntary contributions and claimed it had no political affiliations and that it was not censored or controlled by a government—all fundamental lies undercutting broadcast claims that "truth is the foundation of freedom."[59]

Radio Free Asia's blunt anticommunist messaging made it an easy target for ridicule and resistance. One sign of this resistance appeared in a letter from F. Karim, a Pakistan government employee, complaining to CFA personnel that these broadcasts were obviously US government propaganda efforts and adding that most Asians "were far from convinced that the Uncle Sugar Government was honestly practicing what it prescribed." Karim admitted that communist propaganda efforts had succeeded in recruiting "the majority of Pakistan students" but added that Radio Free Asia's "nay cry of anti-Communism was valueless since the average Asian regarded it merely as an American battle cry designed to subserve Uncle Sugar military interests."[60]

To establish a base for Radio Free Asia operations, in 1952 CFA opened an office in the Philippines. But Philippines-based broadcasts ended the following year as the committee shifted its focus to supporting private and governmental groups supporting democracy and education in that country. While Radio Free Europe was developing robust propaganda operations, there were significant technological issues that undermined similar efforts in Asia. The CIA did not let the lack of radios immediately end CFA plans for broadcast operations. Instead, the committee planned to use balloons to deliver radios to mainland China. Under this ill-conceived plan, "balloons, holding small radios tuned to Radio Free Asia's frequency, were lofted toward the mainland from the island of Taiwan, where the Chinese Nationalists had fled after the Communist takeover of the mainland in 1949. The plan was abandoned when the balloons were blown back to Taiwan across the Formosa Strait."[61]

Radio Free Asia broadcasts had little impact on the desired Asian target populations. The CIA determined that "in mainland China the audience was limited to government officials and those specifically authorized to listen to short-wave broadcasts."[62] With these broadcasting failures, CFA abandoned its radio broadcasts and the committee expanded its support for educational propaganda operations. By 1955, Radio Free Asia had shut down operations entirely.[63]

COMMITTEE COVER AND DAILY OPERATIONS

CIA protocols required some CFA personnel to be briefed on details of CIA-CFA cover operations. This requirement was because the agency maintained "that the concurrence of CFA was essential to any proposal for operations to be conducted under CFA cover."[64] The State Department was also aware of the CIA's role in CFA operations, and there were formal agreements between State, CFA, and the CIA describing "the manner in which the Committee for a Free Asia will operate."[65] DTPILLAR operations sometimes overlapped with those of State, a situation that occasionally created frictions.[66] To reduce these clashes, the CIA apprised State of its activities, reporting on them at monthly meetings.[67]

In some instances, the CIA briefed foreign allies of DTPILLAR operations. American agreements with British intelligence services required the CIA to disclose elements of US intelligence operations conducted in the British colonies of Hong Kong and Singapore.[68] Patrick Judge, CFA's Singapore representative, provided British intelligence officials with "the names of people [to whom] he proposed to . . . give scholarships or other financial assistance. He also was to agree to entertain specific questions they might have about operations in other countries. The station was to relay these questions via our channels for answers that, in due course, he would be authorized to transmit to them."[69]

Agreements between British and American intelligence agencies meant providing the British with assurances that DTPILLAR activities would not incite anticolonial sentiment.[70] Some British officials were skeptical of American intentions and of the committee's ability to enact effective Asian propaganda operations. In late 1952, one Singapore official expressed concerns about committee projects, complaining that whatever good came from these programs was "often vitiated by the clumsiness of their methods" and arguing that the British should do what they could "to mitigate the effects of such propaganda and to exercise a restraining influence where possible on American representatives."[71] These contacts between US and UK intelligence personnel led to the establishment of "monthly meetings at which Pat [Judge] would give them a general rundown on his program, names of people to check, and receive their questions."[72]

As committee programs multiplied, so did the need to hire more personnel with security clearances, and by the summer of 1952 the CIA had a demonstrated need to "speed up security clearances" for CFA employees. When the committee hired "non-witting" employees, the CIA checked its central files and provided a clearance over the telephone within a few hours; for "witting personnel" the CIA undertook full investigations.[73] The CIA expanded operations on university campuses as CFA developed networks with unwitting scholars advancing committee goals. The CIA directed the CFA to develop plans to expand its presence on university campuses by offering "support to schools" and "endowing professorships."[74]

CIA documents describing the committee's guiding principles establish that while much of what CFA did was overt, it would "not be precluded from undertaking confidential activities, *appropriately coordinated*" and aligned with local operational missions.[75] Through such covert means, DTPILLAR engaged in such activities as aiding local groups, "influencing the development of leadership by giving hearing[s] to selected leaders and withholding [them] from others," "openly encouraging the subversion of the Chinese Communist Government," presenting "as truth the probable or possible when its falsity cannot be disproved by the enemy," working to "expose communist informers in non-communist controlled areas more freely than can [Voice of America]," and seeking to "enlist the aid of Asian intellectuals who might be fearful of the association with an official Government program."[76] The CIA directed the committee to prioritize developing "personnel who could be trained for intelligence duties; or stay behind or other covert missions in time of war."[77] The committee also "furnished daily overnight Department of State propaganda guidance and weekly propaganda guidance."[78]

THE RANGE OF CFA ACTIVITIES

In 1953, the committee published *Land Reform: Communist China, Nationalist China, Taiwan, India, Pakistan*, an anticommunist screed posing as an academic book. Free copies were mailed to libraries and journalists with letters explaining that the volume was "not designed to serve as a detailed analysis of land reform, but as a ready daily reference for use by editors, news commentators and educators."[79] Supplying journalists with such predigested DTPILLAR analysis was one of the ways the committee, in direct violation of the CIA's charter forbidding involvement in domestic activities, tried to shape American public discourse regarding mainland China.

The CFA produced internal monthly reports with anticommunist narratives briefing the board and CIA personnel monitoring committee developments. Briefing materials came from open-source documents that committee members encountered in their work. One 1953 CIA document detailed procedures governing meetings between in-country CFA staff and CIA station representatives. CIA security protocols dictated that US embassies were used for meetings between CFA employees and CIA personnel. Sometimes at these meetings CIA station chiefs passed along "embassy biographic files" to committee representatives.[80]

Several FOIA-released documents establish CIA guidelines for CFA country-specific operations. One 1953 CIA document explained that committee staff in Taiwan "should not attempt to propagandize the overseas Chinese to support [Taiwan]," because this population was already "educated in democratic concepts by providing alternative to Mainland [China] education" and because so many elders in this Chinese community were hostile to Chinese communism. The CIA's position was that "U.S. policy specifically does not preclude use of third force groups to obtain U.S. objectives," and it kept open the possibility of undertaking operations at odds with stated US positions, arguing that "DTPILLAR was not bound to follow every turn of U.S. policy and that activist support of Formosa was not required although obviously DTPILLAR could not and would not take an opposing stand."[81]

Special Assistant to the Secretary of State Jesse MacKnight estimated that the CIA and CFA needed a decade to establish a network of individuals able to provide continuity for its programs. MacKnight stressed the importance of identifying local groups not aligned with the United States and then using the committee's nongovernmental status to support groups that had no communist ties. Working through such local groups was vital for achieving the CIA's goals, because "if DTPILLAR could not work with groups which were not tied to U.S. policy, [MacKnight] saw no reason for DTPILLAR's existence."[82]

The CIA cautioned committee employees not to compromise operations by seeking to actively "obtain intelligence information." However, should employees inadvertently collect useful "information of intelligence value to the Agency," they were given secure procedures for passing this information to CIA's Office of Operations. One CIA memo outlining security procedures indicated that Operations had "disseminated six CFA reports on political developments in Dacca and student developments in Japan. Several [Foreign Intelligence] reports on political developments in Burma are based in information supplied by CFA."[83]

The committee's façade as a nongovernmental entity allowed the CIA to establish alliances with groups and individuals whose views diverged from US policy. It also removed the stigma of being associated with the US government. Committee staffer James Stewart worried that if the committee adopted too obvious a pro-American stance, links with local organizations could be endangered. Discussing a 1953 committee proposal to write a book countering Japanese communist claims of abuses by American military personnel in Japan, Stewart warned that "it would not be good for CFA to become known as apologists for the Army," and he cautioned against the committee adopting such a posture.[84] Such concerns were common in committee correspondence during this period, as staff worked to support CFA objectives while not raising local suspicions.

THE JACKSON COMMITTEE REPORT AND THE END OF THE COMMITTEE FOR FREE ASIA

In 1953, President Dwight Eisenhower appointed a committee charged with evaluating the capacities, programs, and actions of US governmental agencies related to international security and countering communist propaganda.[85] The President's Committee on International Information Activities came to be known as the Jackson Committee, chaired by CIA deputy director William H. Jackson. In June 1953, the committee issued to the president a 125-page secret report that reviewed existing programs and proposed more subtle means of disseminating Cold War propaganda.[86]

The report had significance for DTPILLAR for two reasons. First, it recommended that the CIA oversee all global covert programs and propaganda operations. Even more significant, the Jackson Committee's chief of staff, on loan from the Mutual Security Agency, was Robert Blum, whose work on this committee became instrumental in his decision later that year to become the CFA's president just as the committee was preparing to become the Asia Foundation.[87]

Jackson Committee members spoke with key American cold warriors, including Adolph Berle, George Kennan, George Gallup, Walter Lippman, Paul Nitze, and Robert Oppenheimer, who offered advice or dire predictions about a coming increase of Soviet influence and the growing importance of the United States engaging in a global struggle for hearts and minds.[88] The Jackson Committee recommended expanding American psychological warfare operations, moving from blunt propaganda campaigns of the sort developed during the

Second World War toward soft-power programs showering targets with different forms of aid and assistance. The Jackson Committee identified movies as being an effective means for spreading propaganda worldwide, observing how "the American film industry, working with CIA and FBI, has cooperated in removing communists from production units and in withholding contracts until unions provide non-communist labor. With their large overseas investments, American companies can assist materially in combatting communist infiltration of the film industry abroad."[89]

That the CIA faired so well in the Jackson Committee's report was in part ordained by the agency "assisting" the committee, with CIA staff members playing roles in researching and writing the committee's report.[90] The Jackson Committee report reviewed US abilities to counter international communism and also the status of several related classified and nonclassified operations. It evaluated the United States' international anticommunist broadcasting campaigns and differentiated between the broadcasts of Voice of America (VOA) and the National Committee for a Free Europe (NCFE) versus CFA operations. It observed that, unlike the approach taken by VOA, "CFA operates on the concept that a private organization, particularly in Asia, can accomplish results which an official agency by its very nature cannot. It presupposes that the more it obscures its American label the more effective it will be."[91] The report stressed that the CFA's public position as a nongovernmental organ gave it a local legitimacy that VOA and NCFE lacked.

The committee viewed scholar exchange programs as a promising Cold War asset. It concluded that academic "exchanges play a major role in the Soviet effort to influence foreign peoples in the Soviet interest. It is estimated that 45,000 persons are brought to the Soviet Union annually from the free world for training, not only in propaganda but in many forms of political action and clandestine operations. This large group is augmented by other[s], especially from backward areas, who are brought to the Soviet Union for technical training or merely on good will visits."[92] The report recommended emulating this successful Soviet tactic.

The report identified several recent instances when separate covert CIA funding streams had unknowingly funded the same organizations. To avoid such duplications, it recommended making the CIA "exclusively responsible for projects the disclosure of which would 'seriously embarrass the United States Government,' 'seriously discredit the activity,' or 'seriously damage the outlet.'"[93] The Jackson Committee identified a significant portion of the CIA's covert operation spending going to the types of projects supported by the CFA, finding that "substantially more than half of CIA's covert operations budget is used for the covert support of large foreign and international organizations which are either fighting communism directly or actively supporting other United States objectives such as the European Defense Community. Except for the sources of funds, most of these activities are completely overt."[94]

The report recommended increasing governmental reliance on private organizations, arguing that the "gains in dissemination and credibility through the use of such channels will more than offset the loss by the Government of some control over the content."[95] But the report avoided addressing problems inherent in using fake "private organizations," like the CFA, that were covertly controlled by a governmental agency.

During the following year, as the Committee for Free Asia took on its new identity as the Asia Foundation, several of the recommendations made by the Jackson Committee were implemented. The most significant change comprised the foundation's efforts to move beyond blunt propagandistic messages to more nuanced projects, increasingly supporting things like publishing programs, fellowships, scholarships, and other cultural programs propagating positive views of American society while supporting anticommunist groups.

EVALUATING THE COMMITTEE FOR FREE ASIA'S APPROACH TO CULTURE HACKING

Committee staff sometimes disagreed about how to best undermine Asian communism, but after a few years it was increasingly apparent that DTPILLAR's obviously propagandistic approach had achieved only limited success. As early as 1952, James Stewart argued it was a mistake for the committee to focus so much on attacking communism instead of championing the positive features of Western capitalism. Stewart argued that CFA was "adopting the policy of the poor salesman who tries to sell his eggcups by knocking the eggcups of his rivals. A sales line of this type tends to antagonize the prospective buyer—it offends his instinct of fair play; it makes him suspect that the salesman is attacking his opponents' wares precisely because he is unsure of the merits of his own. From the practical point of view, it is self-defeating."[96] Stewart warned that the committee's blunt attacks on communism were "indistinguishable" from the local propaganda efforts by the Soviet and Chinese communists. One of the primary messages sent by these crude efforts was that the US government was "extending the Cold War into Asia" in regions where locals would "not tolerate the intensification of the psychological warfare operations of either the Western or the Eastern blocs in their countries."[97] Stewart urged the committee to fund projects championing capitalism and democracy's strengths—projects that did things like underwriting magazines providing a "platform for a surgical operation on communism," while highlighting Asian achievements and mutual interests that strengthened ties between the United States and Asian nations.[98]

Stewart wanted to build intellectual outlets where deep philosophical issues could be discussed. He championed funding projects like pro-Western intellectual journals that would "serve as a forum for the impartial examination of existing weaknesses and defects in democratic thinking and practice." He understood that Asian intellectuals experienced the same existential crises facing Western cultures, and he wanted the committee to fund a journal aimed at this audience, arguing that "throughout Asia there exists today an intellectual elite, who have had their final training in Western universities, and in the process have lost faith in their own traditional values, without finding a meaning and purpose in life in the secular values of the West. It is within this elite that communism is making its most insidious inroads." Because racism, imperialism, and the shortcomings of capitalism contributed to the lure of communist and nondemocratic alternatives, Stewart supported exploring these issues. In raising these questions, however, the committee left no doubt that the answers would be found in Western democratic models and capitalism. But Stewart argued that if the CFA's sponsored publications were going to be accepted by the Asian intellectuals, they

> must not hesitate to play the searchlight upon the gap between democratic promise and performance. Such a policy will have the additional advantage of exposing the untruths, the distortion and the exaggerations of communist propaganda. In admitting the truth, one is in an advantageous position to point to the measures which are being taken to narrow the gap between ideals and practices; and to lay bare the dishonesty and malice of attacks upon the democratic system by those who have substituted in its place a tyranny and a terror before which the most published failures of democracy pale into insignificance.[99]

Stewart's approach to the Great Game was too nuanced for committee leadership and CIA sponsors, and no specific intellectual journal pursuing these ends was sponsored by the CFA in 1952. Yet, his critique that the committee's blunt propaganda techniques were not suited to the task of attracting the sort of intellectuals DTPILLAR sought to influence was part of a growing criticism that contributed to the Committee for Free Asia soon reinventing itself as the Asia Foundation.

While Stewart's arguments to transform DTPILLAR into a more normal-appearing foundation working with Asian intellectuals would eventually prevail, basic problems with the CIA covertly funding such activities remained. It is not that there is something inherently wrong with the US government, or any government, funding educational exchanges, language programs, fellowships, scholarships, book-buying programs, folklore, or literary projects, even if the ulterior motives for funding these programs are to gain allies or undercut international adversaries. But hiding the basic fact that it is the government, not a private foundation, doing this work corrupts these undertakings and taints all those involved. And when the CIA is the government agency secretly sponsoring and approving these activities, these problems metastasize.

And while DTPILLAR found new life and new successes by transforming itself from the Committee for Free Asia into the Asia Foundation, it could only temporarily bury the basic lie on which all its programs were anchored.

2   The Birth of the Asia Foundation

The controlling fact is that the great foundations have immense sums to disburse. It is the inevitable result that an energetic university president or an ambitious university teacher should think out his plans in terms of what the foundation is likely to approve.

HAROLD LASKI / "Foundations, Universities, and Research"

In August 1953, Robert Blum resigned from the Mutual Security Administration (MSA) to become president of the Committee for Free Asia. Blum had worked at the MSA for several years, and decades later the *New York Times* reported what others had long whispered: the MSA post had been a CIA cover. Twenty-four years later the *Times* claimed Blum had resigned from the CIA to take on the Asia Foundation presidency, a role of central importance to the CIA.[1] Although there are some reasons to question the *Times*'s claim that his MSA position had been a CIA cover, his CIA work on DTPILLAR operations while president of the Committee for Free Asia and the Asia Foundation is clear.[2] The CIA's selection of Blum for the CFA presidency made good sense. He was a former World War II counterintelligence chief with experience in Southeast Asia, and his work on intelligence planning bodies such as the Jackson Committee demonstrated his understanding of the importance of the soft-power programs DTPILLAR supported.

Before the Second World War, Blum taught international relations at Yale. In 1942 he joined the OSS and soon was running European counterintelligence operations, eventually overseeing French operations for the X-2 branch of the OSS. After the war he continued this work with the Strategic Services Unit (SSU) and the Central Intelligence Group (CIG), organizations that would later be absorbed by the CIA.[3] During this postwar period, Blum worked for Secretary of Defense James Forrestal, then took a State Department position supporting the Marshall Plan in France, later becoming the US chief of mission to Indochina under the newly formed Economic Cooperation Administration (ECA).[4] As Emma Best observed, "The ECA, however, was no mere economic agency. According to the CIA, the Marshall Plan's execution was closely coordinated with the Office of Policy Coordination (OPC), which Blum had helped set up. Fittingly, some of the ECA's programs would eventually be transferred to OPC.

This is unsurprising considering the ECA's explicit role in propaganda along with monetary policy."[5] As chief of the Special Technical and Economic Mission (STEM) in Cambodia, Laos, and Vietnam, Blum increased the US presence in the region while working at the forefront of the United States' new use of development aid as an important Cold War tool.

Blum's private correspondence from the early 1950s records him networking with close friends from his years in the OSS as these friends rose to top CIA positions. This correspondence shows "Colonel Bill" Donovan, James Russell Murphy, William H. Jackson, and others urging him to join the agency.[6] As noted above, Blum headed the US Special Technical and Economic Mission to Cambodia, Indochina, and Laos.[7] In Indochina, he worked with the Mutual Security Administration to fund projects supporting various anticommunist groups. This MSA work linked him with the CIA, and as described in Blum's 1965 *New York Times* obituary, this position "involved personal risk for Dr. Blum. On one occasion guerrillas threw a grenade and opened rifle fire on a road convoy carrying him to a village near Hanoi. At another time, a last minute change in plans kept him from taking a route where guerrillas had set up an ambush."[8] Author William Corson described Blum as a "protégé of CIA Director Allen Dulles" and detailed his pre-DTPILLAR work in Vietnam, for which he was dubbed by General Jean de Lattre, commander of the French expeditionary forces, in a quote that appeared in the Pentagon Papers, as "the most dangerous man in Indochina."[9] This so-called most dangerous man was the person DTPILLAR sought to transform the Committee for Free Asia.

At MSA, Blum had grown frustrated with the limitations imposed on the programs he supported as a representative of a US governmental agency. The bureaucratic weight of the MSA wore on Blum. His hopes that the organizational structure and opportunities to transform the CFA could provide the organizational agility lacking at MSA helped draw Blum to CFA. The administrative dexterity that came with the committee's status as a (fake) private organization excited Blum.

Journalist Emma Best argues that while Blum was a staff member for Secretary of Defense Forrestal, he played a significant role in helping design the United States' postwar intelligence agencies. Best found that Blum's work on the McNarney Report (known as NSC 50) directly led to the firing of Roscoe Henry Hillenkoetter as director of central intelligence and that Blum played a significant role in the creation of what would become the National Security Agency.[10] Blum's Jackson Committee contributions influenced President Eisenhower's support for the types of soft-power programs that Blum later implemented for CIA DTPILLAR operations. Best noted that Blum, while working on the Jackson Committee, "suggested they look at their current and potential ability to conduct covert operations, which would inform their discussion of who should have responsibility for them. Blum was particularly interested in the extent to whether U.S.-identified propaganda should be replaced by non-attributed propaganda and whether or not psychological warfare was 'a technique in its own right or an illusion that risks distorting the proper conception of foreign policy as a whole.'"[11] These formulations prefigure the work Blum later oversaw as he transformed DTPILLAR operations.

Not long after the Jackson Committee submitted its report to the president, Blum wrote his friend Max Millikan, a former assistant director of central intelligence at CIA and then director of MIT's Center for International Studies (CENIS), that the committee work "inspired" him to quit his job and move to San Francisco to take this new position. The CFA, he wrote, was moving "definitely away from a propagandistic, anti-Communist, pro-American tone and is geared to providing encouragement and assistance to local groups and individuals capable of strengthening the non-Communist forces throughout Asia."[12] Blum reformed what had been a blunt anticommunist propaganda instrument, reshaping it into what appeared to be an independent nonprofit educational and cultural foundation.

REBRANDING THE COMMITTEE FOR FREE ASIA AS THE ASIA FOUNDATION

During Blum's first year as CFA president, he familiarized himself with the workings of the organization by visiting field offices, meeting with staff, and getting up to speed on the range of programs they offered. After six months he began re-visioning what programs could support DTPILLAR's anticommunist goals, considering programs that better fit the more subtle visions of the Jackson Committee report.

By 1954, CFA early propaganda programs had created enough problems for the organization that pressure mounted for the committee to change its tactics as well as its name. In September 1954, a year after Blum's presidency began, the Committee for Free Asia changed its name to the Asia Foundation. This name change marked a significant pivot in the organization's strategy.[13] With the name change came a visibly new approach to programming. A June 1954

CIA memo, "Evaluation of Operational Capability" of the Asia Foundation, explained that the old name "proved an impediment in the establishment of the character desired for CFA. It has a political connotation and irritates Asians, proud of the fact that they are already free."[14]

When DTPILLAR took on its new, rebranded identity, the CIA issued a revised secret statement of purpose and mission for the Asia Foundation:

STATEMENT OF PURPOSES IN DTPILLAR ARTICLES
OF INCORPORATION, 13 SEPTEMBER 1954

a. To make private American support available to individuals and groups in Asia who are working for the attainment of peace, independence, personal liberty, and social progress.
b. To encourage and strengthen active cooperation, founded on mutual respect and understanding, among voluntary organizations—Asian, American and international—with similar aims and ideals.
c. To work with other American individuals and organizations for a better understanding in the United States of the peoples of Asia, their histories, cultures, and values.
d. To solicit and receive funds for the objects and purposes herein set forth and to administer and use such funds for the promotion of such objects and purposes.

DTPILLAR MISSION

The mission of DTPILLAR is to encourage, assist and support non-Communist Asian individuals and groups in the efforts to strengthen their societies and institutions in ways which support the attainment of U.S. policy objectives.

This mission is based on the premise that it is primarily Asians themselves who must overcome Asia's problems, and that outside aid can play only a supporting role. Implementation of this mission requires the stimulation of constructive action through the greatest possible Asian initiative and participation.

In pursuing its mission DTPILLAR will give priority attention in programming toward (1) counteracting the appeals of communism, (2) promoting viable ties with the US/West, (3) redirecting extreme nationalism, (4) eradicating irresponsible neutralism/non-alignment, and (5) inculcating concepts of freedom and democracy.[15]

Blum expanded the number of foundation field offices in Asia, connecting unwitting American and Asian scholars in ways that harnessed their intellectual productivity and expanded DTPILLAR's social network. The covert intelligence experience Blum had acquired overseeing European OSS operations prepared him for this work.[16] Blum pressed the board to start fundraising. While there were ample CIA funds to finance projects, Blum hoped that bringing funds from legitimate outside sources could improve the appearance of the foundation's legitimacy, though these fundraising efforts largely failed.

REORGANIZING THE COMMITTEE AS THE FOUNDATION

In 1951, DTPILLAR had a staff of 116, with another 56 people hired the following year.[17] By 1957 there were "about 140" employees, and the foundation was sponsoring a diverse array of projects.[18] These included projects like bringing Burmese, Japanese, and other Asian scholars to American universities; translating Boy Scout literature into Burmese and Korean; funding an East Asia teacher training program at the University of California; helping the Camp Fire Girls mail seeds to people in Asia; arranging book-buying programs; offering "citizenship education" in Ceylon, Pakistan, and the Philippines; disseminating an American business curriculum; offering summer course work for scholars not specializing in Asian studies; producing Asian radio commentaries; and doing economic analyses of Asia. The foundation funded programs at organizations such as the Carnegie Endowment for International Peace, the Association of Asian Studies, Institute of East Asiatic Studies, the Nieman Foundation for Journalism, Japan Society, University of Michigan, the National Association of Foreign Student Advisors, and the Stanford Research Institute.[19] These were diverse projects, yet the programs the foundation funded selectively shaped knowledge production in ways aligned with American power.

By 1955, the transformation from the Committee for Free Asia to the Asia Foundation was complete, and with this came a growth in programs. In April 1955, Frank Wisner, the CIA deputy director of plans, authorized the expansion of DTPILLAR operations in Indonesia, Cambodia, and South Vietnam.[20] Early foundation projects included diverse approaches to spreading anticommunist pro-American messages, funding such things as alternatives to Soviet-backed aid projects, teaching villagers about American-style democracy, providing free books and magazines positively portraying the American way of life, or establishing patron-client relationships that promised to be significantly useful later on. Often a primary goal of these projects was, ironically, to increase trust in the United States as an honest and forthright actor. In a 1954 presidential report, Blum stressed it was "vital to the future of the United States and of Asia that misunderstandings and suspicions on both sides should be replaced by genuine friendship and cooperation."[21]

In Singapore, the foundation sponsored a teen day camp called the Vacation Life Camp. The Union Press Organization organized the camp and its agenda, which featured procapitalist and pro-Western civics activities. There were debating courses, essay contests, speech contests, and other activities. The foundation report on the 1960 camp session included photographs of students participating in a debate session, with captions of an exchange in which one debater asked, "Do you mean to tell me that you admire a mean, miserly, miserable millionaire rather than a man of high virtue just because the former has more money and can live in the lap of luxury?" while the procapitalist rebuttal argued, "Whom you like better is another thing, but I assure you that a successful businessman may contribute much more towards the prosperity of a community than any of these helpless idealists," thus crudely championing capitalist ideology that idolized "job creators."[22]

Some foundation efforts to nurture relationships with Asian intellectuals had clear anticommunist goals, while others had less obvious political messaging. Programs funded visiting scholars, speaking tours by American writers or university professors, and other means of connecting intellectuals from different cultures who sometimes had no political messaging beyond showcasing the Western intellectuals. Robert Blum was concerned that Japanese intellectuals were drawn to Marxist critiques and had minimal concerns about threats of communist totalitarianism. He worried that Japanese writers sometimes incorporated Marxist dogma and anti-American critiques in their writings. Blum believed these Japanese intellectuals would be "more receptive" to anticommunist analysis "if they could discuss communism with Europeans whose experience has been closer to that of the Japanese, who had felt communism at first hand and who could effectively demonstrate the vast differences between theoretical and practical communism." To help nurture such anticommunist intellectualism, DTPILLAR sponsored a six-week, twenty-two-city tour of Japan by select European anticommunist intellectuals. Blum later included Japanese intellectuals in US-based seminars pressing pro-American agendas.[23]

As discussed in greater detail in chapter 5, foundation staff sometimes collected intelligence that had actionable uses by the CIA. One 1955 CIA memo observed that because Asia Foundation representatives had regular interactions with "a great variety of Asian leaders and governmental figures," they were "frequently in a position to get information not otherwise available to the Agency. Between 1 December 1954 and 1 March 1955, DTPILLAR reports have resulted in 21 CS [CIA's Clandestine Services] and CO [Clandestine Operations] disseminations."[24] These routine interactions between foundation staff and government employees of Asian nations helped the CIA gather information and establish contacts with individuals working for foreign governments.

Some Asian governments welcomed foundation anticommunist activities because they worried that communism could threaten their hold on power. One 1955 CIA memo reported Burma's prime minister praising foundation representatives for their anticommunist work, adding that the "Prime Minister of Ceylon has publicly defended DTPILLAR against communist and opposition attack. In Pakistan DTPILLAR has received the active cooperation of many official and semi-official bodies."[25] But not all Asian countries welcomed foundation interventions in local political discourse. In some instances, the CIA lamented that because of "poor public relations" originating during the days of the Committee for Free Asia, the foundation had difficulty in the mid-1960s establishing a presence in India, "where its activity would be particularly useful to U.S. objectives."[26]

DTPILLAR funded several programs bringing leading Asians from the fields of medicine, journalism, and business to tour the United States; it also helped the Junior Chamber International bring young Asians to the United States.[27] The foundation's Department of American Operations supported several US groups with ties to Asia, sponsored programs to bring refugees from communism to the United States, and funded operations counteracting communist propaganda programs.[28]

Increases in Soviet aid and Soviet advisors in Afghanistan pushed the foundation to increase activities there. In a 1955 foundation report on a recent trip to northeastern Afghanistan, country representative Harold Amoss Jr. complained about "the problem of communist imperialism" growing from "Russian intervention in the affairs of Afghanistan, and the buttressing of social, political and economic structures within the country, rather than one of organized indigenous communist party activity." Amoss characterized Soviet aid as trying to "take over all Afghan territory north of the Hindu Kush," and he projected that the Soviets understood that if they successfully "controlled the northern provinces[,] the rest of Afghanistan would collapse like a pricked balloon because this is the economic heart of the country."[29]

Because of Soviet successes with these aid programs, Amoss recommended that the foundation develop programs to send "young Turkic-speaking men to Turkish military schools, fund the study of meteorology, scientific based farming techniques, modernizing gold mining methods, and simply funding the spread of decent schools." Amoss wanted the Afghanistan government to increase its presence in rural areas, with modernization projects serving as a way of bringing a positive governmental presence while undercutting Soviet authority. He worried that "loss of control in these provinces could be tantamount to losing the entire country at this time."[30] While Amoss voiced deep concerns, his proposals called for only minor innovations such as "increasing the flow of reading materials into this region," even while Soviet programs aggressively brought expensive new farm equipment to rural areas.[31]

SURVEY: PROGRAM INFORMATION SERVICE BULLETIN

Beginning in the early 1960s, the foundation produced a series of internal reports under the title *Survey: Program Information Service Bulletin*, which provided an instructive overview of the sorts of projects DTPILLAR funded. These bulletins preserve some of the internal dialogue that emerged among foundation staff. *Survey* was a typewritten magazine publishing stories on Asia, and its issues reported on a range of topics. For example, the December 15, 1964, issue (vol. 2, no. 3) contained such reports as "Hill Tribe Programming in Thailand," "ASAIHL Math Education Seminar," "Teacher Training Program at Northwestern University," and "Housing and Home Finance Agency Training Program in the US," and it included a "Chart of Communist Party Alignment in Asia."[32] Some issues printed public talks or summarized foundation area programming, and frequently the articles contained political critiques or blatant anticommunist analysis. Because of the US-centric political focus of the *Survey* articles, foundation leadership understood that dissemination of the bulletin outside the foundation could be problematic, and in 1964 foundation staffer James J. Dalton warned employees receiving *Survey* that, "in order to minimize the risk of any possible embarrassment resulting from material contained in it, we are reverting to the original practice of sending the *Survey* under the designation 'Confidential' to all career Foundation employees overseas." Representatives were warned to use "discretion in showing individual issues" to other staff members and were reminded issues were only for use within the foundation.[33]

In a 1964 *Survey* article, "Foundation Buddhist Programming," William Klausner described the Thai government's mandate that Buddhist priests not become involved in political matters. Klaussner explained that despite this ban, highly educated Buddhist priests were increasingly becoming important political figures in Thailand. He described the foundation's "principal objective in its Buddhist programming" as being "to channel and guide the intellectual energy of these priest leaders into positive educational and social activities which will result in a stronger and more social[ly] and politically stable community."[34]

A 1964 *Survey* article, "Functions of the New York Office," described the foundation office's interactions with visitors, reports written, and attention to financial matters. The passage below describes this office's commitment to tracking Asian news reports and the activities of nongovernmental organizations working in Asia, explaining that at the New York office

> a substantial amount of time is given to reading and interpreting the periodicals and reports received from other foundations, organizations with which we have program contacts, and all kinds of groups which are interested in Asia and have programs in Asia. Even a careful reading of the daily press and press releases is useful because we have found that news items of special interest to the Foundation may be carried in the eastern editions of a newspaper which are not carried in the western edition. A recent example of this was the information about the Ford Foundation's grant of several million dollars to a consortium of universities interested in international development. A careful reading of reports and periodicals enables us to relate our program to the programs of other groups with similar interests, to interpret our program in this light of theirs in discussions, and to ask pertinent questions about their programs on matters of special interest to the Foundation. Similarly, in interpreting the work of The Asia Foundation to other organizations, we find it necessary to try to keep abreast of periodic reports from all the field offices.[35]

This shows that foundation staff were monitoring the work of legitimate foundations and searching for projects that overlapped with DTPILLAR interests in Asia. Through such mundane tasks, the Asia Foundation used both witting and unwitting staff to collect and digest information that had other uses at CIA headquarters.

A 1965 CIA report observed that after a dozen years of Asian programming, the foundation was "firmly established in Asia with an excellent range of contacts in the 13 countries where its Representatives are working closely with Chiefs of Station and Ambassadors to catalyze, support and make more effective Asian initiatives which advance U.S. policy objectives."[36] The CIA reported that by 1965 there were 17 residential offices in 13 countries, with 300 TAF-funded projects under way and that the foundation employed "157 Americans (most are witting of the CIA/TAF connection) and 240 foreign nationals (non-witting)."[37]

The CIA considered the foundation's 1965 cover to be "good, as evidenced by the fact that Asians continue to invite TAF to program in sensitive areas of their national life." The CIA noted that because the Ford and Rockefeller Foundations were frequently attacked by the Chinese Communist media for being arms of American policy, they could consider such attacks on the Asia Foundation as merely routine, adding that "within US academic and Foundation circles, TAF is accepted as a respected and experienced institution, but is subjected to occasional allegations from certain individuals that it is connected with and supported by ~~CIA~~ [handwritten correction: the sponsor]."[38]

FINANCES AND CIA EFFORTS TO HIDE DTPILLAR FUNDS

The CIA's September 1954 revised "Statement of Purposes in DTPILLAR Articles of Incorporation" not only outlined DTPILLAR's mission as it shifted from the Committee for Free Asia to the Asia Foundation, it also described how the CIA was to fund the foundation. The prescribed funding protocols included procedures for DTPILLAR staff to submit "detailed budget request[s]" that were reviewed by the CIA's Budget Division, whose staff made final adjustments to requests and then, in consultation with the CIA's Covert Action staff, approved final budgets and developed covert means of funding the foundation designed to hide the true source of funds.[39] The document described the CIA's practice of using "individuals acting as ostensible donors and appropriately cleared with the Central Cover Staff" or working with "Agency established national organizations in coordination with the Central Cover Staff" who covertly received millions of dollars from the CIA and then "contributed" these CIA funds to the Asia Foundation, effectively laundering CIA money and maintaining the fiction that the Committee for Free Asia and Asia Foundation were private, nongovernmental organizations.[40]

A 1953 CIA memo, "DTPILLAR-Cover-Fund-Raising," summarized plans to improve the organization's cover by better concealing that it was funded by the CIA.[41] The CIA proposed establishing a "non-profit charitable foundation" known as the Fund for Asia to fundraise by creating a plausible public funding stream for an operation running purely on CIA funds. To explore this possibility, the Asia Foundation established its Finance Committee.[42]

The East Coast–based Fund for Asia was supposed to provide a plausible public fundraising organization to help the foundation claim it had "a credible public source of funds which it now lacks."[43] The CIA identified fifteen men "prominent in the fields of business, law, education, publishing and diplomatic" whom the agency had consulted when selecting the officers governing the Fund for Asia.[44] Author James Michener, who was witting of CIA links, took on a leadership role in the Fund for Asia.[45]

In 1953 the CIA outsourced the Fund for Asia's fundraising activities, contracting with Harold L. Oram, Inc., for $7,000 a month with an anticipated annual fundraising goal of $200,000. The budget projected $84,000 in overhead expenses, while planning for expenditures that consumed 42 percent of earnings from fundraising, or about 3 percent of the 1953 annual budget, simply to provide cover. The CIA's operating plan stipulated that "the fund-raising will be more than self-liquidating and result in a substantial amount of public funds.... DTPILLAR will reimburse itself from such public funds for actual expenses incurred for the fund-raising. The remainder of such public funds will be retained by DTPILLAR and expended for programs approved by the IO Division [International Organizations Division]." The CIA stipulated that it would manage all publicity for Oram's fundraising activities, and all members of the Finance Committee and Oram's employees had to undergo CIA "operational clearances."[46]

At the May 17, 1955, board meeting, Blum discussed foundation fundraising activities, including contributions by "various foundations and other organizations," which likely included CIA pass-through foundations.[47] In the end, little came from such discussions about moving the foundation away from its total dependency on CIA funds, and it continued to run on CIA funding. The establishment of the Fund for Asia was an unsuccessful effort to provide financial cover for this CIA operation and never came close to meeting anything like the targeted funding levels.

During this period, the foundation's board was all male, predominantly white, American, and moneyed. Some individuals joined as established business leaders with interests in Asia, while others had academic or political backgrounds; many were liberal anticommunists embracing the views that soon led the United States into the Southeast Asian anticommunist wars. Most were business tycoons, and a few were celebrities.[48]

During DTPILLAR's first decade, the CIA channeled $76 million into the Asia Foundation (table 1). It was a large enough sum that in 1964 the foundation's board used the size of this "investment" to push the director of central intelligence (DCI) to increase the foundation's budget, essentially arguing that it was now too big to fail:

> The Board wishes to go on record as feeling that it would not be discharging its obligation if it did not call forthrightly to the attention of the Director [DCI] its belief that the $76,000,000 investment in the Asia Foundation will become a wasting asset unless it is given increased financial support now and in the years ahead. The Board feels that this is a time of crisis in Asia and a time of increasing challenge and opportunity for the Foundation. If these challenges are to be met, if these opportunities are to be exploited, the sights of the Foundation must be set at a higher level.[49]

To give some idea of the relative size and significance of how much this $76 million spent by the CIA during DTPILLAR's first decade, this was over half the amount of money that the Ford Foundation spent between 1950 and 1960 on all their overseas development projects.[50]

By 1964, the CIA was struggling to decide what to do with the scattered accumulation of small monetary donations that the foundation occasionally received. The foundation always accepted these rare donations as a way of supporting the pretense that it was not owned and run by the CIA. Because CIA DTPILLAR funds had always been the CFA and the Asia Foundation's secret source of operating funds, the latter had never established any formal bureaucratic means for processing or allocating actual donations, referred to by the CIA as "bona-fide contributions." This created bookkeeping problems for the CIA until a 1964 CIA Covert Action staff "secret project approval notification

TABLE 1 Funding for secret project DTPILLAR, 1951–1958

Dates of funding activity

ORIGINAL APPROVAL	FEBRUARY 7 [HANDWRITTEN: 1951]
Project renewal	April 8, 1955
Amendment 1	April 18, 1955
Amendment 2	May 23, 1956
Amendment 3	June 4, 1956
Project renewal	December 18, 1956

Funds used since initiation of project

FISCAL YEAR	AMOUNT (US$)
1951	150,000.00
1952	1,469,966.95
1953	3,914,799.96
1954	3,111,102.06
1955	5,117,586.64
1956	5,660,711.28
1957	6,589,568.29
1958	6,800,000.00 budgeted

Source: CIA DTPILLAR 2, 9, 4.

report" authorized the foundation to spend these contributions as part of their budget. Before this policy change, the CIA required these occasional donations be tallied and returned to the CIA, but because the foundation received only minuscule amounts of money from non-CIA sources, the CIA acknowledged this was not worth the bookkeeping effort. These outside funds averaged only "about $30,000 per year," which was such a small percentage of the budget that the CIA acknowledged that tracking this "created housekeeping and cover problems." These paltry non-CIA funds were too insignificant even to provide window dressing to hide the CIA's role as the only meaningful source of foundation funds.⁵¹

This CIA secret report advocated for the continuation of CIA covert funding for Asia Foundation operations and summarized the success of its programs. Programs touted by the CIA included ongoing programs in Cambodia, Franklin Press publishing contracts in Afghanistan, the sponsoring of a Japanese academic journal, new foundation offices, funding of "Buddhist circles," the "development of access to new leaders through use of Congressional and Nieman Fellowships, and the Harvard International Seminar," and the "distribution to date of 4,355,170 books and 944,136 journals to over 10,000 recipients in Asia."⁵²

This CIA report explained that the Asia Foundation's primary "covert mission is to support the attainment of US policy objectives. It does so by assisting Asian individuals and institutions in their efforts to strengthen their own societies and institutions, giving priority attention to programs which: (1) counteract the appeals of communism, (2) promote viable ties with the US/West, (3) redirect extreme nationalism, (4) eradicate irresponsible neutralism/non-alignment, and (5) inculcate concepts of freedom and democracy."⁵³ The CIA explained that the foundation was required to lie about seeking to accomplish these five objectives guiding its work, insisting that "as a covert political action instrument, TAF publicly eschews any relationship between US official goals and TAF program objectives."⁵⁴

From the CIA's perspective, these lies were necessary because "the entire scope of TAF programming is open to scrutiny by host governments," members of the press, and "non-witting Americans." While these five CIA directives could not be publicly divulged,

> by openly declaring its intention to assist Asians in activities designed to promote social and economic progress, and by carefully cultivating its public image as a private foundation, TAF is able covertly to support US government and [Central Intelligence] Agency missions in Asia. Its modus operandus is to provide the means through which Asian groups and individuals, ostensibly acting in their own interests and for their own purposes, actually commit themselves to points of view and courses of action which support US national interests. By carefully adhering to this modus operandus and taking pains to preserve cover TAF has established access and influence at all levels of society in the

countries of Asia where it has been represented during the past twelve years. During FY 1964 TAF was able to utilize its special position and capabilities to make further significant contributions to US government and Agency goals."[55]

The CIA listed a dozen examples of ways the foundation successfully carried out this agency mission. These included the high value to the CIA of the foundation remaining in Cambodia after other US organizations had been expelled, its abilities to influence "Afghan Government policy at the cabinet minister level," opening up North Borneo to an American presence, reducing suspicions in India that the foundation might not be a bona fide organization, and sponsoring research projects on communist China.[56]

In evaluating the foundation's effectiveness, the CIA observed that DTPILLAR programs were being increasingly accepted in Asia. The CIA bragged that its control over the foundation created an asset unlike any held by any other "government, including the communists, [and it] has among its assets an independently-chartered organization with capital and personnel capable of making such wide a varied impact throughout Asia."[57]

The CIA approved of F. Haydn Williams's management of the foundation since becoming president in January that year, with one document noting that Williams "demonstrated a lively interest in keeping TAF programs on target and has shown great readiness to work closely with CIA. Under his leadership, good TAF-CIA working relationships should continue, and operational objectives of the project should be enhanced."[58] Williams understood his role, and he provided the outcomes the CIA sought. He was a valuable asset to the CIA, and his close relationship with the agency raises questions about what contacts he may or may not have maintained with the CIA after the foundation stopped receiving CIA funds in 1968.

CIA ENGAGEMENT WITH FOUNDATION STAFF

A 1963 memo discussing agency oversight of the foundation illuminates some of the ways that the CIA hid funding during this period.[59] CIA Covert Action staff secretly played vital roles in some foundation functions, including sometimes being responsible for making significant foundation decisions. The CIA insisted all foundation trustees be "approved by [Covert Action] Staff prior to election in accordance with charter and by-laws of the corporation." Covert Action staff also approved the selection of foundation presidents and all "Executive Committee members and key staff officers."[60] In order to monitor alignment with US government policies and with DTPILLAR's mission, CIA Covert Action staff reviewed all DTPILLAR-sponsored programs. The CIA maintained the right to "eliminate, modify, adjust or change the emphasis of the activities contemplated by DTPILLAR."[61] The requirement that CIA Covert Action staff approve all foundation grants shows that the agency was shaping academic research agendas.[62]

The CIA's careful protocols for passing agency funds to the foundation included altering payment dates and geographical locations and the identifying information on accounts transferring funds so as to hide the source of these funds. CIA staff used third parties to pass CIA funds to the foundation following "a schedule of established monthly reimbursements . . . prepared by CA Staff each fiscal year and forwarded to the Budget Division for approval and to the Central Cover Staff." This schedule established "a pattern of funding that is staggered as to time, amount, and geographic origin of funds, and the funding mechanism or method to be used for each advance of funds." There were several means for passing these funds, including using "individuals acting as ostensible donors and appropriately cleared with the Central Cover Staff."[63]

Until 1968, the members of the Asia Foundation's board of trustees were props creating a public fiction, while many of their most important duties were secretly performed by the CIA. The board's most important powers were superseded by the CIA's secrecy rules—rules that bypassed the foundation's legal documents of incorporation. The board's primary function was to create an air of legitimacy for a foundation that was, if not illegitimate, then not what it pretended to be.

Given the absolute dependency on CIA funds and the extent to which agency personnel were required to approve decisions, most board members had to be aware the foundation was run by the CIA. The CIA's language covering the specifics of these relationships left open the possibility that one could be elected to the board and remain unwitting, but if this occurred, it must have been rare. The CIA specified that "each person elected to the Board of Trustees of DTPILLAR after date of authorization of this Plan, and who is made witting of Agency sponsorship of the activity shall be required to execute a Letter of Understanding and a Secrecy Agreement."[64] These letters of understanding included language indemnifying "directors and officers of DTPILLAR against any liability resulting from actions specially approved by the Agency."[65]

The CIA's administrative plan committed CIA staff to avoid micromanaging foundation presidents' day-to-day management of the foundation's operations.[66]

Most all foundation grantees (while secretly having been cleared by the CIA to receive foundation funding) were unwitting of the foundation's CIA links and remained unaware the CIA ran background checks on them. Several CIA documents detail elements of the agency's background clearance procedures, which included consulting CIA files and the records of other US government agencies. After receiving the results of these CIA checks, the foundation's "DTPILLAR Representative" decided "whether to proceed with the intended purpose, taking into account the advice of the Station and security interests of DTPILLAR." The decision-making power of these representatives was limited; they were not allowed to "proceed against explicit advice of the Station." In instances where foundation country representatives disagreed with the decision of the CIA's chief of station, the latter could forbid the foundation representative from taking any action until CIA headquarters resolved the dispute.[67] The power relations between the field representatives and the CIA were clear; the agency was in charge.

Only in instances where "substantial derogatory information" on grantees was found would CIA headquarters be notified of the results of these background checks, though investigation results on all hired local employees were sent to CIA headquarters.[68] The extent to which any collected derogatory information was saved is unknown, but because the foundation appears to have saved files on every individual job, fellowship, or scholarship applicant—even those immediately rejected from any possible funding—this raises the possibility that information from these background checks was preserved somewhere.[69]

The CIA collected information from the Immigration and Naturalization Service (INS) for these investigations.[70] The CIA's grantee clearance protocol authorized the agency to share classified materials with levels "not higher than 'Secret'" with authorized individuals at Asia Foundation headquarters.[71] The CIA maintained the authority to direct foundation staff to engage in counterespionage operations, as needed. The CIA was prepared to "carry out special security measures of a counter-espionage nature ... [that would] be undertaken with the cooperation of DTPILLAR and, as necessary, will be implemented by DTPILLAR."[72]

Under CIA protocols, there were two categories of foundation employees: those with security clearances who were aware of the CIA's presence, designated by the CIA as "Category I" employees, and those who were unwitting of the CIA's connections, known as "Category II" employees.[73] Because some CIA documents reveal protocols instructing foundation country representatives to at times meet with CIA officers stationed at local embassies, we can assume that all country representatives were aware of the foundation's CIA links.

CIA protocols for appropriate channels of communication and issuing and receiving CIA orders in the field specified that in countries where the foundation operated, the CIA's chief of station briefed "the DTPILLAR Representative on those portions of the Country Team Program which have a bearing on the DTPILLAR mission, bringing to his attention specific areas or problems which lend themselves to DTPILLAR programming."[74] The CIA chief of station also had the authority to suspend Asia Foundation projects threatening to create security problems for US interests.

CIA protocols dictated that most communications between Asia Foundation field offices and their San Francisco headquarters use normal commercial channels (mail, telephone, cable etc.), but there were also more secure channels established for communicating about "sensitive information affecting the security of the U.S. Government generally, or the Agency or DTPILLAR." Such communications used the CIA station chief's secure encrypted communication systems located within the American embassy.[75] While these links between select foundation personnel stationed abroad in field offices and CIA personnel were vital elements of the CIA's control of the foundation, CIA policies also dictated that the agency should mostly not interfere in the day-to-day operation of the foundation. CIA policy established that foundation representatives needed to support CIA station chiefs by "(1) reporting on matters pertaining to Station FI [foreign intelligence] requirements; (2) spotting, evaluation, and assessment of individuals; (3) provision of grants or other forms of support to individuals or organizations of interest to the Station, and (4) provision of access or introductions to persons of potential interest to the Station."[76]

The CIA's caveat that the agency should generally not "exercise direct control" over Asia Foundation projects leaves questions about the exceptions to this "general" rule. Because the CIA conducted background checks of grant applicants, the agency played a significant, invasive role in the foundation's most basic interactions with people from host countries, and the CIA's ability to reject critical academics helped shape the forms of knowledge the foundation produced.

COURTING ROCKEFELLER TO JOIN THE BOARD

In 1954, even as the Committee for Free Asia was changing its name to the Asia Foundation, John D. Rockefeller III was invited to join its board of trustees.[77] When approached by foundation trustee Robbins Milbank, Rockefeller expressed concerns about the difficulties facing the foundation in Asia. Robert Blum later personally approached Rockefeller, offering more information about the political climate in Asia, saying that he was baffled by some of the antagonism facing the foundation, claiming he did not understand why the Indian government was hostile toward it. He explained that these attitudes remained from "the earlier days of CFA when the Committee was engaged in an outright program of direct anti-communist propaganda. It is almost as if the Indian Government, having put in its card files a black mark against us three years ago, has not bothered to bring the record up-to-date." Blum speculated that the roots of this hostility might just be negative feelings in India toward the United States in general.[78]

Rockefeller was unsure about accepting the invitation, and when he consulted with his advisor Francis A. Jamison, Jamison bluntly recommended against joining the board. He warned that the taint of CFA's previous practices brought risks to the foundation and those associated with it. Jamison understood that "the Committee has been regarded with varying degrees of resentment in Asia because it spends a lot of money and is regarded as a propaganda instrument of the United States government."[79] Jamison knew that CFA staff were unwelcome in Indonesia and elsewhere, and he cautioned that any association with the foundation could "jeopardize" Rockefeller's activities in Asia, warning that "in the long run your independent activities may well serve the cause of the United States better if you have no such affiliation."[80]

But the CIA viewed Rockefeller as a valuable asset for the foundation's board, valuable enough that DCI Allen Dulles followed Blum's approach by making a personal phone call to ask Rockefeller to join the board. Rockefeller later sent Dulles a note, writing that while it had been a difficult choice, he felt he must decline the invitation.[81] The foundation tried to attract other Rockefellers to join the board but met with similar failure, and a few months later David Rockefeller also declined an invitation to join the board.[82]

FOUNDATIONS AREN'T LOTTERIES, AND THEY HAVE AGENDAS

Inderjeet Parmar's *Foundations of the American Century: The Ford, Carnegie, and Rockefeller Foundations in the Rise of American Power* critiques the Ford, Carnegie, and Rockefeller Foundations' hegemonic power by connecting the funding priorities of these elite foundations with projects of American empire. Parmar draws on extensive archival records from these foundations to understand how their fortunes support forms of scholarship that align with American governmental policies around the world. Parmar also shows how these foundations have historically funded projects supporting (certain types of) internationalism over isolationism. While some projects supported forms of nation-building, favoring at times neoliberalism and neocolonial relationships, in general these foundations have not supported socialist or communist developments, all the while claiming to not support "political" projects.

Parmar argues that while the projects funded by these foundations did not meaningfully reduce poverty (an expressed goal many sought to achieve), they did establish a brain trust of scholars who were part of "sustainable elite networks that, on the whole, supported American policies—foreign and economic—ranging from liberalism in the 1950s to neoliberalism in the twenty-first century."[83] Parmar shows how these foundations, while not state agencies and effectively maintaining structural independence from the US government, acted as extensions of state interests. Parmar describes these foundations as engaging in "philanthrocapitalism."[84]

Parmar observes that foundations perpetuate a "'nonstate' fiction," using their status as nongovernmental agencies to act as if the directions of their funding priorities were detached from American governmental policies, though their funding policies are in fact linked to governmental policies.[85] Parmar builds a strong critique, and if we compare this situation with DTPILLAR's fiction, at least the "nonstate fiction" of the Ford, Carnegie, and Rockefeller Foundations requires quotation marks, unlike the nonstate fiction of the pre-1968 Asia Foundation. However, the nonstate fiction of these other foundations raises questions about why the CIA was not simply satisfied with the proxy state relationship it had established with other foundations.

One explanation of why the CIA was not satisfied with the level of governmental influence already exerted on legitimate foundations was that in the early 1950s the CIA had become headstrong to a point where it wanted to pull strings directly. In the 1950s, Frank Wisner and others at CIA appear to have decided they shouldn't have to deal with the sort of lag time that existed when working on agency-linked programs or goals through nongovernmental foundations like the Ford, Rockefeller, and Carnegie. Parmar quotes American scholar Robert Spiller's acknowledgment that regardless of different claimed goals, governments and private foundation programs "tended to supplement rather than conflict with each other."[86] With the Asia Foundation, the CIA cut out the middleman, thereby controlling a foundation it could use as expediently as it saw fit without worrying about cumbersome committees and outside views. This move streamlined control, and as long as the foundation could hide in plain sight behind actual nongovernmental foundations, the CIA accomplished these goals.

The Asia Foundation extended the CIA's Cold War mind-set. It tried to harness American intellectuals, to connect with foreign scholars, to collect intelligence, and to limit the growth of Asian communism and the proliferation of critics of Western capitalism. While most of these projects and activities transpired in the open, the CIA's covert sponsorship obscured then-contemporary understanding of all of what these programs sought to accomplish. Because the executive branch had CIA oversight, the president used DTPILLAR to fund anticommunist programs that conservatives in Congress would never have approved. While conservative anticommunist members of Congress conducted McCarthyistic witch hunts, liberal anticommunists used CIA funding fronts to fund soft-power anticommunist projects.

The CIA created the Committee for Free Asia "to aid in the creation of private action institutions and groups in Asia which would provide expanding opportunities for Asians and thus counteract the appeal of Communism."[87] With time, the Asia Foundation tried to undermine specific Asian political movements seeking to build democratic nationalist movements not to the United States' liking. In the 1963 Second Revised DTPILLAR Administrative Plan, the priorities for the mission were to counter communism, promote ties with the West, work on "redirecting extreme nationalism" when "eradicating irresponsible neutralism/non-alignment," and "inculcating concepts of freedom and democracy."[88] Released DTPILLAR documents show no acknowledgment within the CIA that other countries pursuing freedom and democracy might naturally do so in nationalistic ways that pursued neutralism and nonalignment.

Passing as a private foundation had benefits beyond allowing for the CIA to make connections with groups and individuals not aligned with US policy. It also allowed the CIA to covertly fund projects benefiting the United States, while allowing this US government–funded foundation to ignore the tight budgetary restrictions governing financial activities of governmental organizations. The Asia Foundation learned valuable lessons from the mistakes of the Committee for Free Asia. Even a decade after ceasing operations as the committee, the foundation remained cautious about being associated with programs producing clumsy anticommunist propaganda. In 1964, the foundation rejected a proposal from its Borneo representative for a proposed Radios for Sabah project seeking foundation funds to purchase radios for people living in rural Borneo. Foundation staff worried their representative was running a psywar program like those CFA had attempted. Even after the representative, William Fleming, rewrote his proposal focusing on adult education, the foundation rejected it, wanting to maintain some distance from anything that might be viewed as heavy-handed anticommunist propaganda.[89] Other examples of the foundation avoiding funding projects that could expose the latent political context of its work include the 1962 rejection of a funding request by Louis Lazaroff in Ceylon, where he was seeking to finance a loan to Ceylon's Harbor Progressive Workers Union. In their rejection, the foundation explained that even though the proposal claimed "that we could support this particular union because it is 'clearly politically independent,' it seems to us that where the Foundation has been attacked openly for its assistance to much less innocuous bodies such as the youth councils, assistance to a labor group would not remain unnoticed by the left wing unions or the right wing employers, or go unmentioned in the press."[90]

One of the lessons the foundation learned from the CFA's obtuse propaganda tactics was that low-key, soft-power forms of persuasion had the best chance of winning Asian hearts and minds. With this rebranding venture, the CIA hoped a more academically anchored, less abrasive approach by the Asia Foundation could accomplish the same anticommunist goals it had established for the Committee for Free Asia.

3 Sponsored Exchanges, Cultural Programs, Conferences, and Scholarships

Given the conditions of perpetual financial crisis within academic institutions, the large-scale funding programs of foundations prove very attractive to researchers and influence the selection of research topics, research questions, and methodologies.

INDERJEET PARMAR / *Foundations of the American Century*

During the 1950s and 1960s, the Asia Foundation funded numerous projects countering Soviet and Chinese communist propaganda. A 1966 CIA secret report, "Communist Cultural and Propaganda Activities in the Less Developed Countries," summarized agency concerns about the communist cultural programs and propaganda operations that the foundation sought to counter. The CIA worried about the recent growth of Soviet cultural propaganda targeting Eastern Europe and the Global South.[1] New Soviet-funded organizations delivered cultural programming through organizations like the binational friendship societies and cultural centers located in forty countries. Soviet radio broadcasting operations in developing nations increased their output from 550 hours per week in 1955 to 2,268 hours in 1964. Communist-backed organizations screened films, produced art exhibits, and published millions of copies of books and periodicals.[2] The CIA worried that the Soviet Union was winning a culture war in Asia.

If one ignored the particular ideologies of communism or capitalism, there were many similarities between 1950s and 1960s Soviet and American cultural and educational programs. Both frequently brought in outside artists, scholars, or intellectuals for public events, and both supported local forms of visual arts, music, or other expressive forms. Both routinely championed their nation's quality of life, scientific achievements, and opportunities for fulfillment.

The CIA reported that by 1966 communists had "extended more than $60 million in economic aid for information media and cultural facilities."[3] By the mid-1960s the Soviets had expanded their programs supporting peoples of the Middle East and Asia to include new programs focusing on Africa, though the CIA estimated that Asian nations would continue to be increasingly targeted by communists.⁴ The CIA's analysis of the goals and methods of Soviet cultural and propaganda programs would only need the alteration of a few words to describe many of the Asia Foundation's international programs—alterations consisting of swapping out "communist" for "capitalist" and "anti-Western" for "anti-Soviet":

> In general, Communist cultural and propaganda programs are designed to establish and strengthen rapport with the people of the less developed countries. The Communist countries particularly seek to identify themselves with the political and economic aspirations and anti-Western prejudices of these countries. The Communists, however, also use their extensive propaganda apparatus to exploit dissatisfaction and to encourage the overthrow of unfriendly regimes. The choice of targets selected by the Communist countries depends upon the expected receptivity of a group, the type of available media most easily exploited by the Communists, and the importance of the target group. The illiterate and poor are rarely the target of Communist propaganda. They have the least access to propaganda media, exert little pressure on government policies, and usually are not a revolutionary force. Those groups typically targeted are youths and students, young government and military officials, leaders of trade unions, and employees of information media.⁵

Cultural programs developed by Soviet and American patrons often targeted the same groups. Both nations offered similar programs and desired to establish loyal clients, making promises of building peaceful and prosperous nations as they struggled for the hearts and minds of Asian clients.

The CIA understood that most of the Soviet Union's foreign propaganda and cultural activities were run by the Communist Party's Central Committee, but it also understood that with the backing of the Soviet government some "propaganda activities also are carried out at a nonofficial level by 'private' organizations, such as the Council of Soviet Societies for Friendship and Cultural Relations with Foreign Countries, the All-Union Central Trade Union Council, the Union of Writers, the Union of Journalists, and the Academy of Sciences."⁶ This Soviet use of fake "private" organizations paralleled the United States' use of CIA fronts to carry out propaganda campaigns.

The report included a map, "Major Less Developed Country Targets for Communist Cultural and Propaganda Activities, as of December 1965," indicating the broad distribution of cultural agreements, cultural societies, films, exhibits, exchanges, or press representatives. The Soviets' visible presence in India included a large staff and programs financing significant publishing and news operations. The Soviet embassy's information department in New Delhi had 125 employees, and its press section had a staff of 25 to 30 employees who printed, translated, and distributed booklets and produced news stories that often made their way into Indian newspapers.[7] These publishing operations provided Indians with free or inexpensive books, pamphlets, and local and national news coverage, all of which generated narratives championing the interests of Soviet patrons in ways similar to how DTPILLAR publishing projects championed procapitalist narratives.

Beginning in the early 1960s, the Soviet Union established academic centers focusing on Asian, Latin American, and African studies, training specialists in the languages, culture, and history of these regions.[8] These Soviet developments mirrored US universities' postwar growth of area studies as both superpowers struggled for the same hearts and minds scattered across the globe. The CIA observed that cultural agreements between the Soviet Union and developing countries were "often ... the first important Communist step in establishing a presence."[9] The CIA found that, in the years since 1956, "36 less developed countries have signed at least 165 separate cultural agreements with Communist countries." The majority of these were between the Soviet Union and Eastern European countries, but China and the Soviet Union also had a growing presence in Asia.[10] Film and book programs, international scholarships, radio broadcasts, and artistic cultural exchanges were the communists' most significant types of cultural exchange.

To better understand how the Soviet Union used these cultural programs, the CIA analyzed two cultural agreements between the Soviet Union and Nepal. One agreement established an exchange of films, art exhibitions, radio broadcasts, publications, and delegations that were "in keeping with the principles of sovereignty, equality, and noninterference in the internal affairs of other countries."[11] The resulting exchanges under this agreement included displays of Soviet stamps and photographs, the funding of a Soviet lecturer's visit, a Soviet stage ensemble, and two radio experts provided to the Nepalese government. The Soviet Union also hosted a photography exhibition, sponsored an eighteen-member Nepalese cultural delegation and twenty-five Nepalese students, and funded a delegation of Nepalese literary experts' travel to the Soviet Union. Links were forged between Soviet and Nepalese universities, which led to an exchange of textbooks, music, and radio programs.[12] Similar agreements were established between Nepal and China, and the Chinese government financed programs distributing films, art, and books and providing musical performances, as well as academic and journalistic exchanges.

Sometimes such agreements to reciprocate cultural exchanges strained the resources of poorer countries. These strains led "many less developed countries to discourage the Communist participant from sending more cultural groups than they themselves can possibly send in return."[13] Communists used binational friendship societies and cultural centers to establish interpersonal links as gateways for political indoctrination. Between 1957 and 1964 "communist countries established such organizations in more than 40 less developed countries."[14] The CIA used "friendship societies" in similar ways, connecting Americans with individuals in countries of interest through secretly CIA-funded organizations, like the American Friends of the Middle East, in efforts to steer public opinion.[15] The CIA observed that "to conceal their involvement in the activities of the friendship societies and to avoid official objections, the Communists frequently resort to indirect methods of financing these organizations," a tactic mirroring the CIA's modus operandi for the Asia Foundation.[16]

Between the mid-1950s and mid-1960s the number of communist-themed radio broadcasts significantly increased in underdeveloped nations.[17] These broadcasts mixed news, music, or educational programming with programs designed to appeal to a range of demographics.[18] In 1962 the Soviet Communist Party's Central Committee ordered a "sharp increase in the number of hours broadcast" focused on targeted-audience programming.[19] These programs were designed to appeal to women and youth and often provided programming platforms for locals to talk about their impressions of the Soviet Union after traveling there.[20]

In the United States, the CIA sometimes used private publishers, like Praeger Press and Franklin Books, to produce and distribute desired books.[21] The Soviets used their government publishing system for similar ends. Since the 1950s, the CIA had secretly used bookstores in foreign countries, like Pacific Book and Supply in Indonesia, to distribute a variety of books meeting local needs, and the CIA reported that communist nations were engaging in similar operations, by subsidizing the distribution of books and periodicals.[22] The Soviets' foreign language publication program was impressive; in 1964 they "published about 45 million copies of more than 1,500 books in about 40 non-Soviet languages. Of these, almost 28 million copies, consisting of more than 1,000 titles[,] were published in 24 languages spoken in less developed countries."[23] The Soviet

Union used both open and clandestine means to distribute books, periodicals, and pamphlets, including sponsoring libraries, mailing items directly, and distributing materials through international book exhibits, unions, communist front organizations, or embassies. To increase circulation, book prices were significantly reduced by government subsidies. These Soviet-published books were "obtained at substantial discounts with payment frequently made in local currency to the Communist embassy or consulate, often after the shipment has been sold. The transaction tends to be profitable for the local bookseller and involves no outlay of foreign exchange." The CIA worried about the ideological impacts of the Soviets' campaign, as it almost quadrupled the volume of exported books and periodicals between 1955 and 1963.[24]

Communists funded travel for delegations of artists, scholars, musicians, scientists, writers, trade unionists, and youth organizations. These exchange programs tried to create favorable opinions among travelers, and communist hosts stressed themes of "peaceful coexistence" while presenting China or the Soviet Union "as a model society, express[ing] admiration for the national cultures and achievement of the visitors' countries."[25]

KISSINGER'S HARVARD INTERNATIONAL SEMINAR

In early 1956, Representative Walter Judd (R-MN), a foundation trustee, criticized those looking to "guns and money" as solutions for political problems in Asia and elsewhere while "they overlook the intangible factors—matters of human dignity, the spiritual and psychological factors." Judd identified the three "targets" of the foundation's efforts in Asia as being students, books, and "ideas that uphold spiritual values and individual dignity." Judd viewed each target as part of a larger anticommunist program in which "the communists try to get the intellectuals first" with their subsidized "large shipments of communist books." Judd wanted the United States to counter this Soviet effort with inexpensive or free pro-Western publications, arguing that because the communists "are not always talking about communism, but about human welfare, human freedom, and about the promise of the future, in ways that stir men's hearts and arouse great hopes," DTPILLAR should seek to counter this propaganda with programs meeting these same needs while challenging communist claims.[26]

From the mid-1950s onward three tactics—supporting students, supplying books, and appealing to Asian dignity—were cornerstones of DTPILLAR's international educational programs. The foundation's support for the Harvard

International Seminar program exemplified this commitment to supporting select ideologies while appealing to the dignity and values of Asian participants, all while establishing contact with individuals who appeared to have bright futures in Asia.

For most of a decade the foundation provided airfare for Asian participants attending Professor Henry Kissinger's Harvard International Seminar.[27] These seminars began in 1951 and each year brought scholars and other public intellectuals from Europe for weeks of highbrow networking and discourse on politics, the arts, literature, and social science—discussions frequently explicitly including pro-Western or anticommunist themes. The seminar used these close interactions to export American political ideals, since, as participants returned home, they "carried back with them their picture of American freedom and democracy."[28]

Seminar reading lists mixed classics with contemporary, pro-Western, anticommunist essays or novels. The 1961 seminar's reading list included Adam Ulam's *The Unfinished Revolution: An Essay on the Sources and Influence of Marxism and Communism* (1960), and Ulam led a seminar on the psychological conditions necessary for a successful communist revolution.[29] Foundation files include detailed descriptions of the political discussions that occurred during this seminar, descriptions that identify the arguments of individual seminar participants by name. One seminar session opened with a discussion of George Washington's farewell address, stressing his argument that all nations must pursue their own interests. This set up a contrived discussion led by Hans Gresmann, championing Allen Dulles's position that there is no place for neutralism in a world divided by communism and capitalism. Seminar leaders discussed how the Soviet Union "exploited" the anticolonialist and nationalist sentiments of developing nations. Discussions criticizing notions of neutrality continued for several sessions, and foundation records include seven single-spaced pages of notes tracking individual participants' views of the politics of neutrality. A later seminar read J. D. Salinger's *Catcher in the Rye* and considered the meaning of disaffected American youth in the postwar period; no notes survive indicating what individual participants thought of that Ackley kid.[30]

In late 1956, after receiving Kissinger's request for another lump sum of funds to bring Asian intellectuals to these seminars, an internal memo by foundation staffer Richard Heggie presented an evaluation of the seminar and its relationship with the foundation. While Heggie identified several positive outcomes from this relationship, he proposed that rather than providing funds and leaving the participant selection to Kissinger, the foundation could help select participants. He argued that the foundation had provided $20,150 for the previous seminar, yet "seldom has a nominee of a Representative not been selected by Dr. Kissinger." Heggie complained about the "effectiveness" of seminar alumni, noting that in some instances "the Seminar has been used by some participants as a forum for attacks on United States foreign policy." Heggie wanted countries that would be sending participants to establish selection committees, on which no foundation representatives would serve, while country representatives would later review recommendations before passing them along to Kissinger. This proposal left open the possibility that these lists might change as they were passed through foundation hands.[31]

Foundation efforts to control selection of Asian participants upset Kissinger.[32] He complained of his "disappointment in the increasing tendency of your representatives even in countries where they do support us to seek to control the selection procedure entirely." Kissinger claimed he would concur with ninety-nine out of a hundred recommendations, and his objections were based on "a question of principle," leading him to a position in which he could not "turn over to another organization the right to make the selection."[33] The foundation conceded Kissinger's right to select participants.[34]

Foundation attempts to influence Kissinger's selections remained an ongoing struggle. In 1962, "Mrs. Norman Coliver," acting director of the foundation's Program Services Division, sent Kissinger specific participant recommendations from the foundation's Ceylon field representative.[35] Staff recommendations to Kissinger were common occurrences, and in some instances field representatives requested specific individuals.[36]

HARVARD'S NIEMAN FELLOWSHIPS

In 1938, the Nieman Foundation established a $1.4 million endowment that would bring journalists to study at Harvard for a year. The initial Nieman program, shaped by James Conant, Archibald MacLeish, and Walter Lippman, had these practicing journalists reading common texts, engaging in discussions with colleagues, and being encouraged to contemplate their craft. The ties established by bringing Asian journalists to the United States connected DTPILLAR with important Asian opinion makers, while the curriculum strove to shape participants' views in ways aligned with US policy.

The foundation began providing funds for Asian Nieman Fellowships in 1955, and these funds allowed it to select the participating Asian journalists.[37] Of the sixteen Nieman Fellows for 1956, all were men, with nine from the United States and five from New Zealand, Australia, Japan, India, and Pakistan.[38] Harvard's role hosting the Fellows assured an air of prestige and legitimacy as the seminar exposed international journalists to certain American intellectual critiques.[39] The CIA's involvement in the Nieman program was secret until 1977, when the *New York Times* reported that the Asia Foundation had "provided cover for at least one CIA operative and carried out a variety of media-related ventures, including a program, begun in 1955, of selecting and paying the expenses of Asian journalists for a year of study in Harvard's prestigious Nieman Fellowship program."[40]

Sometimes, links between journalists and the Asia Foundation were short-lived, lasting only for the duration of the fellowship. In other instances, contacts with foundation staff continued after fellows returned to their home country, under dynamics in which, as described by Parmar, "foundation networks are system-maintenance systems that *usually*—after a sufficient period of foundation patronage—self-perpetuate. Their self-perpetuation becomes a vested interest of the networks' key constituencies."[41]

Some Nieman Fellows worried their participation in this elite US network could taint their reputations after they returned home. In 1956, Gunupati Keshava Reddy, a well-respected journalist at the *Times of India*, confided to Robert Blum that he "was anxious to visit the Foundation in the United States and that he hoped to help us remove some of the suspicion and misunderstandings with the Indian Government." These suspicions came from rumors Reddy heard from a former Indian consul general based in San Francisco, Azim Hussin, that the foundation "engaged in anti-Indian activity." Hussin told Reddy that the Committee for Free Asia had run on State Department funds "set aside [for] subversive purposes" and that the foundation had created difficulties for Indian journalist Wilfred Lazarus.[42] The foundation's name change only partially distanced it from the CFA's more obvious propaganda tactics. Hussin's guess that the committee was funded by "some secret State Department fund set aside [for] subversive purposes" was not far from the mark, though the truth was more devious than he guessed.

Three years later, G. L. Jain, chief reporter for the *Times of India*, complained to Blum about recent Nieman Fellowship selections from India. Jain complained that G. K. Reddy had been "a bad selection." In Jain's view, the previous year's fellow, T. V. Parasuram, "was a good man, but had little political sense," and

Jain felt the current fellow was another poor choice. To eliminate these issues, Jain wanted the foundation to select Nieman Fellows on their own, without consulting anyone in India.[43] Jain's harsh remarks revealed the political dimensions of and desired outcomes for these fellowships. With time, the foundation increasingly vetted Fellows joining the established network of Asian journalists.

But even with Harvard as a backdrop, as well as a curriculum promoting the promises of Western ideals, not all Nieman Fellows returned home with the views that the foundation envisioned for them. In 1963, after completing his Nieman Fellowship, Vietnamese journalist Nguyen Thai sent a final report to Asia Foundation grantee advisor John Plate, thanking the foundation for the opportunity and summarizing the outcomes of his time at Harvard. After recounting various fellowship activities, Thai wrote that his fellowship had given him the opportunity to reflect on his personal position on the war in Vietnam, and these reflections clarified his opposition to his government. He wrote that, "practically speaking[,] I have become a *persona non grata* for the Diem regime as a consequence of my decision to speak up against the unfortunate situation prevailing in South Vietnam. I had the alternative of keeping quiet and going along with the Diem regime which is still the legal government in power and the 'ally' of the USA."[44]

The foundation wanted Thai to return to Vietnam with the perspectives he had gained at Harvard informing his work, presumably writing again for the *Vietnam Press*, but instead this experience strengthened his resolve against the war.[45] He concluded there was "no possibility . . . to reform from within the Diem regime," but he believed that as an experienced journalist he could help inform Americans about the situation in Vietnam. With these considerations Thai accepted an appointment at the University of Missouri School of Journalism's Freedom of Information Center, though he later returned to Vietnam after Diem's assassination.[46]

NASIM AHMED, VISITING PAKISTANI JOURNALIST

The foundation worked hard to establish connections with foreign journalists. When traveling in Asia, foundation president Robert Blum frequently sought out local journalists at parties or arranged to meet over meals—sometimes inviting them to apply for Nieman Fellowships or for other funding opportunities. Blum's travel reports regularly included information or analysis he picked up from such meetings.

One example of how the foundation sometimes used these relationships with foreign journalists appears in mid-1950s records of ongoing foundation contacts with Pakistani journalist Nasim Ahmed. Prior to visiting the United States as a delegate to the United Nations International Press Institute seminar, Nasim Ahmed, a news reporter from Pakistan, corresponded with foundation representative Lyman Hoover of the New York office. Ahmed wanted to meet with foundation personnel to discuss the foundation's neglect of Pakistani students studying in the West. His letter to Hoover stressed the need for proper hostels or other facilities in London to meet the needs of Pakistani students studying there.[47]

Before Ahmed's arrival, foundation staffer Pat Casey circulated memos stressing the need to support the Pakistan Student Federation, noting that Ahmed was a founder of the Pakistan Society and an important contact for the foundation. Ahmed met with several foundation staff members, as well as with President Blum, and was taken to dinner by foundation staff member Colin D. Edwards and his wife. Edwards reported that Ahmed complained that while there were many Pakistani students studying in Britain, there remained a significant lack of "social facilities" for them at their universities. The Pakistan government had purchased a sizable house that could serve as a student center in London, but it needed remodeling, furniture, and books for a library. Ahmed asked Edwards for foundation help funding these additions so that he could establish the Pakistan Student Federation there, which could connect these students to foundation personnel.[48]

Ahmed's anticommunist bona fides were established with his account of how as a young journalist in London he had exposed a group of Pakistani communists who had taken over the Pakistan Student Federation. He had written "a series of articles exposing the situation and through his influences the membership carried out a new election in which the communists got only 10 votes from the 400 members present." Ahmed stressed that while these communists were no longer in control, their threat remained, and he identified "one of the most active organizers" as a journalist for a Hong Kong newspaper, Mohamed Ali. He stressed that there was rapid recruiting of Asian students by communists in Europe and stated that "Asian students in Western Europe were being made tempting offers of scholarships and fellowships in Eastern Europe by communist student organizations operating from Prague. And that many students were accepting vacation invitations to Eastern Europe, Russia and even Communist China, returning with glowing accounts of the flattering attention they had received and the marvelous things they had been shown."[49]

PHAM XUAN AN

While Asia Foundation projects sought to develop pro-American sentiments, some funding recipients remained, or became, critics of the United States rather than supporters. The most famous such example was Pham Xuan An, now recognized as one of the most successful anti-American spies during the Vietnam War. Under an Asia Foundation fellowship, An traveled to Costa Mesa, California, in 1958 to study journalism at Orange Coast College. His studies led to a journalism internship at the *Sacramento Bee* and a driving trip from California to New York and Washington, DC, where the foundation helped him meet top journalists and wire service representatives. An used these experiences to establish his career as one of the most valuable journalists covering the Vietnam War, working for *Time* and other publications. An's reporting was held in high esteem by America's top journalists covering the war.

After the war's end, Pham Xuan An was exposed as having spied for the North Vietnamese throughout the war, during which he used his position as a journalist and his work for the US military to acquire extremely valuable information from US forces. During the war, An frequently spent late evenings secretly photographing documents. He would then pack the film canisters inside *nem ninh hoa*—grilled pork wrapped in rice paper—or inside rotting fish that he passed along to couriers for the Vietnamese National Liberation Front (NLF).[50]

The foundation first became aware of Pham Xuan An in August 1958, after its Vietnam representative met with Captain John D. Horner and Pham Xuan An. An was then working for the US military in Vietnam, though he was already operating as a spy for the North Vietnamese communists even as US Cold War counterinsurgency warrior Edward Lansdale "arranged for the military attaché in Saigon to take An for a meeting with the Asia Foundation representative."[51]

An was born in Binh-truoc (Bien-hoa), in southern Vietnam, in 1927, and was educated at Franco-Vietnamese High School before working in private business and as a government employee. In 1954, he was "mobilized by the Department of National Defense and assigned to the Director Central of Psychological Warfare," where he worked as a secretary in the Moral Action Office until May 1955. He soon began work in the military's press office, later becoming an interpreter for the US military, then a Vietnamese liaison officer for the US Military Assistance Group (MAG) to Vietnam. In February 1957, he resigned from the National Army and prepared to study in the United States.[52]

In 1958, this Vietnamese spy arrived in California to study journalism. He was a good student, made friends easily, and used this experience to make important journalistic connections that would help him in his work once he returned to Vietnam. After completing his studies, An planned to return to Vietnam in the fall of 1959 with hopes of writing for the *Times of Viet-Nam*. While studying in the United States, he wrote that after graduation, he wanted to get some on-the-job training at an American newspaper, and he drew on foundation support funds and contacts at American newspapers for further training.[53]

The Asia Foundation provided a special "in-service training grant" and made arrangements for the McClatchy chain's flagship newspaper, the *Sacramento Bee*, to host An.[54] At the foundation's request, the *Bee* helped An meet with McClatchy employees working on the international wire service so that An might use these connections when reporting from Vietnam in the future. *Sacramento Bee* staff helped An make arrangements to later meet with newspaper staff in Washington, DC, and New York. The foundation introduced An to personnel at *Vietnam Presse*, opening future employment opportunities.[55] McClatchy staff also arranged for An to meet with members of their Washington bureau, and the Asia Foundation provided travel and per diem funds and arranged for him to meet with individuals at the *New York Times*, *Time*, *Life*, and *Look* magazines.[56] An wanted to spend as much time as possible at the United Nations, and the foundation and *Sacramento Bee* staff helped him secure a press credential providing access to the General Assembly meeting, where he watched Nikita Khrushchev deliver a speech.[57]

Here was an instance where the CIA used the Asia Foundation to unwittingly provide one of the most skilled anti-American spies of the Vietnam War with the opportunities, training, and contacts that were foundations of his espionage cover that would later allow him to pass along intelligence damaging American military prospects in Vietnam. As with other CIA ventures, when trying to manipulate people or culture, the unintended consequences were sometimes as significant as the intended ones.

OBSERVING AND MAKING CONNECTIONS AT CONFERENCES

By selectively funding scholars with grants, fellowships, or academic conference travel and fees, DTPILLAR shaped academic discourse in important ways. Such selections are normal foundation activities, but CIA foundation directives steered funding in specific ideological directions. The influence staff exerted in these selection processes varied, but sometimes Asia Foundation staff shaped the discourse of sponsored events. In one example, while assisting with the planning of an upcoming science symposium in Japan, foundation president Blum provided his own list of scholars to be invited, a list drawing from an already constrained pool of coalescing academic voices from Princeton and Columbia and the Social Science Research Council. Blum helped select scholars espousing liberal anticommunist ideas bolstered by the foundation.[58]

Sometimes organizers planning conferences wrote Blum seeking foundation funding or advice. In one such example from 1956, Henry M. Wriston, then in the early planning stages for an upcoming American Assembly conference, wrote President Blum seeking advice.[59] Blum replied, indicating interest in supporting the conference.[60] Months later, the assembly's associate director, Clifford C. Nelson, asked Blum to "recommend any people from the West Coast who would make good participants" for their upcoming assembly meeting, where US assistance programs and American foreign policy would be discussed. In his reply letter, Blum handwrote seven names of individuals to be invited: Frederick Anderson, Brayton Wilbur, Russell Smith, John McCone, John Condliffe, Admiral Spruance, and Admiral Nimitz.[61] Blum's reply the following week, on February 13, 1957, included a slightly different list of recommended participants—minus Admiral Nimitz and plus R. Allen Griffin (publisher, *Monterey Peninsula Herald*) and William H. Draper ("Chairman of the Board, Mexican Light and Power Company, Mexico City, Mexico[;] was US Special Representative in Europe with rank of Ambassador from 1952–54").[62] Blum also provided information on his proposed additions.[63]

In March, Blum wrote Raymond Allen, chancellor of the University of California, Los Angeles, suggesting specific participants for the upcoming western regional American Assembly conference on "the United States and the Far East." Blum annotated Allen's original list, adding "+" and "−" marks on this list, indicating whether he thought specific individuals should be invited ("+") or not ("−"). Out of the thirty-eight originally suggested names, he recommended not inviting thirty-two individuals on Allen's list, and he recommended only six individuals from the original list. Blum's preferred list championed a local oil executive, select local journalists, and several Stanford University scholars.[64]

Through such exchanges, DTPILLAR corralled academic discourse. Sometimes Blum's responses limited academic freedom, with recommendations reducing the political range of conference discourse. In some sense, such limitations are normal elements of planning any conference programs, but as the Asia Foundation was a CIA-funded entity, these limitations on political discourse deformed the promise of informed democracy in the United States.

The foundation supported several meetings of the covertly CIA-funded Congress for Cultural Freedom (CCF), in which academic papers challenged communism or championed Western democratic ideals. While there was some overlap in the types of CCF programming funded by the CIA versus DTPILLAR-funded programs, the breadth of Asia Foundation programming reached beyond the higher-brow intellectualism that the congress nurtured.[65] The foundation's report on the 1960 Berlin CCF conference noted that "the communist issue was not separately discussed but was of course implied in much of what was said and was referred to frequently. At no time, however, did it appear that the conference was no more than an anti-communist propaganda platform. The general level of participation was high and the intellectual tone sustained."[66] The foundation offered to cover Sidney Hook's New York University faculty salary during a planned 1956–67 CCF-supported Asian tour. Hook planned to lecture on philosophy with his own anticommunist flare, but at the last minute Hook had to cancel the trip.[67]

In 1957, the foundation provided funds to supply 150 libraries in India with copies of CCF's *Encounter* magazine, and it funded a CCF seminar in Pakistan as well as Khmer architecture archaeologist M. Jean Laur's trip to the United States.[68] Professor Q. M. Aslam, MA professor of psychology at the University of Karachi and a member of the Executive of Pakistan Committee of CCF, reported to the foundation on the CCF-sponsored Islamic Seminar held in Karachi in early 1959. Aslam described this meeting as "more fruitful and productive" than the 1957 Islamic Colloquium held in Lahore, which he wrote had been co-opted by communists. Aslam wrote that at this previous conference "the Russians, the Chinese and some of their friends did whatever they could to convert scholarly deliberations into political debates. The Islamic-Western competition in thinking, inevitable in a gathering of this sort, took an ugly turn at times. Speakers showed a tendency to play to the gallery and at least one paper became the subject of fierce controversy: some asking for an excision of some of its parts, others for the retention of every word."[69] Professor Aslam noted that two papers at the 1959 seminar argued that Islam was inherently opposed to the principles of communism, because the latter was "materialistic, Godless and naïve."[70]

Asia Foundation staff routinely attended conferences where they met with Asian professors and students they funded. Staff reports summarized conference papers and meetings with conference attendees.[71] Asian scholars receiving foundation funds to attend conferences were often asked to submit conference reports. Foundation staff themselves routinely attended academic conferences focusing on anticommunism. Staffer Jerzy "George" Lerski reported on an assortment of mostly anticommunist papers presented at a 1964 Hoover Institution conference, "War, Revolution, and Peace." His favorite paper was by Raymond Aron, "The Impact of Marxism in the Twentieth Century," which argued that "in the course of the West's dialog with Marxism some of the American intellectuals subconsciously assimilated certain Marxist assumptions," an argument absurdly including Walt Rostow's book *The Stages of Economic Growth: A Non Communist Manifesto* as an example of this crypto-assimilationist Marxist trend.[72] Reports like this demonstrate that internal dialogues within the foundation at times created anticommunist echo chambers, where dogmas became unquestioned truths while reinforcing intellectual blind spots and ignoring significant postcolonial issues facing Asian nations.

Douglas P. Murray's report on the 1955 Sinocentric World Order Conference discussed political science professor Allen Whiting's criticisms of US assumptions that China would be an "irresponsible nuclear" power or that China would necessarily violate neighboring borders. Murray observed foundation staff attending such conferences and comfortably engaging with academic professionals, and in his view such conferences served as "excellent recruiting grounds for contract personnel, particularly from the academic world." These sorts of potential contacts were important enough that Murray recommended "conference participants from the Foundation should be thoroughly and routinely briefed, particularly by the Personnel Division, in advance."[73]

ASIA FOUNDATION ARTS AND CULTURE FUNDING

The Asia Foundation funded various cultural and arts programs, including grants for purchasing art supplies, sponsoring arts training, and funding folk art surveys. The foundation produced traditional music records, staged theatrical productions, financed folklore projects and musical performances, and underwrote arts festivals, dance troupes, and film projects. In the literary arts, it funded the publication of local books, translation projects, literary magazines, and literary awards, and it paid for Asian scholars to travel to international literary conferences.[74]

Funding arts and culture projects often served dual purposes. These arts projects generally focused on preservation or education, and in broader terms there were sometimes also unstated counterinsurgency-linked outcomes associated with these programs. Consider the brief description below of a Thai project collecting and preserving traditional folk art objects. While fundamentally a cultural arts program, it also supported US-backed counterinsurgency goals in the region. This project used the language of cultural preservation as it brought border patrol police into close contact, under a "friendly" academic pretext, with those they policed in this "Study of Hill Tribes by the Department of Public Welfare." According to this report, "Funds for the Department of Public Welfare to assist in the making of a study of the hill tribes of Thailand and to the Siam Society [will] help in its comparative program with the Border Patrol Police for the preservation of the fast disappearing cultural artifacts which will assist in the study of hill tribes, indicating for settlement, also for the purchase of artifacts and the making of films depicting the use of these artifacts."[75] This program recast Thai border patrol police not as armed agents of the state but as caring preservationists while striving to increase friendly contacts between police and villagers, though it is difficult to imagine villagers easily shifting their views.

Sponsoring cultural programming also connected the foundation with influential members of Asian societies. One foundation document explained that "cultural programming creates an excellent entrée to the artistic elite and the influential patrons of art in the given country." Some programs revitalized traditional arts and strove to enhance "the Foundation's reputation as an intellectual institution." One of the foundation's cost-benefit anticommunist rationalizations for investing the foundation's dollars in indigenous cultural programming was that it "helps destroy the communist propaganda myth about the cultural inferiority of 'barbaric and dollar-minded Americans.'"[76]

While most foundation publishing projects translated Western writing into Asian languages, other projects translated Asian-language works into English, such as a 1962 project for which the foundation provided $182,500 to establish the Institute for the Study of Japanese Social Thought, which translated Japanese political and legal writings into English.[77] President Blum consulted with Grayson Kirk and Wallace Stirling, presidents of Columbia and Stanford, while planning the institute, and the foundation influenced the selection of which specific political works (i.e., those aligned with US policy goals) were translated.[78]

The foundation also sponsored Asian speaking tours for American writers. Selected writers were usually famous authors without polemical anticommunist positions, but on occasion, such as the sponsorship of philosopher Sidney Hook's 1959 Japanese speaking tour, selected writers had blunt anticommunist political messages.[79] But even when selecting writers with less explicit political messages, the foundation played a significant role in the character of the speaking tours. In assisting with the logistics of a 1960 PEN American Writers tour of Asia, Robert Sedwick, the foundation's Program Services Division acting director, helped cull an initial list of three dozen US authors, working with John Farrar (of Farrar, Straus and Cudahy) to make the selection. The archived copy of the foundation's list includes handwritten rankings, with some authors marked as "questionable" and eliminated from consideration.[80]

JERZY LERSKI'S CIA-FUNDED ANTICOMMUNIST TRACTS

For many years the Asia Foundation supported the work of Jerzy Lerski (aka George Jan Lerski), a Polish-born anticommunist intellectual and World War II hero. Between 1954 and 1964, DTPILLAR funded visiting professorships for Lerski in Japan, Pakistan, and Ceylon.[81] Early in the war, Lerski had been captured by Soviet forces, but he escaped in 1939, eventually making his way to Britain, where he joined the Polish army's secret commando unit operating in exile and parachuted into occupied Poland in 1943. After the war he immigrated to the United States and earned a PhD in history from Georgetown University in 1953, and the following year he accepted the first of more than a decade's worth of DTPILLAR-funded positions.

Lerski spent two years working for the foundation's San Francisco office as a program specialist in the Review and Development Department—a job requiring direct knowledge of the CIA's role in funding Asia Foundation operations. The foundation funded another two-year visiting professorship at the University of Ceylon, Peradeniya, where in 1964–65 he wrote parts of a book chronicling the rise of Trotskyism in Ceylon.[82] He was next awarded a research associate position at the Hoover Institution, where with additional Asia Foundation funding he conducted archival research for his Ceylon Trotskyism project. The acknowledgments of his 1968 book *Origins of Trotskyism in Ceylon*, published by the Hoover Institution, fail to mention the central role of the Asia Foundation in producing this work; this omission may have been linked to the then recent revelations of the foundation's CIA ties.

Foundation records contain an incompletely dated (August 25, no year), unattributed four-page report titled "Contemporary Communist Strategy and Tactics" that summarized a discussion by Lerski and several foundation staff members. Lerski argued that while there were no changes in communist doctrine overall, new soft-line tactics designed to broaden their base were evident.

These tactics were designed to weaken Western positions abroad, to "drive a breach between the American government and American intellectuals and opinion leaders," and to weaken the positions of leaders and groups "cognizant of the enduring nature of long-range communist doctrine."[83]

Lerski argued that the communists' recognition of past shortcomings in their tactics did not necessarily mean they would react defensively but that they would likely develop new programs to attract allies. These new programs "may include infiltration efforts in the educational, cultural, youth, and other fields. Thus, it is important that The Asia Foundation develop means, not necessarily of combat, by which it can recognize these long-range efforts in specific areas of activity." Lerski wanted foundation delegates attending international conferences to be aware of such communist tactics and to counter these moves.[84]

Responding to Lerski's analysis, foundation representative James Dalton displayed his abilities as a capitalist dialectician, arguing that "the struggle between capitalism and communism will always be directed according to the dialectic development of world society. Communist struggle will take advantage of all types of conflicts in the social structure." James Stewart argued that this strategic shift could impact the foundation, as Asian members of existing groups would likely be unaware of communist efforts to subvert their organizations. After discussion of the possible roles the foundation might play in preventing such communist infestations, some suggested that the foundation direct anticommunist training. But longtime foundation staffer Harry Pierson clarified that "a direct anti-communist role is denied to the Foundation" but that foundation employees needed to be aware of these intrusive tactics.[85]

EXCHANGE AS PROPAGANDA

While many DTPILLAR-funded exchanges, seminars, workshops, and other programs had clear anticommunist or pro-American connotations, it would be a mistake to interpret all these programs strictly as transactional investments. Not all foundation interactions were as straightforward as simply funding individuals to produce specified anticommunist results. The foundation in a general sense funded programs with various goals, casting generally pro-American seeds on barren and fertile ground alike, but whether the seeds being sown nurtured friends or supported desired ideologies, there was little randomness in the political views expressed through these efforts. Run as a covert operation, the program faced little pressure for the sort of outcome-based assessment that a closely monitored operation might face. Nevertheless, CIA reports repeatedly indicated agency satisfaction with connections made and intelligence produced by the foundation.

The perceived need to competitively match or exceed Soviet spending played significant roles in launching many DTPILLAR programs, but notions that investments in educational or cultural programs, conferences, or seminars were viable weapons for undermining the advance of communism in Asia reveals how the CIA viewed itself, its powers, and its global domain. The agency had no compunction about deceiving Asians, Americans, or others if that deception advanced the cause of anticommunism—so long as no one figured it out.

Specific messages were relayed in the books published and curriculum supported by Asia Foundation dollars—messages linked more to US goals than to anything approaching local indigenous empowerment. As Audra Wolfe has observed, "Despite the Asia Foundation's stated commitment to 'Asian programming for Asians,' the organization did not attempt to create or even encourage the development of indigenous curriculum reform programs. Instead, it provided various kinds of financial and material support for translating and adapting the newly revised US science textbooks for Asian markets."[86] Frequently, the sort of science training the foundation supported aligned with faith-based principles of Rostowian modernization, which required the infusion of technology and Western science into a society for the magic of modernization's anticommunism to succeed. It was a Cold War act of faith that US-linked modernization projects would keep communism at bay.

While there was little hidden about what many of these programs offered and did, the CIA's hidden role as funder and authorizer of the foundation's programs reveals that none of these programs were simply what they seemed to be. Even the most basic interpretation of the covert operation of the foundation, assuming that all of these programs operated exactly as publicly claimed, reveals the CIA deceiving at least three parties: grantees, host nations receiving these funds, and the American public.

The foundation's scholarship, conference, and exchange programs established ties supporting US-style capitalism and democracy, and there were political uses for training Asian leaders in certain ways. As Frank Sutton, a Ford Foundation vice president, observed, "You cannot have a modernizing country without a modernizing elite," and as the CIA had uses for the debt and dependency that came with modernization's programs, the foundation helped train and identify elites who could work with the West.[87] As the foundation expanded into new countries, these programs, along with other publishing and educational efforts, were frequently used as examples of what the foundation could accomplish. But the foundation supported other types of programs that had less to do with cultural or educational exchanges and more to do with quelling rebellions or uprisings through implementing foundation-supported counterinsurgency operations. These programs represent one of the ways DTPILLAR connected with the CIA's better-known, sometimes violent anticommunist Cold War operations, characterized by author Vincent Bevins as the "Jakarta methods." Such links to CIA counterinsurgency goals show DTPILLAR operations as a vital piece of the CIA's larger strategy to subdue, with violence, Asian people's efforts to develop political and economic solutions to the postwar, postcolonial problems they faced in their own lands. It is these strategic ties between the CIA's violent Asian operations and DTPILLAR's seemingly benign soft-power cultural and educational efforts that reveal the disturbing impacts of these programs.

4 How the CIA Tried to Make Friends and Influence People

What I soon discovered was that in accepting [US] "aid," we were infecting ourselves with a virus which poisoned the national bloodstream. I tried to resist their "dollar diplomacy," but it was like an insidious, paralysis-type illness—and by the time the symptoms appeared it was too late to do much about it. Even after I cut off aid altogether, the poison continued its work. Top level "dollar addicts" in our government were prepared to commit treason and maybe to undermine my stop-gap measures, in order to get the dollars flowing in again.

PRINCE NORODOM SIHANOUK / *My War with the CIA*

To understand the CIA's interest in funding what might appear to be innocuous DTPILLAR soft-power operations, it is important to consider the full range of CIA global anticommunist operations during this period. DTPILLAR was but one part of the larger CIA Cold War project. As the writings of Vincent Bevins, Vijay Prashad, Bradley R. Simpson, and many others document, during the Cold War the CIA recurrently used violence to attack a variety of postcolonial movements that did not strictly align themselves with narrowly defined US governmental or corporate interests. In Vietnam, Laos, Indonesia, Iran, Guatemala, and many other Cold War fronts, the CIA attacked political organizations, including popular democratic movements, that it viewed as threatening US geopolitical or economic interests. While DTPILLAR was not bureaucratically part of these violent operations, it was nonetheless functionally and budgetarily part of this same project.

These relatively harmless-seeming soft-power DTPILLAR projects were part of the larger anticommunist operations that included CIA support for violent conflict with nonaligned movements, communists, socialists, and anticolonialist movements around the globe. DTPILLAR was but one of many tools the agency used in this conflict for control over Asian bodies, hearts, minds, and markets, with DTPILLAR's greatest focus being on hearts and minds.

The driving forces behind the Asia Foundation's 1950s and 1960s programming was the CIA's mission to eclipse Soviet and Chinese efforts to win Asian loyalties. By the mid-1950s, the US government was increasingly struggling to match communist programs providing development aid; it began using State

Department agencies like the International Cooperation Agency (ICA), or later the US Agency for International Development (AID), to supply agricultural or industrial technology and training. The State Department's US Information Agency and other agencies provided cultural programming competing with Soviet programs. These programs were sometimes critiqued by Asians because of their US government sponsorship. These critiques made the Asia Foundation, as an apparently nongovernmental organization, an attractive alternative channel for funding Asian cultural programs.

DTPILLAR sponsored numerous soft-power "good neighbor" projects. Some community-building programs boosted the United States' image in Asia, while other programs were more directly tied to US political interests or facilitated intelligence gathering. In 1955, the Asia Foundation hired academic consultants "to study and make recommendations on [the foundation's] major operation policies and programs."[1] These consultants supported foundation efforts to fund the types of cultural programs ignored by the Point Four Program, President Truman's ambitious global development program.

The consultants recommended that the foundation remain nimble and unconstrained by bureaucratic structures so it could easily shift and meet local needs. They favored projects supporting Asian elites. The consultants recognized the dangers for the foundation should it appear too obviously to be supporting political factions or engaging openly in anticommunist propaganda, and they advised that "the Foundation should support anti-communist activities if genuine local initiative and interest are involved" but warned that the foundation risked accusations of "political meddling unless its activities are confined to cultural groups, and local support is sought for its operation by well-established civic groups with broad interests."[2]

These recommendations reinforced existing post-CFA practices. The selection of these academic consultants all but guaranteed a report telling the foundation what it wished to hear—a dynamic as old as the existence of consultants.[3] These consultants had disciplinary expertise in Asia, and each also had significant past links to wartime intelligence circles. George Taylor had served as deputy director of the Office of War Information's Far East Division. Shannon McCune had held various posts throughout the war, including service on the Board of Economic Warfare, and Richard Park's wartime military service in India left the consultants as a group predisposed to approve of the foundation's soft-power programs.[4]

Foundation president Robert Blum's September 1961 monthly report raised concerns. Titled "Growing Communist Aid to Less Developed Countries," the report stressed that the United States' relatively low levels of foreign aid gave the Soviets advantages in Asia. Blum explained that since the early 1950s, the Soviet Union had steadily increased foreign aid there, to a cumulative total between 1954 and 1960 of $3.6 billion, while US aid increases had been sporadic, a situation that would change with the Kennedy and Johnson administrations.[5]

Blum told the foundation's board of trustees that Soviet premier Khrushchev believed "Capitalism and Communism are engaged in a critical competition for favor with the underdeveloped countries; Communism is bound to win because it has a more efficient, rapid better planned system for lifting people out of darkness and poverty." Blum pushed the foundation to the front lines of this struggle, arguing that "the foundation should certainly play a role in proving the fallacy of Mr. Khrushchev's prediction." While directing a claimed "private organization" that was actually a government-funded and directed entity, Blum insisted that free enterprise, in the form of private organizations, could outperform communists' collectivist, government-funded programs. Blum also warned the board that communists could skillfully use the ill feelings and the horrors of colonialist history "to mobilize the dissatisfied intellectual and the impoverished masses in support of the Soviet program."[6] Such intellectuals were prime targets for the foundation's programs bringing Asian scholars to study at elite US universities, where theories of development or modernization had greater prominence than critiques of colonialism or neocolonialism.

In a late 1950s speech, "Peasants, Students, and Communism," Blum argued that "a strange alliance between students—intellectuals—and peasants has been largely responsible for [the] rise of communism in Asia." He observed that it was "usually educated but frustrated men—men in the students and intellectual classes"—who led communist rebellions. These intellectuals promised land reform that would reallocate privately held land to landless peasants as rewards for following them into revolution. Blum argued that "the peasants swallowed the bait of land—for they had little to lose but everything to gain. They formed alliances with the student-intellectual organizers in the hope that any change would improve their lot—and change would be for the better."[7] Blum used DTPILLAR funds to develop programs seeking to capture loyalties and un-frustrate this class of "educated men."

Many of the Asia Foundation programs described in this chapter supported efforts to undermine communist advances in simple ways. Frequently, these programs did little more than fund groups or projects already in place or supported Western organizations whose interests aligned with the CIA's goal of undermining communists. But whether funding new anticommunist organizations or funding existing programs with no visible, direct anticommunist dimensions, DTPILLAR used soft power to attract Asians to join American capitalism's Cold War struggle against nonalignment, unaligned democratic independence movements, and communism.

THE ASIA FOUNDATION AND THE ASIAN SCOUTING PROGRAM

DTPILLAR support for the international Boy Scouts stretched back to the earliest days of the Committee for Free Asia. The latent political ideology of scouting aligned with foundation goals, and foundation leaders viewed scouting "as a bulwark against communism and a means of spreading hygiene and other benefits of civilization among backward countries."[8] The 1950s and 1960s was a period when international scouting increasingly undertook charitable projects assisting underdeveloped nations, though in some Asian nations there developed competing localized scouting organizations that were at times viewed as threatening the westernizing goals DTPILLAR hoped to propagate by funding the international Boy Scouts.

A 1951 CFA report summarized the view of W. Arthur McKinney, assistant to the chief executive of Boy Scouts of America, as claiming that Boy Scout programs "are by their very nature and purpose a help in preventing Communism and winning the following among boys. Like other youth organizations they attempt to avoid partisan politics, but the Scout movement is clearly identified with an emphasis on freedom, democracy, and the development of individual responsibility among boys. In Europe, Communist occupation of countries has usually met with the liquidation of Boy Scout activities and the arrest of Boy Scout executives."[9] Scouting's paramilitary structure also taught values of discipline, subordination, and adherence to external rules.

Between 1951 and 1960, DTPILLAR channeled $400,000 in funds for Asian Boy Scout programs.[10] An October 1960 assessment of the outcomes of DTPILLAR's scouting investment concluded that when "viewed empirically, country by country, the most active youth groups in Asia were found to be those that were off-shoots of political parties. The Foundation encountered increasing difficulties in working safely with such groups. By contrast, in nearly all countries the Boy Scouts were found unidentified with political parties." Still, the assessment concluded that its investment in scouting only "produced results of rather limited significance, with the exception of Malaya, where our translation of the Scouting manual into Chinese helped bring about Chinese Scout troops." The report concluded that "the Scout movement in Asia can be termed a non-communist movement which the communists have not succeeded in subverting, or perhaps have not tried to do so."[11]

After Indonesian independence, multiple Boy Scout groups were formed, but later President Sukarno started his own national scouting organization, which weakened the popularity of the Boy Scouts. The foundation considered funding new administrative personnel who would try and rejuvenate interest in international Boy Scouts, but the director of the World Scout Bureau advised against doing anything "that might smack of interference."[12] When the foundation established scouting programs in Afghanistan, it encountered problems linked to the country's decentralization. Because so much of the country's population lived in far-flung rural settings, it was difficult to oversee rural programs. The foundation's biggest concern in Afghanistan was the possibility that scouting could become a vehicle for local authoritarian movements. While the foundation was comfortable trying to inculcate certain Western values, there were clearly expressed concerns that their scouting work "be approached warily in order to be quite sure Afghans are really interested in a true Boy Scout movement and not the formation of a youth corps not unlike the Hitlerjugend."[13]

The foundation sponsored Asian Boy Scout leaders' travel to the United States for training sessions, during which they met with foundation staff. A 1961 *New York Times* article described how developing nations were authorized to start local scouting units, a process that included "bringing Scout leaders to the United States or Canada for training." This training was often a stepping-stone for Asian scouting leaders' career advancement in government positions, which meant that frequently, when these "potential leaders return[ed] to their native lands they end up in government jobs or industry, to the neglect of the Boy Scouts, as a result of their training abroad."[14] While such patterns of leaders leaving scouting for significant jobs was a setback for scouting, these individuals could become contacts for DTPILLAR staff. By the late 1950s, the foundation had standardized elements of Asian scouting, culminating with a 1962 campaign to standardize the constitutions of Asian Boy Scout units, even while scouting faced growing competition from new youth organizations linked to nationalized patriotic movements in various countries.[15]

Cambodia first established its own national youth organization, known as the La Jeunesse Socialiste Royale Khmère (JSRK) during the Second World War.

Prince Norodom Sihanouk championed JSRK for supporting national unity around his royal presence, and some foundation reports analyzed JSRK's role in helping reduce the possibility of Cambodian political opposition.[16] While DTPILLAR funds helped establish chapters of the Boy Scouts in Cambodia in the early 1950s, by 1956 a power struggle had emerged within the Cambodian Boy Scouts organization (known as Khemarak Kayarith) after a visit between their leadership and the liaison of the Boy Scouts International Bureau. Following this visit, a group of Cambodian scout leaders left the Cambodian Boy Scouts and started their own youth organization, and "in April of 1956 they cleverly secured the Queen's backing for a royalist type of youth group," establishing an organization known as Smakum Kayarith Préh Mohaksatreyeani (Scouts of the Queen). Many of this group's activities resembled those of the Boy Scouts, but their members took a loyalty oath "to defend my country, my nation and their Majesties, to fight body and soul against the anti-royalists."[17] They soon attacked other scouting groups, claiming they were antiroyalist, which undermined the popularity of Cambodian Boy Scouts. In 1957, with the backing of Prince Sihanouk, the Scouts of the Queen was abolished and the JSRK became the premier Cambodian youth organization that all Cambodian children were required to join. Prince Sihanouk led the organization.[18]

The foundation understood the JSRK to be "an instrument for carrying out the Prince's policies at the youth level. At the same time, however, it has a national following and will dominate youth activities in Cambodia while the Sangkum remain in power." The foundation calculated that even though the JSRK was a government-controlled organization, it remained the best route for foundation efforts to connect with Cambodian youth.[19]

After Sihanouk's co-opting of Cambodian scouting activities, foundation reports described the state of Cambodian scouting as "rather depressing," as scouting now focused on Prince Sihanouk as its central figure and had no connection to international scouting. Seeking to address these issues, the foundation wanted to "send the commissioner of the Socialist youth group, which is the Royal group that now has infiltrated and devastated the Boy Scouts[,] to the United States" for training. While the Asia Foundation was hesitant to back a socialist youth organization, one 1958 report shows the foundation calculating that this group would continue to be the dominant Cambodian youth organization for many years. This assessment led the foundation to conclude that supporting the JSRK was the best chance to teach Cambodian youth about Western democracy and the best means of establishing contacts with future leaders.[20] While this proposal was never acted upon, such Cold War gamesmanship—backing socialists who were opposing communists—was a familiar CIA gambit during the 1950s.[21]

In internal foundation memos, the JSRK was sometimes described in derogatory terms, such as a 1958 memo arguing that it was "slowly destroying the Khemarak Kayarith—the Boy Scout [organization] with which we have been working."[22] The tensions were significant enough that the foundation's Cambodian representative, Bud Overton, decided to remove foundation support for Cambodian Boy Scouts in order to not antagonize their Cambodian hosts. Foundation staff had "the impression that the new group has many similarities to the Hitler youth group in Germany—perhaps not as fanatic. However, as [Overton] points out, it is impossible for a youth not to join. If he fails to do so, he is automatically considered a traitor to the state. One of the purposes of the group is 'to give young Cambodian boys and girls the royalist spirit' and 'to orient them towards a military career.'"[23] As the foundation's international Boy Scouts programs failed to compete with Prince Sihanouk's alternative program, foundation staff increasingly criticized these alternative loyalties as embodying fascism, while their organization's own programs spread discipline and uniform order.

DTPILLAR's interest in scouting, whether funding international Boy Scouts or monitoring nationalistic independent scouting programs, shows a sophisticated understanding of the ways such youth programs can shape political identities, and both the Committee for Free Asia and the Asia Foundation did all they could to use this knowledge and these programs to spread pro-Western and procapitalist views, while establishing contacts with prospective future Asian leaders.

THE PEACE CORPS AND THE ASIA FOUNDATION

Asia Foundation interactions with some early Peace Corps activities provide a rare view of a CIA front assisting the Peace Corps, though the foundation appeared reticent to have much to do with this new organization. Four weeks after President Kennedy's executive order established the Peace Corps, Robert Sheeks wrote an internal foundation position paper, "The Peace Corps and The Asia Foundation," exploring how the foundation might engage with this new program. Sheeks recognized shared missions between the two organizations, with both promoting development, education, science, technology infusions, and local athletic programs. While some staff expressed mixed feelings about the Peace Corps, Sheeks noted that the foundation was not prepared "to handle the administrative responsibilities and costs of directly putting more than a very few Corps volunteers to work on projects in Asia. If the Foundation, however, were to receive funds and could supplement its staff for this purpose, it would be the American private organization in Asia perhaps best situated to do a comprehensive job."[24]

Sheeks acknowledged there was "room for concern over the proper relationship of the Foundation to a government undertaking, with its propaganda undertones," but because the Peace Corps's scale of operations was so small, he thought it was too early for serious concerns. Sheeks saw opportunities for the foundation to train Peace Corps personnel, thereby helping to identify appropriate local support personnel, conduct needed evaluations, and "provide policy guidance and local contacts." He also recognized that there could be good opportunities for Peace Corps volunteers to gather information for the foundation, and he proposed that these volunteers could report on how the foundation was viewed in the local communities where these volunteers were stationed.[25]

Along with other foundations working in areas where the Peace Corps planned to operate, the foundation was invited to partnership-building meetings. Foundation staff met with State Department personnel seeking advice on establishing Peace Corps programs in Asia. In Thailand, American embassy personnel and Asia Foundation representative Harry Pierson discussed proposals for local Peace Corps activities. But the foundation remained reluctant to take any official role with the Peace Corps. In internal correspondence, foundation staff concluded that "the Foundation should not attempt to obtain any role in the [Peace Corps], as it would get all the headaches and none of the real responsibility or credit. However, we have several ideas of how Peace Corps personnel might be used in Thailand."[26] It is possible that another reason why the foundation did not take on official roles was the federal directive forbidding members of intelligence agencies from working with the Peace Corps, as specified in the Peace Corps manual.[27]

Still, the foundation helped shape the Peace Corps by less direct means. It provided US embassy staff in Bangkok a prioritized list of programs for Thailand. It encouraged the formation of science clubs, recreation programs, and charitable and social work projects, as well as programs assisting at Buddhist secondary schools, training librarians, and developing applied sociology research programs.²⁸ In Vietnam, the foundation advocated for Peace Corps personnel to join existing International Voluntary Service (IVS) agricultural assistance programs or to work as English-language instructors, laboratory assistants, and in Boy or Girl Scout projects—programs aligned with US Vietnam policy.²⁹ James Stewart recommended that the corps send volunteers to teach English in Japan.³⁰ The foundation representative in Hong Kong recommended Peace Corps volunteers work as staff in the Mencius Educational Foundation, an organization established in Hong Kong by the foundation.³¹ Foundation staff also discussed the possibility of Peace Corps programs for East Pakistan, Singapore, Malaya, Burma, and the Philippines.³²

Some foundation staff strongly objected to having any contact with the Peace Corps. In 1961, foundation staffer John James complained about what he called the Peace Corps's "amateur's approach." James objected to the unprofessional nature of the program, complaining that "this is not the Junior League, although it is becoming very fashionable." He complained about the corps's vision of volunteers "going native," mocking "the visionary ideal of 'living with people'" and insisting that to work properly the volunteer needed to be well rested, well fed, and "clean and uninfested." James wasn't opposed to traveling in the countryside, to experience "dust and fleas" and "revolting food," but he felt as a professional he was better equipped for these travails than were volunteers and that the risks of "tuberculosis, filariasis, liver fluke, typhoid, encephalitis, malaria, trachoma, dysentery and jaundice" were "silly risks for Americans to take."³³ Yet, despite his harsh critique, James recognized that it was "desirable" for the foundation to participate in some Peace Corps–linked activities, such as recommending specific programs or helping assign personnel in countries where the foundation operated.

When the Afghanistan government expressed interest in hosting Peace Corps programs, the foundation quietly undertook some advisory roles while internally expressing caution about becoming publicly linked with the program because of the obvious political nature of the Peace Corps.³⁴ In February 1962, the Afghanistan government requested six Peace Corps English teachers, four nurses, and two trained mechanics. The foundation participated in these discussions, but they insisted their involvement be kept private.³⁵ The foundation's board cautioned the foundation to maintain some distance from the Peace Corps until its policies became better known.³⁶

In late 1961, as Cleo Shook, a Peace Corps program development officer, prepared to take about fifty Peace Corps volunteers to Afghanistan, foundation staff in Afghanistan noted that "Mr. Shook is an old friend of the Foundation's here, having spent about six years in Afghanistan in various capacities."[37] Shook asked the foundation to provide contacts and structure to oversee Afghanistan's initial Peace Corps operations, but the foundation was not encouraging in its response. With time, the foundation maintained increasing distance from Peace Corps programs, though a CIA document from 1964 indicates that the foundation continued to track Peace Corps programs under way in regions where the foundation operated.[38]

A month after the *New York Times* revealed on March 22, 1967, that the Asia Foundation had CIA links, a research specialist at the Peace Corps Training Center, T. Thangathurai, thanked foundation president Haydn Williams for providing materials used to train Peace Corps volunteers. These included materials on the history, politics, and culture of the countries they had been assigned to, information on international relations, and items exposing trainees to "Communism and Communist theory as the chief enemy of the United States and other free nations."[39]

There is a long history of speculation and unsubstantiated claims that Peace Corps volunteers have been CIA agents.[40] While I found no records indicating any such connections, these Asia Foundation limited connections with the program during its earlier days provide some rare examples of a CIA-funded program working with the presumably unwitting Peace Corps in limited ways, and records of the foundation's wariness about working with this new organization while seeing it as having some overlapping potential interests reveal fundamental foundation desires.

COMMUNIST WORLD YOUTH GATHERINGS AND THE WORLD ASSEMBLY OF YOUTH

DTPILLAR monitored soft-power programs run by communist competitors. An October 1953 report compiled information gathered by CFA staff interviewing Asian students attending the Communist World Youth gatherings that had recently been held in Bucharest. This report portrayed the gathering as a heavy-handed propaganda extravaganza, while advocating foundation sponsorship of similar events. Committee staff were impressed by the communists' success in recruiting students from mainstream campus organizations and radical political groups, noting that many efforts by Asian governments to prevent students from attending the gathering had failed or backfired. When the Burmese government tried to prevent Rangoon University students from attending, a dozen Burmese students still traveled to Bucharest, where they were welcomed and provided with delegate credentials. When Indonesia successfully blocked its students from attending, these students held rallies in locations throughout Indonesia during the congress's opening day, drawing public attention to the congress. Japan refused to allow student delegates to travel, claiming they faced dangers in Romania, which led to protests in Japan "against Japanese restrictions and subservience to 'American imperialism.'"[41] Even with these restrictions, thirteen Japanese students arrived in Bucharest prior to the travel ban, and they were given prominent roles at the congress.

The congress lacked representatives from Malaya, Thailand, and the Philippines, "probably," a CFA report concluded, "due to the fact that any such meetings would have been raided as subversive or delegates leaving the country would have been refused re-entry."[42] Asian nations with strong Soviet ties sent large student delegations; India sent 150 delegates, while North Korea sent about 250 representatives. The three US citizens, Douglas Gaskov, Doris Kopelman, and Loria Segal, who attended were made officers of the Communist Party–linked organization, the World Federation of Democratic Youth.

The festival sponsored cultural events, music, films, and art exhibitions that were "heavy on the themes of unity of youth, examples of glorious leaders, good life in the 'People's Democracies.'" The sports competitions were a centerpiece of the festival and were billed as the "largest international athletic meet outside the Olympics." The gathering emphasized themes of athletic competition, friendship, solidarity, and cooperation.[43]

The following year, CFA staff monitoring plans for an upcoming Communist Youth Festival featuring sports and music events concluded that these mixtures of sports and cultural events were one of the communists' most successful recruiting techniques. Staff watched for local "unsuspecting non-political groups" that might be invited to attend the festival, and staff were warned that invitations would likely come from youth groups with apolitical-sounding names. CFA staff asked local groups to provide names of students who might attend communist-sponsored events.[44]

Pat Judge, the foundation representative for Hong Kong, reported on the 1958 council of the World Assembly of Youth (WAY) in New Delhi, which attracted four hundred delegates and observers from over eighty countries.[45] Judge monitored emerging political divisions, recording observations on the harassment of the French delegation by delegates from French African colonies; noting that

British delegates did not appear to suffer similar attacks, he claimed this was because Britain was "believed to be more enlightened in her colonial policies, and the British delegation had fostered a familial feeling among the delegates and members of the Commonwealth."[46]

Judge was disappointed that many participants expressed positions of "complacent" neutrality. He was disturbed that Prime Minister "Nehru, even when appalled by the lawless deeds of the Communists in Kerala Province, still emphasized that he was by no means anti-Communist." Judge was frustrated that delegates from colonial countries were far more concerned about gaining independence than worried about the "problems of communism." Some delegates admitted that, while there were problems with communism, "people in the colonies might be compelled to take that approach if their expectation could not be fulfilled otherwise."[47] US policy decisions to not support broad postcolonialist independence movements in the postwar period were clearly helping the Soviets build international movements in the Global South.

In the years following the 1955 Bandung Conference attended by Asian and African leaders, foundation staff often seemed to view the prospect of nonalignment or efforts to maintain neutrality as implicitly linked to communist alignment. Judge concluded that even with India's distasteful position of neutrality, that country showed delegates the progress they had made as a young nation. By presenting speakers, films, cultural showcases, and tours, India displayed its strength as an emerging, noncommunist new nation full of hopes for the future, though any future not explicitly linked with US policy seemed to present dangers.[48]

THE ASIA FOUNDATION'S INTEREST IN BUDDHISM

DTPILLAR sponsored several fellowships, visiting scholar programs, workshops, and conferences on Buddhism. Some of these programs were unusual for a foundation primarily supporting the economic, political, cultural, and educational improvement of Asian countries. Given the reality that the Asia Foundation was secretly a US government–funded and directed organization, its US government–based financial support for a religious organization was extraordinary (table 2). Between 1954 and 1964, the foundation spent over 11 percent of its programming budget on religious-related programs, with about half of these funds going to Buddhist projects (see table 2).

Historian Eugene Ford's *Cold War Monks: Buddhism and America's Secret*

TABLE 2. Memorandum listing Committee for Free Asia/Asia Foundation spending on Buddhist projects, 1952–1960

Date: August 26, 1960
To: Mr. Lerski
From: Nancy Okada
Subject: Buddhism and Religion: Expenditures and Percentages

FISCAL YEARS	TOTAL PROGRAM EXPENDITURES	BUDDHISM EXPENDITURES	BUDDHISM (%)	RELIGION EXPENDITURES	RELIGION (%)
1952–53		$109,218		$191,050	
1953–54		$98,173		$234,754	
1954–55	$2,473,039	$107,671	4.4	$252,437	10.2
1955–56	$3,713,602	$213,866	5.8	$461,383	12.4
1956–57	$4,330,518	$309,296	7.1	$587,181	13.6
1957–58	$4,162,547	$288,214	6.9	$582,892	14
1958–59	$4,531,065	$264,923	5.8	$475,433	10.5
1959–60	$4,556,283	$172,913	3.8	$292,765	6.4
[1952–60 total]	$23,767,054	$1,564,274		$3,077.895	
[Post-CFA] 1954–60	$23,767,054	$1,356,883	5.7	$2,652,091	11.2

Source: TAF P-130, Mr. Lerski to Nancy Okada, Buddhism and Religion Expenditures and Percentages, 8/26/60 Budget, 1960.

Note: Total program expenditures appears to refer to total annual Committee for Free Asia/Asia Foundation annual program budgets, with percentages of each annual program budget spent on Buddhism and religion programming indicated in the fourth and sixth columns.

Strategy in Southeast Asia (2017) details how, during the 1950s and 1960s, DT-PILLAR covertly channeled US government funds to Asian Buddhist organizations as part of an anticommunist strategy.[49] Ford documents how DTPILLAR supported select Buddhist traditions as political weapons, and he shows how efforts to use Buddhism for militarized or political ends was nothing new, as Japanese occupiers of Thailand during the Second World War had tried to develop forms of militarized Zen Buddhism. During the early Cold War, the

United States explored the possibility of, as Vice President Nixon wrote to CIA's Walter Bedell Smith in 1954, trying to establish a Buddhist "spiritual counteroffensive in Southeast Asia."[50]

Some CFA staff had been uncomfortable with the Committee for Free Asia's involvement with religious organizations. George Noronha worried that "in stimulating the faiths of Asia, CFA will not be stimulating merely a belief in God, or promoting merely these aspects of a faith in which it serves the cause of free institutions and free men. CFA will be stimulating these faiths in their entirety."[51] Now there were disagreements among foundation staff about how to best use anticommunist Buddhists. Some, like William Klausner, thought it would "be a mistake to support or encourage militant anti-communist Buddhist groups even indirectly." Klausner instead favored an approach by the foundation that oriented "Buddhist groups to positive social and educational programming and avoid encouraging their political involvement."[52] Others favored funding these militant anticommunist Buddhists.

Searching for possible avenues to influence anticommunist movements, the foundation sent representatives to meetings with Buddhist leaders.[53] The foundation funded anthropologist Robert F. Spencer's two-month trip to Ceylon and Burma, where he sought "to establish contact and rapport with Buddhist leaders" and then attended the World Fellowship of Buddhists in Rangoon, Burma.[54] The foundation directed Spencer to observe the conference in order to determine which foundation goals overlapped with Buddhist programs and to search for programs that DTPILLAR should support.[55]

In Ceylon, Spencer easily accessed Buddhist circles by expressing interest in learning more about Buddhism, but in Burma he used trickery, claiming he wanted to become a practicing Buddhist. As a result of this lie, Spencer was then "obliged to enter a monastery, to engage in a course of Buddhist meditation, and to demonstrate unswerving adherence to Buddhist principles. Once this was done, and once the various Buddhist leaders with whom contact was made were convinced of the observer's earnestness of purpose, it was possible to obtain data of great value. For an anthropologist, the opportunity for study was a splendid one."[56] I found no records indicating Spencer was chastised for this unethical deception; instead, his findings circulated in foundation reports.

Spencer identified several significant roles played by Burmese monks in twentieth-century nationalist and communist movements, and he discussed several ways Burmese communists avoided bringing Buddhism into their politics. He recorded instances in which communists' critiques of Buddhist teachings fostered anticommunist sentiments. One example came from a speech U Nu delivered at the Sasana Council. In it he attacked the "sinister" claims of communists questioning or ridiculing "Lord Buddha's omniscience." U Nu stated that the council would combat such claims, arguing that "the wisdom of Marx is not for him to question but that he does rise to combat when the wisdom of Marx is compared with that of the Buddha. The knowledge that might be attributed to Marx is less than one-tenth of a particle of dust that lives at the feet of our great Lord Buddha, the contrast is so marked."[57]

Spencer claimed regional variations in Burmese Buddhists' traditions made some groups either resistant or open to communist influence, and he argued that Ceylonese Buddhist traditions made them more easily drawn to communism. He recommended that the foundation support programs designed to limit the appeal of communism to Buddhists in all countries where the foundation operated. At a meeting with young Burmese monks expressing communist views, Spencer learned that communist "propaganda tracts circulated among monks." He collected reports of former monks who became communists but who were later "lost behind the Iron Curtain and are believed to be in Moscow," which dampened enthusiasm for communism among this group of young monks.[58] Spencer believed that the indoctrination of young monks was the communists' most effective recruitment strategy. To prevent this, he recommended "that the Young Monks should be wooed and won for the West" in a process he believed could be easily accomplished given the generally anticommunist feelings and support for pro-Western groups.[59]

Spencer argued that monks' venerated status in Burmese society made them essential allies for regional anticommunist campaigns. He saw monks as "a tremendous force either for promoting continuing adherence to the principles of the free world or for alliance with Communism. The monk can preach in political terms and the crowd will follow; he can control votes. In effect, the continued success of the present government of Burma depends on the monk."[60] Spencer reported monks lacking experience or education were often naïve and easily drawn to Marxism. He argued that "a few well placed, better educated and intelligent monks might conceivably counteract the spread of propaganda for Communism among monks who are more naïve and less critical."[61] This approach aligned with foundation programs sponsoring monks to study abroad, and when these foreign study programs occurred in settings with a pro-Western curriculum, these pro-Western and anticommunist messages were part of the educational milieu.

Foundation staff regularly attended and reported on World Fellowship of Buddhists (WFB) conferences.[62] Richard Gard's foundation report on the fourth WFB conference, held in Nepal in 1956, monitored the intellectual content of sessions and political dynamics among attendees. The extent of the communists' presence impressed Gard, who observed that the Chinese communist delegation skillfully engaged with delegates and that both the Chinese and Soviet delegations donated to Nepalese social welfare organizations. Gard reported that "the communists were well behaved and did not try to propagandize among the conferees. Nevertheless, many Asian delegates remained critical and skeptical of the communist approach."[63] The Chinese delegation worked the crowd, giving Buddhist prayer beads and other gifts to attendees and distributing cash contributions to Nepalese temples and social programs. Soviet and Eastern bloc delegations hosted meals for leaders and donated to local charity programs.[64] Gard affirmed that the foundation's funding of several Buddhist attendees had been a productive means of countering the communist presence.[65]

In 1958, Richard Gard attended the fifth WFB conference, in Bangkok, where he helped translate for the Japanese and Korean delegations, reported on resolutions and other developments, and collected copies of presented papers, later deposited with the foundation home office.[66] Because Gard was a Buddhist, the foundation worried that he could have difficulties maintaining professional boundaries with his work.[67] Gard helped write several political resolutions presented at the conference, which meant that someone funded by the CIA was writing political doctrine for an international religious association.

In 1964, the foundation provided $10,000 in grants funding Asian scholars and Buddhist specialists to attend the seventh WFB conference, held in Sarnath, India. The foundation later collected reports on the conference from those sponsored, and internal memos discussed how Buddhism in general and the conference in particular could open new possibilities for the foundation.[68] After seeking support from the foundation to attend the conference, Holmes Welch, an American scholar of Buddhism, provided a five-thousand-word conference report summarizing daily events and political issues.[69] Welch provided the sort of insider report the foundation sought, and his analysis of the conference's political backdrop aligned with foundation interests in supporting anticommunist Buddhist movements.[70] Welch observed that "Americans need not feel guilty of contamination [of] the purity of the WFB," because the conference's contamination was now "endemic." He interpreted each nation attending as pursuing self-interested political goals and argued that Americans "are as much entitled as the Ceylonese, the Thais, the Russians, and so on to play the game: keep politics out of sight, protest (as did the Malayans, Koreans, Indians, Nepalese, and others at Sarnath) that politics are inadmissible and un-Buddhist, but still pursue political objectives."[71] Welch acknowledged the foundation's political motivations in sponsoring select attendees, and he praised its approach of not dictating who the Hong Kong delegation brought or what they did. Like the foundation's leadership, he believed that the power of such nonintrusive means of waging a political ideological battle with communists was superior to the overly obvious and heavy-handed means he saw deployed by the communists. He understood that "most Asian Buddhists involved with the WFB know what the game is. They do not mind if we play it successfully."[72]

BLUM ON THE FOUNDATION'S BUDDHIST GAMBIT

In a 1960 report to the foundation's board, President Blum explained the strategic importance of the foundation's support of Buddhism-related programs. Blum explained that foundation funds targeted "the young Buddhist movement" in various countries and made connections leading to these young Buddhists' increased "willingness to work with Western organizations." Foundation funding of research and educational programs earned the desired goodwill and established important connections. Blum believed that "in a number of instances, especially in Burma, Cambodia, Thailand, Ceylon and Japan, Buddhist institutions and organizations provide the Foundation's only means of establishing contact with some important elements of Asian society."[73]

A few months later, after meeting with Buddhists at the Vajiraramaya Temple in Ceylon, Blum proposed financially supporting specific forms of Buddhist studies by stressing that Buddhism was inherently linked to democracy, freedom, and individual liberties in ways that made Buddhism incompatible with communism. Blum believed the Vajiraramaya Temple was the right point of contact for these efforts. The foundation approached D. L. F. Pedris, who chaired the Lay Committee of the temple, offering to sponsor activities emphasizing Buddhism's inherent support for democracy and individual liberties and opposing communism.[74]

The foundation's political interest in Buddhism caught the attention of some scholars. In 1965, anthropologist Peter Kunstadter asked representative Harry Pierson if the foundation-sponsored Buddhist projects in Vietnam "had anything to do with increasing their political consciousness, and their ability to influence public opinion."⁷⁵ Pierson replied that most of these grants were "very small and have to do with provision of books, equipment, teaching aids and travel," avoiding the issue of foundation efforts to use Buddhism as an anticommunist weapon.⁷⁶ An internal memo alerted Clare E. Humphrey that Kunstadter had raised these questions, and Pierson stressed that he had avoided directly answering.⁷⁷ The following month, Pierson wrote Kunstadter, first explaining that "nothing the Foundation has done, or could have done, could have increased the already tremendous political consciousness of Buddhist leaders in Vietnam," but then he added,

> as for the *intent* of our work with Buddhists, our purpose has been to channel Buddhist energy and thoughts into non-political activities. If we assume that the prominence of the Buddhists in political affairs will not continue indefinitely and if we further assume that frustration could arise if their ambitions in the political sphere were thwarted, our most profitable efforts should be directed at channeling their activities into constructive, non-political projects. This we have done by stressing the education and social service activities of the Buddhists through aid to the recently created Van Hanh University and the social action program of the Institute for the Execution of the Dharma.⁷⁸

Pierson's lie to Kunstadter diverted attention from the Cold War monk-oriented projects the foundation had undertaken for years at the WFB, claiming the foundation was "not interested nor engaged in projects which would promote Buddhist propaganda."⁷⁹ Kunstadter appears to have dropped this line of inquiry, though this would not be the last time he would raise questions about the foundation's apparent political subterfuge and then fail to challenge the accumulating lies he was told in response to his questions.

WHERE THE CIA'S DTPILLAR SOFT-POWER FUNDS WENT

In 1963, Asia Foundation president Russell Smith explained to Director of Central Intelligence John McCone that, having served as a foundation trustee for over nine years, he understood the foundation's basic operations but "only as President, had [Smith] come to the realization of the depth of the activity."⁸⁰ Because trustees were only aware of projects with budgets exceeding $25,000, Smith had previously had little awareness of many projects. He explained that "the value of TAF operations could not be related to the costs of projects; he had learned, as President, that many low-cost projects could be just as effective as the larger ones." He stressed that because the foundation operated as a private institution, it was able to "work productively in Asia in areas of importance to the U.S. from which official programs are precluded." Smith told DCI McCone that "with respect to [the] relationship between The Asia Foundation and the CIA," there was the "wisdom of those in CIA who had vested in the Foundation sufficient autonomy for it to live up to its private character and assume responsibility for carrying out its mission. In this connection, Mr. Smith stated his belief that without such a degree of independence and responsibility the Foundation would not be able to attract and hold its dedicated staff nor could it hope to sustain the interest and guidance it now enjoys from the Trustees. Mr. Smith described the Foundation's Trustees as anything but 'rubber stamps.'"[81] Smith understood the foundation's links to US strategic objectives as "countering communist inroads in Asia." The reason for Smith's visit with DCI McCone became clear when he "acknowledged that a small percentage of the Foundation's programs were for the sake of 'window-dressing,' public relations, or entrée into fields of interest. In discussing such projects, however, Mr. Smith remarked that since becoming President he had learned that some projects which, at first appearance seem to be frivolous, may have concealed edges or potential."[82] Because budget cuts had been planned for the 1964 fiscal year, Smith's visit was to argue against closing down any programs and for maintaining even those budgets that appeared to have no direct support for the CIA's mission.[83] DCI McCone assured Smith that the CIA's sustained support would allow the foundation to continue playing important roles supporting American objectives in Asia, again stressing his recognition that the foundation was able to perform tasks that no official US agency could.[84]

Many foundation-funded programs sought to shape political, social, or educational developments in ways aligned with US strategic interests. Whether it was a political scientist being funded to develop new programs in Thai universities or a program that seemed purely altruistic, such as women's physical education programs in Afghanistan, the political context and the types of curricula proffered aligned with what were believed to be US strategic interests.[85] As had occurred at other CIA funding fronts, some of the funded projects simply helped establish legitimacy by supplementing the work of established scholars—though the foundation at times used these contacts in other ways.

An overview of the types of projects DTPILLAR funded in 1958, to pick one representative year under President Blum, shows the foundation making inroads with Asian groups and establishing favorable relationships in regions the CIA worried were at risk of going communist. Such inroads included funding things like sports activities for youth at the Kabul Sports Club, schools in Indonesia, a reading room at Hokkaido University Student Union, a Japanese cultural center, a school in Malay, the publishing of Thai scholars' social science research, the funding of a Chinese bookstore in Thailand, the publication of Chinese textbooks in Vietnam, Indonesian social science fellowships, and South Korean social science research.[86] For its fourth year (1958), the foundation brought Asian journalists to Harvard under the Nieman Fellowship program.[87]

Foundation soft-power projects planted seeds with both tangible and intangible results. To pick one representative sample, an August 1958 report on recently funded projects included things like $26,600 for a publishing project in Indonesia; $4,304 for Shafik Kamawi to work toward his doctorate in international law at Harvard; $2,300 supporting a Buddhist university magazine in Cambodia; $6,000 for salaries of Chinese research fellows at Hong Kong University's Institute of Oriental Studies; $5,200 underwriting purchases for the Hong Kong Boys' and Girls' Clubs; $5,315 to support Islamic studies at the McGill University Institute of Islamic Studies; $4,210 for the Indian Cooperation Union; $2,700 for the Delhi School of Social Work; $16,500 for the Inter-Indonesian University Scholarship program; $9,250 to support a mobile education center run by the Japanese Ibaraki Prefecture Settlers Union; and another $4,500 for the Nagasaki International Library program to buy microfilm equipment. In Pakistan, it spent $7,300 for the Bulbul Academy of Fine Arts and $3,000 for the Adult Education Cooperative Society. In the Philippines, the foundation provided $5,000 to pay for Janos Horvath, a leader in the Hungarian Revolution, to teach economics at the University of Philippines. In Taiwan, there was a $10,000 grant for a school of journalism and $5,000 for a YWCA camp for girls.

Back in the United States, $11,000 was provided to the CIA-funded National Student Association supporting Japanese, Thai, and Malayan students for its Foreign Student Leadership Project, and $3,500 was allocated to assist the Japan Society's program funding Japanese "scholars and other leaders temporarily visiting the United States."[88] Through such projects, the foundation established contacts and funded projects that had obvious anticommunist links and appeared to have done little more than advertise that the United States wanted to be a friend to Asia.

CONSIDERING WHAT ACCOMPANIES GIFTS

DTPILLAR funded these soft-power projects to improve the United States' image abroad. While DTPILLAR's public name change to the Asia Foundation signaled a break from the more obvious propagandistic programs and hopes of diminishing suspicions of possible intelligence agency links, it is telling that one of the newly minted Asia Foundation's first acts, by Robert Spencer in Burma, was to use trickery to conduct foundation business.

Many of the foundation's more mundane programs were routinely rationalized to the board as supporting US-backed political ends. Following a 1956 youth uprising in Singapore, the foundation recruited Raymond Kaufman, a physical education instructor, "to help organize the Singapore Youth Sports Center, as a major attempt to channel excess energy of students and other youth from leftist politics into healthy recreational activities."[89]

The Asia Foundation's big lie was the claim it was a private foundation not acting in the interests of the US government. President Blum and foundation staff pushed this bovaristic claim frequently and fervently, and reports of this tactic routinely appeared in board reports, with statements like, "Mr. Blum particularly stressed the private nature of the Foundation and the necessity of maintaining this character in all relationships with the public, pointing out that this private nature permitted it to do many things that a public agency could not do."[90] A 1955 *Newsweek* article quoted Blum claiming the foundation was "not a cloak and dagger outfit. Our purpose is to see what can be done through nongovernmental means to build up free-world strength in Asia."[91]

In a 1955 board report, Blum clarified that while the transition from Committee for Free Asia to the Asia Foundation had marked a move away from direct propaganda, "the organization's direct propaganda activity (Radio Free Asia), which developed in 1951 from the emphasis on the urgent military and political necessity for activity in Asia, was dropped in April, 1953, when it became clear that it was impeding the organization's major effort to build up non-governmental groups in Asia." Blum's use of the phrase "direct propaganda" categorically implied the possibility that "indirect propaganda" might be occurring. Blum acknowledged that most of the original organization goals remained, but now the foundation's assistance occurred through financial subsidies, the provision of textbooks and equipment, support for American organizations assisting Asian countries, and working with nongovernmental individuals and organizations in Asia.[92]

5 Collecting Intelligence

In general the presence of American intelligence facilities in a foreign country can have an important effect on American policy toward that country, especially in the Third World.

VICTOR MARCHETTI AND JOHN D. MARKS / *The CIA and the Cult of Intelligence*

Perhaps the most startling revelation emerging from DTPILLAR documents released via the Freedom of Information Act are declassified CIA materials establishing that the CIA at times used Asia Foundation offices and personnel to gather intelligence during the 1950s and 1960s. While the CIA has released only a small fraction of what had to have originally been a massive collection of DTPILLAR materials, released CIA documents acknowledge that the agency indeed used intelligence provided by the CFA and the Asia Foundation.

These documents include a few rare reports of individual operations, such as a 1963 CIA document recording that, as the Asia Foundation established a new office in the city then known as Jesselton, North Borneo, the CIA sent out a foundation representative who had "received some specialized Agency training" to operate a CIA "forward listening post."[1] More generally, the CIA has released documents recording the number of times DTPILLAR reports led to "actionable intelligence" operations in a given year. For example, the CIA's "intelligence production" numbers recorded that during fiscal year 1963 alone, 147 foundation reports "were disseminated as CS [confidential source] or OO [operations officers] reports of value to the intelligence community. Of this total, 98 were OO disseminations."[2] The CIA summarized these foundation intelligence reports as "generally good quality and for the most part of considerable value."[3] The following year (1964), the foundation provided the CIA with 147 instances of "intel disseminations" (consisting of 49 CS reports, and 98 OO reports), with "operational and background data supplied by Senior Representatives to the COS [local CIA chief of station]," various briefings, and "letters and exemplars."[4]

The CIA reported that foundation "representatives continue to supply the Stations with information which is useful as operational and background data" for the agency. CIA personnel regularly read Asia Foundation representatives' "quarterly situation analysis" reports, and CIA valued these "since they represent unofficial analysis by private Americans with access sometimes not possible for official representatives."⁵ Another way the agency gathered intelligence from foundation staff was through the CIA's routine interviewing of foundation representatives who had been stationed abroad, upon their return to the United States. These debriefings, by "Agency components" and State Department personnel, were characterized by the CIA as being "of considerable interest since the Representatives present fresh views and useful information not found in formal reporting."⁶ While witting committee or foundation employees conducted some intelligence gathering, information in foundation reports sometimes originated from scholars or others who were completely unaware their work would be used in this way.

During 1965, eighty-four foundation reports were disseminated within the CIA. The CIA reviewed its procedures for "Agency handing of TAF raw reports," and the agency developed a program of "Agency training for [TAF] Representatives and Assistant Representatives" that "included instruction on reporting from the field," which the CIA believed would "result in increased dissemination in FY-1966."⁷ The CIA recognized that the foundation's appearance as a private organization could provide cover, and in instances where the foundation remained in country after other Americans had been expelled, it could undertake what the CIA called "cover and stay-behind" operations. In evaluating the foundation's effectiveness in supplying intelligence, the CIA found its "cover and stay-behind potential [was] perhaps best demonstrated during FY-1965 by its ability to remain, fully operative, in Cambodia after withdrawal of all Americans, officials and private citizens."⁸ The following year, the CIA reported which CIA divisions had used Asia Foundation reports and found that "during FY-1966, 41 CS [confidential source] and CO [covert operations] reports were disseminated. In addition, 76 Asia Foundation reports were consolidated under ten Headquarters report numbers and distributed to interested desks in OCI [Office of Current Intelligence], [blurred text likely to read "ONE," for Office of National Estimates] and OCR [Office of Central Reference]."⁹

When the foundation found itself in countries where nongovernmental agencies were being expelled, it tried to remain as long as possible. In April 1962, after Burma's seventeen-member Revolutionary Council banned educators and advisors funded by the Ford Foundation, Asia Foundation, and Fulbright Program, the Asia Foundation was slow to withdraw. While the Ford Foundation quickly terminated Burmese projects and evacuated its staff, the Asia Foundation prolonged its exit, telling employees they would be sent home in six months.¹⁰

These distinct institutional responses to a country's instability marked the foundation as different from actual nongovernmental organizations in rather obvious ways. For example, President Blum's board report for June 1958 discussed the deteriorating political stability of Laos following communist gains in recent elections. While reports of political instability at other educational NGOs normally led their presidents to caution board members about possible staff withdrawals, Blum reported that these developments meant the foundation would likely expand its presence in Laos, writing,

> Early in May, after the elections were held in Laos, I asked our Representative in Cambodia, Leonard C. Overton, to go to Vientiane in order to study the situation there and recommend whether the Foundation should undertake an expanded program in Laos. Up to the present time we have had only a very small program there, operated from our Bangkok office, and we have had no resident representative. Overton returned to Cambodia on June 4, and we have not yet received his full report. He has, however, cabled me that he will recommend the establishment of a permanent office in Laos. It is probable that his recommendation results in large part from the worsening internal situation in Laos as a result of the gains of the communist-led NLHZ party at the recent elections. I am awaiting Mr. Overton's report and at the same time giving preliminary consideration to his recommendation, which we will be able to discuss at the July meeting of the Board. As in the other countries mentioned above, the political situation is Laos is a very difficult one, particularly as a result of the recent elections which saw a substantial gain in communist strength.[11]

The Asia Foundation didn't retreat from situations endangering field staff; it ran toward them. Blum's move to increase the foundation's presence during rising instability makes sense given the high value the CIA placed on the basic information that could be gathered from "cover and stay-behind" operations, but this would be highly unusual for any normal foundation.

While CIA documents provide records of the CIA using foundation reports for actionable intelligence, the CIA has not released any details revealing which foundation documents were used for this purpose. Yet, we know enough about the types of information produced by foundation staff, and desired by intelligence analysts, to make conservative statements about what sorts of information the CIA sought from the foundation. On a basic level, the CIA sought news on political and cultural movements that could impact the stability of Asian countries where DTPILLAR operated. Reports from rural areas outside of capital cities where information was scarce were highly valued. In countries with tribal or ethnic groups that could align with insurgent groups, it sought basic information about potential uprisings, stability issues, or alliances, with a visible hunger for information that could inform counterinsurgency operations. These were broad intelligence interests, and the discussion below covers what available documents reveal about the CIA collecting intelligence from DTPILLAR and provides examples of projects that informed this intelligence collection process.

COLLECTING OPEN SOURCE INTELLIGENCE

Committee and foundation field staff routinely compiled regional news reports gleaned from Asian newspapers, magazines, and radio broadcasts and sent summaries of this news back to foundation headquarters. CFA clipping files indicate a focused interest in regional economic developments, with frequent reports on economic reforms in China. When, in 1952, Chinese communists began closing private banks, CFA staff collected news reports of high-pressure communist campaigns pushing the Chinese public to bank with the Communist Party's People's Bank. Staff summarized news reports of Chinese housewives out doing their grocery shopping being pressured to "either contribute to the Anti-American Korea fund or to deposit some with the People's bank," while other residents were asked to deposit their entire salaries in the bank on payday, being told they could easily withdraw funds as needed, when in truth such withdrawal requests were routinely denied "on the grounds of 'being luxurious.'"[12]

A 1952 clipping file reported a directive from China's Central People's Government Council requiring security committees in workplaces, schools, and public places to monitor and report on public officials. This initiative spawned widespread denunciations of local officials. Such violations were reported at "reception rooms for peoples' denunciations."[13] Another clipping reported problems emerging as Chinese communists' centralization of agriculture spun off self-perpetuating meetings that damaged the agricultural systems they were designed to improve, evolving into regular three-hour meetings each week. These "endless gatherings" eventually "seriously curtailed the farmers' energy, which would be devoted to production, and affected the health of individual villagers."[14] These news digests circulated as open source intelligence briefings within the CIA. The CIA's operations officer reported that because Asia Foundation reports contained useful news summaries, "they are excellently prepared situation analysis and we are pleased to have them for our own reference; they are perhaps the most current in-depth situation reports we have in our office area files."[15]

ASIAN LIBRARIES AND ARCHIVES AS SOURCES FOR RESEARCH ON CHINESE COMMUNISM

In 1958, anticommunist sinologist Karl Wittfogel wrote President Blum, reminding him of a conversation six months earlier, when Blum had mentioned a 1955 Hong Kong–based foundation project that sent "two men to make a trial run of indexing back numbers" of issues of communist newspapers. Wittfogel asked Blum if he could create an "analytical index" from the fruits of this project.[16] But Blum's reply disavowed any knowledge of this project, as he coolly wrote that he was "afraid that there must be a misunderstanding as this is not an activity in which we have been involved." Blum claimed he double-checked this with foundation staffer James Ivy, who also had no memory of any such project, and Blum referred Wittfogel to the State Department, saying that it would likely have knowledge of such studies of Chinese communists.[17] While it is possible Wittfogel confused who had told him about such a project, it is also possible that Blum now regretted mentioning the existence of a DTPILLAR project with obvious intelligence applications to such a notorious anticommunist scholar, one who might bring unwanted attention to the foundation's collection of open source communist intelligence materials. If such an index had been created for the CIA, it would likely have been classified.

DTPILLAR also funded the collection and analysis of textual materials produced by Asian communists. In the early 1960s, the foundation developed plans to purchase several Asian library collections containing documents on Chinese communism.[18] A confidential foundation report identified five important collections of materials on Chinese communism: a collection at the Bureau of Investigation Library at Ching Tan, the Nationalist Party Archives, the National Defense College Library collection, the personal archives of Republic of China vice president Chen Cheng, and the library at the Ministry of National Defense. American scholars had not previously had access to these significant collections, which were poorly organized and contained a mix of classified and unclassified materials.

Foundation documents stressed these collections would allow American scholars to understand the dynamics of the international communist movement in new ways. The foundation noted that with the political and security sensitivities surrounding scholars' access to these records, "one can imagine the reception that would greet a request to use similar records of our own FBI in a study of the American Communist party. It is doubtful that scholars even in the more advanced field of Russian Communist studies have ever had access to such an array of detailed information about the CPSU." Because the Bureau of Investigation ran counterespionage operations in Taiwan, American access to this collection could create difficulties.[19]

Foundation staff worried that if these records were not preserved, their poor organization and storage conditions might lead to them being burned as useless waste paper. During the 1960s, the Hoover Institution Library tried to purchase communist materials from the Mainland Recovery Strategy Board, but these earliest efforts reportedly failed because a Chinese seller mistakenly believed that the Hoover representative was "pro-Communist."[20] The Chen Cheng collection was eventually microfilmed and deposited at Stanford's Hoover Institution Library and Archives.

Because these collections mixed classified and unclassified documents, and because many American scholars did not have the requisite language competency to properly read them without assistance from state translators, Americans were dependent on Chinese translators who, the foundation worried, may have been instructed to obstruct some lines of research inquiry.[21] The foundation also worried that providing local Chinese translators or scholars access to these materials might unintentionally convert them to communism. The controlled access to communist documents demonstrated the depth of these fears, as the foundation worried that "only a half dozen fiftyish, 'sound' Chinese academics are permitted to do any research on Communism outside of official studies. These sometimes pay a price: loss of prestige among many of their colleagues (who consider such research worthless at best and possibly dangerous), loss of the fatter, better-paying academic posts, restrictions in social contacts, and probably a great deal more restraint in the classroom."[22] The proposed solution to these issues was to fund a large-scale microfilming project photographing copies of all important material. The Hoover Library's Eugene Wu began copying some materials, but he was later denied access to the Bureau of Investigation Library.[23]

With foundation funding, Professor Hsiao Tso-liang negotiated an informal agreement to conduct research on the Jiangxi Soviet at the Bureau of Investigation Library. Factions at that bureau later accused him of "'selling state secrets' to the Americans." He was denied access to this collection despite having letters approving his research from Vice President Chen Cheng and other important figures.[24]

The foundation wondered if access to such archives could be purchased by Western scholars, and staff tried to learn if this was a matter of national principle that could be circumvented for a certain price. The foundation believed that the Bureau of Investigation's lack of microfilming equipment could be exploited to help the foundation gain access to these collections, and a foundation report speculated that if they provided $7,000 in equipment and funds for training, then after the material they desired was copied, the bureau could keep the equipment for its own uses.[25] I did not locate foundation records clarifying the outcome of these efforts, but these documents show several instances of DTPILLAR seeking remote access to documents that could help inform Western intelligence and academic historical understandings of Chinese communist political machinations.

AFGHANISTAN, ESTABLISHING "COVER," AND EARLY DTPILLAR EFFORTS, 1953–1958

During the early 1950s, the CFA attempted to establish a presence in Afghanistan to compete with the many Soviet aid programs there. The committee's 1953 draft plan for Afghanistan began with its representative attempting "to achieve cordial relations" with various members of the Afghanistan government, while trying to negotiate "door-opening" agreements with the Education Ministry there. As part of this effort, the committee acquired and distributed free drug samples from US pharmaceutical companies, helped establish chapters of US women's clubs, and assisted 4H clubs in sponsoring projects in Afghanistan.[26]

Because of DTPILLAR's dual filing system, open discussion of intelligence gathering or the mechanics of establishing intelligence covers are rare in the foundation's deposited archival papers.[27] One apparent exception to this tendency is a March 1953 memo from staff member Harold Amoss to James Stewart discussing ways that the committee might establish a presence in Afghanistan. This correspondence discussed the best way for someone placed by the committee to establish "cover" in this territory. In this memo on "Honorary Traveling Fellowship," stamped "Private," Amoss suggested that one way for the

CFA to establish "cover" to work in Afghanistan could be to get a University of California Honorary Traveling Fellowship. Amoss described the simple steps of applying for this fellowship, adding that his PhD in anthropology from UC Berkeley (1951) meant he had met the requirements for this fellowship. This fellowship provided no funding and was essentially an affiliation awarded to a scholar working overseas. Amoss said he could "outline a presentable project for any country to which the Committee" wished to send him. Amoss volunteered that "should the Committee become interested in operating in Afghanistan, *this type of cover would be most practical* for the initial survey period," adding that he had spent time there, had contacts, and spoke "some Persian."[28] Such open discussion of establishing cover appearing in CFA correspondence seems to be a rare lapse of protocols used in committee correspondence and effectively records open discussion of what must have been an ongoing concern.

Amoss was later appointed Asia Foundation representative to Afghanistan, and a report on his 1955 early winter trip to northeastern Afghanistan records him striving to help the foundation outperform the Soviets in the competitive quest for Afghan loyalties. Amoss observed that a shortcoming of the Soviets' effort to establish "communist imperialism in Afghanistan" was that their interventions had not successfully established "organized indigenous communist party activity." Amoss believed Soviet programs eroded Afghanistan unity and threatened to fracture the country; he reported that the Soviets' goal was to "take over all Afghan territory north of the Hindu Kush Mountains."[29]

Throughout the 1950s, internal memos record foundation concerns over the increased Soviet presence in Afghanistan. There were constant reports of a "steady Soviet penetration," and references to military developments like "shipments of Communist arms . . . reaching Kabul at night" added to concerns that increasing numbers of Afghan military forces were training in the Soviet Union and that Russian influence dominated Afghanistan.[30] Hoping to increase American influence, the foundation purchased a radio-linked news teletype machine for the Bakhtar News Agency, which allowed this Afghan news agency to access United Press International news feeds, with wire-service subscription fees paid by the foundation. While Afghan news agencies already had access to Indian and Soviet news sources, this program allowed them access to US news. But soon after US Information Service personnel installed the equipment, hoping local news services might make more US-friendly news reports, the foundation learned that members of the news agency tried to reconfigure the equipment to receive news feeds from TASS, the Soviet news agency.[31]

REPORT ON LAOTIAN TRIBES

The foundation sponsored numerous reports collecting information on Southeast Asian tribal groups. Because tribal populations often found themselves at odds with the states surrounding them, those governments frequently imposed external controls on traditional tribal ways of life, and some foundation-sponsored reports monitored conflicts between tribes and states. Some foundation reports on tribes were based on collected political or ethnographic information of a sort that had obvious uses in counterinsurgency operations seeking to control tribal groups—including information on levels of tensions between villagers and governments.

A "Rural-Border Tribes" report described the Laotian Kha Katou tribe as "greatly feared" by their neighbors because of their knowledge of poisons, possession of magic for defeating enemies, and "rebel sympathies."[32] The government of Laos tried to weaken tribal sympathies for rebel groups and to keep rebels away from villages by imposing restrictions on the sale of salt to rebel groups and other means of limiting Kha rebel movements. Foundation reports monitored governmental efforts to use salt restrictions to "starve out the Kha rebels," and they reported impacts on rebel groups by increased restrictions of movement.[33] But there was little evidence that, other than slightly inconveniencing the rebels, these salt restrictions produced desired results. Kha rebels innovated salt substitutes made from "a salty black liquid from the ash of certain barks," and they found salt by following elephant tracks to locate jungle salt licks. Foundation reports found that despite these efforts the rebels "succeeded in putting fear into the hearts of civil administrators."[34]

The foundation report concluded that army and police operations had not led tribal members to fear rebels but instead increased villagers' anger toward the national army. This situation exacerbated poor conditions in which there were "countless tales of army misbehavior, indiscriminate, arbitrary killing by the army." The foundation collected reports of the army's "arbitrary and sometimes wholesale killings" of villagers for only the "slightest deviation from regulations" imposed by the army. They learned of collective punishment, including one incident in which "an entire village was razed to the ground, and everyone shot after some Lao army soldiers had been ambushed there."[35]

The report included a lengthy account of foundation staff travel into the rural Haut Mekong Province accompanied by a military officer identified only as the "Lao Colonel." The colonel was described as "a very likeable chap" from

Luan Prabang who "would have been completely at home in the bar rooms of Marseilles." Still, this "likeable chap's" behavior distressed the foundation report's author, as the colonel took liberties with local young women in a region "where relationships between the majority of the people and army are delicate at best."[36] The foundation representative reported that

> in most villages this Colonel felt that the local belles of the villages were more or less obligated to submit to him based on the fact that he was a Lao officer in a tribal area. As is always true on this type of trip, there was much dancing and partying and the Representative, even as an old sailor, was a bit shocked by Lao Military behavior. Nevertheless, the Representative and Ravet purposely accepted invitations to tribal parties and sprees in order to see what was going on.
>
> The Colonel claimed that he was probably more genteel than most Lao officers for he felt that he should not just walk into a village and just ask for a girl; it was much more refined, he said, to get them drunk first and give them gifts of imitation jewelry of which he carried quite a quantity in his army bag.
>
> Mr. Ravet and myself, although while participating in dancing in the tribal villages, were just a bit shocked by the Colonel's behavior. But that of another Lao army officer was considerably worse in making unmistakable attempts before each of the populace and almost reducing the girls to tears while other visitors, and the girls' Parents and the chief looked on.
>
> Although we were cordially invited by the Colonel to join in these occasions, we managed usually to ally aside to look at the beautiful opium fields when his invitations got too intense. We were also rather disturbed to see the Colonel getting the village girls thoroughly drunk in the middle of the afternoon by lining them up and passing a bottle of cognac to each one and keeping them drinking. The girls did not like it at all and were close to tears; one of the girls was the daughter of the village chief. We were not happy to see chiefs and parents standing by in many cases bringing new bottles of whiskey, rum, or cognac, at the colonel's orders. *Although we could not speak Lao, the look in their eyes was language enough. If it ever comes to war in this area the Lao army officers will receive nothing but a slit throat from the people they are supposed to protect.* It was also apparent that Somsanith did not approve this behav-

ior but would not in any way interfere due to the powerful position of the army in Laos.[37]

This report conveys the distress of this foundation staffer, who understood such behavior lacked basic human decency and undermined the military-political position supported by the United States. With such boorish behavior by a military officer, it was little wonder rebel support grew among some tribal groups.

THE THAI TRIBAL RESEARCH CENTRE

In 1960, the foundation proposed an ambitious project studying the hill tribes of Thailand. The foundation's proposal stressed that research advances made by Chinese ethnographers studying Thai tribal groups created a significant knowledge gap for the West, one that needed to be addressed. A foundation memo warned, "Peking has an anthropological research institute with 400 people working just on hill tribes." The foundation argued that the knowledge gap this created meant that "the non-communist world's work along these same lines is negligible in comparison with that of the communist Chinese and anything that could be done to increase knowledge of the hill tribes, if only to assist in forestalling communist penetration, would be all to the good."[38]

It was this hunger for knowledge of these tribal groups that led the foundation to fund a 1961 grant to the Thai Department of Public Welfare to conduct a socioeconomic ethnographic survey of hill tribes. Once the foundation approved funding to hire an ethnographer to be stationed in rural Thailand's tribal areas, staff approached several anthropologists and invited them to apply for this position. Among those approached were Harold Amoss (University of Colorado), David Plath and Jay Ingersoll (University of California), George William Skinner (Cornell), Richard Beardsley (University of Michigan), Delmer Brown (University of California), Ted Dongras (Fulbright Program), and Mel Spector (State Department).[39] The foundation eventually hired Austrian ethnographer Hans Manndorff for this position. Manndorff's efforts laid the groundwork for what, in 1965, would become the Tribal Research Centre in Chiang Mai.

In November 1961, Dr. Manndorff arrived in rural Thailand and began fieldwork on the Asia Foundation's Hill Tribes Research Project with supplemental funding from a UN Narcotics Division grant to study regional opium production. The foundation's "Manual for Field Workers among Hill Tribes: Intensive Village Community Study" detailed plans for launching "self-help" projects involving villagers in all stages of development project planning. The manual called for projects "attuned to the 'felt needs' of the tribal villagers concerned" while relying on outside technical assistance. While the manual advocated involving local populations in all stages of research, it also recommended conducting a reconnaissance survey before involving local populations in a public planning process for technical assistance.[40]

The project manual reads like a condensed version of the 1926 colonial classic, *Notes and Queries*, instructing field workers to begin with a community survey, then build plans for community development. The hill tribes survey gathered information on economic and cultural conditions, collected villagers' opinions, and assessed "requirements and essential projects that should be undertaken," and researchers also collected information on the physical environment and economic activities.[41] While the manual recommended collecting villagers' views, it cautioned researchers not to take them too seriously and to separate these views from those of the researcher. The manual provided detailed instructions for structured and unstructured interviews and for recording observations, and it instructed ethnographers to sketch structures, conduct censuses, record food sources, and gather demographic information. The categories of data to be collected reflected the sort of standardized approach to trait indexing pioneered by the Human Relations Area Files.[42]

In 1962, the Asia Foundation took note of anthropologist William Klausner's report on recent Thai governmental efforts to ban opium production in tribal regions. Researchers reported that during exploratory hikes through the tribal areas they routinely encountered opium plots, including some close to the village and tended by elders who did not have the energy to hide their fields in more distant locations. Occasional arrests occurred, but these appeared to be "indiscriminate in nature."[43] Government policies had little impact on the price of opium. Alternative crops to replace opium were discussed, with the usual suggestions of coffee, tea, and fruit being made with little recognition of how their smaller profits would impact decisions. Instead, issues of transportation and other logistical matters were cited as reasons for hill people not abandoning poppy production. There was only a hesitant acknowledgment that locals *liked* smoking opium and that its use was part of their culture. Klausner acknowledged that physical addiction to opium and cultural values favoring opium use hampered opium suppression efforts. He reported that "there apparently is an almost hypnotic quality to the fields of opium poppy in blossom. Most all of the tribal groups are addicted to opium, but the percentage of those addicted varies from tribe to tribe and within a tribe vary from village to village. The socio-economic survey enumerators are obtaining detailed information on the extent of such addiction."[44]

Foundation reports indicated that some members of the Haw tribe worked as enforcers, managing the opium trade with threats and acts of violence. During the course of his ethnographic fieldwork, Manndorff encountered uniformed Thai soldiers involved in opium trafficking, and he documented a great fluidity in Haw roles, noting they were primarily interested in trade and seemed to care little about the Chinese Nationalist troops or other state actors. Klausner observed that some traders "maintain their army connection," some of them even continuing to wear "army uniforms one day and regular village clothes the next."[45] At times, Chinese Nationalist soldiers worked with armed men guarding opium caravans. Klausner observed that

> these troops get double pay; they first extract a levy for opium carried across the Burma or Lao borders, the amount levied depending on the weight of opium that is transported. They then hire out as armed guards of the caravan. They also will accompany any shipments of opium produced in Thailand that are being transferred from one area to another. All of these Haw tribesmen described above in their varied roles are remnants of the Chinese Nationalist troops which fled Communist China and later crossed over from Burma under pressure from government armed forces.[46]

Klausner suspected these armed opium guards were fighting communist forces in Laos or China. At one point, field researchers encountered armed Chinese Nationalist soldiers in uniform, and there were rumors that the Thai army was secretly arming local tribal groups "to enable them to carry out guerrilla activities against Communists in the neighboring area."[47]

Ethnographic fieldwork identified four primary opium trading centers. Klausner reported that "Haw traders sell the opium in the [Chiang Mai] area where it is processed into morphine," and the government failed to locate local processing plants because opium, once processed into morphine, "is then shipped to Bangkok where it is processed into heroin."[48] The area around Chiang Mai took on an increasing importance because of its location within this opium-producing region, and these tribal populations became test subjects for a variety of counterinsurgency research programs.

By early 1963, the foundation had proposed establishing the Tribal Research

Centre in Chiang Mai. This would be run through the Thai Department of Public Welfare, which sought funds from several international foundations and aid organizations.[49] The foundation's proposal to establish a tribal research center was developed by "an informal, unofficial working committee" consisting of representatives from Thailand's Department of Public Welfare, the United Nations, Colombo Plan countries, United States Operations Mission (USOM), the National Economic Development Board, National Research Council members, and the Asia Foundation.[50]

The details of this DTPILLAR-funded vision for the Tribal Research Centre are instructive. The proposal presented the project as addressing pan-Asian regional issues facing "minority hill tribes," while framing tribes as problems needing to be solved. The tribes along the northern Thai border and elsewhere were described as having "presented the Thai government with many serious problems in economic, government and border security matters, which demand urgent solutions." Chief among the identified "tribal problems" was opium. The proposal stressed that after opium use and sales were outlawed in 1958, the Thai Department of Public Welfare became responsible for the welfare of these tribal peoples; responsibilities included providing services (such as stable housing, development, and land settlement projects) that would be identified by Tribal Research Centre projects. From a managerial standpoint, the significant cultural diversity among these tribal groups, as well as growing concerns about tribal insurgents, made this a strategic location in which to locate a tribal research entity. The report envisioned such an entity hosting international researchers and others working with international organizations and governmental agencies.[51]

In mid-April 1963, Klausner and Cornell University anthropologist Lauriston Sharp discussed the foundation's hill tribes pilot project. Sharp planned to work with an ethnographically trained Thai team to survey cultural ecological features of Thai tribal areas.[52] Sharp was flexible about the fieldwork location, and when Klausner suggested either the Chiang Mai or Tak areas, he was open to these possibilities. The Thai Department of Public Welfare was supportive of Sharp's project and volunteered to provide several Thai research associates.[53]

Princeton historian and OSS alum Frederick W. Mote conducted a ten-day visit of the hill tribe area "at the request of the Hill Tribes Division, Department of Public Welfare."[54] Mote provided the foundation with a copy of his report (marked "not for circulation"), which critiqued, in vain, the simplistic notion that any village could meaningfully be classified as either pro- or anti–Nationalist Party, yet these sorts of overly simplified designations were precisely the sort of measures these hill tribe surveys were designed to undertake. Mote complained it was "inappropriate to refer to the villages . . . as KMT [Nationalist-aligned] villages, and it is especially inaccurate to refer to all of the groups mentioned [in his report] by the general and inclusive label of 'KMT's' and to imply that they constitute one coherent group."[55] While solid advice, this was not what the Thai government or US advisors wanted to hear or *could* hear. Much of the institutional inability to understand Mote's critique was embedded in the limited vision the US government had when contemplating these matters.

Manndorff's report on an October 1964 field trip to Mae Sariang, Tak, and Chiang Mai described several immediate negative impacts on Karen people following the recent construction of a roadway into the Mae Sariang region.[56] Manndorff found significant increases in cattle theft, presumably by road workers "or lawless stragglers coming from the lowlands" along the new road. Showing faith in modernization theory, Manndorff claimed the new consumer goods these Karen communities could access through new trade with the outside world would soon improve their lives, yet he appeared surprised these villagers were not entering the cash economy by taking jobs as day laborers on road construction crews. His observations of the impacts this road would have on Karen tribal families expressed concerns about the ways that development would irrevocably change core features of local cultures.

One foundation report described a remote shortwave "subversive radio station" broadcast heard while traveling in rural Thailand late at night. Broadcasting under the name "The Voice of Thailand," the program attacked US development efforts in rural Thailand. The announcer spoke in a central Thai dialect and delivered sharp, humorous criticisms.[57]

Although DTPILLAR was instrumental in laying the groundwork for the establishment of the Tribal Research Centre, in 1965 the foundation informed the center's staff that while it would continue supplying general funds and grants for individual projects, the foundation would reduce its financial support for the center. The foundation's Thailand representative, Graham Lucas, explained that "while the policy of the Foundation was to disengage itself from long-term assistance on behalf of a particular program, nevertheless our intention was not to phase out entirely but to respond to ad hoc requests from government sources for continued assistance, for example, further research on particular aspects of hill tribe development."[58]

As DTPILLAR reduced funding for the Tribal Research Centre, an arm of the US military-intelligence complex came forward with new funds for counterinsurgency research at the center under a program funded by the Advanced Research Projects Agency (ARPA).[59] Many of the Tribal Research Centre's programs aligned with US military and Thai governmental interests in seeking to establish forms of stability linked to overarching counterinsurgency goals. Lucas reported to foundation president Haydn Williams that ARPA "was considering the possibility of putting as much as one million dollars into an enlarged tribal research program and he had discussed this matter at some length with Robert Kickert, an American anthropologist employed by ARPA."[60] Because this research effort would be funded by the US government, the Thai government was hesitant to back such military-linked programs. This reluctance of the Thai government to work with anything having such clear US military connections demonstrates one of the reasons why the CIA preferred to use the Asia Foundation as a nongovernmental organization to support these counterinsurgency-linked operations: when DTPILLAR channeled apparently nongovernment funds for programs, suspicions eased.

In October 1966, Asia Foundation senior research associate John Sutter asked Manndorff to compile a list of anthropological books that could improve "the professional competence of Government officers responsible for planning and directing programs concerned with the aboriginal minority in Malaysia, including Sabah and Sarak."[61] Manndorff's recommendations mixed classic anthropology texts with ethnographic works designed to assist tribal managerial staff.[62]

Among the foundation's last recorded engagements with the Tribal Research Centre was a 1966 proposal by the Hill-Tribe Cultural Minority Program to bring members of Asian tribal minority groups to tour Thai tribal areas.[63] The proposed trip did not occur, but the vision for it reveals the sort of world-as-laboratory approach the center and foundation nurtured. This was to be a sort of counterinsurgency display, in which "the observation tour would be carried out in North Thailand with visits to Department of Public Welfare settlement centers," with plans to use the Chiang Mai Tribal Research Centre as a model showroom. A weeklong "observation tour" and several days for seminars were proposed.[64] The foundation proposed to fund visiting officials from Malaysia and the Philippines, and to avoid political tensions there would be no official Thai governmental presence. Instead, the "relevant Thai government agency would merely arrange the program of visits and the informal seminar following the observation tour."[65] The initial plan was for the foundation to arrange "a seminar and observation tour for selected personnel with responsibilities in the field of hill-tribe/cultural minority programming in the Philippines."[66] This proposed Asian tribal summit never materialized because of political concerns.

At the end of the decade, following whistleblowing revelations by anthropologist Delmos Jones, as well as critical focus from Eric Wolf, Joseph Jorgensen, and other members of the American Anthropological Association (AAA), news of US-backed counterinsurgency operations and Chiang Mai's counterinsurgency programs became well known to American anthropologists, and these revelations spawned a crisis in the discipline. It came to a head at the 1971 AAA annual meeting, where an investigative committee report submitted by Margaret Mead was rejected by the association members for failing to investigate reports that US anthropologists were colluding with military and intelligence personnel in Thailand. Many anthropologists were outraged that Mead's committee had investigated not accusations of anthropologists' involvement in counterinsurgency research in Thailand but Wolf's and others' use of stolen documents in their condemnations of anthropologists engaged in counterinsurgency work and the early condemnation statements by AAA ethics committee members. The backlash against the ethnographic contributions to counterinsurgency operations at Chiang Mai's Tribal Research Centre and elsewhere led the AAA to adopt a strict ethics code prohibiting secret research.[67]

LOUIS CONNICK

During his many years on the Asia Foundation staff, Louis Connick understood how to play the role of the quiet American. He maintained a low profile, conducted foundation business efficiently, sent reports to headquarters in a timely fashion, and routinely reported political and military developments—at times detailing shifting factions, military developments, and political minutiae.[68] The excerpt below, from a routine 1966 memo reporting developments in Laos weeks after a coup, shows his reporting style, as he added backstory details to political events occupying the immediate foreground. Connick reported,

> The Prime Minister held a press conference Friday morning, October 8 which lasted only fifteen minutes. Only three questions were allowed.
>
> The Prime Minister reported that the [Laos] Ministry of Foreign Affairs had sent a telegram to the Minister of Foreign Affairs in Thailand asking the Thai Government to return General Thao Ma and his confederates to Laos. No action has been taken so far.

> In regard to the January 1 elections, Souvanna said that the [Pathet] Lao would be asked to participate. If they didn't, Souvanna said he would not consider the requirements of a general election [to] have been fulfilled, and would feel free to continue to provisional government, leaving the four Pathet Lao posts still vacant. Such a move could well spell trouble.
>
> Souvanna denied the rumor that Neutralist General Kong Le had been ousted as leader of the Neutralist army. Kong Le has been in Bangkok since before General Ma's raid, purportedly for convalescence. Lt. Colonel Thavil Oudanon has been sent to Bangkok to see him.
>
> General Kane Insixiengmay has reported the capture of two more northern strongholds—Nambark and Pak Seng which have been held by the Pathet Lao since 1960.
>
> Kane reported that General Ma and his confederates took off from Luang [Prabang] Thursday, October 20, supposedly to fly sorties against Pathet Lao positions. They didn't return to Luang Prabang that night. The [bombing] took place the next day from Savannakhet.[69]

Connick remained on the foundation staff after its CIA connections were exposed and continued as the foundation's representative in Laos until at least 1968.[70]

Decades later, Connick's nephew, Oakley Brooks, wrote about his uncle's years working for the CIA. In a 2008 article in the *Christian Science Monitor*, Brooks described Connick's preferred use of CIA cover, in which he acted as a "charming humanitarian who ran aid programs in Indochina" during the 1970s while he "moonlighted for the CIA."[71] According to Brooks,

> While Lou led humanitarian efforts on almost every continent, he ran aid and development programs for the Asia Foundation and the US Agency for International Development (USAID) in Laos at the height of the American military presence in Indochina. As part of those postings, he worked for another organization there—the Central Intelligence Agency.
>
> His involvement with the CIA seemed low-level, passing on information here and there about people. He didn't talk about it much. Like a lot of lives lived on cold-war fronts, his remains shrouded in some mystery.[72]

Connick's nephew likely knew few details of his uncle's actual CIA activity, such as whether he was involved only in this sort of "low-level passing on information." In regions where Westerners had a limited presence, even reports of news or of the conditions of daily life became valuable intelligence.

PASSIVE AND ACTIVE INTELLIGENCE GATHERING

After the 1967 *New York Times* story exposed links between the Asia Foundation and the CIA, the foundation insisted it did not gather intelligence. This claim was later used to argue that the foundation should receive State Department funds to allow it to continue its work.[73] We now know that while the gathering of intelligence was never DTPILLAR's primary mission, some foundation employees did gather intelligence prior to 1968 when the CIA severed ties with the foundation, and CIA documents establish that DTPILLAR at times produced valuable actionable intelligence.

Because neither the US government nor the foundation ever provided an accurate public accounting of the CIA's central role in creating, overseeing, and funding the foundation, public misrepresentations of this history became common. Typical of these misrepresentations were the statements made in 1983 hearings of the US Senate's Committee on Foreign Relations discussing the Asia Foundation's past, present, and future. These hearings glossed over the extent of the CIA's involvement in the foundation up to 1967, instead claiming that "the Foundation was funded from its inception through trusts and other foundations which in turn were funded by the CIA. Its activities were not used for covert intelligence operations. They were open and, in some cases, subject to the review and prior approval of host governments."[74]

The foundation's status as a CIA proprietary complicates our interpretations of many of its basic pre-1967 activities. Determining exactly what was and was not intelligence-related foundation work can be difficult to divine. While the vast majority of DTPILLAR-funded programs were not designed to gather intelligence, the fact that the CIA at times consumed intelligence provided by the foundation raises questions about all sorts of activities. For example, it is unknown whether a 1959 program to assist advisors of Asian students studying in the United States was simply the foundation assisting Asian students as a goodwill effort and application of Cold War soft power or if this program also was a means for the CIA to recruit, or gather information on, Asian students who would likely take on leadership roles in future years. While many details remain unknown, given what is known of CIA recruitment tactics during this period it is reasonable to wonder if it sometimes did both. Even with gaps in released records, we know that the foundation recommended that Asian students receiving foundation grants to study in the United States met individually with foundation representatives each year.[75] This would have fit known CIA patterns for collecting intelligence or recruiting agents, but we simply cannot know if such activities occurred in connection with this student program.[76]

By the early-1960s, the CIA was pleased with the amount and quality of intelligence it received from the Asia Foundation. The CIA's refusal to release a significant amount of still classified DTPILLAR records leaves significant gaps in our knowledge of these activities. As is discussed in chapter 9, foundation reports often contained valuable intelligence information, much of it the sort of mundane information on current conditions, underreported in the press, that the agency valued. Many years later, some of those involved in these operations spoke more bluntly about what the CIA had been doing. James L. Woods, Department of Defense advisor and later ARPA counterinsurgency specialist in Thailand, described US operations with the Thai border patrol out on "the outermost fringes of the Kingdom" as "basically a CIA project or at least [they] were getting support and training through the CIA part of USOM."[77] Woods stressed the importance of ethnographic knowledge in this operation, stating that

> there's really a highlander/lowlander split, however, if you had to describe the politics, but then you had the KMT [Nationalist Party-aligned] army or remnants thereof over on the western border and the drug smugglers on both borders and the lumber smugglers. So it was a "Terry and the pirates" kind of environment, and we were basically just trying to collect information. We were also sponsoring basic ethnographies by a number of anthropologists, European and American, at the time, again trying to collect in-depth ethnographic understanding of several selected lesser-known tribal groups. So that's how I spent a rather odd year as the advisor to the dean of the faculty of social sciences at Chiang Mai University.[78]

This was a world where intelligence operatives imagined they were living in a Milton Caniff adventure comic, as anthropologists and other social scientists walked in and out of the panels, frequently, but not always, with little thought about the political roles they were playing, much less how hard Cold War

American officials were working to convince Asians that capitalism's market forces could best meet their needs.

The significance of the Committee for Free Asia and the Asia Foundation's activities at Chiang Mai and their other intelligence-gathering activities is best understood not simply in the individual episodes described here; it is best understood as part of DTPILLAR's contribution to larger, ongoing counterinsurgency operations that the CIA supported as a central part of its Cold War global strategy. During the 1950s and 1960s, this global strategy had a lot to do with the sort of counterinsurgency operations DTPILLAR was involved with, discussed in the next chapter.

6 Foundation Anticommunism and Counterinsurgency Programs

Beware of Greeks bearing gifts.
VIRGIL / *The Aeneid*

While the Committee for Free Asia projected a brash, evangelical commitment to helping capitalism vanquish Asian communism, Asia Foundation anticommunism tried to project a cultivated veneer of academic sophistication. The committee funded openly anticommunist groups, while the foundation often funded organizations with more refined academic affiliations engaging in activities supporting US policies. These activities included projects like translating Boy Scout manuals into local languages, supplying textbooks, or providing newsprint to newspapers publishing stories sympathetic to US geopolitical interests.

DTPILLAR monitored the activities of communist-linked groups throughout Asia. Memos from in-country staff regularly tracked the activities of local communist groups. These reports mixed first- and secondhand observations of communists' interactions with such groups as rural farmers' organizations or labor unions. The following excerpt from a 1953 CFA report shows the committee's interest in monitoring communist activities in the regions where they worked. The report stated,

> Communist activities in Indonesia are being vigorously pushed, although I did not have the impression that the Communists were, by themselves, in a position to cause major trouble. The Communists are reported to be particularly strong in the labor field where they completely control the major labor union, S.O.B.S.I. [Sentral Organisasi Buruh Seluruh Indonesia, or Central All-Indonesian Workers Organization]. Similarly, I was told that they have a strong hand in farmer organizations. There do not seem to be any affective [sic] counter movements in these areas, and it is generally agreed that the present Government, even though it is predominantly non-Communist, is not capable of offering any effective opposition to these developments. The Communists seem to be working through their traditional methods of

financing their own organizations and splitting those of the opposition, which unfortunately is always quite weak.¹

Such reports helped committee staff synthesize what they had learned from monitoring local communists' arguments, tactics, advances, and retreats.

THE NATIONAL MOVEMENT FOR FREE ELECTIONS IN THE PHILIPPINES

While two of the primary causes supported by DTPILLAR operations were anticommunism and prodemocracy campaigns, the specific democratic initiatives supported were selectively tied to outcomes favoring anticommunist candidates in ways that sometimes found DTPILLAR interfering with electoral politics. As CIA-backed coups overthrowing democratically elected candidates in places like Iran and Guatemala demonstrate, the CIA did not care about supporting democracy or fair elections; it cared about supporting regimes aligned with US capitalism. CIA support for democracy only backed certain types of outcomes aligned with US policy. As a claimed supporter of democracy, the committee claimed to provide independent oversight for open and fair elections in the Philippines, yet this support was far from impartial. The CFA began financially supporting the National Movement for Free Elections (NAMFREL) soon after NAMFREL was established in the summer of 1951.

NAMFREL was part of Edward Lansdale's CIA-linked mission to shape democratic movements aligned with US geopolitical interests in the Philippines.² Colonel Jaime Ferrer directed NAMFREL, and soon after its founding he began opening NAMFREL chapters throughout the Philippines. While NAMFREL claimed to support free elections, covert CIA funding flowing through the CFA undermined any such claims; NAMFREL was interested in anticommunist candidates winning elections, not in promoting free elections.³ Desmond Fitzgerald at the Office of Policy Coordination selected Gabriel Kaplan to assist with NAMFREL operations, and Kaplan helped the group incorporate campaign techniques used in US elections. Kaplan had worked with Fitzgerald on US political campaigns, having run (unsuccessfully) for Congress and the New York Supreme Court. Kaplan then followed Fitzgerald to the Philippines after the latter became chief of the CIA's Philippine operation.⁴ Kaplan oversaw registration and voting procedures for Philippine presidential elections, and through NAMFREL he trained election observers on how to detect and eliminate voter fraud.⁵ Kaplan was employed by a CIA front known as the Catherwood Foundation while he prepared for the 1953 elections in the Philippines.⁶

In one CIA report, Kaplan described his mission as being to shape NAMFREL into a neutral civic organization similar to the League of Women Voters or the New York State Association against Election Fraud.⁷ CFA staff backed Kaplan and NAMFREL by establishing a network of local Filipinos supporting various campaign tasks.⁸ Kaplan also gathered support from American service groups, including the Jaycees and Lions Clubs.⁹

Edward Lansdale's operations went far beyond assuring that President Elpidio Quirino's government did not commit voter fraud. As part of the CIA's campaign to sway election results, during the months leading up to the election Lansdale used local media and handbills to spread propaganda about Huk rebels and communists.¹⁰ This was a key moment in the CIA's vision of how it could shape the world by shaping the flow of information and disinformation in foreign election campaigns. As Lansdale biographer Cecil Currey has observed, for Lansdale, this election was "a real opportunity to demonstrate to Filipinos that the ballot was better than a bullet to achieve change in government. He also saw it as a chance to discredit the Huk leadership, which advocated armed rebellion as the only possible solution to the country's problems."¹¹

Colonel Jaime E. Ferrer worked with CFA to build NAMFREL-backed community centers. These centers housed public education programs promoting democratic participation throughout the Philippines. Because Ferrer believed communities sharing the costs of building these centers became invested in the democratic movements they represented, some of the costs of running these centers also came from the communities where they were located.¹² The CFA purchased books for NAMFREL community libraries, and the centers served as public education venues and as distribution points for the CFA's Seeds for Democracy program. In 1952, the Philippines government—worried about foreign interference in domestic political processes—tried to limit the impacts of the centers by not allowing shipments of movie-related materials for these centers to clear customs.¹³

In March 1953, William T. Fleming wrote to CFA acting president Ray Maddocks, warning that the committee faced damaging political exposure for backing these NAMFREL community centers. Fleming advised Maddocks that because President Quirino understood the links between CFA, NAMFREL, and community centers, the best option for the committee was to emphasize that they had no desire to interfere in electoral partisan politics, claiming instead their only interest was in supporting community centers that were good for the whole of the Philippines.[14]

A spring 1953 Associated Press news story reported that President Quirino had attacked the CFA for supporting NAMFREL community centers. Quirino argued that these foreign-funded centers hosted political discussions to improperly influence domestic political campaigns. After the AP story appeared, CARE (Cooperative for American Relief Everywhere) staff members expressed concern that their sponsorship of NAMFREL community centers could put them under attack as well.[15] As concerns over the neutrality of the community centers spread, Acting President Maddocks wrote CARE's George Andres, informing him that the committee was abandoning its support for the centers.[16]

Colonel Jaime Ferrer was upset by the committee's withdrawal of support for the centers, and in a meeting with Philippines representative Fleming, Ferrer claimed "he was going back to the States, where he would say many things about the Committee which 'you will not like.' He added that he would stop at the San Francisco Office and implied he would 'tell them off.' His parting thrust was that following the November elections, *he* would oppose the operations of the CFA in Manila." Fleming reminded Ferrer that the committee's work was "an asset to the Philippines," adding that as the committee ended its enthusiastic support for the centers, he hoped the colonel would not "obstruct them in any way."[17] Privately, the CFA worried about the fallout from its association with Ferrer and the community centers, as well as what he might publicly say to the press in the United States.[18]

Kaplan helped organize Ramon Magsaysay's presidential campaign. He established rural development programs for Magsaysay using funds from CARE, Coca-Cola, and NAMFREL's organizational network.[19] Kaplan borrowed themes and tactics from an anti–rat infestation campaign he had run in a political campaign in Harlem and Hell's Kitchen.[20] Nakano Satoshi has noted that in these elections there were "visible similarities in election fraud" patterns found in US elections, which raised questions for Satoshi about whether "there was not some sort of 'personal technical transfer' from Americans to Filipinos during the early colonial era."[21]

With NAMFREL and CIA support, Magsaysay was elected president in November 1953. With him in office, the United States gained an important Asian anticommunist ally who led the Southeast Asia Treaty Organization's regional anticommunist campaign. In 1958 Kaplan returned to the United States, where he became president of the Community Development Counseling Service, of

Arlington, Virginia, training personnel for international work fighting communism.[22]

Some claim that US backing of NAMFREL did not undermine the legitimacy of local support for Magsaysay. Benedict Kerkvliet, for example, rejects critiques that NAMFREL was a fundamentally American imposition on indigenous democratic efforts, arguing that the movement's support by various local groups had a greater significance than the CIA's backing. Kerkvliet claims that even if one acknowledges that NAMFREL was launched by the CIA, the presence of local Filipino supporters discredits claims of CIA hegemony.[23] Such arguments misinterpret how monied outside support, such as the CIA brought, works in situations in which local voices are amplified by well-funded vested interests. Such critiques downplay the significance of how these outside efforts build specific types of democratic movements favoring one political group, or candidate, over another and how externally funded movements crowd out what might have been other local movements.

Beyond this sort of foreign interference in Asian elections, committee and foundation staff routinely reported on election campaigns and other political events in host countries, often adding nuanced interpretations or backstories on events not covered in the international press. Reporting on the 1960 elections in Laos, foundation representative Gordon Messegee described election results as "very favorable to the West." In one campaign report he described some of the ways the United States tried to sway voters. For example, staff traveling in US-backed jeep convoys that were "heavily guarded by armed police or soldiers" brought food and drinks for villagers attending political rallies. Messegee wrote that if the candidate was one "favored" by the foundation, their "convoy will be supplied with one motor generator, one public address system, one movie projector, one screen and two or three rolls of film and an expert (usually a Thai) to operate this apparatus. All this is supplied by USIS." After a "favored candidate" gave a speech, the USIS screened movies, most often films of Lao cultural events like dancing or musical performances, or perhaps featuring Laotian government or military activities, and one film showing scenes from the United States.[24] Through such forms of support as supplying these rare chances for villagers to watch films, linked with the political campaigns of favored, anticommunist candidates, DTPILLAR interfered in foreign elections, all in the name of democracy.

FUNDING A VIETNAM WAR BRAIN TRUST

While DTPILLAR funded a broad range of academic work, there were significant types of projects the foundation did not generally support during this period—such as work critical of US military policy. The foundation's ability to selectively fund projects and individuals helped produce a fortified intellectual body of work supporting certain types of policies in Vietnam and elsewhere in Asia; in some instances, this meant funding academic work with ideological arguments that would help persuade the nation to remain in this long, bloody, lost war. It wasn't that everyone funded by the foundation supported the war; they certainly didn't. What the foundation didn't do was fund academic projects directly opposing US policies in Vietnam or elsewhere in Asia. However, the foundation did fund a variety of academic research projects whose results contributed to the Vietnam War.

In March 1962, sociologist Howard Kauffman moved with his family from Nepal to Vietnam for an Asia Foundation–funded project at the Cooperative Research and Training Center in Vietnam. Kauffman trained Vietnamese social scientists in field research methods so they could study community organizations, like cooperatives and farmers' associations undergoing transitions. One product from this research was Kauffman's 1,125-page 1963 study, *Cu-Lao: A Preliminary Socio-Economic Study of a Fishing Village and Its Cooperative*, a thorough ethnographic picture of Vietnamese society detailing traditional roles and practices of village life.[25] Kauffman's project went far over budget, but with the support of foundation staff in Vietnam the scale of his study grew as he trained numerous Vietnamese research assistants to conduct socioeconomic field research. While this was a noninterventionist study, it provided important information of the sort desired by US military and intelligence personnel, who were soon designing various counterinsurgency projects drawing on such data.

DTPILLAR funded various Vietnam projects, either directly supporting counterinsurgency operations or indirectly providing data informing counterinsurgency programs. Whenever possible, the foundation worked with other organizations supporting these projects, such as American Friends of Vietnam (AFV), which funded scholarships for Vietnamese students studying in the United States. This presented some boundary issues as members of the Diem government sought increasing control in selecting students for these scholarships. By the mid-1950s, rumors were circulating (some foundation staff believed the French government started these rumors) that the foundation's close relationship with the AFV had become too close and that the foundation was involved in a program "trying to buy votes in Vietnam." AFV executive secretary Gilbert Jonas advised the foundation that it should remove its name from these scholarship programs due to growing suspicions of impropriety.[26] Foundation staff bristled at suggestions they should downplay the American backing of such programs and claims they were influencing foreign political processes, yet this was exactly what the foundation sought to do.

In 1956, years before Michigan State University's (MSU) ties to the CIA were publicly exposed, Wesley Fishel, of MSU's Project in Public Administration, developed a program that funded Vietnamese intellectuals. Fishel provided public services linked to Operation Brotherhood, a counterinsurgency effort supplying medical care and generating goodwill between the United States and the Vietnamese people. Fishel reported that Operation Brotherhood helped improve relations in some areas but that there also had been problems with communists infiltrating the program.[27]

In 1961, at the request of a Catholic bishop in Vietnam, the foundation provided a $16,570 grant financing a "Mobile Film Service for Montagnard Areas" of Vietnam. The grant purchased film projectors, "motion pictures of an educational and informative nature," and other equipment priests used to screen educational movies in remote Montagnard villages. This sort of alliance between the CIA and Catholic Church was advocated for Vietnam by Edward Lansdale and other American counterinsurgency tacticians advising the CIA.[28] DTPILLAR provided $3,300 for a Vietnam "popular Cultural Association" program establishing provincial centers, with teacher training courses for members of mountain tribes.[29]

In 1961 the foundation provided $43,000 to "assist the Cooperative Research and Training Center by providing the services for two years of a rural sociologist to conduct a series of rural studies on economic and social problems in at least one and possibly three pilot villages in Vietnam with emphasis on group dynamics and the problems of a society in transition."[30]

THE MONTAGNARD RESETTLEMENT PROGRAM AND PROJECT STRATEGIC HAMLET

In the early 1960s, the foundation studied the possibility of moving entire Montagnard (Hmong) villages away from Vietnam's highland areas in order to isolate them from Vietnamese NLF fighters moving through the mountain regions.[31]

The proposed Montagnard Resettlement Project would move the villagers to lowland areas, and it was part of the incipient US counterinsurgency strategy in Vietnam, which would later include the Strategic Hamlet Program.[32] In August 1961, Vietnam representative James C. Porterfield justified the foundation's support for these counterinsurgency projects as aligning with foundation objectives "to encourage national integration of the various religions, social and racial group." This aligned with program objectives of assisting the "mutual adjustment of the various religious, social and racial groups, including the mountain tribes."[33] Porterfield's report framed the foundation's resettlement plan as "doing something for" the mountain tribes, as if forced relocations were a gift rather than a disruption of the only life they knew, and stressed that officials "expressed growing concern over the infiltration of the Montagnard but have no funds at their disposal with which to launch a program."[34]

One early resettlement operation moved five thousand Rhade Montagnards to a secured compound near Ban Mê Thuột, a resettlement site selected by Vietnamese civilian and military authorities for its "defensibility and agricultural potential." This resettlement came with armed guards and fortification. Because of fears the NLF would try and "move these people into communist controlled areas," the move occurred quickly and was unannounced.[35] While these security concerns were justified—because this move had such devastating impacts on the lives of the Montagnard people being moved—this secrecy also kept the village from organizing some forms of resistance.

While the foundation helped plan the Montagnard Resettlement Project, there was an awareness that it should not be identified as being directly involved in the planning. The foundation preferred its involvement in such operations to occur out of the public eye and to "not enter the picture until after the relocation has occurred, otherwise we will be identified with an unpopular government policy." Instead, the foundation wanted "to appear to be interested in the community development aspects and to avoid appearance of endorsing a military policy of the government."[36]

This planned Montagnard Resettlement Project never got off the ground and was canceled in the fall of 1961. But a few months later, Roger Hilsman, director of the State Department's Bureau of Intelligence and Research, began work on the Strategic Hamlet Program, whose roots were linked to the DTPILLAR-planned Montagnard Resettlement Project.[37]

Like this recently canceled project, the Strategic Hamlet Program was a counterinsurgency operation designed to weaken support for North Vietnamese forces by engineering the forced relocation of highland villagers en masse to lowland hamlets. "Hamlets" was the euphemistic name for armed, fortified, defensively fenced communities that functioned like detention centers for relocated Hmong villages, in areas away from the NLF. As with the earlier plans to relocate these villages to lowland fortified compounds, the foundation preferred that it only be identified as supporting "humanitarian" components of these operations. In 1964, DTPILLAR supplied 66 villages with 198 classrooms in schools located inside the fortified walls of these counterinsurgency villages. It also provided a grant (235,200 piasters) to Vietnam's Ministry of National Education to pay for the training and salaries of teachers working in the schools in the Strategic Hamlet Schools Program in six provinces.[38] The foundation consulted with several individuals familiar with the program locations on the advisability of specific projects. While the foundation's previous support for the Montagnard Resettlement Project had reached beyond its proclaimed mission, by funding schools and educational projects for the Strategic Hamlet Project, foundation involvement in this counterinsurgency operation provided public cover more closely aligned to its declared mission.

At the January 1963 meeting between CIA director John McCone, deputy director Marshall Carter, and the new foundation president, Russell Smith, it was agreed that because of AID's slow pace in approving strategic hamlet proposals, Smith would accelerate the foundation board's approval of this work.[39] Within the CIA, Cord Meyer coordinated support from key individuals at the State Department to launch a foundation-funded program that included building seventy schools in strategic hamlets.[40]

The foundation continued to fund schools located in strategic hamlets' fortified counterinsurgency outposts. The following year, foundation Vietnam representative Howard C. Thomas Jr. argued that building and staffing schools, medical facilities, and other visible improvements in services would improve the occupants' attitude about this program that had so drastically altered their lives. To bring these improvements, Thomas requested funds to build a hundred schools within strategic hamlets.[41]

Throughout the 1960s, the foundation explored many initiatives supporting Vietnam's tribal mountain groups; among these were projects to strengthen support systems for those who had been impacted by the war. In August 1966, Richard Koontz, a foundation assistant representative to Vietnam, proposed a $14,300 program to send three delegations of Montagnard representatives on a two-week trip to Taiwan, the Philippines, and Malaysia to "to observe tribal affairs activities."[42] These trips were to help Montagnard leaders study how other tribal groups developed more active roles in national governments. This proposal faced several political hurdles. Foundation staffer Bill Evans attached a note to the proposal, describing it as "loaded with political dynamite." Evans believed that "unless the future government of Vietnam decides to continue the government's current policy of paying little more than lip-service to the Montagnard's legitimate rights, this project will only serve to strengthen Montagnard leadership in preparation for eventual civil war. TAF could be denounced by future government for its present role."[43] But even with these risks, Evans believed the project to be one of the foundation's best options for assisting the Montagnard people. He insisted that Vietnamese political leaders be included in these trips. Even though those leaders expressed racist views that the Montagnards were "very inferior," Evans believed it was necessary to include those holding power in any such program.[44] In late March 1967, as part of this program, the foundation funded a seven-member Montagnard delegation visit to Thailand.

By the mid-1960s, US intelligence agencies and civilian policy makers increasingly believed that acquiring greater cultural knowledge about the tribal populations they wished to pacify would be the key to reducing armed conflict in Southeast Asia. This led to increased government funding for projects studying Southeast Asian tribal populations. One of the most significant landmarks of this movement was the May 1965 DARPA-sponsored conference, Tribal and Minority Peoples in Southeast Asia, held at Princeton University.

PRINCETON'S 1965 TRIBAL AND MINORITY PEOPLES IN SOUTHEAST ASIA CONFERENCE

The 1965 Tribal and Minority Peoples in Southeast Asia Conference was organized by anthropologist Peter Kunstadter and sponsored by Princeton's Woodrow Wilson School of Public and International Affairs and the US Department of Defense's Advanced Research Projects Agency (ARPA). This ARPA-sponsored conference invited academics and government personnel to discuss issues facing tribal and minority groups in Southeast Asia.[45] The limited views and approaches of the conference papers show some of the ways that the sponsorship and presence of US military agencies circumscribed the problems and solutions considered by scholars.[46] Conspicuous among the limited views was the absence of academic works critically challenging basic assumptions of US-backed military and counterinsurgency operations in the region.

Upon learning of the conference, foundation staff approached Kunstadter and asked to be invited to participate.[47] Following this request, Kunstadter invited James Dalton to present a paper analyzing the "factors accounting for success or failure of programs [and] areas of needed research suggested by the experience" of the programs funded by the Asia Foundation that linked "central governments and tribal or minority peoples."[48] Dalton replied that Bill Klausner would be better suited to present at the conference.[49]

At the foundation, Harry Pierson compiled biographical summaries on each conference participant and circulated these within the foundation.[50] Pierson worried that any paper presented by foundation employees would be later published in a book that Kunstadter proposed to publish. Because government officials from Thailand and elsewhere had expressed concerns to foundation staff that researchers studied their people without adequately sharing their findings with them, Pierson proposed that the foundation should buy copies of the book that emerged from the conference and give these to Asian governmental officials.[51] The foundation's Review and Development Department instructed Pierson to write a conference paper discussing the foundation's tribal minority programming efforts.[52]

William R. Geddes's conference paper provided a short overview of Thailand's Tribal Research Centre (discussed in chapter 5), recounting a brief history of the center and describing some of the projects undertaken there.[53] Geddes noted the importance of Hans Manndorff's recommendations to establish the center following his 1961–62 socioeconomic survey of the hill tribes, and he stressed the center's role in preserving tribal knowledge, collecting data to help develop projects for economic development, assessing governmental projects to improve conditions for tribal members, and coordinating domestic and foreign studies of tribal populations. Geddes's description of the Thai government and Tribal Research Centre obscured the latter's links to counterinsurgency operations and instead highlighted the general goals of development programs disarticulated from these larger goals. He discussed schemes for transplanting upland cattle grazing as if such economic disruptions would not have dire ecological or cultural impacts; he described census projects with no analysis of how such legibility projects are inevitably used for state control; and his discussion of language education programs did not mention the impacts the coming changes would have on local languages. Geddes's paper did not discuss the political context that had birthed the Tribal Research Centre, and the lack of critical voices at this ARPA-funded conference all but guaranteed these dimensions remained in the background.

Comparing the original manuscript of Geddes's conference paper with the chapter published in *Southeast Asian Tribes, Minorities, and Nations*, we see that he later added a section.[54] In that later addition, he addresses anthropologists' concerns about the Tribal Research Centre's demand that all anthropologists deposit research reports at the center within six months of completing research it had sponsored. Many anthropologists objected, arguing that these conditions "infringe the independence of anthropologists or impede [their] work."[55] Geddes acknowledged that reporting detailed information on the social structure and socioeconomic status of research participants made many anthropologists he consulted uncomfortable; these anthropologists complained that governments could misuse such data for their own ends. But Geddes dismissed these concerns, arguing that "in return for this government effort it is fair that the research workers should supply the information resulting from their studies and assist the development of further research work."[56] Geddes argued this was necessary because the tribal region now had a "great strategic importance," and he claimed the "supplying of the report is the minimum condition under which free anthropological research is likely to be permitted to continue in the area."[57] Geddes cynically dismissed anthropologists' ethical and political concerns by simply redefining "free anthropological research" as being whatever the state decided was of "great strategic importance." These anthropologists' concerns about governmental abuse of this data at the Tribal Research Centre would later prove to be justified.

Pierson's conference paper presented a conveniently curated version of the Asia Foundation's history and approach to tribal research.[58] As the conference approached, however, foundation president Haydn Williams wrote Kunstadter to inform him that although Pierson had been looking forward to attending the conference, he would be unable to do so due to "current demands on Mr. Pierson's time," and the foundation would send James Basche in his place.[59]

Basche attended a single day of the conference, where he presented Pierson's paper. Basche later submitted a report to the foundation summarizing papers and discussions he had heard. He reported that there was little discussion of Pierson's paper, though his audience was keenly interested in learning more about the criteria the foundation used in evaluating grant applications, as well as about how the Asia Foundation cooperatively worked with other private and public organizations.⁶⁰ Basche appeared to be particularly interested in anthropologist Michael Moerman's focus on failures of tribal peoples in military defense roles, and he reported Geddes urging participants working in Thailand to rely on locals at the Tribal Research Centre when conducting field research. Moerman and Kunstadter expressed skepticism of the reliability of this approach. Basche told the participants that the Asia Foundation could fund the training of Thai researchers in Western research methods. British anthropologist Tom Harrisson favored using local researchers and argued that providing locals with research training was "a kind of *quid pro quo* for the foreigners to be permitted to do research in Asian countries." Harrisson warned that there was growing resistance among Asian peoples to being studied by foreigners as objects. He urged researchers to publish their research and share it with local governments, or they could expect decreased research access.⁶¹

Dalton reported that "the Thais are getting more and more concerned about the foreign researchers who come to Thailand," and he advised that the increased use of local researchers could allay these concerns.⁶² Dalton was surprised to hear Geddes, Kunstadter, and Moerman disparaging the use of local field researchers.⁶³

After the conference, Kunstadter wrote Haydn William that he and other scholars had been conscientious about sharing their work upon request, and he wanted to see the foundation do likewise. He noted that some months earlier he had asked foundation staff for a copy of a report on the Union Research Institute and that over the years he had asked for reports on tribal groups of mainland China and for other documents, which he had never received. He now assumed this was because of "an unwillingness of the Foundation to release materials in its files."⁶⁴ A handwritten internal foundation note suggested the foundation "do anything we can to ensure continued access to the work of others" and asked if it would "be possible to send the two reports mentioned to Kunstadter with the understanding that they were not to be reproduced or quoted."⁶⁵ Because of internal concerns that, if the foundation refused to share reports, it might have difficulty accessing scholars' research, the requested materials were shared with Kunstadter.

MILITARY LINKS IN ASIA

Foundation staff expressed ambivalence about establishing relationships with host country militaries. While DTPILLAR supported positive relationships between friendly Asian military forces and the United States, there were ongoing concerns that the foundation needed to maintain some distance from local militaries or risk damaging their image as an apolitical organization.

In 1959, the foundation's representative to Burma, James Stewart, argued that the foundation should reevaluate "the future role of the military in Burmese governmental affairs" and advocated that the foundation develop "a somewhat more sympathetic attitude toward the role of the present army caretaker government." He believed the Burmese army provided a "protective arm" and a "guiding hand" supporting Burmese political life, and Stewart's promilitary views found support among other foundation staff. Stewart predicted the army would play an increasingly significant role in Burmese society and government, which he believed would benefit the foundation's standing.[66] These alignments with allied governments' militaries were common for the CIA but rare among private foundations. Other foundations more commonly sought relationships of stability and continuity with foreign civilian governments and avoided alignments with noncivilian branches of governments.

Some members of the Burmese military expressed skepticism about the foundation's motivations for funding the training of "technicians, professors, students, youth, etc." Colonel Maung Maung acknowledged that the Ford Foundation's and Asia Foundation's programs successfully met local needs, but he also raised concerns about (as summarized by Robert Blum) "why foreigners are engaging in such training plans."[67] Colonel Maung asked President Blum a series of what he termed "silly" questions that Burmese dissidents might raise about the foundation's motives for funding Burmese projects. These included questions about whether it was "to subvert or warp Burmese loyalties that the Asia Foundation is engaged in supporting an international relations training program at the University of Rangoon." He asked about whether the Ford Foundation's program was suspiciously linked to American forms of agriculture. Maung said there were many "potentially dangerous questions" that might be asked, but he assured Blum that "all that would be required in order to influence local Asian opinion would be the appropriate political atmosphere."[68]

The colonel's willingness to dismiss the possibility that the Asia Foundation and Ford Foundation might have undeclared political motives for providing aid, whether sincere or performative, indicates at least one reason why Stewart so strongly favored the foundation's alignment with the Burmese military. This was a relationship of mutual aid, one in which DTPILLAR gained access to a powerful segment of Burmese society, a segment that was willing to overlook as absurd many of the critical reasons why the Burmese people should be skeptical of Western foundations bearing gifts.

The foundation interacted with Asian military forces in several supportive ways. Between 1958 and 1960, the foundation proposed funding a US university–based educational program for Asian military personnel. This proposal began with a January 1959 confidential memo written by John Gange, of the San Francisco office, explaining that recent discussions with representatives indicated that there was no agreement on how the "Foundation could help develop knowledge among Asian military men which would be useful in the event of their direct involvement in civilian affairs." To facilitate further discussion, Gange sent a report by the Japan foundation representative, Robert Schwantes, highlighting Major Jiro Tokuyama's positive experiences with the foundation—first as a recipient of foundation-supplied books, then later as a recipient of foundation funding allowing him to study at Princeton University.[69] Other reports from this period argued for the positive benefits from military education programs.[70]

A 1958 Asia Foundation paper presented at a Hong Kong conference on assisting Asian military and police forces described the needs of those entities, but these identified needs were significantly different from the focus of the Michigan State University Vietnam Advisory Group (MSUG), which ran from 1955 to 1962 with covert CIA assistance.[71] While the CIA's MSUG program focused on counterinsurgency and paramilitary techniques, this Asia Foundation paper stressed the need for well-educated military leaders in Asia. The report acknowledged that the foundation could "not give assistance of a strictly military or technical character," but if programs could be framed as contributing to democratic processes, they could be supported by the foundation. The report also recommended supporting literacy and English-language programs, libraries, athletic programs, and study abroad opportunities in programs supporting economic and social development.[72]

The foundation explored housing this program at MIT or Harvard. Professor Ithiel de Sola Pool argued that Harvard's claimed philosophical commitment to developing civil societies through democratic, nonmilitary means made his institution, MIT, the logical choice for such a military education program.[73] President Blum corresponded with Hans Speier of the RAND Corporation, informing him of the foundation's interest in a program for Asian military leaders.[74] Meanwhile, Richard Heggie traveled to Washington, DC, and the Boston area, meeting with Walt Rostow, Max Millikan, and Henry Kissinger to discuss establishing an educational program for Asian military officers at

MIT or Harvard.[75] Ithiel de Sola Pool recommended against sending a few officers until details were worked out, such as whether participants would enter mainstream classroom settings or have a separate program that isolated them from regular students.[76]

At the San Francisco office, foundation staff were divided in their support for the proposal, and Robert Sheeks questioned the wisdom of enacting a program appearing to "place special priority on military officers, even ahead of civilian officers of government." He wanted to know why the foundation wasn't instead working to expand similar programs for civil servants, and he bluntly asked if "the military is in fact more dangerous [than civilians]" and should thus be judged more important.[77] Sheeks speculated that the proposal was linked to recent military takeovers in Pakistan, Burma, Indonesia, and Thailand, and he wondered if these programs were efforts to adapt American influence to better fit a world of Asian military coups. He argued that these military-focused programs should be funded by the US armed forces rather than the foundation.[78]

John F. Sullivan, director of programs for the Asia Foundation, complained that Sheeks's memo attacked "first the whole idea of working with the military as a special group, and then the particular project idea."[79] Sheeks's objections irritated Sullivan, though he acknowledged that funding the military must be approached with caution, and he admitted there was some validity to Sheeks's suspicion that the proposal was "conditioned by recent military take-overs in Asia." Sullivan defensively added that a written proposal had existed before the coups.[80]

Other Asia Foundation projects that aligned with Asian military and police forces included the 1959 purchase of new police training books for the East Pakistan Police Training School.[81] Some projects were directly linked to armed counterinsurgency training. In late 1959, Burmese colonel Ba Than approached foundation representative James Dalton to request a $10,000 grant to purchase psychological warfare training books for a Burmese military library. But Dalton was displeased that the colonel had not made an official request through the appropriate channels, and he refused to say whether the request would likely be funded until the colonel approached the foundation using government channels. Despite his displeasure with Than, Dalton supported the colonel's proposal to purchase books for the Psych-War Reference Division of his nation's military library. Dalton was impressed by the size and scope of the collection, which he estimated to include two thousand titles. He noted that "the Research Library is used by six special research officers of the Armed Forces. These men are assigned [to do background reading from] various pamphlets, posters, booklets, and radio scripts issued in a steady [stream] by Psych-War in its operations against the Communists."[82] The Burmese Psych-War Division had produced over a million anticommunist posters, two million pamphlets, and four hundred thousand books.[83]

Because the Japanese Self-Defense Forces were so directly tied to the US military, the foundation understood there was little it could contribute to this sector of Japanese society, while there was much that would be risked should suspicions arise over links between the foundation and the Japanese military. Because of these concerns, the foundation generally refrained from supporting programs funding Japanese military libraries.[84] Even with this limited approach, the foundation occasionally contributed to programs linked to the Japanese military, such as a $10,000 grant in 1960 supporting English-language training at Japan's National Defense Academy.[85]

THIN LINES SEPARATING AID AND COUNTERINSURGENCY

DTPILLAR operations supported political movements and rural development campaigns that the CIA believed would spread anticommunism in Asia in ways that sometimes found the committee and then the foundation undermining local political autonomy. In the Philippines, this meant the CFA used NAMFREL to "educate" rural voters in ways that favored Magsaysay. In Vietnam, DTPILLAR supported counterinsurgency operations like the Strategic Hamlet Program or ethnographically informed projects designed to weaken villagers' connections with the National Liberation Front. In northern Thailand, this meant funding studies of tribal groups in the Tribal Research Centre's natural laboratory, where questions of counterinsurgency were always at hand.

There is a long history of the CIA interfering in elections around the globe. Historically, these CIA tactics include backing certain candidates, undermining opponents, engaging in disinformation campaigns, selecting and backing members of royal lines vying for legitimacy, and supporting rebel groups of "freedom fighters" the agency believed could serve US interests. Successful CIA operations rely on the support of local groups who stand to gain from allying themselves with CIA backing. The CFA's support for anticommunist candidates was one manifestation of this CIA strategy, and the foundation's less active role in such campaigns marks one significant difference between committee and foundation approaches.

Some elements of DTPILLAR operations prefigured practices that many Americans would object to on their home turf. Some Americans become outraged at the idea that the United States' global adversaries interfere with US elections in ways similar to how the CIA used the CFA and NAMFREL to interfere in Philippine elections. China's efforts to use Confucius Institutes to shape intellectual discourse on US university campuses in ways similar to DTPILLAR programs, as well as claims of Russian interference in US elections, are examples to consider.[86]

These efforts to influence foreign elections show DTPILLAR operations undermining Asian political self-determination. Here we see DTPILLAR operations extending far beyond things like book publishing, offering scholarships, or cultural programs. The CIA used DTPILLAR to limit the political options of postcolonial Asian nations. With US-supported politicians in power, the United States used its dominant presence in the Philippines to do more than just intervene in local politics; these patron-client relations eased the way for US military bases there to play crucial roles in Cold War military and intelligence-gathering activity, including the Vietnam War and CIA operations in Indonesia.[87]

While the foundation distanced itself from being involved in the sort of political campaigns that the committee had aggressively supported, DTPILLAR's support for other forms of political soft power remained strong. By 1966, the Asia Foundation was funding research on counterinsurgency projects for the Muslim world. In a Pakistan-based project, for example, the foundation supported a program at the Central Institute of Islamic Research that President Ayub hoped would "pacify dissident elements."[88] The foundation also funded research on Thailand's northeast hill tribe region, "identifying many of the problems there for subsequent AID [US Agency for International Development], [CIA] Station, and SEATO Attentions."[89]

As foundation practices shifted, apparently becoming more like those of other educational or philanthropic foundations, it increasingly reached out to other foundations to establish connections that would help camouflage the Asia Foundation's CIA alignments and expand the reach of the foundation at home and abroad. This shift allowed the foundation to outsource some elements of its basic work, a process that further spread the taint of CIA contact and influence to groups and individuals who would otherwise have kept their distance from the agency.

7 Interactions with Other Organizations and Foundations

For the CIA to secure control of so many youth and trade union groups and employ universities and individual scholars to do its subversive work did not mean that the members of such organizations had either knowledge of or agreement with the secret CIA aims; it merely meant that some leaders and individuals could be "bought." That the whole operation had to be kept secret from the American people and from the foreigners who were being guided, indicates clearly that the operation was acknowledged to be reprehensible.

DAVID CONDE / *CIA—Core of the Cancer*

Many of DTPILLAR's successes were the result of the Committee for Free Asia and the Asia Foundation's ability to work with other organizations with overlapping interests. These relationships helped DTPILLAR acquire expertise, draft behind others' reputations, and blend in with actual nongovernmental organizations. Among the many organizations DTPILLAR sought to work with were noncommunist labor unions in Asia. DTPILLAR supported various Asian labor unions and labor organizations with hopes of undermining communist-linked labor movements. Some of these projects brought in American labor experts or union representatives to provide instruction to noncommunist Asian labor groups.

After news reports of communist rebel groups forming in Ceylon in 1954, CFA staff wrote a paper, "Indications of Communist Strategy in Asia," analyzing how "an overall communist policy of internally organized violence, internationally coordinated, [was] being implemented in Asia [which] could form the essential strategy of post-Korean action in Asia."[1] The committee's Research Division expressed similar concerns as it studied how Asian communists used labor unions to advance their cause.[2] By 1955, the foundation was funding anticommunist Asian labor unions as a tactic to undermine communist inroads throughout Asia.

In 1955, the foundation's internal labor policy identified "concern for labor developments in Asia" as a vital anticommunist strategy to strengthen democratic institutions and spread the foundation's values.[3] The initial labor programs supported labor education and welfare groups. Recognizing the foundation's limited knowledge of labor issues, President Blum directed the foundation to draw on the expertise of existing labor organizations such as the Congress of Industrial Organizations (CIO), American Federation of Labor (AFL), the International Labor Organization (ILO), and the anti-anticommunist International Confederation of Free Trade Unions (ICFTU) for this cause.

In the mid-1970s, the Church Committee hearings in the Senate revealed the existence of several CIA programs using US labor unions to undermine communist labor movements in Latin America, Asia, and Africa. These hearings revealed that the work of former communist turned anticommunist Jay Lovestone with the AFL's International Affairs Division (IAD) was directed by the CIA as part of agency efforts to support non-Marxist international labor organizations.[4] Tim Shorrock's research in the AFL-CIO's archives establishes that during the early 1970s the AFL-CIO's American Institute for Free Labor Development (AIFLD) worked with the CIA to divide Chilean labor movements in order to overthrow Salvador Allende.[5] In South Korea, the AIFLD followed US government policies designed to undermine independent labor unions.[6] Christopher Gerteis established that the CIA used the AIFLD to suppress communist-linked labor unions in Japan during the 1950s.[7]

As part of the first wave of CIA-backed union activity, in 1954 the foundation formed a partnership with the anticommunist West Pakistan Federal Labor group to build a labor leadership program there. They founded a labor institute in Karachi, where "outstanding Pakistani, American and British union specialists [trained] 40 senior leaders and 80 potential leaders annually" and supported programs training Ceylonese labor leaders in Karachi, with hopes that such programs would spread throughout Asia.[8] The foundation also funded several worker education programs in East and West Pakistan.[9]

The foundation sponsored Seiichi Katsumata, chair of the Diet Policy Committee of the United Socialist Party's month-long 1955 trip to the United States, where he studied US labor and political systems. Foundation staff worried that Katsumata would embarrass the foundation by focusing on American labor problems. To limit this possibility, the foundation and the Institute of International Education controlled access to American labor leaders and others viewed as problematic. By the end this trip, Katsumata was complaining that the foundation had excessively stage-managed his visit. The foundation reported that Katsumata "developed the impression that the individuals whom he interviewed could have been carefully selected by the Foundation in advance." Foundation staff defensively claimed that the only time Katsumata explicitly had minders was during a scheduled lunch with Eric Hoffer. Katsumata became so disenchanted with the intense oversight that at one point he threatened to abandon the trip.[10]

The CIA's covert support for anticommunist unions created contradictions for the capitalist owners it sought to serve. In June 1954, CFA staffer Frank Robertson found that an Indonesian program funding the translation and distribution of pro-union anticommunist pamphlets was increasing complaints about capitalist exploitation. Robertson acknowledged inherent contradictions in the committee's support of trade unions in areas ripe for Western economic exploitation, and he worried that although supporting anticommunist labor unions was important, a tension was building with US businesses interested in establishing factories in places like Indonesia. These capitalists worried that "helping educate an anti-Communist labor force, is thereby working against their interest. Unfortunately, foreign management in Indonesia today does not seem to differentiate much between Communist and anti-Communist labor, but tends to take the colonial view that labor is a threatening force to be dealt with only as a last resort."[11] These tensions existed to some degree everywhere the CIA backed labor organizations, but the agency's calculation was that the benefits of undermining the spread of communist labor movements outweighed the risk that noncommunist labor movements might seriously threaten capitalism.

JULES WEINBERG, LABOR CONSULTANT

In 1956, the foundation hired longtime CIO representative Jules Weinberg to help reshape union practices in West Pakistan. Between 1956 and 1959, Weinberg worked with the West Pakistan Confederation of Labor Institute and the All-Pakistan Confederation of Labor, where he established the International Labor Advisory Service, a resource for regional labor organizations. Before leaving for West Pakistan, Weinberg met with two important US labor leaders, Victor Reuther and Jay Lovestone. Lovestone was the CIA's key labor consultant developing the agency's international labor union strategies. Lovestone endorsed the personnel Weinberg selected to work with in Pakistan, and he supported foundation efforts to build a Pakistan-based union movement separate from the ICFTU. Weinberg reported, "Lovestone said that so long as the Pakistan Labor Institute was conducted along national lines, he could see absolutely no conflict with ICFTU."[12]

Unlike CIA-linked Lovestone, American industrial labor organizer Victor

Reuther was critical of the foundation's approach to union activities in Pakistan. Reuther derided the foundation as playing "the State Department's game in Pakistan" against the best interests of the workers. He told Weinberg that "he did not consider the Pakistani labor movement a true trade union movement, and it was being used in the 'game' to establish ideological and military bases in Pakistan, which was being played off against India." Reuther understood the entire program was a waste of resources that could be better used elsewhere in Asia to help workers organize.[13] Reuther criticized Weinberg's strategy of providing direct grants to Pakistanis aligned with foundation goals, arguing that it was spawning "a corrupting influence" that would undermine the legitimacy of the ICFTU in the region.[14] Weinberg acknowledged Reuther's concerns, but he did not recommend the foundation alter its approach.[15]

During his three years as a foundation consultant, Weinberg compiled dossiers on individuals active in Pakistan's labor movement. One seven-page memo, for example, provided detailed backgrounds on Karachi labor activists, describing individual skill sets and connections to networks and power structures.[16]

In 1957, the foundation gave $5,000 to Malayan miners and supported AFL-CIO and ICFTU representative George Weaver's work with them.[17] In 1958, the foundation sponsored the National Union of Plantation Workers' sending local labor leaders to a conference in the Philippines. In Japan, the foundation funded research on labor disputes; in Pakistan, it supported the Workers Education Society and founded a labor training institute's course in collective bargaining, and it provided workshops on basic economics.[18]

In some documents, the foundation appears ambivalent about Weinberg's work supporting trade unions in Pakistan. Weinberg made no secret of the fact that the foundation's decision to refrain from direct involvement in building up a strong labor movement in Pakistan was a mistake. He repeatedly criticized foundation failures to support the sort of class consciousness critique and solidarity needed to build an effective labor movement. The foundation remained unmoved by Weinberg's insistence that (as Louis Lazaroff summarized) "the Foundation is not being sufficiently honest with itself in understanding why it is supporting trade union education and in addition that the strength of any program in the labor education field depends on whether or not the program will enable the trade union movement to organize and bargain effectively. As a trade union man [Weinberg] feels it important that we recognize this, but he has never made it clear how we should do so given the limitations of our present organization."[19] This critique exposed a core shortcoming in Weinberg's work:

because the CIA's interest in supporting noncommunist unions was only to undermine communist-linked unions, the necessary commitments to class interests were lacking, which undercut his ability to develop effective union building.

An undated draft letter from Weinberg to President Blum bluntly identified the problems with the foundation's union work in Pakistan. Weinberg reported on the favorable media coverage of the Workers Education Society, as well as his launching of the Trade Union Institute, noting that the Pakistan government had declared Weinberg "a 'good influence' on their workers." Weinberg understood his programs needed to be more directly tied to the formation of Asian unions and to engage in more direct labor actions. He complained that he was "not satisfied with the present working arrangement with The Asia Foundation . . . because I feel that the direction in which we are traveling is not conducive to the healthy growth of labor programming."[20] With time, these restraints on his ability to develop unions increased Weinberg's frustration, eventually leading to his resignation in 1959.

The foundation funded several Japanese and Korean trade union projects in the 1960s, and it coordinated local union projects working with large US-based unions, including the AFL and CIO.[21] In 1961, the foundation funded Union Research Institute's efforts to strengthen noncommunist Hong Kong unions.[22] In 1960, the foundation spent $450,000 supporting labor unions aligned with Western political and economic interests.[23]

MINGLING WITH OTHER FOUNDATIONS

A May 1955 *New York Times* story, "Problems of Charitable Foundations," which described regular meetings of staff from thirty foundations based in New York City, caught the attention of foundation staffer John F. Sullivan. Sullivan suggested to Lyman Hoover that a foundation representative attend these meetings.[24] Hoover believed the foundation could establish invaluable contacts at these gatherings. In a report, he noted that these foundation meetings occurred because of "the scare resulting from the Reece Committee activities."[25] Foundations were concerned that many of the new small foundations were illegitimate entities formed for tax evasion and that, "by establishing some liaison, they hope to protect the legitimate foundations."[26] It seemed advisable for a CIA front to join a group formed to protect legitimate foundations from the taint of being associated with foundations that were not what they claimed to be.

In August 1955, Lyman Hoover attended his first foundation representative meeting in New York City. Hoover later briefed President Blum and provided a list of foundation representatives attending. Attendees discussed foundation practices, project evaluations, and other topics relating to foundation administration. They planned to meet monthly, and Hoover recommended that a foundation representative regularly attend these meetings.[27] Hoover's list of foundation representatives attending included five foundations that would later be revealed to have ties to the Central Intelligence Agency: the Asia Foundation, J. M. Kaplan Fund, Josiah Macy Jr. Foundation, Jessie Smith Noyes Foundation, and the Benjamin Rosenthal Foundation, Inc.[28] The presence of so many CIA-linked foundations transformed these meetings into a Cold War farce, as the various foundations ostensibly met to protect their members from accusations of funny business while almost a quarter of the members were secretly drawn from foundations with CIA links.[29] These meetings fulfilled the CIA DTPILLAR policy directive that foundation staff develop "close relationships" with non-CIA-linked private organizations and use these relationships to gain "moral and material support from such organization."[30]

NOEL BUSCH IN THE NEW YORK OFFICE, 1959

Noel Busch became the CFA's Tokyo representative in 1952, was the foundation's Bangkok representative from 1954 to 1958, then in the 1960s became President Blum's special assistant in New York City. Born in 1906 and educated at Princeton, Busch was an experienced journalist, having been a *Life* magazine war correspondent during the Second World War, covering developments in Africa, Asia, Europe, and South America. He later became an editor at *Time* magazine and the *New York Daily News*. Busch was a prolific writer, authoring a dozen books, and was a popular contributor to the *Atlantic Monthly, Horizon, Saturday Evening Post*, and the *New Yorker*.[31] He was the sort of suave Ivy League liberal intellectual the foundation and agency sought for their anticommunist work.

In a 1977 article in the *New York Times*, Busch reminisced that back in the 1950s while he was reporting for *Time*, the CIA had asked him to use his journalist credentials "to interview an Asian political figure for an in-depth profile" for the agency. Busch told the CIA that this person of interest had no journalistic significance to *Time* or other news publications, but the CIA agreed to pay him $2,000 for the interview and article. Busch said he later learned that the CIA's primary interest in this interview was "to flatter this guy through an approach by an American correspondent."[32]

The Hoover Institution's Asia Foundation Collection includes materials from Busch's 1959 work as the foundation's special assistant to President Blum. These records include Busch's detailed reports on foundation meetings—meetings ranging from those with wealthy patrons of the arts interested in bringing Asia collections to US galleries, to visiting Asian ambassadors and meeting with staff members of other foundations. Some reports show Busch meeting with other foundations to seek funds for Asia Foundation activities; some of his meetings were with foundations that years later were revealed to be CIA fronts or pass-throughs. There are records of dozens of meetings with representatives from powerful organizations discussing foundation programming opportunities, which may or may not have also involved activities more closely linked to agency intelligence agendas.[33] These remain unanswered questions.

In March 1959, Busch met with Edmund Rosenthal, of the Rosenthal Foundation, at Rosenthal's Fifth Avenue office in New York. Busch reported that Rosenthal "was one of the founders of the New York Foundations Group and also one of the executives in the American Playing Card Corporation."[34] Eight years later, the Benjamin Rosenthal Foundation would be identified in a *Congressional Quarterly* report as a private foundation operating as a CIA conduit.[35] Rosenthal's foundation supported various educational projects, and he expressed interest in the roles played by Buddhist priests in Asia, saying that he might be interested in supporting such projects. While not committing to any specific amount, Rosenthal indicated his foundation funded about $200,000 in programs a year and that a $10,000 grant was "considered rather sizable."[36]

Six months later Busch and Rosenthal again discussed the possibility of the Rosenthal Foundation funding Buddhist monks' travel to the United States. Rosenthal discussed these plans with his foundation's attorney to determine how this might be accomplished given the foundation charter's specific charge to fund projects associated with "relief." Rosenthal asked Busch several questions about the sources of the Asia Foundation's funding. Busch reported stating that it was funded from "contributions," and he claimed the foundation "had not made a custom of reporting all its contributions since some of the major contributors preferred for various reasons not to have their contributions published."[37] Rosenthal appeared at this point in time to have no knowledge the foundation was CIA funded.

Busch routinely interacted with other foundations, establishing contacts, spreading information about the foundation's mission, and telling other organizations how he could assist them if they wanted to work in Asia. Several reports record moments of surprise as other foundation representatives learned Busch was not meeting with them to seek funds but was instead making contact to offer to help them work in Asia. Busch's 1959 meeting with Rockefeller Brothers Fund representative Charles Noyes generated such a reaction. When Noyes asked Busch if the Asia Foundation might want a grant from the Rockefeller Foundation for projects of mutual interest, Busch replied that this might be possible but that receiving such grants would be secondary to foundation desires to help facilitate Rockefeller's Asian work that overlapped with the foundation's interests. This response surprised Noyes, who was "much impressed by this offer on our part and said that it was a completely new thing in his experience of foundation work but quite possibly one of considerable value. He said that he would bear it in mind for future planning of his foundation and that, when opportunities presented themselves, he would make it known to other foundations."[38]

In a 1959 meeting with the New World Foundation, discussing a possible project to distribute birth control in Asia, Busch sat with Raymond Rubinow, a consultant to the CIA-linked J. M. Kaplan Fund.[39] During the lunch portion of the meeting, Rubinow provided details on the history and goals of the Kaplan Fund, explaining that the fund's money came from the fortunes of the company behind Welch's grape juice. After Rubinow expressed interest in financing some Asia Foundation projects, Busch arranged a lunch at the Princeton Club the following day to discuss such possibilities. At this Princeton Club lunch Rubinow provided more information on J. M. Kaplan and his political involvements, which included his close relationship with Adlai Stevenson—a relationship Busch suggested might be used to get Stevenson to join the Asia Foundation's board.[40]

GATHERING NAMES: DTPILLAR AND PROFESSIONAL ASSOCIATIONS

Committee for Free Asia and Asia Foundation records demonstrate that both organizations collected and retained information on individuals they encountered. During the 1950s and 1960s the foundation appears to have maintained records on every individual who applied for funding or to participate in foundation programs. The extent to which they maintained these records was unusual for a foundation; their volume is so extraordinary it raises questions about whether this practice was part of a CIA information collection effort.

Because under the Freedom of Information Act the CIA only released a small portion of DTPILLAR internal communications, we do not know if the foundation did such thorough collecting for intelligence purposes. But these records show the foundation persistently sought and established contacts with scholars from Asia. Because of the difficulties of identifying individual scholars and their works before the advent of the internet and search engines, the compiling of such collections of names could have served a crucial basic intelligence function during this period. Mimeographed lists and published directories and rosters of scholars listing languages spoken and areas of expertise were important and powerful tools needed and funded by the incipient national security state during the early days of the Cold War. During this period there are documented instances of the CIA approaching professional associations seeking this information in order to compile lists of scholars working around the globe.[41]

In the mid-1950s, the foundation began subsidizing Asian scholars' membership fees to about thirty professional organizations. These grants sought to increase "contact between these associations and Asian professional colleagues at the graduate or post-doctoral level."[42]

Among the organizations with these subsidized memberships were the American Anthropological Association (AAA), American Economic Association (AEA), American Mathematical Society (AMS), American Personnel and Guidance Association (APGA), American Philosophical Association (APA), American Political Science Association (APSA), American Sociological Association (ASA), and American Studies Association (ASA).[43] The Asia Foundation reported that "in most cases these grants are used to assist Asian scholars in this country by enabling them to participate in regional or national meetings of the American associations . . . and sometimes make it possible for scholars in Asia to obtain membership in these professional associations at reduced cost."[44] These programs were popular with both the professional associations and the Asian members receiving these subsidies.

Typical of these programs was the agreement between the foundation and the American Anthropological Association. In 1956, the foundation awarded an annual $2,500 grant to make "it easier for Asians to subscribe to the *American Anthropologist*" journal and to "provide small sums to enable [Asian anthropologists] to come to scientific meetings if they are already in the USA."[45] This program also funded a three-year AAA membership, including receipt of the AAA's flagship journal, *American Anthropologist*, all for the cost of one dollar.[46]

AAA publications advertised the availability of these subsidized memberships. Over the course of a decade the AAA used Asia Foundation funding to underwrite association memberships for hundreds of Asian scholars. The AAA's records are incomplete but include ledgers listing over 413 individual recipients, as well as several institutional recipients.[47] Records from the 1961 distribution of AAA subscriptions show the "breakdown of subscriptions to the American Anthropologist under the Asia Foundation Amount by country: East Pakistan (1), India (38), Japan (101), Indonesia (5), Thailand (1), Korea (5), Formosa (4), Philippines (4), Ceylon (3), Andaman Islands (1), and 'Others' (5)."[48]

The AAA collected the names and addresses of Asian anthropologists participating in this program and gave these to the foundation.[49] When AAA staff forgot to send along these lists identifying recipients and their contact information, foundation staff wrote them asking for this information before sending reimbursements. Among the AAA's archival materials from this program are announcements of special offers for graduate students from Asia studying in the United States to receive foundation funds to attend conferences, where they could meet with foundation staff. Such arrangements raised the possibility of recruitment efforts, or the passive collection of intelligence from these young scholars; at a minimum the grants established first contact with Asian intellectuals who might later become significant regional figures.

One reason why the foundation sought out anthropologists was because they were viewed as being "especially concerned with a heart-problem that is implicit in the Foundation's activity in Asia: culture change." But the foundation also worried about growing suspicions in Asia about American anthropologists. Nevertheless, the foundation frequently remained in contact with these grant recipients, nurturing ties with them through book funds and research funds provided by local foundation offices.[50]

These AAA membership subsidies continued until soon after the foundation's CIA ties were exposed in 1967. This revelation led to soul searching among AAA leaders about whether they should continue receiving the funds. Eventually the AAA executive board discovered they had fallen behind in submitting invoices for reimbursements and had thousands of dollars due from previous years. Internal AAA memos show leadership agonizing over the issue, but they eventually decided to collect the reimbursements—even though this meant providing the foundation with the names of participating Asian anthropologists—before terminating the relationship. Although members of the AAA board were suspicious of the CIA, there was no concern expressed in their correspondence that the foundation might forward to the CIA the membership lists they had provided.[51]

When replying to anthropologists seeking assurances that they had not been unwittingly funded by the CIA, the foundation lied about the extent of their links to the CIA. In reply to a 1968 question about whether the AAA had in fact been receiving CIA funds for years, the foundation's Patricia Flanagan told AAA executive secretary Charles Frantz that all foundation funds were mixed together in a "general fund," so "under these circumstances, it would be impossible to determine the source of the funds for any particular grant made by the foundation."[52] This lie obscured the fact that the CIA had been the foundation's only meaningful funding source and that it was a CIA subsidiary. Flanagan claimed that it had always been the foundation trustees' policy not to make public their donors' names or how much they contributed. Because the CIA was the primary "donor" to the foundation, this was likely an actual policy. Flanagan claimed "the Foundation does not accept funds from sources alleged to have any connection with the Central Intelligence Agency, nor has it ever been supported by other intelligence branches of the United States Government."[53]

Foundation documents show no record of the American Psychological Association (APA) or the American Sociological Association (ASA) or other social science associations inquiring about or protesting the foundation's relationship with the CIA after the 1967 revelations in the *Times*. Instead, the APA and ASA continued to forward lists of their funded Asian scholars benefiting from foundation funds.[54] The Society for Applied Anthropology (sfAA) received the same membership supplement funds the AAA received, but unlike the AAA it did not appear bothered by revelations of foundation-CIA links and continued receiving these funds until 1970, when the foundation ended the program.[55]

THE NATIONAL STUDENT ASSOCIATION AND FOREIGN STUDENT LEADERSHIP PROGRAM

The Asia Foundation occasionally funded other covertly CIA-funded organizations, such as the US National Student Association (NSA), which received a foundation grant in 1960. These grants funded the NSA Travel Grants for Student Leaders, as well as the Foreign Student Leadership Program, both of which brought Asian students to the United States for conferences—an activity that brought these students directly into the foundation's orbit.[56] The foundation took steps to make it appear as if it were not involved in selecting the Asian students awarded these NSA Foreign Student Leadership Program fellowships. Privately, foundation staff explained that they did not want "to have the ill-will of the persons not selected and their families and friends," but because the foundation still wanted to "be sure about the suitability of the individual selected," staff made arrangements to see the NSA's list of applicants and privately let the NSA know if these individuals met their approval.[57]

Foundation staff sometimes used their connections with students and staff affiliated with the NSA studying abroad to gather information on Asian political developments. In 1958, foundation staffer James Dalton submitted a report detailing information on University of Rangoon campus political developments that he learned about from his conversations with James C. Scott, who was an American student, University of Rangoon Rotary Fellowship awardee, and future political scientist.

Scott supplied Dalton with details about the relative power of the Students' United Front (SUF) and other political groups on the University of Rangoon campus; the SUF was a Burmese popular front organization, forming coalitions between communists and other leftist groups. Scott described the SUF's recruiting process, telling Dalton that "the SUF leadership spends much time cultivating the high school students through the means of ABFSU [the All-Burma Federation of Students Union]." Scott reported that the most powerful campus voting bloc appeared to be the new first-year students, who had been cultivated to have favorable opinions of the SUF even before arriving on campus. Scott told Dalton that

> the recent "student conference" held at the University of Rangoon under the sponsorship of the Nu-Tin government was an excellent means by which the SUF and the ABFSU strengthened their grip on the high school leadership[;] only those high school student leaders were selected for attendance at the conference who owed their loyalty to the ABFSU and the SUF. Leadership of those two organizations cared little about the nature of the resolutions adopted by the conference. They were far more interested in getting individual student leaders, at the high school level[,] into their debt.[58]

Scott saw no reason to think that other student organizations would be able to challenge SUF's grip on power. He reasoned that SUF organizers had to have an off-campus funding source because the small dues that members paid could not have added up to the funds they used for their expensive ongoing campaigns at high schools and elsewhere, as well as on campus during elections.

Scott advised Dalton on what political strategies the foundation could pursue to gain influence on campus, and he thought it best for the foundation to not meddle directly in campus politics. According to Dalton's reporting,

> Scott believes that projects such as student counseling and the recreation center will be of help at the University. He notes, however, that the Foundation cannot and should not concern itself with matters of student politics—but that such politics can and will adversely affect all efforts by Burmese and foreign groups to improve the standards of the University. He thinks that the faculty can prevent some kinds of difficulties through the right kinds of action but that, fundamentally, it will be up to the leaders among the Burmese students to see the danger of allowing politics to overwhelm educational improvements.[59]

James Scott reported it was common for students on campus to criticize the West, citing examples of domestic racial issues and international problems in South Korea, the Philippines, and Vietnam. He reported that many students were swayed by literature distributed around campus that contrasted Western failures in South Korea with the strong growth of the Soviet economy.[60]

While this conversation transpired nine years before the Asia Foundation's relationship with the CIA was revealed, the specificity and probing into internal campus student politics might reasonably spark questions in a student being pumped for such information. When I asked James Scott what he remembered about this meeting with Dalton that occurred six decades earlier, he told me that when he had studied in Burma on a Rotary Club Fellowship in 1958, he had twice knowingly met a CIA officer based at the US embassy in Rangoon. He told this CIA officer "what little I knew about student politics."[61] Scott wrote me, saying,

> I was interested (as a student activist myself) in the political battles between the minority students (Karen, Shan, Kachin, Chin, PaO) and the Rangoon University Students' Union (RUSU), then controlled by self-described communists. I lived in a dormitory (Old Staff Chummery) for teaching assistants and did some economic research. (Rangoon University had some internationally known economists on its faculty[,] U Hla Myint and U Aye Hlaing). I got a couple of threatening letters from what I assumed were RUSU partisans. I took fright and moved to Mandalay University (teaching assistant dorm again, New

Staff Chummery) where I had no contact with student politics and spent all my time travelling by motorcycle and studying the Burmese language, until I returned to the US.[62]

Scott told me that he had no specific memory of Dalton, but he speculated that he might have met him once when he "escorted Lucian Pye (a political scientist from MIT who later wrote something—shallow and forgettable—about Burmese personality and politics) around Rangoon. Pye was interested in student politics."[63]

ASSOCIATED STUDENTS OF AFGHANISTAN

The foundation regularly provided funds to the Associated Students of Afghanistan (ASA), a US-based group for Afghanistan students studying in the United States. This support included funds to cover the costs of the ASA's annual meetings. The foundation regularly sent staff to observe and report on these meetings.

In 1961, Jerzy Lerski attended the eighth annual ASA convention in Boulder, Colorado, as a foundation representative. There were about one hundred Afghan students in attendance, a number representing about half of all Afghan students then studying in the United States. Lerski reported on conference discussions of political developments and noted the absence of Pakistani representatives, a shift reflecting the collapse of diplomatic relations between Afghanistan and Pakistan. The foundation funded about a quarter ($1,000) of the convention's costs, while the CIA's American Friends of the Middle East (AFME) provided the remaining funds ($3,000). In other words, unbeknown to the participants, this event was entirely funded by CIA front organizations. Lerski reported that the foundation's "presence at the meetings provides us with an opportunity to explain our contribution to Afghanistan's development, our basic philosophy, and *modus operandi*."[64]

In 1966, the foundation sent a summer intern, J. Michael McGinnis, to report on the thirteenth annual ASA convention.[65] McGinnis's report provided notes from sessions he attended, as well as financial documents and impressions of some association members. His notes included a three-page appendix, "Personalities Noted," comprising paragraph-long entries on individual students catching his interest. These entries were narrative evaluations of students, sometimes with assessments of how approachable students were or of possibilities for working with them in some future unspecified context. Sample entries include the following:

ARSALA
A person who is a student, but did not appear on the student list, and had no part in the official handling of the convention. He ran for President of ASA/USA against Shahryar and almost won. He is a very affable person and was regarded highly at the convention. Possibly someone to watch.

ASSIFI, Abdul Tawab
The 1965–66 President of ASA/USA. Assifi seemed to be fairly articulate and quick-witted, but as an executive he was very poor. I say this not only because the convention, the highlight of ASA/USA's year, was so bad, but also because be seemed to have made very little progress in unification of the body throughout the year. ASA/USA's programs during the regular year were nil except for the newsletter and its editor. In spite of this, I do not feel that he could be labeled as corrupt to the extent feared by some in correspondence with the Foundation. It had been suspected that Assifi was using the office for his own political advantage in Afghanistan and using the Association's money for his own secretary and personal phone calls to Kabul.[66] In particular answer to these charges, I very much doubt that the office is highly enough regarded in Afghanistan to be used as a political stepping-stone, and in regards to the finances, a simple check of the budget of last year and the previous year will clear him of guilt. In short, I think he was a President who just did not know how to be an efficient executive."[67]

McGinnis characterized the meeting as unorganized and chaotic. He recommended the foundation provide funds for the newsletter but felt they should withhold funds the following year until a final version of the annual convention's program was submitted.

In 1967, after the *New York Times* revealed the foundation's CIA ties, the ASA's executive committee "unanimously voted to sever all relations" with the foundation. ASA president Ishaq Shahryar declared that the ASA deplored "activities of any organization which disguises itself and attempts through covert actions or intentions to influence in any way, misdirect, or contaminate students' minds." Shahryar announced that the ASA knew of no direct "wrongdoing or arm twisting" by the foundation.[68] The foundation responded, saying they regretted the ASA's decision and claimed they had never attempted "to influence or direct your members or policy in any way."[69]

In the spring of 1967, *Ramparts* published "How the CIA Turns Foreign Students into Traitors." The article reported that the CIA had six full-time officers whose primary job was to recruit foreign students studying in the United States to become CIA spies. CIA recruitment officers used Department of Defense cover and pseudonyms. *Ramparts* based its story on a source "intimate with student recruitment" who explained that typically a CIA officer would telephone a foreign student, identify himself as being from the Department of Defense, and then inquire how the student was doing while studying in the United States. Under this pretext, the CIA officer arranged meetings with the student, while the CIA ran security checks. The CIA then tried to have further meetings with the student during which the agent eventually "asks the student to perform some small service for which he is 'rewarded' with $10 or $20 for 'expenses.' However, the student must sign a US government receipt 'for service rendered.' If the student should [later] threaten to blow the story, he can be threatened by the vouchers which can be turned over to his government's embassy." At the end of this process, the CIA asked the student to "engage in subversion against the student's government" for large cash payments, as much as $10,000, with promises of allowing the students to permanently live in the United States at some future date, after having completed their assigned task. The CIA then trapped these students by asking them "to write out a contract in his own handwriting, and the agreement," which could be used by the agency at any future moment to blackmail a student reconsidering this decision.[70]

"Numerous foreign students" told *Ramparts* that CIA officers had approach them on American college campuses. Most were afraid to be identified, but one Afghan student, Abdul Latif Hotaki, told his story on the record. Hotaki began studying agricultural journalism at California State Polytechnic College in 1957, and efforts to recruit him to work for the CIA occurred four years later in a meeting with the ASA president, Zia H. Noorzay, in Berkeley. A CIA officer approached Hotaki during a visit to Noorzay's apartment, and the recruitment pitch stressed that the CIA's interest in him was to maintain "friendship" between the two countries, telling him that "money was no object" in securing his help. Noorzay told Hotaki he had first been approached by the CIA through American Friends of the Middle East, and he encouraged Hotaki to accept this offer, telling him that the money and "scholarship aid" were good deals.[71] But Hotaki did not agree to help the CIA, though the agency tried two other times to recruit him—once during the 1962 ASA annual convention, held in Washington, DC, and another time at AFME's San Francisco office. He was told that if he helped the CIA, "scholarships would be available for me to attend Harvard, Stanford, or any other university I wanted to go to." After rejecting these three recruitment efforts, the US Immigration Service began harassing Hotaki, threatening to deport him to Afghanistan even though he was married to a US citizen and had two children who were citizens.[72]

Ramparts described the CIA's support for the Afghan Student Association as a "convenient vehicle for entrapping the foreign student and turning him into a puppet."[73] The magazine identified "CIA-financed educational and cultural organizations" as the environments fostering the CIA's recruitment of foreign students, and it described AFME as "one of the chief arms of the CIA in the world of foreign students," one that channeled CIA funds through its department of student affairs.[74] The article described AFME's Student Affairs Department work with educational organizations, like the Institute of International Education, using their funds to shape the policies and activities of these student organizations. The *Ramparts* article detailed how AFME shaped the policies of other student organizations as well, such as when in 1961 AFME withheld funds from the Iranian Students Association after the group opposed the Shah of Iran.[75]

Finally, *Ramparts* named "the prestigious Asia Foundation" as one of the Afghan Student Association's funders, stating that the foundation "received money from at least three CIA conduits."[76] Following the publication of this *Ramparts* story, some members of the Afghanistan government and the greater Afghanistan community tried to dismiss the significance of these revelations. UCLA economics professor Nake M. Kamrany published a letter to the editors of *Ramparts* complaining that "your account of the Afghan students and their association was inaccurate, misleading, without foundation, and deplorable. May I repeat that your entire story was based upon the testimony of a single individual (Abdul Hotaki) who has openly claimed of his intentions to remain in this country permanently, and who has had personal grudges against the people he has named and implicated."⁷⁷

At a March 1967 event at the National Press Club, Afghanistan's prime minister, Mohammad Hashim Maiwandwal, answered a question from a reporter about the *Ramparts* claim that he had "personal knowledge of attempts by the CIA to recruit an Afghan student as an agent." The prime minister said he had no such knowledge, insisting he had "the greatest faith in the integrity of our young people and their loyalty to their country."⁷⁸

OTHER FOUNDATIONS' POLITICAL INFLUENCES

In a collection of Ford Foundation archival documents, I found an old issue of *Current Digest of the Soviet Press* that translated an undated *Komsomolskaya Pravda* article, "The Fords and Foundations." This article examined Henry Ford's use of US tax law to avoid estate taxes by setting up a foundation that retained 90 percent of his wealth within a family-controlled corporation that continued to influence governmental policies decades after his death. Among such work was the Ford Foundation's financing of academic research on postcolonial nations following the Second World War, work the article interpreted as making these newly established nations increasingly vulnerable to American capitalist designs. Although the prose in this piece was strident in places, the analysis of these wealthy foundations pursuing the self-interests of founders was more astute than most articles covering the work of the Ford Foundation appearing in the American press during this period.⁷⁹ The article claimed that during the years following the Second World War, American foundations increasingly funded projects designed to increase US global power. The article critiqued the Ford, Rockefeller, and Carnegie Foundations' projects studying new nations and "spreading democracy"—or more accurately, spreading certain forms of democracy in the postwar world:

> After the Second World War the wave of the national-liberation movement rocked entire continents. The peoples of Africa and Asia started throwing the colonialists out of their territories. At the same time a long file of military, economic, political and all kinds of other missions of the USA moved in. They included missions organized by "philanthropic" organizations, in the first place [was] the Ford Foundation. The money of the Fords began flowing to Syria and Iraq, Turkey and the

U.A.R., India and Pakistan. Using subtle tricks and the usual political demagoguery, the bosses of the foundations strove to impose their way of thinking and their ideas on these countries. They are trying with all the forces to place the economies and politics of these countries under the dominance of the American monopolies. The Ford Foundation spends millions of dollars a year in the underdeveloped countries.

The young states that are starting to build their economies have an acute shortage in housing, industrial enterprises, raw materials and food products. But it would be useless to try to find even one plant built with Ford money. Foundations like the Fords' prefer to spend their dollars training businessmen and government employees, viewing them as their future puppets, and libraries stuffed with books eulogizing the "American way of life."[80]

Despite the blunt political tone of this Soviet analysis, it accurately identified some of the ways these private foundations carried out work aligned with the same political missions supported by DTPILLAR operations.

CONSIDERING WHAT EMERGED FROM THESE CONTACTS WITH OTHER GROUPS

DTPILLAR's engagements with other foundations and organizations extended the CIA's reach. Some of these activities connected foundation staff with scholars working in Asia, while others established connections with organizations engaged in work aligned with DTPILLAR goals. These connections helped establish an air of legitimacy at home and abroad. At times this helped foundation staff gather intelligence, and growing institutional connections helped expand DTPILLAR's contacts with significant organizations and individuals.

In many of these DTPILLAR programs involving other organizations, the CIA opportunistically used its partners in cynical ways. DTPILLAR's support for certain labor union activities was self-serving. The agency's interest was not to organize unions to improve the lives of exploited workers by improving working conditions; it wanted to subvert communist-linked union movements. DTPILLAR's interest in working with other foundations also appears to have been motivated by desires to seek camouflage among "normal" foundations and to find other groups that could help carry out its anticommunist mission. CIA funding of professional association memberships helped DTPILLAR connect with Asian scholars and future leaders.

DTPILLAR's use of students within the United States and in Asia betrayed basic trust, and had those impacted by these tactics known of this duplicity at the time, there would have been significant fallout for the CIA, the foundation, and for other, unwitting foundations. Some of these activities depended on individuals being willing to provide the intelligence the CIA sought, as when James Scott reported information on Burmese campus political developments while studying abroad as a Rotary exchange student. In other instances, such as DTPILLAR secretly funding and monitoring Afghanistan Student Association meetings, the CIA tried to shape foreign organizations to serve American interests.

Even though John D. Rockefeller III had rejected the foundation's 1954 invitation to join the board of trustees (see chapter 2), three years later President Blum explored possibilities for coordinating some foundation activities with Rockefeller's Asia Society. In January 1957, Blum and Rockefeller met during the latter's stopover in San Francisco, as he departed on a two-month Asian tour. Rockefeller told Blum that "he hoped our two organizations would work very closely together and that he saw no reason for conflict or duplication." Rockefeller maintained some institutional distance, however, explaining that the Asia Society mostly worked in the United States as a "service organization," not as a foundation.[81]

Filling a gap left in the Asia Society's budget by a loss of funds from a different covertly funded CIA organization (the American Committee for Cultural Freedom), in 1957 the Asia Foundation provided a grant of $5,000 to Rockefeller's Asia Society.[82] These funds supported some new Asia Society programs and helped with hospitality expenses for prominent Asians visiting New York City, "a function previously handled for the Foundation by the now dissolved American Committee for Cultural Freedom."[83] Ironically, Rockefeller had previously been reticent to appear linked to the Asia Foundation because of its association with crude American propaganda operations, yet just a few years later his own foundation was comfortable using Asia Foundation funds to fill funding gaps left by the shuttering of this organization.

The CIA hoped Asia Foundation programs would routinely work in conjunction with the Ford, Rockefeller, and Carnegie entities, as well as other foundations operating in Asia. This was one of the reasons why Asia Foundation staff routinely met with staff of other foundations. Overlapping funding sources helped strengthen the appearance of the legitimacy of DTPILLAR programs, which helped ensure these programs' viability—so long as links to the CIA remained a protected secret. In some instances, programs launched by the Asia Foundation were later funded by others, allowing the foundation to outsource the CIA's mission to private foundations. One example of this occurred when Asia Foundation projects funding college education programs in the Philippines led to a $230,000 Ford Foundation grant to Philippine colleges working on rural development.[84]

Whether it was projects supporting anticommunist unions, connecting with students studying in Asia under nonfoundation programs, funding Asian student associations, or sponsoring Asian memberships in third-party professional associations, during the 1950s DTPILLAR skillfully developed techniques for using existing organizations to establish contacts with Asians, using these connections to advance their soft-power anticommunist goals.

While foundation engagements with other organizations brought varied outcomes, a common theme emerging from these interactions was the foundation's collection of names or dossiers on prominent or up-and-coming Asians or scholars of Asia. Much remains unknown about what all was done with these names.[85] Because the CIA and the foundation have not released records collected under the foundation's dual filing system, and because other related documents remain classified, we are left to wonder what sort of recruiting may, or may not, have occurred. While this dimension of these interactions remains unknown, we know a lot about the ways the foundation used these engagements to build networks of scholars, journalists, and Asian nationals who showed themselves willing to support various projects undermining Asian political developments not aligned with US political-economic goals.

While DTPILLAR-funded operations helped increase foundation contacts with others, DTPILLAR also developed more direct means of altering Asian narratives by shaping the production of books, magazines, newspapers, movies, and other means of spreading news reports and entertainment, as the foundation sought not only to expand its connections with others working in Asia but to shape the thoughts of those it reached through these media.

8 Books and Movies as CIA-Funded Propaganda

Propaganda in some form or other lurks in every book.
GEORGE ORWELL / "The Frontiers of Art"

While the Committee for Free Asia was established primarily to broadcast propaganda to Asian listeners, technical problems soon led the committee to switch operations from broadcasting to publishing and distributing anticommunist books, magazines, and movies. These print and visual media proved to be effective means for connecting with Asian audiences, whether they were rural villagers seeking technical information to improve agricultural production or audiences seeking escapist pleasure in action films with pro-Western, individualist heroes and communist villains. DTPILLAR funded these media in campaigns generating pro-American sentiments and casting shadows of distrust on communists.

In the mid-1970s, the US Senate's Church Committee investigations into CIA illegal activities included inquiries into the agency's covert funding of book publishing during the 1950s and 1960s. The Senate's final report summarized what the CIA sought to achieve in these publishing campaigns, which included CFA and Asia Foundation projects before 1968. The Senate learned from the CIA's chief of the Covert Action staff that covert book publishing and distribution operations sought to

1. get books published or distributed abroad without revealing any US influence, by covertly subsidizing foreign publications or booksellers
2. get books published that could not be "contaminated" by any overt tie-in with the US government, especially if the position of the author is "delicate"
3. get books published for operational reasons, regardless of commercial viability
4. initiate and subsidize indigenous national or international organizations for book publishing or distributing purposes
5. stimulate the writing of politically significant books by unknown

foreign authors—either by directly subsidizing the author, if covert contact is feasible, or indirectly, through literary agents or publishers.[1]

Following these goals, the CIA's covert funding of Asian publishing projects sought to shape the thinking of targeted audiences without creating suspicions that these books were published by a US government propaganda operation.

Various scholarly works analyzing how CIA fronts influenced the arts and culture during the 1950s and 1960s document CIA funding of projects ranging from literary magazines like *Paris Review* to supporting American abstract impressionist painters, as part of efforts to undermine communism.[2] One of the most impressive studies of CIA publishing ventures was undertaken by Rutgers University professor Sol Chaneles, who died in 1990 before completing this work, leaving tantalizing fragments of his book manuscript, which he had titled "CIA and the Books." Surviving portions of this manuscript are archived at George Washington University's National Security Archive, though its fragmentary state leaves holes in the story Chaneles pieced together.[3]

Chaneles determined that the CIA's secret involvement with book publishing extended practices initiated by the Office of War Information (OWI) during World War II, when the OWI secretly underwrote the publication of books to boost American support for the war.[4] Using wartime agencies like the Council on Books in Wartime (CBW), the US government assisted with the publication of over a thousand books, including books characterizing the enemy in distorted ways that aligned with the American war effort. While most of these wartime subsidy operations ceased at the war's end, Chaneles argued that the early Cold War's CIA publishing operations essentially extended or revitalized elements of these wartime programs. His research traced how individuals like Harper & Row's Cass Canfield drew on their wartime intelligence work when later undertaking CIA covert publishing operations.

Chaneles examined how the State Department's psychological warfare unit, known as the Committee on Books Abroad, relied on members of New York's publishing establishment—people like Harper & Row's Canfield, Thomas Crowell's Robert Crowell, and Macmillan's George Brett—to oversee covert publication efforts. Chaneles traced how Marshall W. Fishwick, director of the Wemyss Foundation, helped channel CIA funds for CIA publications, and he described the revolving doors between the Department of State, CIA, and the publishing industry.[5]

The CIA's intrusion into academic publishing in the 1950s and 1960s was substantial. As the CIA admitted in Church Committee testimony, the agency "produced, subsidized, or sponsored" over a thousand books prior to 1968; a quarter of these were written in English, and "many of them were published by cultural organizations," using methods that left many authors unaware the CIA had subsidized their work, though in some instances there was "direct collaboration between CIA and the writer."[6] The CIA's use of DTPILLAR to publish and distribute books undermining Asian communism was part of this larger CIA project, and the significant number of surviving records from DTPILLAR operations provides a rare opportunity to consider how these programs worked and what the CIA sought to gain from these efforts.

EARLY COMMITTEE FOR FREE ASIA BOOK PUBLISHING AND DISTRIBUTION

Prior to the Second World War, Hong Kong was an insignificant publishing hub. Its publishing distribution network then largely consisted of newsboys and a central news district at Lee Yuen Street East. During the war, as a response to the restrictions of the Japanese occupation, a decentralized distribution system known as the "general agent system" developed. As these distribution groups began charging increasing rates, many publishers and retailers welcomed a wave of inexpensive communist-subsidized publishing operations that began in the late 1940s.[7]

Because Hong Kong was a British Crown colony, DTPILLAR operations needed to align with British policies. In general, "Hong Kong permitted the US authorities to use the American Consulate as a processing plant for human intelligence," and similar arrangements existed for DTPILLAR's publishing, distribution, and filmmaking operations.[8] While the official British presence in Hong Kong may not have been aware of all of DTPILLAR's operations, the publishing and distribution programs sponsored by DTPILLAR there were acceptable to the British. It is unclear what level of communication or disclosure the CIA had with its British intelligence counterparts, but given that the CIA disclosed some DTPILLAR operations to British intelligence in Singapore during the 1950s, it is reasonable to assume similar levels of disclosure to MI6 occurred in Hong Kong.[9]

During the early 1950s, Hong Kong's press and printer associations proliferated. Many had communist affiliations, though only some presses published explicitly political content. The growth in publishing provided the communists with significant reach beyond Hong Kong, as Hong Kong became a base for producing communist publications distributed throughout Asia.[10] The demand for printed materials by overseas Chinese populations was large, and the growth of mainland Chinese publishing networks in the early 1950s helped feed this overseas demand.

From its earliest days, the committee supported the publishing and distribution of Asian-language books denigrating communism. In 1952, when CFA began supporting select Hong Kong publishing projects, Chinese communists dominated local and global distribution markets. The committee understood that with monetary subsidies it could fund significant anticommunist publishing ventures and thereby help spread these publications throughout Hong Kong and abroad. Beginning in 1952, the committee began subsidizing several small Hong Kong publishers, the most prominent among them being the Union Press and the Asia Press. But even with increased production, distribution problems remained. Because Hong Kong's distribution networks were dominated by communists, only six bookstores sold CFA-backed books. In 1953, with careful planning and targeting a select group of books, Union Press and Asia Press expanded distribution into bookstores that previously sold only books distributed by communist interests, eventually reaching a total of thirty-four Hong Kong shops. By the summer of 1953, this program was so successful that "the major bookstore into which Asia Press had first pushed its books entered into an agreement with the Press under which the store agreed to throw out all Communist books and concentrate on the sale of free world books."[11]

Two years later, sixty-nine Hong Kong bookstores stocked DTPILLAR-backed books, and the Union Press and Asia Press opened offices elsewhere in Asia. The communist press distribution network reorganized "under the new titles Yiu Lo Hui, or Recreation Club, to avoid attracting too much attention on the part of government authorities." By the mid-1950s, the competition between DTPILLAR-backed enterprises and communist presses and distribution networks in Hong Kong intensified, culminating in the July 1956 formal registration of the foundation-backed Hong Kong Publishers and Distribution Association. The association had connections with publishers in Thailand, Vietnam, Cambodia, and Indonesia to help distribute foundation-backed publications.[12]

While the State Department backed various USIS publication programs, the CIA used DTPILLAR to support similar distribution and publication projects. This sort of replication of activities might appear to be a waste of American energies, but when problems arose for State Department–backed programs, the (fake) independent status of the committee or foundation provided relative freedom of operations. For example, when in 1953 Hong Kong authorities protested USIS publication activities in Hong Kong, the Committee for Free Asia continued similar work unimpeded, under the guise of being a nongovernmental operation.[13]

OPERATION BROOMSTICK

In 1953 the CIA launched Operation Broomstick, a program using the CFA to weaken the reach of Hong Kong communist booksellers. In early 1953, CFA Hong Kong representative Delmer Brown met with an individual identified by the code name "Fiction" to discuss Operation Broomstick.[14] "Fiction" was Chang Kuo-sin, author of the anticommunist memoir *Eight Months behind the Bamboo Curtain*. Operation Broomstick was "a project drawn up by Fiction and aimed at 'sweeping Communist influences from the bookstores' of Hong Kong." Broomstick sought to get local booksellers to refuse to sell communist publications and to increase sales of anticommunist books. Broomstick, designed by Delmer Brown, used Fiction to buy up large numbers of "the most virulent Communist books" from booksellers while coaxing these booksellers to return other communist books to publishers claiming they couldn't sell this stock.[15]

Operation Broomstick compensated booksellers for lost revenue from books they would not be selling, paying them to remove unsold communist books from the shelves, then returning them for refunds months later. As for the copies of communist books Fiction bought, Brown planned to "obtain Communist books for a bonfire" he thought "would attract considerable attention and serve to speed up the shift of other bookstores to the democratic side."[16] Brown appeared unconcerned about obvious comparisons to historical book burnings by fascist authorities.

An undated CFA document described proposed activities for "Fiction Enterprises." These activities included sponsoring anticommunist books and movies and instigating forms of anticommunist agitation drawing on "various intellectuals, writers, authors, journalists and artists." Chang Kuo-sin was the key individual working on this project. Fiction Enterprises was described as revealing the truth about communism, helping the people to understand that, "like other swindles," communism "is fronted by an attractive camouflage. We must tear apart that front and show the inside to the people."[17]

By the summer of 1953, Delmer Brown had misgivings about the relative risk and value of the programs Chang, as Fiction, was conducting. Brown worried about Fiction's tendency "to build all of his projects and programs around himself in a manner that attracts attention and gives an exaggerated impression of the size and of extensive CFA support in spite of CFA efforts to keep all CFA help from being disclosed."[18] But by September 1954, Fiction's operations had produced impressive results. The Asia Press sold "more books in Indonesia than in Singapore and other anti-Commie countries," and Operation Broomstick was supporting many anticommunists in Hong Kong. Fiction next wanted the foundation to hire anticommunist "teachers for Chinese schools in Malaya," and he proposed that the Singapore government could screen teachers while the committee could support newspapers that would publish anticommunist columns. Fiction also wanted the foundation to weaponize flood relief by offering such relief aid to China, because "if Commies refuse, it will hurt them." Fiction recommended the CFA send a telegram "to Mao Tse-tung offering aid if: Red China will stop selling rice to accumulate war goods; (if) Mao will stop refusing Red Cross and other foreign offers of help."[19]

One 1954 plan tasked Fiction with embedding anticommunist messages in Hong Kong films financed by DTPILLAR. The committee's Tokyo representative, John W. Miller, developed protocols for DTPILLAR-backed films and formalized roles for committee staff to "serve as a subtle type of Watchdog" as they supported work Fiction supervised and made sure anticommunist plot devices remained in the final cut of the films produced.[20] This "watchdog" executive producer oversaw film productions, including keeping films on budget and on schedule, monitoring daily rushes, and ensuring anticommunist messaging.

Miller proposed Fiction have a direct stake in the success of the operations he managed and be paid with stock in the committee's company, Asia Pictures, Inc., "perhaps in lieu of some of his salary," in order to keep him interested in the commercial success of the films he made. When it was suggested some of their films circulate on the international art film market, committee staff expressed concerns that much of the messaging was obvious propaganda and that such international exposure could backfire. Worrying that Fiction's work would be seen as "instruments of Nationalist China's public policy," Miller warned that "Fiction's film should not seek deliberately to propagandize for fear that the stigma of propaganda be attached."[21]

Between 1955 and 1959, Asia Pictures produced nine films. Several actors and directors, most notably director King Hu, later became famous, though CFA-financed films at Asia Pictures achieved little critical acclaim. Charles Leary has described the overall tone of Asia Pictures' films as "consistently 'subtle,'" noting there were few "overt political claims ... made in any of the films. Most of the films are family melodramas" set in past periods or the present.[22]

ANTICOMMUNIST PUBLISHING PROJECTS BEYOND HONG KONG

During the first half of the 1950s, DTPILLAR's Hong Kong anticommunist projects reached beyond Fiction's work in research, publishing, and filmmaking. In 1954, the committee sponsored Robert J. Lifton's Hong Kong–based study of "the psychiatric aspects of Chinese Communist 'Thought Reform' or 'Brainwashing.'"[23] Because the committee worried that funding such propagandistic work could threaten its cover, Delmer Brown asked Lifton "to avoid publicizing [his] affiliation with The Asia Foundation, though later the Foundation reversed this decision."[24]

The committee's funding of Lifton's brainwashing research shows the CIA using a funding front to finance a project that likely would not have survived a normal foundation's peer review process. When the committee asked Yale University's David N. Rowe to evaluate Lifton's work, Rowe explained that while Lifton asked important research questions, his lack of experience with the Asian cultures he wished to study presented serious problems that would undermine the entire project.[25] While the Ford Foundation's peer review process rejected Lifton's proposal, CFA ignored these concerns and funded Lifton without even asking that he address the serious concerns Rowe raised.[26] This ability to ignore fundamental aspects of peer review provided significant "value" to CIA fronts, allowing the agency to fund what independent peer reviewers concluded were flawed projects; this increased the likelihood of the agency producing low-reliability research findings that fit agency preconceptions. These are troubling prospects for the production of reliable science, and it did not bode well for the policies such research was used to justify. But this greenlighting of projects of interest to the CIA was a vital function of CIA fronts.[27] In the case of Lifton's research, his book *Thought Reform and the Psychology of Totalism: A Study of "Brainwashing" in China* was published in 1961 as a trade book by Norton. It became a popular work shaping American Cold War views of China, though its representations of "brainwashing" were sensationalistic.

The committee acquired translation and republication rights for many popular novels, and staff evaluated which books should be translated, weighing both literary value and pro-Western messaging. The committee's 1953 correspondence includes a rejection of a Japanese literary agent's suggestion they translate Paul Bowles's *The Sheltering Sky*. Staffer Ann Byington was disgusted by the suggestion, because "the story concerns a degenerate American couple and a so-called gentleman friend who go to Africa in 1939 because they don't like American life."[28] Instead of translating Bowles, they translated Norman Vincent Peale's *The Power of Positive Thinking*, as well as books on agricultural techniques and Burmese translations of overtly anticommunist books with titles like *Forced Labor in the Soviet Union*.[29]

In 1954, the committee purchased the Burmese-language publishing rights to George Orwell's *1984* and *Animal Farm*, paying the author seventy-five dollars for each title.[30] CFA also sponsored the anticommunist comic strip "Guy Gullible in Muscovia," which appeared in the *Malay Mail*. Committee staffer Robert Sheeks mailed a sampling of the "Guy Gullible" strips to the CFA president, recommending the committee publish the strip in other Asian newspapers. The daily strip chronicled the misadventures of Guy Gullible as he experienced the failures of the dystopian communist society "Muscovia," where he had hoped to find a worker's paradise, and instead found only a corrupt party machine duping the people.[31]

In 1953 DTPILLAR supported Burmese anticommunist operations by providing the Burmese army's psychological warfare section with 150 tons of newsprint, which the military used to publish a popular magazine mixing anticommunist messages with news and popular culture stories.[32] Committee-sponsored book-buying programs purchased anticommunist books for Burmese military libraries and Burmese teachers college libraries.[33] The committee also funded a Malayan Chinese Association project "printing and distributing 20,000 basic civics textbooks to Chinese schools there." While presented as simply an effort to provide textbooks to underfunded schools, this was also an ideological project, one that replaced "books which had previously made the schools ideological breeding grounds for communist insurrections."[34]

By the mid-1950s, DTPILLAR supported numerous Asian newspaper, magazine, and book publishing operations, while Hong Kong remained the base of the foundation's most important publishing projects. The foundation's October–December 1956 quarterly activity report for Hong Kong provided a historical overview of publishing in Hong Kong, tracing how it had become the center for "the free Chinese publishing industry," with money exchanges, knowledgeable publishers, minimal censorship laws, and transportation networks to Chinese communities worldwide. Books were popular gifts to nations hoping education would help in their modernization efforts. Like the foundation's music, film, and travel programs, foundation-backed book projects were popular, upbeat topics of discussion during President Blum's meetings with foreign leaders.[35]

In the mid-1950s, the foundation began funding Franklin Publications (later renamed Franklin Books), a New York–based small press specializing in the overseas republication and translation of books by American authors.[36] Decades later the *New York Times* described Franklin Books as part of a small group of "'legitimate publishers that received CIA subsidies' to aid in the publication of books supporting views aligned with American foreign policy." This 1977 *Times* article also identified the Asia Foundation and "another small foundation" as the CIA-linked funders of the press. Franklin officials claimed they were unwitting recipients of CIA funds.[37]

The Asia Foundation and Franklin Publications developed a cordial and cooperative relationship. In the mid-1950s, as Franklin moved from working primarily in the Middle East to expanding operations into Asia, foundation staff met with Franklin staff to share information on regional needs for Western books. In 1958, Franklin Publications' publisher, Darius C. Smith, wrote President Blum to say that "some of our mutual friends have suggested" the foundation might support an Afghanistan-based publishing program, which would involve Franklin Publications renting the Afghan Ministry of Education's printing press in order to publish textbooks.[38] The foundation's assistant representative for Afghanistan, John A. Banning, helped select the press's new publications manager and had involvement in other managerial decisions.[39]

When backing local publishing projects, the foundation sometimes reshaped anticommunist Asian book narratives by excising passages that included critiques of the United States. When translating an anticommunist article from the *Nippon Times* depicting a totalitarian communist takeover of Japan, the foundation removed passages portraying the American postwar occupation as its own form of totalitarianism.[40] In evaluating Walt Rostow's *The Prospects for Communist China*, published in 1954, James Stewart criticized the author's efforts "to be as objective as humanly possible" while having "summarily brushed aside a wealth of material from the anti-communist Chinese sources," suggesting Walt Rostow might not be anticommunist enough for the foundation's translation project.[41] Stewart concluded that Rostow's "book is certainly not going to bring about Asian awareness of the communist conspiracy. On the contrary, it might encourage some Asians who believe that communism, admittedly a radical surgical process, might be the very cure-all."[42] This attack on a fellow liberal anticommunist shows how narrow the range of acceptable foundation anticommunist messaging was during the mid-1950s.

The foundation worked with outside groups, such as the Committee on Books Abroad, a State Department advisory group, and it asked Human Relations Area Files director and Committee on Books Abroad chair Mark May to establish "a vast international program of subsidized book distribution" that would select affordable anticommunist, procapitalist texts and college textbooks.[43] May stressed the ideological significance of this work, quoting Stalin's argument that communists "must storm and take the citadels of learning," and he claimed that communist book programs were adapted from Nazi propaganda techniques developed in Latin America as wartime efforts to gain allies.[44]

By the end of the 1950s, the foundation's book program had distributed over a million books and 250,000 copies of journals throughout Asia.

TIGER BALM MAGNATE AW BOON HAW

Because DTPILLAR viewed newspapers as important conduits for influencing opinions about communism, capitalism, and electoral politics, the Committee for Free Asia courted newspaper magnate and cofounder of the Tiger Balm empire, Aw Boon Haw. The committee established an ongoing relationship with Haw based on their shared antipathy toward communism. Aw Boon Haw was born in Burma in 1882, the son of small herbal medicine shop owner. He later moved to Malaysia, eventually founding his Tiger Balm business with his brother, Aw Boon Par, and purchasing an Asian publishing empire. Aw Boon Par managed much of the daily work at the Tiger Balm plant, while Aw Boon Haw managed the publicity and branding of the company. The Asia Foundation's dossier on Aw Boon Haw observed that "a knowledge of the Aw family is important in any intelligence study into Aw Bo[o]n Haw's newspapers. Family affairs are deeply involved in both his publishing and medicine enterprises." The report claimed he had entered publishing—against his brother's wishes—to sell more Tiger Balm, and he found financial success in publishing while using newspapers to increase Tiger Balm sales. His business plan had thus "paid off, and he soon was recognized as one of the most influential, as well as wealthy, overseas Chinese leaders. Even today, he proudly displays photos showing him with Generalissimo Chiang Kai-shek, and other high Nationalist officials."[45] The CIA's interest in Aw Boon Haw was as old as the agency itself, with 1947 memos showing the CIA tracking his newspaper empire and monitoring news of his 1949 arrest in Singapore.[46]

Aw Boon Haw spent the Second World War in Hong Kong, where he expanded his newspaper empire and his influence increased among a growing overseas Chinese readership. His brother and one of his sons died during the war. He had four wives, described in the foundation's dossier as having different statuses and stations linked to the countries where they resided (Burma and Hong Kong) and their roles in providing him heirs (the foundation reported that wives three and four "were taken when the first two failed to give him children"). He adopted three sons, had a daughter by his second wife, had a son by his third wife, and another by his fourth.

The foundation's (undated) "Report on Aw Boon Haw's newspapers" reported that he purchased newspapers in Singapore (*Sin Chew Jit Poh*), then Penang (*Sing Ping*), and Hong Kong (*Sing Tao* and *Sing Tao Wan Pao*), relying on close friends or family to handle important managerial roles, and he hired well-known journalists to boost readership.[47] He also financially backed a Hong Kong football team, an enterprise also linked to his promotion of Tiger Balm. Aw Boon Par hired his friend Ling A-ming to manage the day-to-day operations of the Singapore newspaper; the latter also later ran the newspaper in Hong Kong while Aw Boon Haw took on a more symbolic managerial role, and new newspapers were opened until a struggle for control of the publishing empire broke out between Aw Boon Haw and Ling A-ming. During the war, Aw Boon Haw established a sort of peace with the Japanese that later led to collaboration accusations.

In 1951, concerned that Aw Boon Haw's newspapers did not have the sort of unified editorial policy that might be expected in a chain of same-owner newspapers, CFA staffer Harold Nobel proposed the CFA work "to get the old tiger balmer to America and to persuade him to visit and talk at length with American owners of chain newspapers." Nobel wanted the State Department to sponsor such a visit, while the committee helped approach Aw and tried to influence him to adopt a strong pro-American editorial policy for all his newspapers. Nobel wrote they should "lay it on thick with the old boy, so that he would not feel that he was just another leader grantee. Perhaps the Committee could help in this phase."[48]

The committee/foundation dossier on Aw Boon Haw detailed complex machinations involving the acquisitions of newspapers in China and southern

Asia, with interruptions of war, infighting, purges, the occasional paradoxical ownership of competing communist and anticommunist newspapers (with Aw Boon Haw supporting anticommunist politics, while maintaining his deepest loyalty to survival), twists of fate like an airplane crash killing his trusted son, communist revolutions, and a world war toppling plans, four wives providing a stock of competing heirs (adopted and family born), all as prologue for the appearance of the Asia Foundation as a would-be player in Asian publishing schemes.

Robert Blum described Aw's newspapers as among the best funded in Asia, well edited, and adept at surviving in a difficult political climate, noting that there "are wide variations of policy. His two Chinese papers in Hong Kong, for instance, are extremely anti-communist, although I understand there are some leftist staff members." Blum recognized Aw was a skilled operator, able to continue publishing in Singapore by mostly following the "Peiping line" while maintaining such uncommitted policies in his newspapers that he "was out of favor with the Nationalists for some time because he refused to take a personal stand against the communists, apparently in the hope of retaining control of his vast properties on the mainland. He has since become publicly disillusioned."[49]

When Aw Boon Haw died in 1954, the committee worried about his vast newspaper empire's uncertain future. When CFA staff met with him right before his death, he had confided that "his sons have been disappointing and [he] fears that they might close down all the newspapers after his death. 'What they want is money,' he said. 'They would not allow the papers, most of which are still losing money, to continue. Then I would lose plenty of face.'" Foundation staff concluded that "his fears are not entirely groundless," and "his heirs would not hesitate to close down the Singapore papers (which have lost S.$2,100,000), and perhaps also the Hong Kong Standard which has to be helped along by the money-making Sing Tao Jih Pao [*Sin Chew Jit Poh*] each month."[50]

An unsigned, undated draft CFA memo (with penciled and typed edits) discussing likely developments following the death of Aw Boon Haw speculated that his profitable Hong Kong publications would likely fall under the control of his widow, Tan Kyi-kyi, and would be managed by Miss Sally Aw. The committee knew the Singapore newspapers were losing money. Aw's four sons lived in Singapore, and CFA staff speculated about whether they would sell these newspapers to cut their losses and raise capital. The committee did not know who Mr. Aw's will would designate as the new owner of his Bangkok newspapers, which had long been run by a third party, and the committee speculated that one of Aw's sons might inherit that newspaper. Whatever the disposition of the newspaper, the committee wanted a role in the editorial stance of these newspapers, and the CFA planned to "cooperate with the Aw family to (a) [*sic*] keep the newspaper chain intact on the side of the free world, (2) to develop it into a strong, independent group of newspapers through more coordinated editorial directorship, (3) to develop the newspapers as the anchors of [an] overseas Chinese informational, distribution and organizations program."[51]

The committee felt it needed to take steps to keep the newspapers from "falling into leftist hands" and to strengthen the newspapers' support for democratic movements. This unsigned memo advised the committee to strive "to graft CFA's programs into the newspaper." Committee staff speculated, "If Mr. Aw's will create[d] a family council to run the newspapers, CFA would have to deal with the council as a whole. Otherwise, individual local controlling bodies would have to be approached tactfully—for either local cooperation or overall cooperation, with the latter, of course, more preferable." The CFA did not wish its role running the newspapers to be publicly known, so instead the committee proposed "to keep its role secret so that any credit for the growth of the Aw papers will go to the Aw family. [The CFA] will furnish the know-how and *clearly defined* financial backing to make the redevelopment possible."[52]

One proposed strategy was for CFA to "convince" the Aw family that new publishing equipment would be needed, and if the family hesitated at the expense, they might "need some outside help, such as mortgaging the new equipment to CFA for a period of years." The draft memo's final page listed the primary eight Aw family members likely to be involved in these developments and provided a brief description of their roles in the family.[53]

Whatever role the foundation might have played in these struggles following Aw Boon Haw's death, the death of his son Aw Hoe in a plane crash three years earlier had placed Aw Boon Haw's daughter, twenty-three-year-old Aw Sian (aka Sally Aw), in line to inherit the publishing empire. Aw Sian continued to combine shrewd business practices with the sorts of editorial policies established by her father, and released CIA records show the agency monitoring her work.[54]

LEVERAGING NEWSPAPER DEBT

Offering loans to establish debt obligations was one way the Committee for Asia could gain control over a newspaper's editorial policy, and though in at least one of the instances when the committee began applying this leverage it drew unwanted critical attention from the committee's own staff. Because some CFA and Asia Foundation staff had no knowledge they were part of a CIA-funded operation, there were always risks that these unwitting staff could raise objections to some of the blatant efforts to shape political developments in host countries. One such staff pushback occurred in early 1954, when CFA Burma staff member Colin D. Edwards wrote a memo to Harold Amoss expressing his own "disquiet" over arrangements being made with the Rangoon newspaper, the *Oway Daily*. Edwards worried that the committee's proposed interference with the newspaper's editorial policy could present "a grave danger that one of the guiding principles of this Committee (as I see them) may be contravened." After learning the CFA had taken the title to the newspaper's property as collateral for a US$5,000 loan to the newspaper, Edwards internally expressed concerns.[55] In his memo to Amoss, Edward wrote

> that the Committee is becoming involved in a "deal" by which it is paying a newspaper in a foreign, sovereign country to alter its editorial policy. Open mention is made in the memorandum of "sufficient control to achieve the desired results," which is interpreted as "printing editorials and stories that are definitely anti-communist." I personally would like to see more Asian papers print articles and editorials exposing communist methods of subverting the ideals and liberties of Asian peoples ... but not at the expense of the principle that no foreign individual, government or group should control the editorial policy of a newspaper in another country through the covert exercise of financial support. In other words, I do not think that "buying an editor" fit in with the ethical standards of conduct which I have always believed this Committee maintained.[56]

Beyond these ethical issues, Edwards also argued that these arrangements would likely in the long run damage the reputation of the committee, damage he believed could undermine the credibility of CFA throughout Asia. He pressed hard for the loan to the press be made without editorial restrictions.[57]

Edwards's interpretation that CFA was hijacking the *Oway Daily*'s editorial policy was correct, yet his naïveté seems akin to a mafia enforcer being shocked that customers' kneecaps were occasionally broken. A few weeks earlier, Marvin McAlister reported to President Blum that the committee would not provide the newspaper with its needed financial assistance "until such time as the *Oway*, by printing editorials and stories that are definitely anti-Communist, shall prove to our satisfaction that the officials with whom I am dealing have sufficient control to achieve the desired result."⁵⁸

CIA FILM DREAMS

As with publishing operations, Hong Kong was an important production base for DTPILLAR's film efforts. The Hong Kong government, while anticommunist, "largely tolerated" the Communist Party's "production of left-wing films, so long as they did not in the government's judgement pose a substantial threat to the basic colonial situation."⁵⁹ DTPILLAR film productions had a relatively small audience base, so many of its films were produced for export to Asian destinations with large Chinese audiences. While never able to compete with Hong Kong's major filmmaking figures, such as the Shaw Brothers, DTPILLAR-backed films had some success in countering the communist messages from their Chinese and Soviet competitors.

The committee and foundation routinely monitored Soviet and Chinese cinema propaganda campaigns. A 1954 memo analyzed the Rangoon screening of a Soviet movie, *The Circus*, which told the story of a white American circus performer who was shunned after giving birth to a Black baby out of wedlock, only to eventually find acceptance and protection from American racism in the Soviet Union.⁶⁰ Staff reported Chinese and Soviet communists had approached Rangoon theater owners and offered each theater a payment of "five thousand kyats per week on a twelve-week contract, the entire sum of sixty-thousand kyats to be paid to each theatre in advance, if the theatre agreed to show exclusively Russian and Red Chinese films during that period."⁶¹ The foundation countered these operations by backing a series of films depicting daily life in Burma.

There were other ambitious DTPILLAR projects that were never completed. Laura Harrington pieced together the story of CFA's failed efforts to produce the film *Wayfarer*, a biopic telling the Buddha's life story, "as a bloc-building strategy to draw Asian Buddhists away from the Communist orbit and into the Free World."⁶² Harrington found that the script's political elements raised concerns among some Asian Buddhists, and these concerns led to the abandonment of the project.

Another way DTPILLAR impacted Asian filmmaking was by increasing the prominence of certain Asian films. Sangjoon Lee's research shows how the Federation of Motion Picture Producers in Asia "chiefly functioned as a base camp for the foundation's motion-picture project that aimed to 'strengthen the influence of the anti-Communist elements in the Federation' and 'to orient the Federation towards the west instead of the east.'"[63] In 1954, the foundation started working with organizers of Tokyo's Motion Picture Producers of Southeast Asia Film Festival to alert festival attendees of "possible communist infiltration and other maneuvers." Staff encouraged the "production of non-communist films" by donating an expensive, commercial-quality movie camera as a festival prize. The foundation kept its donor list private, instead publicly describing the donation as coming from the US Association of Motion Picture Producers. Among the well-known Hollywood figures Blum tried to recruit for this effort were directors Cecil B. DeMille and Frank Capra; and producers Eric Johnston, president of the Motion Picture Association of America, and Frank Freeman, vice president in charge of production at Paramount, as well as Herbert Yates, president of Republic Pictures, though Blum was unsuccessful in these recruitment efforts.[64]

CIA records from a 1960 DTPILLAR audit indicate auditors identified unusual financial and record-keeping practices dating back to the days of the CFA's early 1950s Hong Kong filmmaking projects. For example, auditors found records indicating that in 1954 the committee lent former CFA employee Charles Tanner $25,000 to establish "himself as a recognized motion picture producer in Hollywood." Six years later Tanner had "as yet failed to accomplish these objectives," and "although he has confirmed his indebtedness and his willingness to repay the loan, he has stated that he is not in a position to do so at this time."[65] Tanner had previously worked for the State Department on film projects in Korea and the Philippines, and from 1953 to 1955 he had been the committee and foundation's liaison with the Hollywood film community. The audit determined that the foundation had invested $397,000 in Asia Pictures Limited and $764,000 in the Asia Press.[66]

The extent of Tanner's efforts remains unknown, though some documents establish him as working with Hollywood figures known to have had CIA connections.[67] For example, in November 1953, Carlton Alsop, whom Frances Stoner Saunders identifies as a CIA officer operating in Hollywood during this period, met with Tanner to establish contacts for the committee.[68] Committee records from this period include a file with a list titled simply "Persons to Contact" and the names of approximately thirty people involved in filmmaking, ranging from Cecil B. DeMille and Walt Disney to Stanley Kramer, with most names on the list having the notation "no previous contact."[69]

President Blum corresponded with director Cecil B. DeMille in 1954, thanking him for meeting with and helping Tanner and telling DeMille he had "read with deep interest [the] report on conversations with you and other leaders in this American motion picture industry." Blum's letter acknowledged DeMille's awareness that the foundation's interest was in "countering communist infiltration and penetration" of Asian film markets and also indicated that DeMille had expressed interest in assisting the foundation in their efforts. Blum also wrote of plans to try and visit the director in Hollywood, but I found no record of anything concrete coming from these interactions.[70]

Throughout the years of DTPILLAR's involvement in Asian film production there were recurrent concerns that the allure of filmmaking had become a distracting, time-consuming task for foundation staff, drawing them away from other less-enticing duties. Correspondence from 1953 shows staffer James Stewart worrying that Robert Sheeks and other staff were distractingly enamored with prospects of becoming film producers. Stewart cautioned staff against becoming too directly involved in the details of movie productions.[71]

Sheeks had discerning cinematic tastes—he admired the work of Akira Kurosawa and other gifted Asian filmmakers—but these standards left him underwhelmed by the less refined films DTPILLAR financed. Sheeks oversaw distribution and production of films in several Asian countries. In an October 1953 report he summarized the progress of the films under production and being considered for production in Malaya. Among the films he reported shipping to San Francisco were *The Fight against an Unseen Enemy* (which military personnel did not think should be released), *Fight in Malaya*, *The Kinta Story* ("a good little documentary on the defense plan in the Kinta Valley"), *The Knife* ("re-enacted story of the resistance of two village Malays to terrorists emphasizes the cooperation between the public and the armed forces in eliminating terrorists"), *Jungle Fort*, *Tomorrow Is Theirs*, *Before the Wind*, and *Formosa—Blueprint for a Free China* ("an idealized film concerning youth in Malaya").[72]

A LESS THAN MIGHTY ASIAN WURLITZER

These sorts of culture-hacking efforts funding publishing, film, or media ventures are among the most studied of the CIA's funding front operations of the 1950s and 1960s. And as with the sorts of programs documented by Saunders in *The Cultural Cold War*, or by Wilford in *The Mighty Wurlitzer*, DTPILLAR's media programs were designed to discredit communists' claims and to propagate pro-American, procapitalist messaging. With these media ventures, DT-

PILLAR cast a wide net, both mimicking the similar forms of propaganda undertaken by the Chinese and Soviets and occasionally innovating new uses of media.

The foundation's motivations for supporting specific DTPILLAR projects are sometimes difficult to understand. Some agency-funded projects appear to have sought nothing more than establishing a positive presence in a region of interest to the CIA. One such mundane example was the foundation's 1957 grant financing the construction of a theosophical library in Pakistan.[73] This seems an unlikely project for the foundation, for beyond a library's circulating of books, the spiritual mission of the Theosophical Society would seem to run counter to the foundation's mission. However, 1955 documents show the foundation backing the project because it would establish "a public library and its full services will be available to all groups irrespective of religion."[74]

The CIA's desired outcomes for DTPILLAR publishing operations appear in many instances to have been different from those of covert CIA publishing operations in Africa and elsewhere during this period. As Peter Benson argues in *Black Orpheus, Transition, and Modern Cultural Awakening in Africa*, some of the CIA's foreign publishing projects appeared to have had less focus on the politics of the projects they funded and more focus on establishing contacts with local intellectuals. Caroline Davis's examination of the impacts of the CIA's 1950s and 1960s covert funding of African literary projects found only limited impacts on specific works produced by funded African authors, but she found a significant increase in the presence and importance of US publishers in Africa.[75] However, among the more significant outcomes she identified coming from these secret CIA publishing operations were the formation of social networks and ongoing connections with African intellectuals as up and coming regional figures of significance.[76] While the DTPILLAR-funded publishing programs described here usually had more direct anticommunist messages than those examined by Davis, these Asia programs also sometimes created significant long-term networks linking the agency with those they secretly funded.

These covert CIA efforts to manipulate news and entertainment in propagandistic ways show Americans using deceit to try and persuade Asians to reject communism, and these uses of deceit tainted the products and results of these programs. When they involved tactics like book burning and the culling of intellectual critiques, they betray totalitarian streaks that have long been present in CIA covert operations claiming to be fighting for freedom and liberation. When these duplicitous CIA publishing operations were exposed in the mid-1970s, the final report of the Church Committee found "two reasons for concern. The first is the potential, inherent in covert media operations, for manipulating or incidentally misleading the American public. The second is the damage to the credibility and independence of a free press which may be caused by covert relationships with the U.S. journalists and media organizations."[77] DTPILLAR's media operations at times generated both these troubling outcomes.

At a minimum, the CIA's interest in these 1950s and 1960s book projects sought to establish positive feelings about the United States, but there were other desired outcomes as well. In some instances, Rostowian visions of modernization drove the establishment of bookshops that would sell subsidized books that could assist Asian nations in their evolutionary progression to modernization and its promise of mass consumption. An examination of a 1951 catalog of the CIA-backed Indonesian Pacific Book and Supply's stock shows an impressive mix of classic American works of fiction and biography, mixed with a large selection of books pushing horticultural sciences, engineering, and a variety of mechanical innovations.[78] In many of these transactions, the goal may have been nothing more than to inculcate positive associations with Americans who had made these books available at very low, highly subsidized prices—an outcome with some value given the similar efforts by Soviet or Chinese communist subsidized publishing operations. But there was also the more obvious culling of intellectual strands viewed as unfavorable to US economic and political interests, and DTPILLAR took measures to limit which ideas were propagated.

But as with the foundation's filmmaking and newspaper ventures, anticommunist or pro-Western narratives were the common threads linking many of the CIA's sponsored media ventures during the 1950s and 1960s. Most of what is known about the CIA's book publishing programs during this period shows the agency funding the writing, publishing, and distribution of academic works promoting anticommunist messages wrapped in the respectability of what appeared to be normal academic publishing. Yet, in the committee and foundation's often clumsy efforts to infuse anticommunist messages into low-budget Hong Kong action films, we find parallel propaganda motifs shared with their more highbrow academic campaigns.

In the mid-1950s, the foundation's interest in being involved in the Hong Kong film industry cooled, and by 1958 it was willing to just give Chang Kuo-sin full ownership of Asian Pictures, as the foundation pulled out of film work.[79]

After the Committee for Free Asia transformed itself into the Asia Foundation, it continued to support various book and publishing operations, but it increasingly supported projects reaching out to Asian intellectuals and supporting academic ventures, while funding fewer projects aimed at capturing the popular imagination in the way these 1950s film projects had sought to do.

9 Asia Foundation Reports as Active and Passive Intelligence

The Field Representative has been the core of [Asia] Foundation operations; there is one for nearly every Asian country in which the Foundation has an ongoing project. He (they have always been men) is usually assigned to a country for several years and his immersion in local affairs affords him an expertise which quite naturally influences Foundation decisions on country projects.

BEVERLY J. BREWSTER / *American Overseas Library Technical Assistance*

Committee for Free Asia and Asia Foundation staff stationed or traveling abroad routinely sent reports back to headquarters describing local developments. During Robert Blum's years as president, he traveled for a significant amount of time in Asia, where he met with staff, Asian educators, intellectuals, journalists, politicians, and other local leaders. The reports generated by CFA and Asia Foundation staff collected significant information on a range of local developments; these reports often contained details and backstories that would otherwise be difficult to acquire in a world where news traveled slowly through official channels.

How these reports were used outside of foundation offices remains unclear, but what is clear is that CIA sponsors had access to foundation reports and that the CIA reported occasionally receiving actionable intelligence from the committee and foundation. During the 1950s and 1960s, staff generated thousands of short field reports describing political developments, with frequent observations concerning local attitudes toward communism. For example, in a 1954 report on a trip to Borneo, staffer John Carroll's chronicles of his travels included a list of the 117 individuals with whom he spoke. He sent this report back to headquarters with notes about each of them. His reports were rich with detailed descriptions, such as this passage reporting on villages in North Borneo, where he observed that

> Communists are almost as rare as the dodo. . . . In Sarawak, the Communists are not strong, but they have been more active than in North Borneo. Pro-Communist teachers reportedly are still working in some of the secondary schools. On August 9, 1953, the Sarawak government

declared a state of emergency after a group called the Sarawak Indonesian People's Liberation Army raided a village near Kuvching and identified the Army tentatively as a group of immigrant Chinese possibly based [near] Pontaianak in Kalimantan. The Government closed the frontier, brought the jungle equipment from Singapore, and mobilized its 1000-man constabulary.[1]

Other field reports were more mundane, detailing the minutiae of daily life or the problems of running an office in a foreign country.

While there was great variety in details or focus in these field reports, they shared textured details of developments, moods, and attitudes gathered from on-the-ground-perspectives from all over Asia. Different representatives produced varying narratives. There were often ethnographic sensibilities that included statements about the attitudes, stability, disquiet, or incipient movements in distant locales far from staff offices in San Francisco and New York or at CIA headquarters in Langley, Virginia.

JAMES STEWART'S WARTIME TRAVELOGUE

During the early 1950s, as the committee was establishing itself abroad, staff frequently met with Asian governmental personnel to discuss possible programs. Following these trips, staff usually wrote lengthy reports noting the individuals they met, often including vignettes reflecting the local political climate. The staff were often products of solid liberal arts or journalistic educations; many had studied at elite universities, which meant that most were excellent writers, sometimes producing narratives that sounded like the work of seasoned literary travelers. To give some sense of the quality and coverage of this work, below are some entries excerpted from James Stewart's seven-thousand-word, six-day diary of his 1952 trip to the Korean Peninsula during the Korean War. In his "Private-Confidential. Conversations in Korea," he wrote,

> Sunday Morning, Sept. 28, up at six. Packed, ate breakfast and proceeded to George Paik's home by Pusan taxi at 7:30 a.m. Pusan taxis are lettered A and B. They operate on alternate days. Sunday was B day. Other incidental intelligence on Pusan: the crowds which are phenomenal are rated less than a year ago. Still, it is impossible to walk down any Pusan street without being jostled. Often one must brush his way

through merchants and soldiers and beggars. The little boy beggars work in gangs. When they see a well-dressed Korean lady—and there are many, many of them—they push up against her and harry her until she gives them some money. Seoul people control 60 to 70 per cent of Pusan's business and industry. Traders of all kinds are making money, but there is an acceleration of business toward the close of day because good merchants do not want to keep any currency overnight. It may depreciate by morning, they say, and they would prefer to have acquired some new goods in place of the old. Behavior of UN troops, according to my personal observation, was very good except for the driving. The driving is hideous. Surely, some way can be found to have only Korean drivers on UN vehicles in the Communication Zone.

Houses of prostitution are openly permitted. For a while, rather detailed sign boards were permitted but the authorities thought this was not in good taste. So that now there are such signs as SUNSHINE LAUNDRY, short time 20,000 won; longtime 40,000 won. The signs proclaim developing and enlarging inside! All such signs for such houses are painted light blue—the UN color. No one is quite sure whether this is attempted Eastern courtesy, satire, or availability of UN paint on the black market. The price of gasoline on the black market is lower than the official price not by the Korean Government. Gasoline and oil are the main black market commodity in Pusan today. Percentage of stolen vehicles is very low although the actual number is considerable[.] General Herren said in one day's round-up 140 stolen jeeps and trucks were recovered. Some 18 were being driven by assemblymen and several by missionaries or church groups.

But the description of Pusan would be terribl[y] erroneous if it did not include the fact that suffering is widespread and acute. There are, perhaps, a hundred thousand families whose standard of living has sunk and sunk until now the children are taking to the streets and husband or wife or both are sinking into abject despondency. Certain government salaries (the cash part less irregular payments of rice, salt, cotton cloth, etc.) are no more than 40,000 won a month. A pack of Camels on the black market sells for 60,000 won. Suicides in Pusan are all too frequent and there seems to be an increasing group of people—men and women alike—who mentally are at the border-line of insanity. I saw twice rather refined looking women walking down the street suddenly burst into tears. I saw innumerable sudden fist fights among men and boys and one hair-pulling fight between women. I am sure there is a point at which most of us crack up. For many Koreans that point is even now being reached. There are occasional tableaux to be seen from vantage points in Pusan which look for all the world like the opening scenes in the old H. G. Wells movie, The Shape of Things to Come. The result of communist aggression in Asia has been to create a stupendous class of wanderers, no place to go[,] an increasingly hazy remembrance of where they have come from, shuffling along in an epitome of aimlessness. . . .

George Paik on Sunday morning checked the three names of potential workers for the Committee carefully. He then said they were all right. He would try to guide them, giving our Committee translation and acquisition-of-manuscripts program as much attention as he could. He said he was delighted with our proposed program because it fits in so well with an ambition he has always had which is to create something called a Book Depot. He said this would be a Mobile library for intellectuals consisting of the best contemporary Asian writings against communism and in support of Asian-type freedom and independence. He said all countries needed more books in their own languages and he thought that the best books for translations in Asia would be books written by Koreans, Chinese, Indians, etc. We discussed the establishment, perhaps in India of a "Modern Library of Asia." We thought perhaps a standard-looking edition, despite the variety of languages[,] might be attractive and gradually establish itself as the best in a tremendous field for live fiction and authoritative historical analysis. . . .

Back at the hotel, I ran into Ahn Ho Sang, former minister of education, the German-trained lame-brained super-nationalist; the last man in Korea that I wanted to see. He was his usual disagreeable self. It was all America's fault, he said. He had warned that the communists would come down. The State Department had sold out the Korean people. Now everything was lost. The government was not good (he happens to be out of office), the economy is no good, the Korean army is not good. I took exception to the last point. He insisted, said the Korean troops didn't have enough food. This is an outrageous charge. Ahn shook his finger at me. You accused me of being a fascist, he said, but now look at the state of our country. We must arm the students, we must kill the communist sympathizers, and so on. I reminded him that I had never used the term fascist, and that I thought he and I had gotten along very well in the past. I wanted to get him to admit he was delivering a canned speech. He smiled a little weakly. After 20 minutes I managed to break away. He made the standard remark: anything he could do for the Committee he would be glad to do, he said. No thank you, Dr. Ahn, no thanks!

Later in the day I met General Lloyd of UNKRA [United Nations Korean Reconstruction Authority] and Mr. Plimsole, retiring Australian representative of UNCURK [United Nations Committee for Unification and Rehabilitation of Korea]. Plimsole gave me a solid half-hour of his evaluation of the Korean situation which I found most helpful. In brief, he felt that while the President had exceeded his constitutional authority, the compromise solution whereby his amendment was passed making the presidency a general elective office was the best possible solution to a "sticky" situation. He said he was glad to be leaving, but that he had learned a lot in Korea. He too spoke about the unfortunate intemperance of the opposition. He could offer no solution to the problems of Korea. Perhaps because of his UN position he did not respond when I said I thought the only hope was for the truce to fail and for the UN line to be pushed northward somewhere above the Pyongyang-Hamhung line. He seemed sorry to hear that the Committee did not contemplate a large-scale program in Korea. He rather thought that a new and vigorous information program bringing political enlightenment to the Korean people was indicated. I said the UN would have to develop such a program with the ROK authorities. He didn't see much hope in this. He said he looked forward to this new assignment—he has been named Australian Minister and Chief of Mission in Djakarta, said he would keep the Committee in mind and recommend good works for us when he thought of them.[2]

While many of Stewart's entries recounted conversations with government figures, in this entry his prose also captured some of the human tragedy of Korea—the hopeless damage spilling over from the front lines to spread out across the countryside. Stewart's frustrations appear on the surface of these reports. His feelings enriched the report's narrative in ways that must have captured the attention of those reading this report stateside, and these personal insights provided rare views of a rapidly changing situation half a world away.

COLLECTING TRAVELERS' REPORTS

The foundation regularly sought reports from scholars or others traveling in regions of interest. In one instance, the foundation reached out to political scientist and propaganda specialist Harold Laswell upon learning he would be traveling in Asia in 1962, and arrangements were made for him to meet with staff in Hong Kong. Later, Laswell submitted a seven-page research proposal, "The Importance of Studying Corruption."[3]

CFA board member Walter H. Mallory mailed the foundation twenty-three reports during a 1952 Indonesia trip. These detailed local suspicions about US interests in the region.[4] Mallory's reports revealed much about Americans' misunderstandings of Indonesia. He expressed discomfort at Indonesians' criticisms of the United States and was surprised to find "colonialism and capitalism are lumped together with the other Western abhorrence." His ethnocentrism left him dismayed that Indonesians were not more grateful that Americans had died fighting for Indonesia's freedom during World War II. Mallory concluded that "the animosity toward the West stems from dissatisfaction with Dutch rule over the past 300 years. We, in America, we're told that The Netherlands was the model colonial power. But this was true only in the sense that they wrung the maximum profit out of the resources of these islands, and out of the sweat of their inhabitants."[5]

Mallory reported on meetings with Indonesian political figures discussing efforts to limit the power of Indonesian communists. Hadji Agus Salim, an Indonesian revolutionary leader and erstwhile foreign minister, told Mallory that "no Mohammedan can possibly be a Communist," and he critiqued the United States' approach, saying, "Don't keep telling us to oppose Communism, and don't keep telling us to fear it . . . for that is negative. Tell us, rather what we can do to make a better life for our people, and a better world for our people to live in." Mallory asked, "But isn't that exactly what we are trying to do in the Point IV program, give people a better standard of living[?]" Salim scoffed at Mallory, saying that, like the Soviets, all that Mallory could do was to "think on the materialistic plane." Salim lectured Mallory on Indonesia's disinterest in being a Cold War pawn, saying that Western aid "was to buy my support—not simply to help me."⁶ These local critiques were alien to Mallory, and while he did not seem to understand them, he understood the importance of sharing them with CFA headquarters.

Mallory observed a street demonstration he estimated had from five thousand to fifteen thousand protesters surrounding the National Palace. The police guard held a line with their "fingers on triggers, and rifles and tommy guns pointed toward the mob. A sound truck arrived and President Sukarno came out and spoke to the people. They were mostly laborers and young boys. They smoked and talked among themselves, and it was obvious that they had not the slightest knowledge of why they were there, or what the affair was all about. The President spoke for about an hour and a quarter."⁷ Mallory's arrogant dismissal of protesters' ability to understand why they were protesting expressed his distance from those he reported on.

Mallory's wife also collected political information. Some of her observations came from local interactions, like those she had at a Women's International Club, where she observed that out of the eight Indonesians in the club, four were socialists and two were communists. She was "surprised at how frankly some of them talk."⁸

EAST PAKISTAN'S MAN OF THE PEOPLE

Foundation staff sometimes reported on their encounters with famous Asians. One such profile appeared in an unidentified foundation staff member's six-page report to President Blum providing a first-person account of his 1957 audience with Abdul Hamid Khan Bhashani, an East Pakistan political icon. This encounter occurred outside Bhashani's home on a crowded public street in Kagmari where there was "a carnival atmosphere with tea shops, vendors of [betel] nut and tobacco everywhere." Bhashani was described as a controversial figure who was "called at the same time, by different people, a Communist, a tool of [Prime Minister Suhrawardy] . . . , a tool, a demagogue, a man of compassion, ignorant, illiterate and ineffective, an astute politician, the most powerful man in Pakistan's politics today, a has-been." While some in West Pakistan called him a communist, his East Pakistan supporters saw him as their spokesperson, and many of the poor at this gathering revered him.⁹ The report described the scene as a growing crowd assembled, waiting for Bhashani to appear: "I waited among the mélange of farmers, assembled Awami Leaguers, and government officials of nearly all ranks. There was a feeling in my mind that a page had been taken from a book on Gandhi, though the parallel cannot be carried too far. Here were the common people squatting patiently awaiting their turn to see Bhashani. They were being fed out of his bustling kitchen. I was told by Mr. Stockwell Everts of the U.S. Consulate in Dacca that there was free food for all at Kagmari."[10] Foundation staff eventually met with Bhashani, who expressed admiration for the democracies of the United States and Britain. Learning of the foundation's work, he showed approval, given the foundation's (claimed) nongovernmental affiliation. The report observed that "the paradox of the situation was striking. The Maulana, barefoot and dirty like most of his constituency outside, sitting on his straw mat with a grimy 'toupee' on his head, was interrupted constantly by telegrams from all parts of Pakistan and probably from the country's top minister's government. A stack of official looking correspondence, held down by jars of curd, occupied one corner while children perched on the windowsills outside and they, and beggars, farmers, and the curious in general peered in."[11] Bhashani voiced dissatisfaction that most international aid was allocated to West Pakistan and that West Pakistan controlled the army. He complained that foreign aid workers in East Pakistan stayed in posh quarters and ate fancy foods while telling locals what they should do differently—as if they understood what they critiqued. Bhashani wanted technical knowledge from the West, saying that what was needed was "your technicians, your books, your professors, your knowledge" and adding that once these had been provided he would know that the West understood their problems. The foundation representative noted, "As I listened to his recommendations as he embellished them in detail and with some eloquence, I was struck by what could easily be considered a thesis on the work of the Asia Foundation and its orientation to Asian needs. I tried several times to interrupt to tell him about our books program, our seeds program, our bringing in program and project personnel, our constant desire to give leadership opportunities and develop leadership qualities among Pakistanis and other Asian peoples. Again, it was a case of his wanting to soliloquize."[12] Bhashani described his "regional autonomy" plan that could bring a power balance for East Pakistan, stating that if there wasn't regional autonomy by 1960, he was prepared to "fight." He ended by saying that some had called him a communist, but that this was not true, that he was a socialist, and he viewed socialism as having the promise of solving East Pakistan's problems.

After an hour-long lecture in Bengali, his son-in-law translated what he had said into English. The foundation report described him as sincere, concluding he was not a communist and stressing that "he is revered by the masses" and that these views were widespread throughout East Pakistan. He spoke in plain terms and did not take on the stereotypical role of a Muslim holy man always quoting scriptures.

The foundation concluded Bhashani would likely accept foundation books, seed packets, and assistance from agricultural specialists, as well as foundation funding for his cultural organization. The report stressed the importance of remaining in contact with Bhashani and keeping him interested in foundation programs, even suggesting that the foundation try and "put him under some obligation to a private American organization, thus deflating the balloon he has floated opposing American aid as ineffective."[13]

THE COMMITTEE'S BLUNT ASSESSMENT OF NEHRU

In 1952, CFA representative James Stewart speculated on how the proposed policies of India's prime minister, Jawaharlal Nehru, could shape that country's relationship with the United States and the world. Stewart was surprised the Ford Foundation had increased operations in India, though he did not believe Ford's projects would have much impact. He worried India's communists could not be "defeated by the expedient of sending a couple of American children to Indian schools." He was suspicious of Nehru's attacks on Chiang Kai-shek. He worried India had only a shallow commitment to democracy and that, "like many other government leaders past and present, [Nehru] is beginning to confuse the welfare of his country with the well-being of himself."[14]

Stewart correctly predicted CFA would face difficulties operating in India under Nehru, and he advised sending a committee representative to Nehru and to the US embassy to explain exactly what their programs could accomplish. Several early CFA programs supported Indian students, providing books and other materials to "counter the flood of cheap Communist literature ... sold throughout India, in bookstalls, railroad stations, and public squares."[15] Stewart understood that the committee's "work in India will be complicated by the fact that there is in that country a minority of over-educated, highly articulate intellectuals who espouse the policy of neutralism. While our strategic enemy throughout Asia is Communism, our tactical opposition is neutralism." Stewart wanted "to shame Indian intellectuals into a realization that the position of which they seem to be so proud is not one of valor or dignity but is born of moral cowardice."[16] Stewart's tactic of shaming intellectuals was not adopted, though many programs were designed to undermine neutrality. DTPILLAR increasingly relied on positive reinforcement strategies of funding intellectuals who showed promise for ultimately thinking in ways aligned with the West, and Stewart's strategic views moderated over time.

KLAUSNER'S 1960 TRAVELS IN LAOS

In the early 1960s Catholics were the only missionaries working in the remote tribal areas of Laos. When William Klausner learned from Buddhist priests in Laos that there were no plans to expand Buddhists' presence in these remote regions, he saw an opportunity for the foundation to support Buddhists undertaking development projects in this region. He suggested to the foundation's Laos representative that he cooperate with the Ministry of Religion there and local ecclesiastical officials to "work out a plan to give special training in education and medical programming to selected Buddhist priests of Kha origin."[17] These priests would travel to tribal areas and implement foundation-sponsored microdevelopment programs.

Klausner wrote that while many of these tribal groups still engaged in "certain animistic practices," he reasoned they "might, after lengthy contact with Buddhist priests, accept the new faith and the leadership of the priests who could then exercise that leadership to bring about improvements in the social, medical, and educational spheres."[18] These proposed Buddhist missionary projects envisioned basic counterinsurgency goals of establishing regional stability in ways aligned with state power. Klausner was concerned some priests might be aligned with rebels, noting that several priests had recently left the priesthood to join rebel groups, but he expressed no concern about US government funds financing attempted religious conversions.[19]

Klausner recounted stories of disrespectful soldiers fueling villagers' resentment of the Laotian army, as drunken soldiers raped women, shot pigs, and committed other violent acts.[20] He reported that Lao villagers' belief in magic was used for political ends. In one story a political faction "established themselves as leaders by using ordinary parlor room magician tricks and one was particularly respected because of the amazing things he could do with one of his eyes; an ordinary glass eye used to advantage."[21] He collected stories of genies allying with politically powerful humans, as well as of humans who could turn into animals or become invisible and were reported to be allies of political figures. Klausner wrote, "It is important to realize that not only the villagers, but officials believe in these stories" and that these beliefs helped maintain positions of power. He recognized that "although we may tend to disregard these stories as foolish and unimportant, they are a very valuable key to understanding the villagers' mentality, what is important and meaningful to [them], and what factors may affect the leadership role of an individual."[22]

BLUM'S TRAVELS

The CIA approved of the changes President Blum brought as he prepared to transform the Committee for Free Asia into the Asia Foundation. One 1954 CIA memo observed that under Blum's leadership "for the first time, the beginning of the new fiscal year finds CFA led by a person in whom CIA, the Committee for Free Asia, and the staff of CFA have the greatest confidence. Robert Blum has squeezed some of the water out of the organizational structure, has defined CFA's targets more sharply and has refined its methods of operating."[23] Chief among the new "targets" Blum identified were Asian intellectuals, and he courted Asian elites with new academic programs.

Blum's busy international travel schedule had him meeting with Asian leaders, scholars, reporters, future political leaders, embassy personnel, and foundation field staff. While traveling, Blum reported on these encounters, sometimes traveling with a Dictaphone and using embassy pouches to send home dictation for transcription. These reports read like ready-made intelligence dossiers, and Blum's personal papers archived at Yale include collections of enlarged glossy photographs of dozens of groups of people, meticulously labeled with the names of those he met.

The CIA sometimes used Blum's reports as intelligence briefing documents. Examples of Blum reports released by CIA under FOIA include his "Report on Visit to Cambodia, November 24–28, 1954," and his "Report on Visit to Vietnam, November 20–24, and November 29, 1954."[24] His travel reports contained profiles of public and private individuals in Afghanistan, Burma, Cambodia, Hong Kong, India, Indochina, Indonesia, Laos, Nepal, South Korea, the Philippines, Thailand, and other political hot spots of the 1950s and 1960s.

Blum's meetings with journalists abroad allowed him to gather local information and to generate positive publicity for the foundation. While visiting India in 1955, Blum met with A. M. Rosenthal, then Delhi's *New York Times* correspondent, to discuss Indian policy and the rise of the Soviets' status in India. Rosenthal confided in Blum that from a US perspective, he believed that "the next month or so was going to be a very dangerous one because of the inevitable negotiations for large scale Soviet aid to India."[25] While traveling to Laos in November 1960, Blum met with *Time* magazine correspondent Jerrold Schecter, who briefed him on recent political developments and interviewed Blum, leading to a favorable *Time* magazine article stressing that "the Foundation has developed a unique and very important approach to foreign aid."[26]

Blum often wrote brief evaluative profiles of scholars he met during his travels. Typical of the sort of information he included in these short dossiers is this passage from his 1954 visit to Indonesia, recounting his encounter with Cornell political scientist George McT. Kahin. In it Blum reported as follows:

> Kahin said that the situation in Indonesia was not good and that the government was spending a lot of time talking about the international position of Indonesia as a member of the Colombo group in order to distract attention from domestic failure. He said that Sukarno was a revolutionary by training and experience and could not adapt well to the requirements of stable political life. There was no evidence that Sukarno was a doctrinaire communist, but Sukarno had told Kahin that he admired greatly what the communists had done, for example, in bringing about unity and political stability in China and their ability to organize their youth. Kahin does not think that there is an early danger of a communist take-over but is worried that political disintegration is gradually setting in.[27]

Such reports by Blum contained candid evaluations of political developments or summaries of the personality traits of individuals he encountered.

Memos and correspondence record Blum working alone and with others to compile information on scholars working in Asia. One undated memo indicates that Shannon McCune told Blum how to access State Department materials, advising Blum to "make a list of all of the Ford, Fulbright, Carnegie, Rockefeller, Guggenheim, etc. awardees who are going to Asia and see that these lists are sent to the Field representatives." Contact with these awardees was facilitated by San Francisco staff passing along information to field staff.[28]

Blum's November 1955 trip to India coincided with visits by party secretary Nikita Khrushchev and Premier Nikolai Bulganin. Blum used this charged political moment to try to establish an official presence in India by introducing "the Foundation to the Indian authorities and non-governmental leaders in a [more] favorable light than they had known it in the past." His efforts to establish an India office failed, but he remained hopeful, writing that he had made some progress and "it has now become possible, moreover, to continue or start certain types of work in the absence of a resident representative, without running the risk of being accused of subterfuge as was the case in the past."[29]

Blum briefly met with Prime Minister Nehru, though Nehru seemed tired and "spoke very little." Blum was unsure if Nehru was paying attention. However, after Blum

> explained the recent history of The Asia Foundation and some of the difficulties that had arisen in our relations with the Indian Government, he murmured that our name was not a very happy one, but it was obvious that he was thinking of the name Committee for Free Asia, and I pointed this out to him. I showed him a copy of our brochure, pointed to the names of our Board members and to the three purposes of the Asia Foundation as listed in our charter. He seemed to look at the brochure rather carefully, and in response to my prodding commented cautiously that the purpose of the Foundation as listed seemed sound. He added, however, that India did not want propaganda to be conducted in India by foreign organizations, that the line was a very hard one to draw, and that there was also a danger that competitive propaganda would start.[30]

Blum reported his interactions with various Indian officials, ministers, private citizens, educators, university administrators, journalists, and others, noting which individuals or organizations appeared open to the possibility of working with the foundation or receiving foreign funds for programs.[31]

Following Khrushchev's visit to India were visits by Burma's prime minister and the Saudi king. These official visits confirmed India's Cold War ascendancy. The political implications of these visits were obvious, as India's Vice President Radhakrishnan cautioned Blum during his visit: "We know that we are being courted by many suitors.... Do not think that we are gullible."[32]

Three years later, Nehru still did not trust the foundation, and Blum, understating Indian skepticism of the foundation, insisted against abundant evidence to the contrary that Nehru was "the only high official in India who seems to retain an unfavorable attitude toward the Foundation."[33] The following year Blum met with leaders from the Committee of World Brotherhood in India and planned an "All-India conference to deal with the problems of creating democratic institutions and Asia." The foundation used contacts within the Committee of World Brotherhood to get permission from the Indian government to help fund the conference, and during the planning stages the foundation established that "the main participants would come from every political party within India except the Communists and would be representative of various professions."[34] With selective funding for specific forms of democracy, the foundation supported hand-picked individuals and groups, while denying funds to those who might not support American interests.

After a 1956 meeting with Indonesian prime minister Ali Sastroamidjojo, Blum reported that the prime minister "said that he and his government had not been adequately informed by us concerning the Foundation's purposes and activities; we had, he said, merely set up an office and were working in many fields."[35] When the prime minister asked about connections between the Committee for Free Asia and the Asia Foundation, Blum stressed that the foundation "conducted no propaganda whatsoever to which he commented obliquely that there were many kinds of propaganda: was not the mere fact of giving aid a form of propaganda?" Later, the prime minister mentioned accusations that the foundation had interfered with elections in Ceylon, but Blum dismissed claims that the foundation engaged in any political activities.[36]

During the summer of 1957, Blum traveled for six weeks in Asia, writing reports from each stop along the way.[37] In Burma, he found "the general situation appears to have deteriorated somewhat, due largely to the worsening economic position and the inability of government leaders to make up their minds on major government policies, including to end the armed troubles." He described Afghanistan as "trying to toe a narrow line in foreign policy while taking advantage of aid opportunities offered it from both the USSR and Western countries," while Pakistan showed "political uncertainty." Still, he found potential in "an atmosphere where there are innumerable opportunities for useful activity and few restraints," which allowed "considerable freedom" for the foundation. Blum reported on conditions in Thailand just days before Field Marshal Pibul's successful coup, observing that "political change seemed imminent." He foresaw trouble for Singapore's coming independence, reporting that "no one was very confident how self-government for Singapore, scheduled for next year, would actually work out," but he also reported that Malaya had confidence in its independence.[38]

Following his September 1957 visit to Afghanistan, Blum wrote of finding that significant changes had taken place over the previous two years, reporting that "the country is run to a large extent as a police state, although it is probable that the repression does not directly affect the lives of the vast majority of the population." He described the new government as isolationist and lacking due process, as it had imprisoned former government officials "without formal explanation and released [them] with equal unpredictability."[39]

Blum's confidential board reports sometimes included notes on meetings with Asian dissidents. A 1957 Thailand report described his meeting with Nai Kukrit, a Thai writer "who was recently released from jail where he had been put because of criticism of the American Ambassador." Blum found Kukrit to be "very complimentary of the work of the Asia Foundation," telling Blum that the foundation was one of the few American appendages not subject to criticism for backing the Thai government.[40]

The negative associations linked to the CFA stigmatized the foundation for years following its name change. After a 1957 visit to Burma, Blum reported with some irritation that the Burmese government suspiciously monitored the foundation's activities, yet government representatives still told him they appreciated the foundation's work. Blum conceded that "some of the troubles we had with regard to the agreement [with the Burmese government] were a part of the legacy from the earlier days when the Committee for Free Asia was engaged in direct anti-Communist propaganda and work conducted in a less than public manner."[41]

BLUM'S REPORTS AS INTELLIGENCE GATHERING AND ANALYSIS

When Blum traveled to political hot spots, his reports included analysis of recent developments that were otherwise difficult to come by. In November 1960, just hours after his arrival in Vietnam, rebels launched a thirty-hour coup against President Ngo Dinh Diem. Blum noted drily in his report that "as a result of this attempt and of the accompanying disturbances in the city, my entire schedule was upset," though these events provided opportunities to gather information on these developments, which included frank assessments of how dire the situation appeared.[42]

From the Philippines, Blum reported concerns that governmental failures to provide basic social and economic services empowered communist critics, and he worried that governmental failures to take advantage of foundation programs would further weaken the government.[43] An unplanned trip to Singapore led Blum to report his surprise on just "how precarious the situation" there was with Lee Kuan Yew's coming to power on an anti-Western platform.[44]

In Laos in 1961, Blum reported political ambivalence among locals, who told him "they are not quite sure what they can do with their independence now that they have it."⁴⁵ He described a "continued state of insecurity in Laos" while pitching foundation programs designed to bring certain types of stability aligned with American interests.⁴⁶ Blum frequently reported on the local impacts of the United States' communist competitors in the countries he visited. One 1960 report from Cambodia observed,

> There is a good deal of evidence in Cambodia of Russian and Chinese aid, especially in the form of plants and institutions, such as the new Russian hospital and factories, plants and apartments provided by the Chinese. According to some reports that I heard, the Cambodians who have returned from Communist China have been critical, reporting that conditions there are bad. On the other hand, there is no openly expressed pro-nationalist sentiment among the Chinese residents in Cambodia although privately most of the older generation of Chinese feel that way. The younger generation tends to be pro-Communist whereas government officials tolerate the Communists and are much influenced by bribes.⁴⁷

Evaluating the chances that US aid programs could generate positive feelings toward the United States, Blum characterized Cambodians as "diffident, not energetic and sometimes cautious in dealing with Americans."⁴⁸

Blum's 1961 reports on Burma's deteriorating economic and political conditions described "increased restlessness and even open hostility towards the Burman Government of the various minority groups." He viewed the roots of these groups' harassment as coming from the official establishment of Buddhism as the state religion.⁴⁹ He noted increasing Burmese suspicions that the United States was secretly "helping the KMT [NLF] forces in Burma and giving support to the insurgents." Blum possibly knew about CIA covert support for these NLF forces, through Operation Paper, which made illegal arms shipments to the NLF, but he downplayed these suspected CIA covert activities to Burmese officials.⁵⁰ He dismissively reported that "it may be however that some Burmese merely keep this alleged suspicion alive as a means of demonstrating that the insurgents have no genuine support within Burma and as a means of discrediting them."⁵¹

In 1958, Blum described Cambodia's Prince Sihanouk as "erratic," noting "the communists have been able to make considerable inroads through flattery and propaganda. It is doubtful, however, whether they have immediate plans to try and take over control of Cambodia. For the present, it probably suits their purposes better to use Cambodia as a base from which to harass neighboring Thailand and Vietnam. Prince Sihanouk seems so confident of his ability to master his country's many problems that he is probably insufficiently aware of the seriousness of the communist danger." Blum took comfort in Sihanouk's public anticommunist stance and reported that in private conversations he said "all of his enemies could be found at the receptions of the Soviet Embassy."[52]

Blum's reports frequently described how local political issues created difficulties for foundation prospects. A 1958 report on the status of Indonesian development recorded how postponed elections, rising fuel prices, and new mining laws "angered the communists." The US ambassador told Blum that because of these issues, President Sukarno's "government did not want to risk being associated with the Asia Foundation." Blum described the growing strength of the Indonesian Communist Party (PKI) in Java, noting especially the party's growth in rural areas and that "so far the Government has not developed any effective program to combat it. The communists are still close to Sukarno and this is a situation that causes a good deal of concern to the other parties. The communists, moreover, succeed in frightening and paralyzing others and create in them a fear of being known as anti-communists, which is identified in many minds as being pro-colonialist and pro-American."[53]

Because of his previous work for the Mutual Security Administration, Blum knew key Vietnamese political actors, and he drew on these connections during his travels. In 1958, Blum visited with President Diem several times, and he wrote detailed reports on his conversations with Vietnam's leader, as well as with some of Diem's critics.[54] Blum's 1958 report from Vietnam interwove observations on rural changes with reports on his conversations with political leaders. Tran Van Do confided that Vietnamese "disunity existed because Diem behaved as a conqueror in South Vietnam, and he always showed favoritism to Central Vietnam," while his favoring of Catholics spread unease. Blum reported that when he asked, "What would happen if Diem were to disappear?" Tran Van Do coolly told him "that the problem would not be a serious one and that the Army might possibly take control."[55]

Blum's reports frequently included impressions of locals' support for political leaders or noted shifts in political stability. He routinely populated his reports with names of the local sources providing the views he relayed. The excerpt below, from a 1963 report on a visit to India, exemplifies his penchant for presenting analysis with vignettes incorporating local views:

Nehru's own position has been weakened, although it is doubtful that he has lost much popular support in the country. Some of his earlier critics have seized upon the Sino-Indian affair to emphasize his deficiencies, but in addition there are others, especially among the younger intellectual and professional groups, who were sympathetic to Nehru before but feel today that he is not the man to lead the country. Some of the men in this latter group have changed their position markedly during the past years. For example, G. K. Reddy, Head of the Delhi Bureau of the *Times of India* who had some difficulty a few years ago obtaining a visa to come to the United States because of his suspected left-wing leanings told me regretfully that if only the Chinese attack had lasted two weeks longer Nehru would have been thrown out of office, and the Indian effort could have been mobilized more effectively. It is not expected, however, that Nehru will step down soon, nor is there any clear consensus regarding his successor.[56]

Blum described the subtleties of Asian political factions, often presented in contexts stressing how these divisions related to US policies or possible developments favoring US interests. For example, his analysis of political divisions among Japanese intellectuals was more than a description of cultural differences between groups; it contained potentially actionable information of use to Americans interested in trying to shape elements of Japanese society. This sort of social mapping certainly had many possible uses for a foundation focused on choosing which intellectual factions to fund. Blum noted that divisions between Japanese intellectuals continue

> to be badly split between the Marxists and the others, although such a line is obviously somewhat arbitrary, and there is an important group of non-Marxists left or liberal who are very careful to draw a line between themselves and the conservatives. It is in this middle group that one is most likely to find individuals who are sufficiently representative of the prevailing intellectual climate of Japan without being ideologically committed to a dogmatic Marxist position. The fact that some of these persons are looked upon by the Japanese government or the American Embassy as "progressive" or "anti-American" should not deter us from seeking their cooperation where they are properly qualified.[57]

This does not seem like a mapping of Japanese intellectual divisions for its own sake. Blum noted divisions in ways that could be used by the Asia Foundation and by others interested in furthering anticommunist schisms in Japanese intellectual circles.

BLUM'S AFGHANISTAN OBSERVATIONS

Most of the foundation's late 1950s Afghanistan programs sought to improve academic and economic conditions, while also improving perceptions of Americans, capitalism, and Western democracy. This included soft-power projects like establishing a women's welfare society, building public libraries, funding a small industry guidance center, building schools and classrooms, and funding a research arm of the Ministry of Commerce devoted to studying economic change.[58] In 1962, Blum described Afghanistan's rapid changes and new opportunities there to compete with Soviet economic development programs, claiming that "the climate for Foundation activity is better than ever before."[59] Soviet programs to improve women's status pushed Blum to create the position of advisor in women's activities at the foundation and to increase educational initiatives focused on women's education.[60]

The passage below, from Blum's report on a 1960 visit to Afghanistan, shows the sort of focus and detail typically included in his Dictaphone-recorded travel reports:

> In the evening I had dinner at the home of Harold Schwartz, head of the ICA Mission. Ten years ago, Schwartz was Agricultural Officer in the Mission to Indo-China of which I was the head. Schwartz had invited senior personnel from the Embassy and the ICA Mission in order that I might talk with them about the features of the new aid program. When he was in Washington a month ago, he had heard that I had filed a minority report and was pleased with this because my views corresponded with those of the Mission here in Afghanistan which is fearful lest the situation and needs of the very underdeveloped country such as Afghanistan are not properly understood within the framework of the new foreign aid program. There was also some discussion of the effect of the present crisis with Pakistan on the foreign aid program, inasmuch as all border traffic is closed and in a trial run yesterday an ICA

truck was turned back to the Afghan authorities when it headed for the Pakistan border. The entire ICA effort is now seriously threatened unless border traffic can be reopened[,] as the ICA program depends heavily on the transportation of goods, supplies and equipment through Pakistan.[61]

Neocolonialist notions of superiority permeated these reports, revealing views of racialized Western salvation exported to what were regarded as "backward" peoples in ways that sublimated relationships of debt, obligation, and indentured client status that came with such "gifts" from the West. In a February 1961 report from Afghanistan, Blum ethnocentrically proclaimed that

> it would be well for project people to remind themselves once in a while that they are bringing the benefits of centuries of civilization to people who have not gone through the pain of earning it. We are delivering it in ready-made packages . . . a sort of "instant culture." There are elemental dangers in this: the dangers of choosing the easiest, the pleasantest, and the worst of what is offered. The Afghan tends to drive a car not for transportation but for psychological release; he tends to listen to music not as an exercise in the arts but as an aid to daydreaming; and even the best educated of the men see nothing in ballroom dancing but a jolly, new sexual indoor sport. Here again there is no specific alarm to sound . . . it's merely a hint against tripping on the line of least resistance.
>
> It is easy, either from unconscious conviction or from specious evidence, to give the impression that we are members of a superior race. This sense of being a favored breed is at its strongest when the need arises for the exercise of authority or firmness, or when patience is running low; but it can be displayed unwittingly in the manner of driving a car, or dealing in the marketplace, or merely being alive. It is important, of course, to maintain one's prestige and authority; but it is well to be cautious of sinning on this point while doing it. There are times when the temptation is overwhelming.[62]

Blum understood the dangers of openly admitting these colonial feelings of technological, political, economic, and moral superiority, yet such feelings were difficult for him to sublimate and at times they were apparent in foundation reports.

ENGAGING WITH AN AMERICAN SPOOK AND AN OLD BRITISH HAND

Blum was unimpressed with what he saw during a 1961 visit to Nepal, where he explored the possibility of establishing a foundation presence and described Kathmandu as a "primitive" city. He reported on his meeting with "an Embassy man named Redford" who "spoke as if he knew about the Foundation but he did not discuss any matters in detail although he expressed the hope that the Foundation would be able to develop some activity in Nepal."[63] The "Redford" Blum met was likely Ralph H. Redford, who is listed in the 1960 *Foreign Service List* as the US embassy's second secretary/economics officer, which was likely embassy cover for CIA work.[64] Redford's career as a CIA officer is confirmed in an oral history of John M. Steeves (deputy chief of mission, Jakarta, 1953–55) in which Steeves identified Redford as CIA chief of station in Indonesia during the early 1950s.[65] Blum also meet with Biswa Dandhu Thapa, minister of education and of national guidance, and Blum reported that Thapa was "in the United States when the King took over direct power, and when he returned to Kathmandu [he] was put in jail for a few days before arguing himself out and finding himself Minister of Education and National Guidance. He talked to me volubly and almost without interruption for over an hour until I asked to be excused for another appointment."[66] The foundation did not develop a viable plan to establish programs in Nepal.

Blum also described an encounter with a British expat identified only as Mr. Himsworth, a UN employee who had been stationed in Nepal for five years and working as a public finance advisor to the government.[67] Blum's Himsworth conjures images of the sort of "Old British Hand" found in the writings of Graham Greene or Evelyn Waugh, a type of expat now lost to history. Blum wrote that

> Himsworth has been in Asia for about 30 years having spent 25 years in the British Colonial service. He is cheerfully pessimistic about the situation in Nepal; thinks that he has accomplished nothing during his five years here, and has no illusions about the future. He said that there were two central points that needed to be grasped. One is that the Nepalese are the most likeable people in Asia and the second that they are the most incompetent. All foreign aid must recognize these facts. Several years will be needed during which new ideas and institutions are introduced and only after this period will development start, or to

put it differently, the spark that has been produced by the foreign aid activities will set fire and the Nepalese will then be able to take some of the responsibility themselves. According to Himsworth much of the American aid has been wasted because this really has not been grasped. The Americans, arguing from a Western outlook that is theoretically correct, have felt that they could expect a maximum performance from the Nepalese whereas in fact this is just not possible. Himsworth believes that in this respect the Indians have been on much sounder ground. Himsworth said that he felt by far the best USOM project is the new ropeway that will carry freight to the Indian border. In this case, the Americans are doing the job themselves.

Himsworth went on to say that the Nepalese at the present time are suffering from foreign aid indigestion and he suggested that if The Asia Foundation wanted to do something useful for the country it should stay out. There are now about ten foreign aid programs: American, English, Russian, New Zealand, Ford Foundation, British, WHO, German, Chinese and United Nations.[68]

Himsworth's cheerful pessimism appears well informed and voiced a rare realist's view of the unlikelihood that the global superpowers' projects in this remote corner of the world would have meaningful impacts on the quality of life of the people. Finally, Blum noted that "Himsworth said that if in spite of all of these conditions The Asia Foundation felt a real urge to work in Nepal it should confine its activities to the hill country and stay completely out of the Kathmandu valley. Some of the best people in the country were in the hills and if Nepal is to develop into something more than it is today the leadership will come from the hill people[,] certainly not from the people of the Terai, which is the border just along the Indian border."[69]

Blum did not appear impressed by Himsworth's wisdom or his assessment of Nepalese development prospects, but he dutifully recorded these views.

AFGHANISTAN TRAVELOGUE, BEFORE THE FOUNDATION'S COVER WAS BLOWN

The narratives in foundation field reports sometimes served dual uses. As internal foundation documents, they informed the board and staff of developments and issues facing employees working in distant settings. But with CIA access to these reports, the documents sometimes became valuable raw intelligence sources, with on-the-ground reports providing useful information on current local attitudes or awareness. It would be difficult to overstate the significance of seemingly mundane reports from remote corners of Asia in an era when some regions lacked even reliable telephone service, but foundation staff nevertheless regularly produced a wealth of observations on conditions there. Staff reports provided ongoing snapshots of developments half a world away, informing decision-making processes at the foundation's San Francisco and New York offices, as well as in the Central Intelligence Agency—as confirmed by declassified CIA reports mentioning "actionable intelligence" provided by DTPILLAR reports.

The details provided in President Blum's dictated travel reports show not only the thoroughness of his work but also document DTPILLAR's efforts to push the US Cold War agenda throughout Asia. These reports show Blum meeting with heads of state who at times welcomed foundation programming and at other times remained distant and untrusting of what Blum was selling. But the foundation president remained persistent in his efforts, and even when his hosts correctly stated their good reasons for not believing the foundation's claims that it was not part of a US government propaganda operation, he persisted in his efforts and denials. In this sense, these reports record not only DTPILLAR employees passing along information on these distant lands but also the persistent efforts of DTPILLAR staff pushing CIA Cold War agendas in areas where they were both welcome and unwelcome.

This practice of the CIA reading Asia Foundation reports, and sometimes using them as actionable intelligence—no matter how rare these actionable intelligence instances were—was a betrayal of trust. Every time President Blum or other foundation staff bristled at and denied accusations that the foundation was linked to the CIA or other branches of the US government, these lies compounded foundation betrayals.

It is impressive how many of these field reports provided extensive details on life in remote regions of Asia. A good example of this sort of narrative appears in a March 1966 report from foundation staffer John E. James. The narrative describes his almost two-week road trip through rural Afghanistan, during which he stayed in villages and met with local leaders, workers, and teachers. James's record of this trip to Kandahar and Bost reads like a passage from Graham Greene's *Traveling without Maps*, as James described the sudden coming of spring as he drove south:

There is a scattering of green on even the most inaccessible hills, and Kootchia shepherds have their flocks dispersed among them. Their dull brown tents punctuate the rock valleys. Now and then, a moving family, its goods disposed on donkeys or camels, with babies—lambs, mostly, but now and then a child, rocking contentedly on top of the bundles.

Between Ghazni and Kandahar, the road, a good one built under American supervision, runs through some of the most desolate territory I've encountered. Except for the mountains, some miles away on each side, the only relief is rocks and a rare camel there. There is not even the relief of cactus, as there would be on the American desert, or a mesquite or other desert shrub. Yet this unrelieved landscape has, here and there, a man working on the road, or a shepherd, watching his flock from a slight rise, and now and then, a green depression that means water, agriculture, and settlement. Now and then an orchard is in bloom, the delicate rose and pink of peach apricot blending unobtrusively with the drab khaki background. All colors are subdued in this landscape.

The farmers grub out the camel thorn, pile it in windrows and carry it home to burn. Yet it is humus, if it were turned under the ground and allowed to rot there. Of course, their plows don't turn the ground, as a moldboard plow would. Instead, they scratch the surface down to about four inches. If they did use the camel thorn for humus, what would they burn?[70]

Just twelve months later, whatever cover such backcountry travel had provided for Asia Foundation affiliations was blown, as news of the foundation's CIA ties hit the pages of the *New York Times* and the foundation's survival came into question.[71] These revelations would lead to the termination of the CIA's funding of DTPILLAR, forcing the foundation to find other, non-CIA funding sources and to rethink some of its practices.

10 Suspicions

There are strong reasons to suspect that the covert U.S. agencies use the U.S. social scientists' expertise acquired through field research abroad. This utilization is usually "sanitized" through seemingly respectable organizations.

SATISH SABERWAL / Observation in "The Problem," 1967

From the Committee for Free Asia's earliest years there were suspicions about CIA connections, but it wasn't until March 1967 that the public learned that the Asia Foundation had indeed received agency funds. However, it hadn't taken long for critical Asians to suspect the committee had CIA ties. In 1952, L. Natarajan wrote in his book *American Shadow over India* that the CFA was "close to American Intelligence."[1] Natarajan was suspicious of the committee's Crusade for Freedom funding, and after establishing the links between the CFA board, foundation staff, or the OSS, Natarajan observed that the board's international business interests were the sort of common connections the CIA frequently used.[2] While Natarajan made some unsubstantiated claims about other organizations' CIA links, the truth about CFA's CIA roots supported his suspicions of Americans bringing gifts of foreign aid.[3]

In late 1952, B. G. Fernandes, a student at the University of California, Berkeley, wrote the editors of a CFA publication, the *Asian Student*, questioning who really authored its articles. Fernandes found it odd there was no list of the officers or editorial board, and he doubted that the publication had any Asians on its editorial board. He challenged the editors to publish his letter and to answer his questions about the identities and nationalities of *Asian Student* staff, writers, officers, and editorial board members.[4]

Fernandes's letter generated commotion among CFA staff as they drafted several versions of a response. The final letter adopted a positive, seemingly open tone, while conceding that "there are no Asian[s] on the list of Committee members itself." Removed from the committee reply was draft text claiming that they "will not be satisfied until the newspaper fully reflects the diverse views of the several Asian national and professional groups studying in American universities." Instead, the response claimed that "there are in truth, a large number of Asians on our staff. These men and women are working in fields for which they have trained themselves both academically and professionally. Many of them are radio specialists and journalists, other advisers and administrative supervisors of programs." The reply's tone was friendly, though defensive, and Fernandes was invited to come and visit with staff.[5] Another rejected draft reply, from George M. Keller, director of the foundation's American operations, avoided identifying any characteristics of the individuals working for the *Asian Student* and took a brisker tone.[6]

Fernandes responded to foundation staffer Holbrook Bradley's letter, thanking him for his reply, writing that he and others

> regarded your Committee with reserve since we first came to know about it. There are a number of reasons for this which I need not go into at the present time. But our reserve and our interest were increased with the publication of your paper. We wanted to know more about you, and I discussed your organization with one of your employees whom I expected from your editorial to be among your student editors.
>
> I was surprised to be told that neither this employee nor any of the other Asian students on your staff had been invited to take part in the editing of your paper. My informant who did not show any ill will towards you but was merely to questions [*sic*] resigned I believe soon after because of a feeling, among other reasons, that Asian[s] are generally given an inferior position in your Committee.[7]

Fernandes did not wish the committee to think him "uncivil," but he saw nothing to be gained by further engagement with staff, and he reiterated his request that the *Asian Student* publish his initial letter, stating that if they were not going to publish his letter that they provide an explanation for not doing so.[8] If anyone from the committee answered Fernandes's questions, I could not locate it among the committee's deposited records. These sorts of suspicions about who was behind the committee and foundation persisted for years.

The committee regularly encountered suspicion in the Asian nations where its representatives worked. Their early reception in Burma was a good example. In October 1952, CFA representative James Stewart traveled to Burma, where upon arrival he was detained by government officials after being reportedly mistaken for another individual named Stewart.[9] After Stewart left Burma, communists planted a story in a local newspaper claiming that Rockefeller Foundation president Dean Rusk had issued a statement that the Committee for Free Asia "is running KMT" [Chinese Nationalist troops].[10] The newspaper later published a retraction, but a few days later this was undermined by a *Rangoon*

Daily editorial criticizing the CFA's lack of Asian staff and questioning why an American outfit was trying to free Asia while it had such significant racism at home. The editorial asked, if the committee considers "that they are justified in carrying out anti-Communist activities, they should do it openly under that name and we do not wish to obstruct anyone who is doing what he thinks is right. But if they try to make use of Asian peoples instead of carrying out the work honestly [then] Asian people will eventually suffer and [this] we cannot stand. Our country is neutral and we cannot tolerate any attempt to influence the people and the clergy."[11] The committee weathered such accusations by issuing denials of wrongdoing. But the accusations accumulated.[12]

DESPITE THE NAME CHANGE, SUSPICIONS REMAIN

The Committee for Free Asia's name change to "The Asia Foundation" was meant to distance the organization from the committee's crude propaganda efforts, yet residual clouds of suspicion continued to follow the foundation. It sought a strong relationship with the Indian government, but its suspicions of the foundation's unstated political mission remained. The complexities of India's multiparty politics and US resistance to India's nonaligned political status made some Indians consider the likelihood of unstated links between the foundation and US imperialism. In 1955, Indian diplomats complained that foundation employees were obsessed with "learning names and specific data on communist delegates attending an international conference" as foundation staff suspiciously collected information on Indian conference attendees.[13]

A hand-edited draft foundation document from April 1955, "Principal Allegations by the Government of India and Its Diplomatic Representatives against the Asia Foundation," described Indian government employees' suspicions about the foundation. The document stated that since 1951, Indian government officials had accused the committee and foundation of six forms of wrongdoing or misrepresentation:

1. "The Foundation is a political organization serving political ends."
2. "The Foundation is an 'agent' of the U.S. Government."
3. "The Foundation is closely associated with, or supported by, the 'China Lobby,' Senator [William] Knowland, Wall Street and oil interests in the United States."
4. "Foundation representatives are engaged in intelligence activity."

5. "The Foundation's policy is anti-Indian."
6. "The Foundation's activities in Burma have disturbed the Burmese Government which has discussed the question informally with the Government of India."[14]

A revised version of this report internally circulated within the foundation under the title "A Review of Indian Attitudes toward the Asia Foundation."[15] This in-house document developed talking points to rebut these accusations, weakly stressing differences in the articles of incorporation of the committee versus those of the foundation while failing to address the critique's substantive issues, much less admitting the existence of DTPILLAR.

President Blum, in a report on his spring 1956 India visit, vented that the foundation's problematic relationship with the Indian government grew from the CFA's previous anticommunist campaigns. The foundation had been renamed, but distrust remained, and Blum appeared genuinely surprised that the name change hadn't repaired the organization's reputation. Blum reported on a pleasant meeting with Prime Minister Nehru during which government officials expressed approval of some foundation programs, such as the Nieman Fellowships. But India still would not allow new foundation-sponsored programming.[16]

Throughout his presidency, Blum had to address foreign officials' concerns over rumors of foundation ties to intelligence agencies. In late 1956, Blum wrote a four-page letter to the Indonesian foreign minister, Ruslan Abdulgani, expressing concerns over Indonesian prime minister Ali Sastroamidjojo's suspicions of the foundation. During Blum's visit to Indonesia the previous summer, the prime minister had declined to meet with him, but Blum persevered and ultimately arranged a meeting during a November 1956 visit to the Pacific nation. In this meeting, the prime minister told Blum that the "anti-communist propaganda approach of the Committee for Free Asia was quite unacceptable in Indonesia," while Blum assured him that the organization had been completely remade and did not engage in propaganda. Blum pitched the many programs the foundation had to offer, but he remained unsure whether the prime minister had altered his skeptical view of the foundation.[17]

In the late 1950s, one of the ways the foundation reached out to Indian scholars despite having no official presence in India was to meet prominent Indian academics when they traveled to the United States to attend conferences. Foundation representatives read conference programs to learn which Asian scholars would attend, then foundation staff approached individual scholars and requested meetings. Frequently, staff took these visiting scholars to dinner during conferences, and later on foundation staff would write reports on these meetings and submit them to foundation headquarters. A typical example of these meet-up reports arose from a 1957 dinner to which Louis Lazaroff and Thomas Rusch took Indian anthropologist Mysore Narasimhachar Srinivas, a professor at Baroda University. Accompanying them was UC Berkeley political scientist Richard L. Park. The report shows nothing unusual or improper about the dinner, other than the undisclosed interests of the sponsors and the foundation collecting more information for its files. Srinivas encouraged the foundation to provide social science research funds for India, saying that among the younger generation of Indian scholars "there was a gradual disillusionment among them in particular with the economic theories of the Keynesian model makers and the Marxists and an increasing interest in the field of so-called Indian 'institutional' economics."[18]

While attending the Fifth International Congress of Anthropological and Ethnological Sciences, held in Philadelphia in 1956, US folklorist Moe Asch noticed Chester Roberts's conference nametag stating his Asia Foundation staff affiliation, at which point Asch aggressively asked Roberts if he was with "that bunch who was out to Americanize the world." Asch told Roberts his negative impressions of the foundation came from his interactions with foundation personnel at American Library Association meetings. Roberts spoke with Asch for some time, and after about forty-five minutes, Roberts claimed Asch revised some of his views. Roberts reported that "this talk with Asch was my first encounter with an anti-Foundation attitude at the Congress but it was not my last." Most of the approximately fifty or so attendees he spoke with "held mild to strong unfavorable attitudes" about the Asia Foundation. He attributed most of these negative attitudes as responses to the activities of CFA rather than the foundation. Few of those he spoke with believed the foundation had really changed its "orientation" when it acquired its new name. Roberts found that a few of the people he spoke with

> refused to believe that we were not a part of CIA and to some I was apparently suspect personally. I continually encountered a great deal of curiosity as to what an Asia Foundation representative was doing at the Congress. I rather quickly learned to leave my notebook in my pocket while talking with other people. After I had gotten to know Dr.

Masao Oka, head of the Japanese delegation and Foundation grantee, he admitted that he had been reluctant to seek our assistance because of the bad name which we had throughout Asia. He added that he did not want our assistance to be widely publicized. He also mentioned that he knew of several other people who had refused to seek Foundation assistance in Japan.[19]

The head of the Indian delegation at the anthropology conference, B. S. Guha, refused to be introduced to Roberts, and an interpreter for Japanese attendees told Roberts he had "heard a number of disparaging things about the Foundation." John Donahue (of Michigan State University) told Roberts he had refused a foundation scholarship on advice from a faculty member who had told him it wasn't a good idea to have this association listed on his résumé. Roberts reported that even two years after the name change

> one of the most embarrassing problems which I encountered was that of explaining to someone that although there was a historical relationship between TAF and CFA[,] that CFA was no longer in existence and that the Foundation was operating under a different set of principles and premises, only to have him take out a calling card of one Huan Wen-Shan of the New School for Social Research, New York, which bore the legend in one corner "consultant for the Committee for Free Asia." This made me look rather ridiculous and I am sure that my protestations that the card was in error was not accepted by some, [and] I was never able to find Huan Wen-Shan to ask him personally about the card. I have since talked to L. E. Yuan who knows of him and who has told me that the man is on the consultant list for the Foundation. If this is correct, we should most certainly buy him some new calling cards![20]

But not all scholars were scared off from meeting with foundation representatives. Roberts provided a more positive report on meeting with Japanese anthropologist Masao Oka, who used foundation funding to attend the anthropology congress. Oka was interested in discussing the possibility of the foundation helping fund a pan-Asian anthropological organization. To ascertain whether there might be more widespread support for the establishment of such an organization among anthropologists, Roberts asked several attendees about their interest in this idea. Among those he spoke with was anthropologist Raymond

Firth, who supported the idea, suggesting they also should consider adding Australian members to this proposed association.[21]

A few days after first raising the possibility of a pan-Asian anthropological organization, Oka and some colleagues sought out Roberts, explaining he had discussed this idea with others but had not suggested Asia Foundation sponsorship "because the Foundation as CFA 'had such a bad name throughout Asia.' It was at this time that he said he did not wish to have his connection with The Asia Foundation published and that he told me that he had accepted our grant only after he had been assured that The Asia Foundation was now a different type of organization than had been CFA."[22] Professor Guha, of the Indian delegation, was "extremely anti-TAF and nationalistic" and would clearly challenge the legitimacy of the pan-Asian anthropological organization if the foundation was associated with it in any way. Roberts tried to stress that the foundation would have little to do with this proposed new organization, perhaps only funding an initial organizing conference. He added that they "would not be in direct support of the conference or of the organization but rather an interpersonal relation of assistance to individual delegates such as our assistance to him to attend the Congress."[23] This seemed to reassure Oka.

Professor Oka also told Roberts that Guha was working on an "evaluation of the social and cultural consequences of industrialization in India" and planned to study these same forces in postwar Japan. He then asked Roberts if it might be possible for the foundation to channel a grant for this research through the Japan Society. It is unclear if Guha (who had disparaged the foundation) was aware that Oka had approached Roberts about this possibility, but Roberts said he would discuss this with the foundation representative for Japan, Robert Hall.

Roberts reported on the Soviet delegation attending the anthropology congress, indicating that the group included an archaeologist, a physical anthropologist, and a cultural anthropologist. He wrote that it was "apparent from the start that the Russians were out to make a good impression and they apparently did. One was a quiet, scholarly looking gentleman, the other a short energetic fellow and the third was a huge, bulky, thick necked NKVD type. I later learned that my analysis was wrong—the NKVD man was the scholarly looking anthropologist! The bulky one was actually, to all reports, the nicest of the bunch."[24] George Tomashevich, of the University of Chicago, reported to Roberts that the Russians were impressive and had produced good anthropological scholarship, and Professor Oka was impressed that these Russians knew more about Japanese anthropological developments than the American anthropologists did.

Because Roberts's most successful outreach to anthropologists at this conference occurred when he spoke for himself and not the foundation, he recommended that this approach be used at the upcoming annual meeting of the American Anthropological Association (AAA). Through such means, the foundation added yet another layer of disguise; this CIA-founded and funded organization thus presented itself as a private foundation, and this "private" foundation had these "individual employees" undertake their work at this conference. He believed that this approach was crucial when trying to approach anthropologists, who, he noted, "are usually in close personal contact with their overseas colleagues and whose antithetical attitudes towards us might prove most harmful in overseas areas." He suggested that "the Foundation might even encourage their representative to the AAA or similar meetings to prepare papers for presentation."[25]

The contrast between Roberts's experience at this anthropological congress and his experience at the American Political Science Association meeting later that week revealed significant differences in disciplinary orientations. He observed that "coming from the Anthropological Congress to the Political Science Meeting was somewhat like stepping from one world into another and the longer I stayed with the political scientists the more depressed I tended to become over the wide gulf which separates them from their more earth-bound colleagues in the social sciences."[26] While Roberts was not met with the same sort of suspicions among the political scientists, he was differently alienated by the highly theoretical, quantitative, and abstract jargon that predominated at these meetings.[27]

VACILLATING SUSPICIONS IN INDONESIA

Since the early days of the CFA, many Indonesians and scholars working in Indonesia had been suspicious of the committee. After visiting Professors Lauriston Sharp, George Kahin, and other scholars at Cornell University in 1953, Harry Pierson was troubled by Kahin's skepticism of the committee's declared interests in Indonesia. When Kahin asked why there were no Asians on the committee's board, he was told that because it was an American organization, it was "unavoidable that its executives should be Americans," and he was assured that they always sought advice from Asians. Pierson tried to convince Kahin that the same would be true of Asian foundations focused on the United States, but Kahin was not impressed with these claims.[28]

Pierson asked Kahin what changes he would like to see in CFA's approach to Asia, and he was told they should finance a new journal that published critical articles from both the political left wing and the right, with an editorial board representing Asian scholars. Despite these doubts, Kahin provided Pierson with names of scholars to consider for such a project, and Pierson reported these to President Blum, with the proviso that Kahin had cautioned Pierson that "he did not want anyone in Indonesia to know that he had given us these names as he was afraid it would 'queer' his research. For the record, these names are [Soekiman Wirjosandjojo] and Jusef Wibisono, both of the right wing Mashumi Party; and [Ignatius Joseph Kasimo Hendrowahyono] of the Catholic Party."[29]

The Indonesian government had a long history of distrusting the committee and foundation's claimed intentions. In late 1956, the Indonesian government asked the Asia Foundation to cease operations in Indonesia.[30] In April 1957, an agreement between the foundation and the Indonesian government prohibited foundation activities that involved a wide range of groups, from veterans and youth, to journalism and labor education.

In the summer of 1957, Indonesian foreign minister Subandrio explained to foundation representative James Stewart Indonesia's political stance, telling him,

> You call us neutral, but this neutrality does not mean we do not take a stand for democracy. We will remain Indonesian and we oppose communism for ourselves. But we can only win this struggle ourselves. [We] cannot allow Indonesia to become the place of struggle between forces led by the U.S. and those led by Russia and China. If you (The Asia Foundation) try to conduct an anti-communist program in Indonesia, then we cannot prevent Soviet or Chinese organizations to work openly and subversively and in subversion they are the experts and you cannot win. Just imagine, if the Chinese were permitted to operate freely; they could paralyze our economic life.[31]

This statement articulated the political forces governing Indonesia's efforts to remain autonomous during the Cold War, and it also identified the political pressures facing the administration, pressures that soon contributed to the Indonesian government's decision to expel the foundation.

But in the fall of 1957, the Indonesian government suddenly appeared ready to reverse course and establish formal relations with the foundation; the government submitted a list with a half million dollars' worth of funding requests to the foundation. The foundation was caught off guard, and they were puzzled where the idea for this amount came from while they continued discussions with governmental officials, though little came from these meetings.[32] In February 1958, communist ministers in the Indonesian government "asked for the immediate expulsion of the Foundation at a Cabinet meeting.... A compromise was apparently reached in a decision to ask the Foundation to wind up its affairs in June 1958." The foundation reported that it had "received official notice from the Prime Minister of Indonesia to terminate the resident program of the Foundation by June 30, 1958. No explanation was given for this request. It is not certain whether this move, which is one in a long series of steps taken by opponents of the Foundation in Indonesia, will be final."[33]

These developments made it difficult for the foundation to accomplish much of value to the agency in Indonesia. In a secret report, the CIA conceded that "it is most doubtful that any normal Foundation would insist on continuing operations in a country where it was not generally welcome or invited, or where its financial grants were not at least graciously received."[34] While the Asia Foundation was obviously not "any normal foundation," the CIA decided that if these conditions continued, the foundation would voluntarily withdraw to avert public scrutiny—while publicly stressing that it was communists and members of the left-wing press making these demands. The CIA noted that "there is no reason to believe that the absence of TAF programs or representatives in Indonesia would impair covert capabilities in the country," and so the agency "recommend[s] withdrawal for the Asia Foundation's program[s] from Indonesia."[35] The CIA's International Organizations Division had "already suggested to the Station that the Foundation voluntarily withdraw as expulsion appears certain. However, even if expulsion should be averted, the objectives of U.S. foreign policy might be well served by an immediate voluntary withdrawal of the Foundation from Indonesia until such time as the Government might invite its return. Such a withdrawal should be accompanied by a request (if not demand) for a public investigation of its total operations."[36] When the foundation withdrew from Indonesia during the summer of 1958, the *New York Times* reported that it had spent about a quarter of a million dollars a year in Indonesia, describing its programs as primarily providing books and other teaching supplies, financing "study by Indonesians in the United States and Canada," and assisting "in the development of cooperatives and rural welfare project[s]."[37]

When the Indonesian government closed the foundation's Jakarta office in the summer of 1958, staff reported that the government gave "no reasons for its action. All of our activities for the past year have had either the approval or tacit assent of the governmental ministries concerned, so the Foundation has given no legitimate cause for criticism of its work in Indonesia. There is every reason to believe that the action of the government is due entirely to internal political pressures during this present period of national crisis."[38] Within the foundation the expulsion was framed as an expression of the larger shift in governmental positions toward all things American, as a report the following month explained: "The Foundation, like other American organizations, is feeling the effect of the political unrest and uncertainty in some of the countries where we are working. When such situations occur, it is inevitable that foreign organizations should come under attack and be subjected to various forms of pressure."[39]

The foundation publicly insisted the expulsions and growing problems in other countries were unfair and without merit, rationalizing the backlash against them by pointing out that "foreigners are always convenient whipping-boys when there are domestic troubles."[40] The foundation remained concerned that this Indonesian expulsion might represent only the first of a coming wave of expulsions as other Asian governments adopted skeptical approaches to Western soft power.

An internal foundation report on the Indonesian expulsion noted that in a final meeting with the foundation representative, Prime Minister Djuanda Kartawidjaja provided details on the expulsion but also expressed hopes that the decision might be reconsidered, and requests were made to budget $25,000 for some small projects that would allow some continued governmental contacts.[41]

Indonesian suspicions of the foundation remained for years to come.[42] In a 1961 report on his meeting with Madame Supeni, Indonesia's roving ambassador and acting head of the Division for Asian and Pacific Affairs of the Foreign Ministry, Blum was told that decisions about the foundation's future status in Indonesia rested with President Sukarno, and the foundation needed to answer past accusations of intelligence ties. Blum assured her these accusations were baseless and that senior governmental officials knew this.[43] Indonesians' suspicions of the circumstances surrounding the foundation's past expulsion were a recurrent topic in Blum's report.[44] Blum put concerted effort into getting the Indonesian government to allow the foundation's return. He stressed positive outcomes from the foundation's book programs in Indonesia and pitched future projects that could fund Asian students' travel to American universities.[45]

NEW ASIA TRADING COMPANY

In late 1953, the CFA began trying to purchase the Ceylon-based New Asia Trading Company (NATC). The committee proposed buying the company, thereby making it possible to locally distribute textbooks and popular books to compete with inexpensive communist publications. The committee tried to hide its ownership of NATC by listing individuals without visible ties to CFA on the ownership documents. The committee planned to spend about 5 percent of NATC's budget purchasing copyright permissions, 25 percent on author fees and translation costs, 45 percent on production and printing, and 25 percent on administration and distribution of pro-Western books.[46]

Ceylon representative Holbrook Bradley used local lawyers to register the company. Rather than publicly declaring that CFA held 140 shares of the original stock of the company, the ownership of this controlling interest was instead listed as "held by a suitable nominee." This public deception hid the committee's control of the company. The committee then had "Bradley's position as a director of the company filled by a suitable figurehead associated with the firm selected as the nominee holding CFA's 140 shares, such that this figurehead is listed on every directory of board members of Ceylonese companies." The company issued new stock, and the CFA report laying out this scheme recommended that "the stock in the company should appear on the surface to be held by a fairly diverse and reasonably numerous set of stock holders." These deceptions were designed to hide covert control of the company.[47]

The Committee for Free Asia instructed the New Asia Trading Company to buy several printing presses and then hire administrative staff experienced in publishing, with hopes their publishing ventures "could compete significantly with other publishing establishments in Ceylon." The committee understood that NATC's expansion in the publishing market would impact an existing publishing "cartel agreement," and CFA hoped to later enter into "binding agreements on distribution" with local people.[48] James Stewart estimated that NATC would generate enough revenue to become financially self-sufficient and that close ties with the government could support the committee in other ways.[49] It is unclear if the CIA ever used NATC for activities beyond this book program, but once the Asia Foundation's secret ownership stake in the company became public knowledge in 1965, accusations that it was a front for espionage proliferated.

In 1965, Soviet writer V. Chernyavsky published an article, "U.S. Intelligence and the Monopolies," in the Russian journal *International Affairs* describing how US intelligence agencies used businesses for intelligence operations. Chernyavsky wrote that "frequently U.S. intelligence establishes its own business firms which are merely camouflaged spy centers," and he then named the New Asia Trading Company as a CIA asset used for Asian operations.[50] Chernyavsky did not provide sources for this claim, but he correctly identified NATC as a CIA asset.[51] Following Chernyavsky's article, several anticolonialist writers, most prominently Kwame Nkrumah in his book *Neo-Colonialism: The Last Stage of Imperialism*, identified the New Asia Trading Company as a "CIA firm" and repeated Chernyavsky's claim that it ran US spies in Asia.[52]

As with other CIA-run businesses operating as publishing houses or bookstores in Asia during this period (such as Pacific Books, in Indonesia), questions remain about exactly what CIA activities, including possible intelligence-gathering or covert operations, these businesses undertook beyond publishing and distributing certain types of books and magazines.[53]

CAMBODIAN TENSIONS

As the US presence in Cambodia rapidly grew during the mid-1950s, so did local distrust and unease. The US embassy in Phnom Penh expanded from only six American employees in 1954 to over seventy the following year, with another two hundred Americans coming to Cambodia as military advisors. This growth spawned distrust and resentment among locals, and communist broadcasts from Radio Hanoi exploited these concerns, warning that "the American imperialist has come to replace the French colonialist."[54]

The foundation's plans for Cambodia in 1955 stressed the importance of appearing to remain neutral in a region with rising communist movements. These plans recognized the important political roles played by village temples and noted that while it was forbidden for Buddhist leaders "to play politics[,] the hierarchy's relationship to the people makes it almost inevitable that its ideas and feelings on given subject[s] will be communicated widely." A foundation report found "there is little evidence today that the Communists have been successful in penetrating Cambodian Buddhism, but at the same time there is no national indication that the monks are anti-Communist. Rather they are non-Communist, a distinction conducive to political neutralism and wholly in keeping with Buddhism as practiced in Cambodia."[55]

Because Cambodia lacked a central newspaper or local film industry, the foundation sponsored programs targeting these needs with materials hostile to communism. The foundation also wanted to increase the Cambodian government's use of nongovernmental organizations, while funding extant local democratic movements, local educational and health programs, and anticommunist Buddhist groups.[56]

Also in 1955, the foundation tried to sponsor the placement of several American anthropologists in rural Cambodian villages, to learn more about local cultural practices. Cambodian foundation representative Leonard Overton argued that beyond a few missionaries, Westerners with knowledge of Cambodian culture were valuable but scarce. Overton argued that Americans must improve their knowledge of Cambodia, calling it "almost incriminating to compare what we know about Cambodia with what we do not know," at a moment when Cambodia's geopolitical strategic value was growing. The lack of ethnographic data on village opinions, on the "influence of Buddhism upon the people and upon their political policy," on diverging political ideologies, on basic demographic or diet data, and scarce data on the level of rural support for the government were significant gaps. To fill these gaps the foundation recommended funding some broad rural ethnographic surveys.[57]

Overton spoke with the embassy's political section chief, other US government employees, and the UN's Technical Assistance expert about this proposed ethnographic project. Overton concluded it would be best if the Ford Foundation funded the project, and he asked the San Francisco office to contact potential funders or researchers to explore the possibility of such a project. For two years foundation and National Research Council (NRC) staff continued exploring ways to fund American anthropologists' Cambodian fieldwork. While there was a steady stream of foundation memos supporting Cambodian village ethnographic research, there was growing awareness that because of local suspicions, this work should not be associated with the foundation and that it should be done with the appearance of independence brought by a university project.[58] The NRC encouraged anthropologists to apply for Ford Foundation funding for this research. The Asia Foundation believed Cornell was "the logical American university to carry out such a project," and as staff considered the "ways we might work in this field that would be acceptable to the Cambodian government," they decided that anthropological research was less threatening than more overtly political research projects.[59] In the end, the Cambodian government was too suspicious of ethnographic proposals to permit foundation-supported fieldwork, and Ford did not fund any of the proposed projects.

After these efforts to fund anthropologists to study Cambodian culture failed, the foundation focused on funding less suspicious traditional educational and publishing projects. Finally, in November 1963, the Cambodian government declared it would stop receiving "all military, economic, technical and cultural aid" from the United States, but because the Asia Foundation claimed it was a nongovernmental agency it was not asked to terminate programs or sponsored activities.[60] Representative Overton filed a twenty-one-page analysis, "The End of American Aid: What Happened in Cambodia," detailing how the foundation came to remain in Cambodia as a nondeclared American outpost after Cambodia terminated all US aid, a development that left the foundation in a unique position. Overton chronicled the long decline of US-Cambodian relations, with Sihanouk's miscalculations, border incursions, and threats real and imagined from external enemies analyzed in some detail and written up in a format ready made for others in Washington to reuse for briefings as needed.[61] In December 1963, Cambodian police began "surveilling residences occupied by members of the official American community and . . . trailing some individual Americans."[62]

In 1964, South Vietnamese troop incursions into Cambodia increased tensions between Cambodia and the United States and threatened the foundation's remaining Cambodian operations. During the March 11 riots in Phnom Penh, protesters vandalized the US and British embassies, prompting other protesters to march on the Cambodian embassy in Washington, DC.[63] These increased tensions led the British embassy to reduce staff, and the US embassy launched a voluntary evacuation of American dependents.[64] The foundation monitored protests and took precautions:

> During working hours, tours were made of the city in order to determine whether demonstrators were massing and local employees were dispatched to monitor the agitators in front of the Ministry of Information. By these measures it was hoped that there would be sufficient warning to escape the office in the event that the mob decided to attack. A precarious escape route was laid out over roof tops and backyards of neighboring buildings but in the final analysis it was decided that this was more dangerous than the mob. As a show of insouciance, however, work was begun to whitewash the external portion of the office facing the sidewalk and to touch up the Foundation's sign, although a small brass sign identifying the Foundation in Cambodian as an American cultural organization was removed—permanently.[65]

On April 1, two US-trained Cambodian pilots shot down an American pilot in an L-19 observation aircraft after he entered Cambodian airspace from Vietnam.[66] Tensions remained high, and the following month a thousand students, monks, and pedicab drivers led an anti-American protest march on the Cambodian National Assembly building. Battles were also spilling over the Cambodian border. Overton observed that "from the Foundation's point of view, this new dimension of tension presents a serious menace. If it reaches the point where individuals or various government departments refuse to deal with the Foundation because it is an American organization, then the end will have been reached in Cambodia. For many it is probably already incongruous to accept financial assistance from an American organization at a time when more and more, from a local point of view, the U.S. is at war with their country."[67]

A 1965 foundation report noted that Cambodia was increasingly aligned with communism, adding that "the extremely personal politics of Prince Norodom Sihanouk, the abdicated God-King of the Khmers and present Chief of State, dominate the daily life of the country to a degree almost unequalled in present-day nation-states and permeate all government policies and decisions."[68] A "nearly fatal blow" to US-Cambodian relations came in late October 1965, when a US-backed South Vietnamese military plane "strafed and bombed a Cambodian border village, killing six and wounding about a dozen."[69] This incident spawned anti-American protests in Phnom Penh, protests that led the US embassy to evacuate nonessential personnel and dependents. The following month, Cambodian forces shot down an unarmed US transport plane. Because of the growing hostility toward the US government, the foundation reported being in the unique position of having "free access to all [Cambodian] government ministries and departments where the officials are easily accessible, generally quite friendly and open to discussing their problems," and the foundation increased Cambodian program expenditures.[70]

This deteriorating situation led to the cancellation of AID projects, and diplomatic relations devolved to a point where the foundation reported that "outside of the Asia Foundation and IVS [International Voluntary Service], there is no American aid coming into Cambodia except for the money which is allocated to cover the Cambodian students still studying in the U.S."[71] In February 1966, Asia Foundation staff member John Bannigan was expelled from Cambodia under accusations of being a spy, and the foundation's Cambodian office was closed. In a letter to all foundation representatives, President Haydn Williams wrote, "Many of you have already sent in newspaper clipping[s] and summaries of radio reports regarding the closing of the Foundation's Cambodia office and the unfounded charges against the former Representative there."[72] Williams included a letter sent by Norodom Kantol, Cambodia's minister of foreign affairs, which confirmed the closing of foundation offices but did not state why Bannigan was expelled. Cambodian newspapers made nonspecific charges that the foundation engaged in "subversive" activities. The China News Agency claimed that Bannigan was expelled for "collecting intelligence."[73] President Williams wrote to Ralph Harris, foundation assistant representative for Cambodia, saying that he

> was quite distressed to read of the curious charges made against John Bannigan. I'm certain that you . . . better than most of us, know full well that someone has misinformed His Highness. I have had a long and detailed discussion of the matter with John and he assured me that he is at a loss to know how these unfair charges could have gained credibility when all of his actions during the fifteen months he worked in Cambodia were completely open and [free] from any illegal or political implications or intentions. Please reassure the local staff people who know and worked with Mr. Bannigan that we have complete faith in his innocence of such activities.[74]

President Williams sent a memo to all representatives providing the foundation's official story of the closing of the Cambodian office. Williams stressed that "there was no request from the Royal Cambodian Government at any time to close our office." Williams's public position was that if staff members were not welcome, the foundation had no reason to remain. He categorically denied that John Bannigan had "abused Cambodian hospitality to carry out political activities." He claimed that any such political activities "are completely inconsistent with The [Asia] Foundation's purpose and fundamental nature."[75] The China News Agency was reporting that foundation employees had engaged in "espionage activities." Williams denied accusations of foundation spying, arguing that China had claimed that

> all Americans abroad are "espionage agents" and all American organizations, private or governmental, are "agents of American imperialism" and therefore natural targets for charges of espionage and subversion. Yet Peking's apparent tactic of focusing attention on The Asia Founda-

tion may reflect the Chinese Communists' real anxiety about the effectiveness of private American assistance to Asian cultural and education programs. The Asia Foundation in Cambodia was the only American organization in the country and a natural target for Communist attack, despite the fact that Prince Sihanouk had personally encourage[d] our work there during my audience with him in December 1964.

As you know[,] Peking through its various agencies has, over the years, made the same charges several times and has tried by every means to discredit and undermine the work of The Asia Foundation as well as the Ford and Rockefeller Foundations, CARE-Medico, missionaries and similar American groups wherever possible. The Asia Foundation's record of philanthropic, non-political programming for almost 15 years in almost every non-Communist country of Asia is proof enough of the falsity of these deliberate fabrications and distortions of the truth.[76]

Williams was splitting hairs in claiming the foundation had not been expelled from Cambodia; he might have more accurately said they left before they were officially expelled.

COMMUNIST ATTACKS ON THE FOUNDATION

In 1965, foundation staff member L. E. Yuan wrote President Williams summarizing a lengthy article published in the communist newspaper *Guangming Ribao* (Guangming daily), which argued that American foundations operating in Asia were extensions of Western imperialism. The article attacked the Rockefeller and Asia Foundations as agents of American imperialism. It critiqued American foundations as ideological manifestations of "monopolist-capitalists['] desire to escape income tax and inheritance" while influencing public policy and engaging in "criminal activities." It also claimed that the Ford Foundation was "behind the rebellion in Indonesia." The Asia Foundation was accused of having "persistently assisted the rebels in Ceylon," of having "financed the establishment of the 'Youth Council' in order to conduct subversion activities and to endanger the independence and sovereignty of Ceylon," and of colluding with the Rockefeller and Ford Foundations to assist Tokyo Bank's "hostile attitude toward and plotting against Communist China." The article claimed increasing numbers of Asians "realized the hypocritic and reactionary aims of American Foundations," stating that "as early as 1962, the Burmese Revolutionary Council ordered the suspension of all Ford Foundation and Asia Foundation activities in Burma. At the time, many newspapers in Burma exposed the criminal activities of those American foundations committed in support of the expansion of American imperialism. They pointed out that these foundations are all tools of American monopolist capital and are vampires wearing the [benign] masks, and that their infiltration activities were in reality methods to corrode Burma's politics, economics and society."[77] Yuan sent Williams a translation of the shorter version of the story (which did not mention the Asia Foundation by name) appearing in Hong Kong's *Sing Tao Daily*.[78]

Other expressions of ongoing suspicions about the foundation's CIA links came after its CIA ties were made public. In an oral history interview, US diplomat Princeton Lyman spoke about being on the Korean Peninsula in March 1967, while working as AID's Korean program director, when news of the foundation's CIA links broke. Lyman met with Korean friends who had been funded by the foundation and asked them if they were shocked by this news. He said, "Their reaction startled me; they were not surprised because they considered that all U.S. funds—for assistance programs, for publications, for public relations, etc.—came from the CIA or its equivalent. All U.S. funds in their view were intended to buy Korean loyalty." Lyman had not expected this cynicism from his Korean friends.[79]

It wasn't just Asians who speculated that the Asia Foundation had CIA ties; members of the American expat communities sometimes questioned the foundation's cover story. As Paul McGarr noted in his essay "Quiet Americans in India," during the 1950s *New York Times* correspondent A. M. Rosenthal "confided to his editor back in the United States that local CIA staff working under the guise of Treasury experts, Air Force contractors or members of specialized bodies, such as the Asia Foundation, were generally known to Indian government officials and journalists."[80]

A HISTORY OF BROAD CIA SUSPICIONS

From the earliest days of the Committee for Free Asia until the spring of 1967 there were ongoing unverified suspicions in many of the Asian countries where the committee and foundation operated that it had CIA ties. The foundation became adept at weathering claims of CIA links, generally falling back on explanations that all US organizations routinely face such false charges. The more these suspicions and claims of CIA collusion accumulated, the more the foundation tried to use the multiplicity of these claimed "false" accusations as a way of supporting their (false) claims of innocence.[81]

But with time, it wasn't just Asians who grew suspicious about the foundation. In 1966 the *New York Times* ran a series of articles covering the growth of protests opposing CIA recruiting efforts on US college campuses. These news stories derailed efforts to establish a new Indian-American foundation.[82] They also spread fears within the CIA that exposure of the agency's links to the Asia Foundation could occur. Beginning on April 25, 1966, the *New York Times* ran a five-part series by Tom Wicker, John W. Finney, Mac Frankel, E. W. Kenworthy, and others examining the CIA's involvement in a range of covert activities, including reliance on American scholars with the assistance of various front organizations, though the Asia Foundation's CIA links were still unknown to the public.[83]

These stories prompted the 303 Committee—the interagency committee reviewing and authorizing covert operations—to consider the possibility that the foundation might soon be exposed, as public awareness and concern over such CIA-academic links were growing. One 1966 CIA report stated that

> in the wake of the *New York Times* series on the Agency, TAF's domestic U.S. cover faced clear challenge. On 8 July 1966, the 303 Committee met to consider TAF's situation. TAF's effectiveness and value to the U.S. Government were strongly reaffirmed and the Agency was authorized to undertake a number of measures to shore up TAF's ostensible [sic] private image. These include: TAF to see bona-fide private donations for operations and endowment fund purposes; Agency to provide funds for endowment purposes; and effect TAF-AID project contracts on a highly selective basis. The decision to improve cover is being implemented step-by-step and will be cleared finally with appropriate individuals in Congress.[84]

A November 1966 CIA memo expressed agency concerns that the Asia Foundation "does not function effectively, given the cost of this program, as a covert political action instrument except in rare cases." The agency was worried about what it called the foundation's "cover problems" given the increasing likelihood that "Ramparts or some other publication" could expose covert ties to the CIA. The FE/CA (Far East/ Covert Action) chief recommended "a complete break with CIA, which, as we see it, would not really reduce the effectiveness of TAF as it now operates" and that TAF rely on "a different and acknowledgeable source of US government funds, i.e., the White House."[85]

As the next chapter shows, these concerns within the CIA were well placed, as the thin veneer hiding connections between the CIA and the Asia Foundation would soon be removed. While the foundation was forced to admit it received CIA funds, a deluge of released information about other CIA funding fronts and other CIA programs, some agency bravado, and a good amount of luck prevented the public from learning the extent of the CIA's involvement in founding and directing the foundation.

11 Exposed CIA Fronts and the Fate of CIA Orphans

Getting caught is the mother of invention.
ROBERT BYRNE

In the mid-1960s, a flurry of alternative press investigations documenting CIA use of funding fronts soon led the mainstream press to join the hunt. The first major story investigating a CIA front was Sol Stern's 1967 *Ramparts* investigation into the agency's secret funding of the National Student Association (NSA). Stern revealed that since the early 1950s, the CIA had secretly been funding the NSA, which was functioning as an anticommunist operation that spread pro-Western propaganda, occasionally collected intelligence, and helped shape the agenda of this large international youth organization. Rank-and-file NSA members had no idea it was CIA funded, but after taking office, newly elected NSA presidents, sworn to secrecy, were privately told of the CIA's secret funding of the association.[1]

Like DTPILLAR's Committee for Free Asia, the National Student Association's CIA funds were first established through Frank Wisner's Office of Policy Coordination. Later these funds came directly from CIA budgets and had agency oversight. As Karen Paget shows in her book *Patriotic Betrayal*, it was anticommunist liberals within the CIA who envisioned using progressive organizations like the NSA as anticommunist instruments. By 1967, the NSA had become completely dependent on covert CIA funding, but unlike the Asia Foundation the leadership of the NSA was elected by rank-and-file members—college students across the United States—which meant there was a rotating group of individuals elected as leaders who were then sworn to secrecy and told of the CIA's hidden role. This elected base of student leaders who knew the source of NSA funding created risks for the CIA.

When the CIA learned that the *Ramparts* NSA exposé was in the works, the agency took steps to discredit the reporters, even going so far as to plan blackmail operations to try and stop the story's release.[2] Once the CIA determined it could not stop the article's imminent publication, it planned a press conference to disclose, before publication, the existence of the program in order to steal the magazine's thunder while shaping the narrative of what it would then call a "former" relationship with the NSA. But *Ramparts* scooped the CIA by quickly taking out a full-page advertisement in the *New York Times* disclosing the basic details of the forthcoming story before the agency could preemptively disclose it. This was a news story that shocked the public in ways that are difficult for later generations to understand. It heralded the government's betrayal of public trust, undermining faith in government.

Two significant developments followed the *Ramparts* story, one journalistic, the other political. First, within weeks of the article's publication, the mainstream and alternative press began publishing various news stories revealing previously unknown CIA funding fronts, conduits, and the names of foundations, groups, and organizations that had unwittingly received CIA funds. It was during this rapid wave of stories that the Asia Foundation's receipt of CIA funds was disclosed. These disclosures led to the second development—the political one—following this story. The political fallout from the disclosure of the CIA link to the NSA and the secondary stories revealing more CIA fronts and fund recipients was significant. Amid increasing talk of congressional investigations, President Lyndon Johnson rushed to reduce the political damage by appointing a commission led by his undersecretary of state, Nicholas Katzenbach, to investigate these revelations and quickly issue a report with recommendations.

Stern's *Ramparts* article quoted former NSA president Phil Sherburne saying that most of the foundations funding NSA programs "were merely passing along CIA money." The pass-through foundations identified in the article included such organizations as the Independent Foundation, the San Jacinto Foundation, the Foundation for Youth and Student Affairs, the Sidney and Ester Rabb Foundation, and the J. Frederick Brown Foundation. And while the Asia Foundation was identified as an NSA funder, *Ramparts* (incorrectly) reported that "CIA money did not pass through the Ford Foundation, the Rockefeller Foundation, the Asia Foundation, and other groups which had also funded NSA international programs in the past."[3]

Even though the *Ramparts* story mentioned the Asia Foundation in passing as a non-CIA asset, the journalistic scramble hunting groups with CIA funds was getting underway, and it was only a matter of weeks until the *New York Times* exposed the foundation's receipt of CIA funds. In February 1967, just days after *Ramparts* released its NSA story, the *New York Times* revealed that the CIA had funded the American Newspaper Guild. This article included a single sentence linking the Asia Foundation to the CIA, noting that "another fund that has been linked to the CIA is The Asia Foundation, which helped finance a three-month journalism seminar for South Vietnamese journalists last year in Saigon."[4] This mention made no claims of how strong this link was, but it again placed this connection in public view.[5]

On March 19, 1967, CIA headquarters sent a secret memo to sixteen redacted recipients announcing that a public statement would be issued by the Asia Foundation's board of trustees two days later, on March 21.[6] Although the identities of the recipients of this memo are unknown, it appears to have been addressed to overseas foundation representatives. The memo said staff would be the "primary public spokesman for [the] foundation in your country," and these employees were told to "stick to statement, avoid amplification and your own interpretation." Headquarters told staff to "put foundation in best possible light." The memo stressed that it was "important to make the point that you and local staff have had nothing to do with sources of funds, which is entirely responsibility of trustees, that you and staff have never been approached or influenced by U.S. government or used for political or intelligence purposes." The memo coached employees to fake surprised reactions to this news but "not undue embarrassment. Be proud of the foundation and its work and confident that it can continue to serve Asian needs."[7] It is unclear what exactly either the CIA or foundation leadership knew about the story coming out in the *Times*, but they knew it would soon be published.

On March 21, 1967, the *New York Times* printed Wallace Turner's article, headlined "Asia Foundation Got CIA Funds—Trustees Deny Influence—Bar Future Hidden Aid," revealing to the world that the CIA used the foundation to fund academic and humanitarian projects in Asia, though the *Times* story failed to state the foundation's complete reliance on CIA funds, as well as the CIA and Office of Policy Coordination's role in creating both the Committee for Free Asia and the Asia Foundation.[8] Instead, the story left the false impression that the foundation—like groups such as the American Newspaper Guild or dozens of other organizations recently revealed to have been receiving CIA funds through CIA pass-throughs—had only occasionally received some funds from the agency. While these CIA revelations were damaging, this bold misdirection was quite successful.

The *Times* story reported that "the Asia Foundation, a private American philanthropic organization, said today that it had received money indirectly from the Central Intelligence Agency. The foundation's trustees issued a press release in which it was said: 'The trustees wish to state that in the past they have also knowingly received contributions from private foundations and trusts which have been recently named as having transmitted Central Intelligence Agency funds to private American organizations.'"[9] Foundation assistant public affairs officer John Bannigan admitted that the board knew "the foundation was accepting money from the Federal Government," a statement far short of admitting that the board knew the foundation ran on CIA money, much less that the CIA was the foundation's only significant source of sustained funding, or that the agency had created the foundation. Bannigan instead said "he did not know whether they had been aware that the Federal money had come from the CIA," and he "declined to reveal the sum of the subsidy from the intelligence agency" but claimed the foundation would "no longer accept hidden Federal subsidies."[10]

Most of the *Times* story was based on the CIA-approved press release. This statement was a series of lies and half-truths claiming that the trustees ran the foundation without CIA interference and that the foundation had not been influenced by the source of these funds, insisting that foundation staff "have not been used or influenced in any way, directly or indirectly, by any contributor to the foundation." For the short-term future, even the claim that the foundation would stop receiving "hidden Federal subsidies" was a lie.

The article identified some current and former foundation board members, noting several prominent trustees, including ambassadors, a university president, the Ford Foundation president, and captains of industry.[11] Turner acknowledged that the previous month's *Ramparts* story on the CIA funding of the NSA had directed attention to the CIA's secret funding of various other foundations, noting that "other articles involving foundation connections with the intelligence agency were being developed."[12] While Turner's article correctly revealed that the Asia Foundation had knowingly received CIA funds, by following the central narrative of the CIA-crafted press release, the story misrepresented the extent and nature of this relationship. The story made it appear that the foundation only occasionally received small amounts of CIA funding. Because the foundation admitted that it had received *some* CIA funds but not that it had always been funded by the CIA, it hoped no one would ask for proof of the less-damaging statement. It was a claim that would not have held up to even the lightest scrutiny. In hindsight it seems odd that the *Times* reporter or other journalists did not demand the foundation provide a list of its financial backers or ask to see their last financial audit's list of incoming funds.

It is difficult to understand why Turner, *Ramparts*, or any other reporters failed to pursue this most obvious follow-up question. Perhaps the best explanation is that the foundation simply appeared to be just another organization exposed for receiving small amounts of supplemental funds that came from the CIA—like all those secondary individuals and groups the foundation had itself funded, who were now embarrassed. One mitigating factor was that the sudden rush of CIA funding revelations published in the weeks following the *Ramparts* NSA-CIA story allowed the foundation to blend in and hide among all the groups whose only connection to the CIA had been the occasional receipt of funds in the past. The fallout from these revelations was remarkably small and short-lived, and even as the foundation scrambled to control the damage—publicly insisting it would no longer receive any CIA funds—it was secretly trying to negotiate one last significant CIA payment to get it through one more year until it could secure a large non-CIA-linked governmental funding source that would allow it to survive.

REACTIONS TO THE *TIMES* REVELATION OF CIA TIES

As news of the Asia Foundation's CIA links spread around the world, several countries called for investigations into the foundation's international operations. Members of India's parliament demanded investigations of the foundation, arguing that its activities threatened India's national interests. Indian foreign minister M. C. Chagla requested a governmental investigation of the CIA's activities in India. Ramnath Umanath, of the Indian Communist Party, claimed in India's parliament that Leonard Weiss, the US embassy's minister counselor for political and economic affairs, and Howard B. Schaffer, secretary in the embassy's Political/Economic Section, were CIA agents. Umanath called for the expulsion of Weiss, Schaffer, and Robert F. Rayle, US embassy second secretary. Others raised questions about CIA influence occurring through Asia Foundation financing of the Indian Society of International Law.[13]

Surprisingly, this exposure of the foundation's CIA links did not immediately lead to its expulsion from India. At the end of August 1967, TAF India representative Richard Heggie reported that in his talks with Indian government officials there was still uncertainty about what the impact of these revelations would be on the foundation's status in India.[14] Months after the CIA revelations, foundation staff in India remained prickly over public characterizations of the foundation as a "CIA conduit"—in one memo Heggie described this characterization in the Indian press as "particularly reprehensible."[15] Finally, half a year after the *Times* revealed the Asia Foundation's CIA ties, the Indian government froze all foundation activities.[16]

In early 1968, the Indian government formally ordered the foundation to suspend operations in India.[17] News reports quoted government officials saying "there was no chance that India's decision could be reversed. They declared the Government accepted at face value the foundation's assurance that it was no longer taking CIA money but found the whole matter had become 'too embarrassing.'"[18] The foundation's closure of its office in India on July 31, 1968, left many local people and organizations in a tough spot. Unwitting Indian journals that had received subsidies, organizations participating in free book programs, and scholars expecting fellowships were suddenly left without funding, and the damage caused by the foundation's expulsion was felt for years to come by recipients who had had no knowledge of the CIA connections.

As they prepared to leave India, staffers sought organizations to which they might give books and other foundation materials.[19] Individuals from several institutions receiving foundation funds wrote letters expressing regrets that the foundation was leaving. India representative Heggie recounted his dinner conversation with S. P. Sen, director of the Institute of Historical Studies. Sen had received significant foundation funding over the years, and following the revelations he had become the target of local resentment. Sen was one of several Indian intellectuals targeted in a petition presented at a meeting of the twenty-ninth session of the Indian History Congress.[20] This petition, supported by 228 delegates, "strongly condemn[ed] the practice pursued by certain foreign agencies of financing research of historical nature in India with a view to either extending their ideological and political influence or collecting information of use to their intelligence service."[21] The petition demanded that Indian scholars refuse such funding.

But three months after this dramatic condemnation of the foundation, Heggie reported that Sen was in high spirits because he had just received authorization from the chief minister of Kerala to write a biography of a communist leader of the independence movement. He felt that after being under the dark shadow of CIA-linked accusations, this procommunist work "gave him some protection against the charges that had been made about the Institute." He remained concerned about claims of CIA influence and asked Heggie to provide letters from the Ministry of External Affairs documenting that the ministry had approved all the past foundation funding he received. He also worried that his historical journal would suffer without foundation funds, and he was assured his current grant would continue for the present. Sen appeared to be a fair-weather friend of the foundation, happily shifting to writing procommunist works when doing so led to funding, though he expressed some worries about claims being made by a "leftist group" that he "had been selling dossiers on communist leaders to US agencies." Sen said these accusations arose over disclosures of his contractual agreement with Columbia University professor Donald Zagoria, under which Sen's institute had "sent material on communist leaders at a set fee."[22] The ease with which a scholar like Sen switched from foundation-sponsored work aligned with Western capitalism to procommunist writing projects is perhaps one measure of how much weaker these purchased Asian loyalties were than the CIA imagined.

Fallout from the CIA funding revelations echoed throughout Asia for years. Asian publications ran editorials and letters to the editor identifying individuals who had received foundation funds, denouncing them as CIA tools, or worse, CIA agents. The Indian magazine *Link* claimed in its issue of June 25, 1967, that American scholars Norman Palmer (University of Pennsylvania) and James Roach (University of Texas) and others at the South Asia Studies Center had CIA links simply because they had been funded by the Asia Foundation.[23]

A 1967 article by Emanuel Phadnis in the *Hindustan Times* argued that because all Asia Foundation projects had been approved by the Indian government, its activities had been monitored and therefore had little chance of penetrating India. Phadnis wrote that he didn't "see how the [Indian Society of International Law, a grant recipient] serves CIA purposes any more than another institution which is believed to have been supported by another [CIA] conduit-fed foundation to set up a chicken farm." Phadnis pointed out that even while receiving foundation funding the institute continued its "blasting of Americans for what they are doing in Vietnam."[24]

One article in the Indian press, headlined "Warning against CIA-Fed Authors," carried dire warnings from Raghunath Singh, former chair of the National Shipping Board, that with the revelations of CIA funding of Indian writers, the "ramifications are bound to be adverse[,] as writers who are receiving money from foreign sources apart from debasing themselves are also apt to corrupt the minds of the public."[25] Singh did not appear to consider the possibility that some or all of these authors had unwittingly been linked with the CIA; he characterized such connections as "derogatory and unpatriotic" and called for the exposure of individuals and organizations involved with the CIA, as well as for an Indian governmental inquiry. Other news stories from this period carried statements from organizations declaring they had not received CIA funds or, in some cases, that they had no knowledge that the funds they received had originated at CIA. These innocence-proclaiming organizations included the International Press Institute, the National Union of Seafarers, the AFL-CIO, the writers group PEN, and the Boston Symphony Orchestra.[26]

In a 2014 interview, David Steinberg, a former foundation representative based in Seoul, described his meeting with the South Korean prime minister to discuss news reports of the foundation's CIA links. Steinberg recalled "getting the cable from San Francisco, the cable that was probably almost six feet long explaining [that the TAF was a CIA front] . . . and making an appointment to see the Prime Minister. He was rather embarrassed to have to deal with me on this particular subject, and he really didn't want to know—or maybe he knew already."[27]

Yet, even while expressing relief that this CIA funding era was over, more than four decades later Steinberg offered a classic liberal anticommunist rationalization for the foundation having once run on covert CIA funding: he insisted that the right-wing forms of anticommunism unleashed by McCarthyism had made it impossible for the US government to openly fund the soft-power liberal anticommunist programs that the foundation had provided for groups like the Japanese Socialist Party. Steinberg argued that the CIA wanted the sort of "independent judgment" that foundation staff had developed by being in country, and decades later he still viewed these CIA-funded programs as having made valuable contributions.[28]

After the Asia Foundation's CIA funding was exposed, Franklin Books sought funds to bail out the Franklin School Library Project in Kabul and cover a financial shortfall. The foundation had given Franklin Books programs $22,000 the previous July for this library program.[29] Its goal was to set up libraries in fifty schools and to purchase twenty-seven thousand Persian-, English-, and Arabic-language books for them.[30] Three months after the CIA revelations, Franklin Books requested an additional $16,000 to make ends meet.[31] Three years earlier, the foundation had lent Franklin Books at least $100,000, and under the loan agreement this Afghanistan library project allowed Franklin to pay back the borrowed funds in local currency.[32] After the CIA funding revelations, the foundation allowed Franklin Books to pay back the loan in local currency, at an estimated rate of 1 million afghanis per year.[33]

KATZENBACH, RUSK, AND FORD CONCERNS ABOUT "CIA ORPHANS"

The Johnson administration moved quickly to limit damage caused by the *Ramparts* investigation of the National Student Association's CIA links. Because of a growing awareness that other CIA fronts would soon be exposed by journalists, President Johnson worried that if he did not control the story, congressional investigations could unearth even more damaging information about other CIA fronts. On February 15, 1967, the day after *Ramparts* announced its coming NSA-CIA story in the full-page *New York Times* ad, President Johnson appointed Undersecretary of State Nicholas Katzenbach to chair an ad hoc committee (to become known as the Katzenbach Committee) that would investigate the extent of the CIA's use of foundations and make recommendations for corrective action.

With Katzenbach as chair, the committee consisted of John W. Gardner, who was a former Carnegie Foundation president and cabinet secretary (Health, Education, and Welfare), and Richard Helms, director of central intelligence. The three-member committee worked quickly, and in late March 1967, the Katzenbach Committee's report to President Johnson was completed.[34] The committee studied the extent of the CIA's use of foundations and developed recommendations designed "to help assure that such organizations can play their proper and vital role abroad." The report provided few specific details on CIA links with foundations, and it avoided making inquiries that would have revealed the extent of such operations. It also avoided doing obvious things like producing lists of known CIA-linked programs. These omissions clarified that the committee's job was to help President Johnson sweep the whole issue under the rug while finding ways to preserve organizations dependent on CIA covert funding. The report's two main recommendations were that the US government stop covertly funding programs "to any of the nation's educational or private voluntary organizations" and that the government develop a "public-private mechanism to provide public funds openly for overseas activities of organizations which are adjudged deserving, in the national interest, of public support."[35]

The committee recommended a strategic shift away from sprawling covert CIA programs run through foundations. After privately reviewing the status and funding of each of the (unidentified) foundations secretly receiving CIA funding, the Katzenbach Committee concluded that each of these CIA-funded organizations could feasibly stop receiving CIA funds by the end of 1967.[36] Yet, because the committee did not publicly name these organizations, the report left many fundamental questions unanswered, including basic questions about the extent and reach of these secret CIA funding programs. Almost a decade later, the Senate's Church Committee Report found that during the years between 1963 and 1966, once they excluded grants from the Carnegie, Ford, and Rockefeller Foundations, "CIA funding was involved in nearly half the grants ... made during this period in the field of international activities," and CIA funding was involved in more than a third of "the physical, life and social sciences" grants during this period.[37] This was a remarkable revelation that most histories of American academia covering this period continue to ignore.

The Katzenbach Committee's report acknowledged the need to fund education programs meeting national security needs and that governmental directives and support were needed. The committee did not issue clear directives on how to accomplish this, but it approvingly noted that organizations like the Swedish Institute of Cultural Relations and the Smithsonian Institution successfully mixed public and private funds for education-linked projects.

Soon after receiving the Katzenbach Committee's findings in April 1967, President Johnson appointed an eighteen-member committee chaired by Secretary of State Dean Rusk (which came to be known as the Rusk Committee), to consider the Katzenbach Committee's recommendations.[38] In December 1967, the Rusk Committee proposed several options to fill funding shortfalls caused by the cutoff of funds for CIA fronts, including a stop-gap funding bill that would cover these organizations for one year, providing them with time to secure other income sources or to move existing programs to a new "semi-public interdependent organization" that would continue these projects.[39] They estimated that a proposed $5 million appropriations bill could fund "the neediest of the student, religious, union, cultural and other groups subsidized for years by the CIA, to counter Communist influence abroad."[40]

The Rockefeller Foundation Archives contain documents, compiled by David Bell, recording Ford Foundation communications, press clippings, reports, and correspondence showing Rockefeller Foundation staff consultations with governmental and private agencies over these 1967 CIA funding revelations. These records include discussions about what would become of programs with CIA funding after the true source of funding had been exposed. In these documents, these soon-to-be-unfunded programs were referred to as "CIA Orphans."

Merrimon Cuninggim reported to the Danforth Foundation trustees about a March 2, 1967, meeting between the Katzenbach Committee (Katzenbach,

Helms, and Gardner) and representatives of the Carnegie (Alan Pifer), Ford (McGeorge Bundy), Rockefeller (George Harrar), and Sloan (Everett Case) Foundations, along with William Marvel and Herman Wells from Education and World Affairs (EWA), a nonprofit organization established with initial funding from the Carnegie and Ford Foundations and having an abiding interest in strengthening international educational opportunities.[41] Cuninggim summarized the following points discussed at the meeting:

> Certain assumptions were present in, and/or certain points of agreement emerged from, Washington and other conversations, as follows:
>
> 1. The covert policy of support of private agencies by the CIA has been not only stupid but wrong.
> 2. The extent of practice of this policy is greater than has thus far been made public.
> 3. One of the reasons this policy developed was that foundations were not supporting legitimate private efforts abroad.
> 4. Much of the general public and perhaps more surprising, many academic people seem not to be greatly disturbed by the disclosures; largely for two reasons, (a) failure to discriminate between a good action or result and a bad method, and (b) failure to realize how bad the method of clandestine support for even good projects has actually proved to be.
> 5. The damage has been immense to the reputation and actual programs of legitimate groups, to their believability as truly private agencies, independent of government influence.
> 6. The spillover of suspicion onto innocent groups has been serious; they are suspected at home and their work is compromised abroad.
> 7. To cut off covert support is only a first step, essentially negative; we need to take some positive action to enable these groups to perform their proper and useful functions, and thus to be able to represent our free society openly and honestly.
> 8. A public-private agency through which to channel support for legitimate groups seems to be the best solution, an agency on somewhat the British Council model.
> 9. Private foundations ought not to be expected to pick up the pieces of the present disaster, and probably won't do so except in isolated instances.

10. But foundations might contribute a great deal both to the planning and to the support of some kind of public-private agency that would serve as a long-range solution to the problem.[42]

These foundation representatives asked Education and World Affairs to quickly develop potential plans for securing new funding for CIA orphans.

EWA's William W. Marvel worried that the US government might not enact meaningful reforms curtailing the CIA's influence on cultural and educational programs. After meeting with members of the Katzenbach Committee and foundation representatives, Marvel found "a tendency to downgrade the urgency of the problem; to argue that since the disclosures of CIA support of private educational activity abroad had not *really* damaged the U.S. 'image' overseas too seriously, we need not feel pressed to make basic changes; that this would be an awkward year to convince Congress to make major institutional or organic changes and to put up large sums of new money."[43]

EWA worked quickly and in two weeks had drafted its "Report on a New Instrumentality for Government Financing of Private International Activities in Education and Related Areas," which considered possible applications of the findings of the Rusk and Katzenbach Committees' inquiries.[44] This confidential draft report found that the problems facing US higher education following these CIA revelations existed because "our country has not established satisfactory arrangements for public support of a number of important private programs and activities in international education."[45] EWA proposed to solve these problems by establishing new public and private non-CIA-linked funding sources for international education.

EWA recommended the development of new programs that had total autonomy from the government, with financing from both public and private funds. The organization favored the operational flexibility of the British Council model, which worked with both individuals and organizations, and supported long- and short-term programs. The EWA report argued that this new program "should be insulated from short-run foreign policy considerations not only by its being 'situated' remote from the foreign-military-intelligence agencies" but also by not funding "highly political" programs.[46]

The report identified several possible courses of action. The first would be for President Johnson to order the CIA to end all involvement in education and cultural programs. Other proposed courses of action all assumed that the president would terminate all covert CIA funding for cultural and educational programs. Once this occurred, new funds could be budgeted for international educational activities or a private sector foundation could administer large grants from the federal government. One option proposed a new governmental agency, administered like the National Science Foundation, be established to administer funding for these programs. Finally, the report proposed establishing a new federally chartered and funded national institute "largely under private control and management [which] would be created through cooperative planning and action between the executive and legislative branches of the government on the one hand, and representatives of major interested private organizations and foundations on the other hand."[47]

Congress introduced several bills to address revelations of CIA interference in public life, but there were difficulties building support for any one specific solution to the problems facing suddenly defunded CIA orphans. EWA identified five proposed bills seeking either to use existing public/private agencies or foundations to take up the activities of exposed CIA operations or to develop new funding sources or agencies to carry on this work. These bills did not make it out of committee, however.[48] Congress remained mostly silent concerning what it would mean for various organizations to switch to open sources of funding while trying to carry out essentially the same tasks once supported by covert CIA funding.

Senate Bill 981, sponsored by Senator Ralph Yarborough (D-TX), amended Title 1 of the International Education Act of 1966 to authorize funds for students to travel to international youth conferences. Senator Eugene McCarthy (D-MN) introduced Senate Bill 1334, establishing the Fund for International Public Service to fund and oversee "international programs and projects in the national interest." House Bill 6990, sponsored by John Monagan (D-CT), would have established the federally chartered American International Cultural and Educational Council, which would use mostly private funds to finance international labor and educational projects previously funded by the CIA. HR 7745, sponsored by Donald M. Fraser (D-MN), sought to establish the Institute of International Affairs using federal funds for international education projects. HR 8724, sponsored by S. Benjamin Rosenthal (D-NY), would have created the federally funded American Council on International Education to support "overseas activities of private American voluntary associations."[49]

The EWA report's appendix A proposed, "a new federally chartered and funded national institute largely under private control and management."[50]

This proposed institute would inherit and oversee most CIA orphan programs but with transparency of funds, oversight, and activities. The proposed institute's structure was modeled on existing bodies like the National Research Council, the National Science Foundation, and the National Academy of Sciences. By June, a more polished proposal expanding this initial draft document had been circulated. It described in some detail the structure of a proposed new federal agency overseeing US international educational funding.[51] But all of these proposed solutions were beyond what was politically possible.

In May 1967, the Ford Foundation's David Bell sent McGeorge Bundy a memo on "CIA Orphans—Rusk Committee staff thinking" that also circulated within the greater foundation community. Bell maintained close contact with Rusk Committee members, White House staff, and budget personnel, and his memo summarized what he believed to be the most likely developments. Bell observed that many CIA orphans ran educational or cultural exchanges or technical assistance programs with similarities to programs financed by AID or other US governmental programs. He argued that if these existing agencies took on these programs, increased budgetary lines would be needed, but this solution had the advantage of avoiding new legislation or creating new organizations.[52]

Bell proposed that the Agency for International Development play an active role in the "political development movement." This made some institutional sense, he explained, as "AID has for some time had contracts with the International Development Foundation, a CIA orphan which has been working to organize Latin American campesinos and slum dwellers in Peru and Chile, and arrangements had been virtually completed, prior to the recent revelations, for AID to finance all of IDF's work in Chile after June 20th of this year."[53]

Bell acknowledged that in many instances "the kinds of political action that have been conducted with CIA funding cannot conceivably be funded by government overtly—for example, action through an American labor union to stimulate a strike intended to bring down a foreign government."[54] However, Bell recognized that even while CIA-funded foundations would no longer carry out clandestine activities, the "CIA can of course continue to operate directly in such cases, under normal control system, but they could not use a U.S. private organization as an intermediary."[55] Still, Bell admitted that "it is entirely clear that many of the CIA orphans would find this far from a satisfactory solution, just as many other private, non-profit organizations working abroad do not find AID, CU, and USIA funding very satisfactory."[56] The reason, he continued, is essentially that the private organizations would like to have government financing for programs they themselves have worked out and want to undertake—whereas the government agencies in general feel themselves to be under a mandate to accomplish specific purposes, and look at the private organizations as possible instruments to carry out those purposes. Once in a while the two approaches coincide, and the desires of the private organization fit quite well with the program and priorities of the government program (witness IDF in Chile, or to take a non-CIA example, the work of the National Rural Electric Cooperative Association, financed by AID, in Latin America and elsewhere). More frequently, however, the private organization must chop and change its proposals in an effort to fit into a governmental program, an effort which, even if successful, often leaves everyone concerned feeling bruised and exhausted.[57]

Fundamental arguments ensued over whether it would be best to establish a new governmental source of funding that could address these needs or whether existing agencies should undertake these tasks.

Bell explained that the rationale for taking taxpayer funds and giving them to nongovernmental organizations to do the government's work was "to strengthen educational and other public-interest institutions abroad and to improve mutual understanding between the U.S. and other countries."[58] Bell acknowledged there could be problems with some AID or USIA programs overlapping with these proposed projects, but he believed these redundancies could be eliminated. Like others during this moment, Bell's concerns did not primarily focus on whether the United States *should* engage in the activities that had been funded by the CIA's funding fronts. The Cold War logic of soft power was a given, not to be questioned. Instead, his and the Ford Foundation's primary concern was to determine how to best continue these CIA-created operations under new funding sources.

In response to Bell's memo, McGeorge Bundy proposed that when devising replacement funds for CIA orphan programs, they should use political channels designed to bypass congressional members critical of the CIA. Bundy advocated that "people ought to put their minds on the question of organizing any new setup so that it does not go to Congressman Rooney."[59] Bundy would have been happy to continue doing an end-run around Congress, thereby avoiding CIA critics, and he believed these problems needed the right political spin. For

Bundy, the lesson of CIA orphans appeared not to be that there was an inherent problem in running covert programs supporting CIA goals abroad; the problem was how to avoid getting caught.

Others at the Ford Foundation had different responses. Eugene S. Staples believed the best way forward would be to force CIA orphans to openly compete with other organizations for State Department funds. Staples favored creating a "new quasi-public authority to channel public funds to private groups interested in working overseas." He encouraged Bell to remain focused on which specific activities should be undertaken abroad and then to think about how these activities could be funded under a "quasi-public authority."[60]

F. C. Ward worried about involving new private organizations that might not have regional expertise. Ward believed a solution to the CIA orphan problem could be found by considering the Asia Foundation and the African-American Institute as "structural prototypes" of how new agencies could work. Like the Asia Foundation, these new institutes "would be staffed on a long-term basis by men and women competent in academic and cultural matters and encouraged to remain for long periods in a given country or region in order to become thoroughly acquainted with its intellectuals, academic and non-academic, and fully acceptable to them."[61] This vision came close to describing the home that would be built for several CIA orphans, yet these descriptions assume that something built in secret by the CIA, with hidden parts and undisclosed agendas, could become normalized simply by switching to a public funding stream. It was an approach that ignored the political issues embedded in the roots of these programs.

At the Ford Foundation, Francis X. Sutton described this mishmash of post–Rusk Committee efforts to preserve the work of CIA orphans as efforts to devise "a governmental agency to support international activities which were in the national interest, had a quasi-political character, and yet ought not to be conducted by a governmental agency."[62] This was, of course, the main reason why the CIA had created these now orphaned organizations in the first place. Sutton quoted Beth Webster, who characterized the CIA's covert funding of the International Commission of Jurists as "stressing the worthwhileness of the activity and the impossibility of doing it on a governmental basis."[63] Such solutions looked to government-funded private organizations as what might be thought of as a way of openly laundering government funds, by having private foundations delivering programs meeting the US government's approval. While DTPILLAR had used secret CIA funds to similar ends, these post-CIA orphan plans would use "clean" State Department funds and actual private foundations for similar ends, with the assumption that as long as non-CIA funds were flowing, few would care about the past of these programs.

By May 1967, two CIA orphan groups, the World Confederation of Organizations of the Teaching Profession and the American Society of African Culture, had approached the Ford Foundation seeking private funds to cover activities threatened by the public exposure of their CIA links. Sutton estimated that the CIA's covert funding of these two front foundations had totaled around $12 million annually, "exclusive of Radio Free Europe[,] of which about $8 million was accounted for by the Asia Foundation."[64] Sutton advised Ford staff to exercise caution and to not make overly specific inquiries into the details of previous budgets for these organizations, as some in Washington might become concerned over such inquiries.

THE ROCKEFELLER FOUNDATION WEIGHS IN

Like the Ford Foundation, the Rockefeller Foundation prepared internal reports evaluating impacts on foundations in the wake of the CIA revelations. As news of the CIA's use of legitimate and front foundations spread in early March 1967, Rockefeller family advisor John E. Lockwood wrote a private memo to John D. Rockefeller III.[65] In it he mulled over questions these revelations raised for the Rockefeller Foundation:

> May a private charity knowingly permit members of its staff to be full or part time agents of the CIA? What should a private foundation say if it is asked to share the financing of some other agency with the CIA? What about a proposition from the CIA that it wants to withdraw and requests private foundations to bail it out? Should they do so? What is our attitude towards the assertion of pressure upon foundations from high sources? . . . What should now be done about those organizations which have publicly been identified as the recipients of CIA funds? Are they all dead ducks or are some still salvageable? Should they be salvaged? How does one draw a line between those that can and should be and those that can't and shouldn't?[66]

These political and ethical questions cut to the core of the Asia Foundation's existence, but there were no clear answers forthcoming from Rockefeller or from the foundation community. Yet, given that the Rockefeller Foundation had long funded projects aligned with US internationalist policies and rotated personnel between foundation and governmental positions, Lockwood's framing of these questions ignored many of the ways that Rockefeller had already been complicit with US agencies.

The first draft of the Rockefeller Foundation's report *Philanthropy and Public Interests: Central Intelligence Agency and Foundations* critically assessed the harm brought by exposure of the CIA's use of clandestine activities involving private scholars. The report explained that these recent disclosures had spawned a new "game of 'CIA watching'" that was damaging the agency and foundations and creating difficulties for scholars and students working abroad. The report was concerned that these uses of "clandestine funds can have a most devastating long term effect" on international programs, generating worries that there would be attempts "to discredit an entire student movement [such as the National Student Association] as supported by tainted funds given and no personnel contacts with the Agency, but the appearance cannot be effectively removed that there might have been such."[67]

A later draft of this memo argued that "so far as possible, government support of private activities and private organizations should be open," but this later draft lacked a direct critique of clandestine use of private foundations for intelligence purposes. This draft viewed the primary hazard of intelligence agencies in the field as being the "risk of achieving an immediate goal" of gathering needed intelligence or of training "at the expense of the destruction of the philanthropic agency." It argued that "the impairment of the reputation of all philanthropic agencies is a very difficult and great risk."[68] Following this line of reasoning, the Rockefeller Foundation report argued that the best solution to these problems was to end all clandestine funding programs.

The Rockefeller report also considered instances in which academics received only small portions of their backing from covert CIA funds. They rationalized that such tinctures of CIA funding diluted the agency's impact on the resulting academic work. They did not pursue another logical interpretation—that any Rockefeller Foundation project also funded by only small amounts of CIA money was using Rockefeller funds to subsidize a project sought by the CIA for its own purposes. The report asked if there existed "projects with substantial publicly identified clandestine support now in mid-stream" and, if these could be identified, what should be done.[69]

HAVING THEIR HEGEMONY AND EATING IT TOO

Decades after the Katzenbach Committee considered how the CIA had infiltrated and covertly shaped various domestic programs using front organizations, Nicholas Katzenbach (no longer needing to provide cover for a sitting president) reflected on the dangers these CIA secret sharers presented to democracy, education, and global relations. He acknowledged that because covert activities are by nature secret, they are rarely accountable and they "run counter to every governmental principle we proclaim, because it is always the end that justifies the means." He noted the hypocrisy of Americans demanding open governmental processes at home while feeling "free to interfere covertly with governmental processes elsewhere—to do things we would be horrified to find being done here at home." After leaving public office, Katzenbach became so opposed to covert activities that he advocated banning them all together.[70]

Today, there are few surviving documents in the released Asia Foundation papers detailing staff reactions to the public acknowledgment of receiving CIA funds. One collection of folders with foundation "office announcements" from the summer of 1967 provides evidence of a significant exodus of employees just months after the CIA's sponsorship became public.[71] Some foundation personnel took leaves of absence soon afterward, such as James Stewart, who took two years' leave of absence working as the Japan Society of New York's executive director from 1967 to 1969.[72]

While the US public was startled by news of CIA funding fronts, reactions to proposals for what should be done were mixed. Many Americans appeared comfortable continuing these same operations with more transparent funding. Former FCC chair Paul Porter told the *New York Times* that the CIA front program had accomplished positive results and that it was "too bad the CIA got caught." Even CIA critics like Senator J. William Fulbright (D-AR) favored finding a new means of funding exposed CIA-funded projects. Some, like Milton Eisenhower, former president of Johns Hopkins University, admired these programs but conceded that simply shifting new funding to these same programs would result in the "new" effort being "discredited before it began."[73]

Even after the Asia Foundation was publicly linked to CIA funding, the *Times* and other news outlets stated that the foundation was uninvolved with collecting intelligence, efforts to contact or track foreign nationals, or agency propaganda efforts. Typical of media representations of the foundation's relationship with the CIA was a December 1967 *New York Times* article on the Rusk

Committee's efforts to find new funding sources for CIA orphans; it described the Asia Foundation as simply having provided "technical assistance to underdeveloped countries," such as facilitating "the establishment of rice cooperatives and [helping to] write the South Korean Constitution," as if "helping" write another country's constitution were a nonpolitical act of "technical assistance."[74]

Two months after the foundation's CIA links were disclosed, the State Department asked Congress for $3 million to fund the Asia Foundation; most ($2.5 million) of this $3 million was directed to the foundation through AID—in many ways a natural agency for continuing the forms of soft-power counterinsurgency programs the CIA had financed at the Asia Foundation for years—with another $600,000 channeled through the Bureau of Cultural Affairs.[75] A May 1968 arrangement secured bridge funds for some CIA orphans, like the Asia Foundation, while leaving others unfunded.[76]

While the Asia Foundation and other CIA orphans scrambled to find new overt funding streams, what was missing was a clear public explanation of what exactly was the relationship between the CIA and these organizations. Congress and the press failed to hold the executive branch responsible for these programs. In this sense, the Katzenbach Committee had been very successful in keeping criticism away from the Johnson administration and in avoiding even the most basic disclosure of how much money had gone to which CIA orphans, much less identifying all the orphans or admitting that some of the fronts hadn't merely run anticommunist propaganda programs but had also generated intelligence for the CIA.

But as the next chapter shows, beyond this public posturing of inquiry, the CIA had plans underway to save the foundation. The agency had created DT-PILLAR, and it would help launch the foundation's new life as a transparent, publicly funded entity. This exposed covert government program that had pretended to do the work of a private foundation would now be reborn as an actual private foundation, running largely on government funds, devoted to continuing many of its original tasks.

12 The CIA's 1967 Termination and Liquidation of DTPILLAR

Honest and independent scholarship was possible in the early area institutes, but the academic integrity of the institutes themselves was compromised by a secret and extensive network of ties to the CIA and the FBI.

BRUCE CUMINGS / *Parallax Visions*

While the Rusk Committee debated how best to secure continuing funds for CIA orphans, the CIA followed those discussions and considered the best way for the Asia Foundation to continue operating. At a May 27, 1967, meeting, the 303 Committee agreed that, if needed, they would provide enough funding for the foundation to complete the year. The 303 Committee also approved funding for "a substantial carryover into FY 1969."[1] Even as the foundation board declared that the Asia Foundation would no longer accept CIA money, the executive branch and CIA agreed that the agency could continue secretly funding the foundation until it could operate on its own.[2]

An internal June 5, 1967, CIA memo, from John M. Clarke, director of the CIA's Planning, Program, and Budget (PPB) Division, outlined several possible ways to fund the foundation. Clarke discussed the possibility to "surge fund the Asia Foundation for 1968"—a plan in which the CIA would dump a significant sum of money into the foundation's coffers before the end of the fiscal year. This would allow it to subsist for months or years until ongoing operating funds could be secured. Jim Clark at the CIA's Bureau of the Budget had indicated that he "would have no difficulty with such a release in principle. He stated, however, that the Agency must be prepared to replenish this money in the Reserve from its 1968 appropriation, irrespective of any program cuts made by the Congress."[3] Clarke worried that channeling CIA surge funds could lead to a congressional intervention and the loss of these funds. He urged the CIA to "defend its budget as it now exists before the Congress with the intention of putting the [redacted] budgeted for the Asia Foundation into the reserve to offset the equal amounts used for surge funding."[4] Clarke recommended "making inquiries on the Hill" to "explain the advantages of funding [it] now."[5] He proposed securing funds under a congressional continuing resolution to finance the CIA's existing budget appropriations, with proper notifications to Congress. But this would mean that the foundation continued to secretly receive CIA funds.

Even with the end of CIA funding, the Asia Foundation's board "assured the [Central Intelligence] Agency that the Foundation will continue its present policies and areas of interest and its normal functions and procedures." In preparation for ending CIA funding, the agency advised the foundation to cut "overhead and program costs as soon as possible to a level which is more commensurate with the anticipated levels of support from other foundations, overt government grants and contracts, channels to be developed by the Rusk Committee and donations from private individuals and corporations."[6]

On June 6, 1967, an unidentified CIA branch presented DCI Richard Helms with a proposal titled "Liquidation of CA [Covert Action] Staff Proprietary Project DTPILLAR."[7] This decision followed the Katzenbach Committee's recommendation to terminate the CIA's relationship with the Asia Foundation. The 303 Committee had already decided on May 27 that "overt U.S. Government support should be provided to help sustain the Foundation in the future," and they "approved a terminal Agency grant of ▇▇▇▇▇▇▇ to be funded through covert channels. This amount, together with an estimated ▇▇▇▇▇▇▇ in savings and reserve funds available to the Foundation at the end of its current fiscal year, 31 July 1967, will provide funds for FY 1968 expenditures without a prejudicial curtailment of activities, and should allow a sustainable carryover into FY 1969."[8] This hidden CIA maneuver provided the foundation with funds for more than another year of operations, keeping the organization afloat while it transitioned to non-CIA funds.[9]

Although CIA financing of the foundation was ending, agency personnel believed that the sort of programs the agency had established would continue. Still, CIA personnel worried that the lack of CIA "field station support," "headquarters guidance," "security traces," and "establishment of priorities" would negatively impact "the Foundation's day-to-day capabilities to provide support for U.S. Government policies in Asia."[10] But the CIA was confident that foundation personnel would still "have access to U.S. policy guidance through the designated liaison officer in the Department of State."[11] It appears here that the CIA's hope for the post-CIA foundation was that the State Department would take on some of the guidance and support roles the CIA had provided since DTPILLAR was established in 1951.

The CIA liquidation report's "disposition of personnel" section identified only one CIA employee working for DTPILLAR, described as "the foundation field representative in Vietnam." The CIA reported that this employee would "remain in his position until a satisfactory non-Agency replacement, now planned by September 1967, can be made in order to avoid the security risks which may be involved in an earlier dismissal or resignation. After that he will be given an assignment which will not compromise the Foundation. His cover salary and other costs after July 1967 will not be reimbursed to the Foundation. Contracts and arrangements with all other personnel will be the responsibility of the Board of Trustees."[12] The foundation's 1967 Vietnam field representative was Leonard C. Overton, who appears likely to be this CIA employee.[13]

The CIA was caught in a bind. It needed to terminate its Asia Foundation relationship as quickly as possible, but if it did so without providing enough "covert financial support" for 1968, the foundation would collapse.[14] The CIA was unsure if it should use reserve monies to quickly fund the foundation so it could immediately seek private funds or whether it should wait for the start of the 1968 fiscal year and "attempt to pass funds to the Foundation then." The CIA worried that if they waited for congressional appropriations, which could take another half year, the foundation might not survive.[15] In June 1967, John M. Clarke, CIA director of Planning, Program, and Budget, authorized the CIA to release $8.5 million as a cash reserve to help tide over the Asia Foundation during its post-CIA transition period.[16] To assure continuity for foundation programs while they sought new funding, the CIA's Office of Finance was "authorized to write off the balance in the DTPILLAR investment account after the processing of the July 1967 financial statement submitted by the Project, plus any part of *the 8.5 million terminal funding which has not yet been recorded in the investment account at that time.*"[17]

As CIA ties to the foundation ended, CIA-witting foundation employees purged agency-linked records from foundation facilities. The CIA's DTPILLAR liquidation document mentions the foundation's "overt files," thereby implying the existence of "covert files." The former were to "continue under the Foundation's present records management system." CIA documents confirm the foundation maintained "a secure file of correspondence and documents executed in pseudonym," and the agency mandated that these records "be made available to a representative of the CA [Covert Action] Staff to determine its disposition."[18] Following this agency directive, the CIA removed "secure files" as the foundation cut its CIA ties.

The CIA planned on establishing a "U.S. government liaison after agency disassociation" to maintain institutional continuity and indirect connections with the foundation through the 303 Committee's State Department liaison member. The 303 Committee was to "designate an officer in the Department of State to act as liaison with the Foundation on matters of national interest and as coordinator for negotiations between the Government and the Foundation on matters of overt support. For as long as is required the CA [Covert Action] Staff will make available to the Department representative an Agency officer who is knowledgeable of the project and Foundation affairs."[19]

The closest thing to a news story ever acknowledging that the pre-1968 Asia Foundation had been entirely financially dependent on the CIA for its existence appeared in a February 1968 *Washington Post* article headlined "State Dept. to Ask Congress for Asia Foundation Funds."[20] In this article the *Post* reported that

> the total money requested, some $3.1 million[,] is expected to meet about half the Foundation's budget and help replace funds it had been receiving through Central Intelligence Agency conduit organizations.
>
> The foundation acknowledged last Spring that it had been receiving CIA money but announced that it would accept no more from such sources.... AID and State Department officials explained that they are now going to ask Congress to pick up CIA's tab because they consider the Asia Foundation is and has been doing valuable education and cultural work abroad and think this should be continued with above-board, openly acknowledged U.S. Government help.[21]

While not stating it directly, this statement that $3.1 million would cover only about half of the budget hole created by the lack of CIA funding announced to anyone paying attention that the foundation had long been covertly receiving at least $6.2 million a year from the Central Intelligence Agency.

In 1968, AID requested $2 million "in general support for The Asia Foundation and another $500,000 for a book distribution program," as well as another $600,000 in funds from the State Department's Educational and Cultural Affairs Bureau for "educational and cultural projects."[22] The foundation's budget had been $8 million, but publicly this figure appears to have been cut in half for the year to follow, presumably because the foundation could secretly draw on "terminal funding" the CIA provided. Because I could not locate records on the specifics of this transitional funding, and my inquiries to the current president of the Asia Foundation did not yield any specifics of such funding, the amount involved remains conjecture. While this $8.3 million in CIA funds appears in some CIA documents, the actual transfer of these funds remains undocumented.

The 1968 *Washington Post* story continued to spread the disinformation that "part of [the Asia Foundation's] financing comes from private contributions from individuals and institutions, many of them in the San Francisco area." This created the false impression that maybe only half the foundation's funding had come from the CIA, although this story finally reported that the CIA had been providing the foundation with millions of dollars a year.[23]

Even with declassified CIA documents indicating the agency's ability and desire to provide the foundation with enough surge funds to survive the next fiscal year or longer, it remains unclear how large the CIA's surge payment to the foundation was. The funds provided by Congress for the following year are known, and that amount would not have been enough to sustain the foundation. Thus, given the CIA paper trail establishing the agency's ability to provide these funds, it appears that the foundation used a final CIA surge payment to get through the following fiscal year or two, during which time it lobbied for significant State Department funds for the coming years.

CONGRESSIONAL AID FUNDING HEARINGS AND CIA ASIA FOUNDATION INQUIRIES

As the Asia Foundation transitioned from CIA to State Department funding, Congress expressed concerns that many of the foundation's projects replicated programs at AID, USIS, USIA, or other State Department agencies. There were also questions about whether the foundation would simply continue what had been CIA-designed operations with State Department funds. During 1968 congressional hearings, Representative Garner E. Shriver (R-KS) asked AID's John Bullitt about funds requested by AID for the Asia Foundation.[24] Bullitt testified these funds were for academic programming and book programs in Asia. Upon hearing this explanation, Representative Shriver asked if this was just a continuation of what the CIA had been doing. Bullitt avoided confirming that the foundation had been doing CIA work, replying instead that

> this would be essentially the same kind of activities that the Asia Foundation was doing when it was financed by the CIA. My understanding of this is that generally speaking in most countries in Asia, the Asia Foundation has a very high reputation. It has operated in quite a nonpolitical way. When the news came out in Rampart[s] magazine about this source of financing, and we were considering whether or not to

continue the Asia Foundation's activities through AID and other financing during the interim period when they might be able to get private financing, we made a very thorough canvass of the countries in Asia where it has been functioning, and the results were generally very favorable, except as I recall in—[25]

But Representative Shriver interrupted Bullitt, bluntly asking what the purpose of the foundation was. Bullitt explained that "essentially it was a private foundation that was partly financed by the CIA. The purpose of it was, or its operations were[,] to promote the education of Asian leaders, non-Communist Asia leaders, to provide them with scholarships, with opportunities to study, to provide educational materials and the like." Shriver asked Bullitt if the foundation was established by the CIA. Bullitt said he did not know and repeated the perhaps technically true (if one counted occasional minuscule outside funds) but fundamentally misleading statement that "it was partially CIA-financed."[26]

At this point, Representative Silvio Conte (R-MA) asked, "Why should CIA get involved in anything like this?" Bullitt avoided answering the question, instead saying this had happened long ago. Conte did not like his evasion and told him,

> I don't care if it started 20 years ago. My questions is, "Why should CIA get involved in something like this?" This is one of the tragedies, that the Congress and the American people do not know what the budget of CIA is, and nobody can get underneath that veil to determine what they are doing.
>
> I was amazed to hear about this CIA involvement when the information first came out last year. CIA was involved in it and was exposed, so AID is going to take it over. I imagine this is going to have a real great impact with the Southeast Asian nations when they know this.[27]

Bullitt replied that AID had not been involved in the Asia Foundation's CIA connections; Conte accepted this but asked if these were the types of activities that AID undertook. Bullitt agreed that they were, then Conte said, "That's exactly right. Yet here was something that CIA was doing all along. The Congress, members of this committee, the Appropriations Committee, outside of that inner circle, that handles that CIA budget, none of us would have known about it. It certainly would not have had my blessings had I known about it. That is why I am disturbed. I certainly want this to be a part of the record."[28]

Representative Conte identified five areas where the foundation would concentrate its programming: "strengthening the institutions of law and public administration," "community and rural development projects promoting the democratic process," "social, economic and cultural, institution building on a selective basis," "book distribution, local publishing, and library development," and the "creation or strengthening of Asian regional institutions and patterns of cooperation."[29] Conte asked Bullitt how this list related to the CIA's activities. Bullitt again responded hesitantly, assuring Conte that he was not as knowledgeable about CIA activities at the foundation as was his boss, William Bundy, who was assistant secretary for the Bureau of East and Pacific Affairs in the State Department.

Conte assured him that he was not alone in not understanding what the CIA was doing with these programs. Bullitt misleadingly testified that "essentially" the Asia Foundation "was not an operating arm of the Agency's operations. This was an effort to provide funds to an organization that then operated quite independently as I understand it of the CIA to accomplish these objectives. They were seeking to strengthen generally the ability of Asians to create and continue free institutions."[30] Conte asked why AID was not running these programs instead of a CIA-funded group. Bullitt did not have an answer. The *Congressional Record* notes that some "discussion off the record" transpired, followed by Representative Donald W. Riegle (R-MI) stating on the record that "it is inexcusable that Mr. Bundy is not here or someone of ranking authority who can speak for him," clarifying that this was not a critique of the committee but of the State Department, implying that State was avoiding publicly explaining exactly how the CIA had been using the Asia Foundation for all that time.[31] Representative Riegel argued that without Bundy or the secretary of state providing testimony on the CIA's past connection to the Asia Foundation, "we ought to adjourn our hearings until such as time as they can" testify.[32] Riegel stressed how much this absence of knowledgeable witnesses disturbed him.

Later, William Bundy did appear before the committee and Representative Charlotte Thompson Reid (R-IL) noted that the requested funds for AID were essentially replacing CIA funds. She then asked Bundy, "What arrangement do you now have—or will you have—with the Asia Foundation?"[33] Bundy's response was in the form of a prewritten statement outlining an AID plan to provide a $2.5 million grant to the Asia Foundation for 1969 so that it could "continue its valuable development work in Asia." He said that in the next few years the foundation planned to "become independent of U.S. Government assistance."³⁴ He compared this funding to that provided by AID to other organizations, like the International Executive Service Corps or the International Planned Parenthood Federation.

In response to a question about how unwelcome the Asia Foundation would likely be in Asia after these CIA revelations, Bundy recited an impressive litany of the foundation's past expulsions from Asia countries. He claimed there had been no single reason for these expulsions, a statement clearly misrepresenting the overarching pattern of suspicion that the foundation was a tool of Western hegemony—suspicions now verified by these established CIA links. Bundy testified that,

> In the case of Burma, the Asia Foundation was asked to leave along with all foreign private and semiprivate foundations including the Ford Foundation, the British Council and the Alliance Française in April 1962. This was due to the Burmese Government's decision to restrict its contacts with foreign nations to government contacts.
>
> In Cambodia[,] the Asia Foundation left voluntarily in January 1966 several months after Cambodia had suspended relations with the United States. The Cambodian Prime Minister wrote a letter to the head of the Asia Foundation saying that when circumstances permit, the Cambodian Government would be willing to consider the return of the Foundation.
>
> The Asia Foundation was asked to leave Indonesia during the Sukarno period. It has not reestablished an office in Djakarta, but the foundation, at the initiative of the Indonesian Government, has financed the international travel of Indonesians attending international conferences, carries on some activities in the book field, and may become more active in the training field.
>
> The Government of India stated on February 15, 1968, that it was terminating the India programs of the Asia Foundation, The Asia Foundation subsequently announced that its office in India would close on or about July 31.
>
> According to present information, the foundation's programs in 14 other Asian countries have not been affected.³⁵

While Representative Riegle had earlier claimed he would get straightforward answers out of Bundy or some other knowledgeable official, if any answers were forthcoming about the extent and intent of CIA financing of Asia Foundation activities, they do not appear in the congressional record. Bundy's testimony instead stuck close to the misleading minimalist version of CIA involvement in Asia Foundation activities that had appeared in the available newspaper stories.

RELEASED GOVERNMENT DOCUMENTS ON POST-CIA ASIA FOUNDATION FUNDING

A collection of declassified State Department documents from the Johnson administration years includes a June 22, 1966, document identified as Memorandum 132. This memo documents that government efforts to secure non-CIA funding for the Asia Foundation began almost a year before the foundation's CIA ties were exposed.[36] These developments grew from concerns that journalists' investigations into the foundation's CIA ties could expose it as "a Central Intelligence Agency proprietary, [that] was established in 1954 to undertake cultural and educational activities on behalf of the United States Government in ways not open to official U.S. agencies."[37] The memo expressed concern that journalists' "inquiries will lead to a published revelation of TAF's CIA connection. In the present climate of national dissent and in the wake of recent critical press comment on CIA involvement with American universities, we feel a public allegation that CIA funds and controls TAF would be seized upon, with or without proof, and magnified beyond its actual significance to embarrass the Administration and U.S. national interests at home and abroad. Some immediate defensive and remedial measures are required."[38] The memo argued that the foundation's best hope for long-term survival would be to end total financial dependence on covert CIA funding. Legitimate public sources of funds needed to be secured, and the memo concluded, "In the long run, we feel TAF's vulnerability to press attack can be reduced and its viability as an instrument of U.S. foreign policy in Asia can be assured by relieving it of *its total dependence upon covert funding support from this Agency*. In the belief that TAF contributes substantially to U.S. national interests in Asia, and can continue to contribute if its viability is sustained, CIA requests the Committee's study and attention to possible alternative means of supporting it."[39]

A few weeks later, the 303 Committee again discussed funding options for the foundation, with White House press secretary Bill Moyers and CIA's Cord Meyer joining the discussion. The committee considered how much money would be required to create an endowment to sustain the foundation if CIA funding ended. Meyer raised the possibility that a new governmental institution might be required to perform such needed work. The record of the meeting states that Meyer

> cited a speech by Eugene R. Black at the recent Wesleyan University commencement dealing with grants in aid. It was emphasized that substantial private contributions and those of foundations are inhibited, if not precluded, by CIA association with such organizations as The Asia Foundation. Mr. Rostow pointed out that the CIA had many times taken up the slack when other agencies were unable to come up with funds. Mr. Meyer's suggestion was greeted with considerable interest, and Mr. Helms suggested that any committee on this subject be headed in the White House in order to give it sufficient impetus. Mr. Moyers agreed to approach Mr. Harry McPherson and urged that talks continue between Mr. Meyer, Mr. McPherson and other interested parties. It was noted that although the committee would not operate under 303 aegis, its determinations and findings might well have a bearing on future proposals before the 303 Committee.[40]

A month after the *New York Times* exposed the foundation's CIA ties, the 303 Committee met to discuss the termination of the covert funding relationship with the Asia Foundation and to consider the relevant recommendations made by the Katzenbach Committee. The 303 Committee referred to the foundation's postexposure press release as "a carefully limited statement of admission of past CIA support."[41] "Limited" in this context was a euphemism for what might more directly be termed limited truth or lying, as the foundation trustees' statement followed the CIA's script that misled the public about the extent of agency involvement in the foundation. The memo written after this 303 Committee meeting in May 1967 explained that the foundation trustees

> sought to delimit the effects of an anticipated exposure of Agency support by the American press and, if their statement or some future exposé does not seriously impair TAF's acceptability in Asia, to continue operating in Asia with overt private and official support. To date, the March 21 statement has produced no serious threat to TAF operations in Asia, and the Trustees are now prepared to attempt to acquire the necessary support for TAF to go on as a private institution, partially supported by overt U.S. Government grants. This will take time and

TAF meanwhile faces the immediate problem of the need for funds during FY 1968.⁴²

With the end of the fiscal year approaching, the foundation had only enough funds to cover costs for three more months. The CIA made it clear that the foundation was important enough to their Asian operational vision that they were "prepared to provide whatever assistance remains within its authority and competence to offer."⁴³ To ensure that the program continued throughout the following year, the foundation's board "with the encouragement and support of CIA" stated it would no longer accept CIA funds—proclaiming that it was "imperative that this declaration be supported by normal or near-normal TAF operations in Asia over the months ahead. [Four lines of text redacted here.] It has further authorized the Trustees to seek pledges of support from heads of private foundations and other prospective private donors; but, as a practical matter, no immediate results can be anticipated."⁴⁴ The CIA hoped to supply funds for one final year, but if the foundation was unable to secure other funds after that, "the Agency recommends that serious consideration be given to phasing down or terminating the Foundation."⁴⁵

A 303 Committee memo from June 1968 establishes that while the foundation was supposed to have secured its own funding or be closed by that time, it was still without an ongoing funding source, yet it remained open. By June 1968, Walt Rostow was looking to the foundation's board with hopes they could raise the millions needed from the private sector, while the 303 Committee looked toward the Department of State, especially AID, for financial support. There was no clear path forward, and the memo concluded with the observation that "if there were deep sighs for the good old days of straight covert funding, they were not audible due to the hum of the air conditioner in the White House Situation Room."⁴⁶

CIA funding for the foundation appears to have ended with a final surge disbursement to help it survive the transition to other funding sources, but even with new funding there remained organizational continuities linking the CIA to the foundation. There was the continuity of remaining foundation staff who had been aware of CIA ties. This included some country representatives, but the most significant of these employees was Haydn Williams, whose role as president had guaranteed past direct involvement with the CIA. It is remarkable that the foundation, board, staff, the CIA, or concerned members of the public did not demand that this most obvious connection to the CIA be severed; Williams instead remained president for another twenty-two years. This leadership continuity inevitably raises possibilities of informal backchannel connections continuing after the CIA's funding of the foundation ended with the final 1967 surge payment, but even without any such contact, Williams remaining as leader after the CIA era ended has a very bad look.

The CIA document transcribed below is presented in its entirety because it establishes the CIA's interest in ensuring the foundation's survival and continuity of mission after severing the ties between them. The date of this memo is unclear, but it appears to have been written around August 1967. It discusses the approaching final payment of the CIA's terminal funding of the Asia Foundation, as discussed in the June 1967 TAF liquidation plan, and includes a copy of a signed August 1967 memorandum of understanding outlining the terms of the CIA's withdrawal from its involvement with the Asia Foundation.[47]

MEMORANDUM FOR: Executive Director-Comptroller
VIA: Deputy Director for Plans
SUBJECT: Terminal Funding/The Asia Foundation
REFERENCE: TAF Liquidation Plan,
Approved 20 June 1967 by the DCI

1. On 10 August the final increment of terminal funds in the amount of ▮▮▮▮▮▮, was passed to the Asia Foundation (TAF). As you know these funds were U.S. Treasury Bonds and Notes in Bearer form. The passing of these Bonds and Notes was effected securely and smoothly, witnessed by ▮▮▮▮▮▮, Chief, Monetary Division, and an officer of this Staff who observed the placing of these funds in a safety deposit box in the Wells Fargo Bank in San Francisco. An appropriate receipt was obtained from the Chairman of the Board, President, and Controller of TAF.

2. Prior to the passage of Bonds and Notes to TAF, we asked key members of TAF's Executive Committee to sign a terminal Memorandum of Understanding (attached). This Memorandum was approved by the Office of General Counsel and the Deputy Director for Support prior to our forwarding it to TAF for their signatures. The language of the Agency's Administrative Plan, which has been binding upon TAF since 1963, refers to the Agency as the "sponsor," therefore the attached Memorandum contains similar language.

3. In order to complete our Project liquidation records, it is requested that you sign the attached Memorandum of Understanding for the Agency.

██████████

Acting Chief
Covert Action Staff
Attachment:
Memorandum of Understanding

[Stamped: Declassified and released by Central Intelligence Agency Sources Methods Exemption 3B2B Nazi War Crimes Disclosure Act, Date 2007]

MEMORANDUM OF UNDERSTANDING

The undersigned acknowledge that upon conveyance of funds hereinafter, referred to as terminal funding, the Trustees of the Asia Foundation assume full responsibility for all aspects of the Foundation and obligations of the Foundation and declare their intent to apply all its assets in furtherance of the present purposes of the Foundation as described in its Articles of Incorporation and amendments thereto.

The balance of the terminal funding, to be delivered to the custody of the Chairman of the Board, the President, and the Controller of the Asia Foundation in August 1967, constitutes full and final Sponsor financial support to the Asia Foundation and upon delivery, the Sponsor relinquishes its claim to all assets of the Foundation, thereby terminating its proprietary relationship.

Upon completion of terminal funding the Administrative Plan (known to the Foundation as Plan 63) and all other Sponsor controls are rescinded. All classified material in the possession of the Foundation will be returned to the Sponsor for safekeeping as soon as practicable.

The Foundation management will effect liaison with the Department of State with regard to U.S. policy interests in Asia and initiate requests for contractual arrangements with other elements of the United States Government. The Sponsor will provide staff support as appropriate to the Department of State during a transitional period, the duration of which will be determined by subsequent agreement between the parties concerned.⁴⁸

This agreement clearly "rescinded" the CIA's "sponsor controls." DTPILLAR ended, and the Asia Foundation ceased to be a CIA asset. This document was signed by one identity-redacted individual designated as "signing for the sponsor," as well as foundation chair Russell G. Smith, foundation president Haydn Williams, Turner H. McBaine (member, Executive Committee), and Mortimer Fleishhacker Jr. (member, Executive Committee). Because the CIA made its final payment—of a redacted amount—in US Treasury bonds and notes in bearer form, this was an untraceable transaction—no one outside the transaction would know the amount, route, or expenditure of this final covert CIA payment or where exactly this CIA money was spent.

The CIA's memorandum of understanding clarified that this final payment terminated the CIA's relationship with the Asia Foundation. It also established that the foundation was not simply cut loose to do as it pleased. It was now tethered to the "Department of State with regard to U.S. policy interests in Asia" and would "initiate requests for contractual arrangements with other elements of the United States Government." The document clarified that the CIA "will provide staff support as appropriate to the Department of State during a transitional period, the duration of which will be determined by subsequent agreement between the parties concerned," and it stressed the importance of mission continuity regardless of sponsorship.⁴⁹

While the terms of this liquidation are clear, the CIA's redaction of this declassified document withholds a vital detail of the arrangement: the amount of money paid in the form of nontraceable bonds in the CIA's final surge payment. The amount of this final CIA payment is crucial for understanding how this CIA orphan survived while struggling to secure new funding. Without knowing the size of this payment, we cannot understand how the foundation survived during the years immediately following July 1967, as the reported funds provided by the State Department for 1968 appear to have been only enough to cover about half the annual foundation budget. Further, if the CIA provided a sizable final surge payment designed to wean the foundation from total dependence on CIA funding, this would change our understanding of *when* the foundation stopped subsisting on CIA funds.

Because the Committee for Free Asia and the Asia Foundation were run as a DTPILLAR operation, the foundation never produced public reports listing sources of funding. At the time, foundation staff claimed this was to protect the privacy of donors, which was technically true given that the CIA wished to keep its funding secret. In 1968 the foundation issued its first financial statement to the public. Beverly Brewster's 1976 analysis of these first financial statements raised questions about the source of the funds listed in this first released foundation financial statement. The unresolved issues surrounding the origin of these first reported funds complicates our understanding of exactly how financially "post-" these first post-CIA years were. Brewster's analysis implied that the foundation was still partially subsisting on this final surge payment made in untraceable bonds, noting that in 1968 the foundation's

> security capital amounted to approximately $6 million, which would yield an income, at the rate of eight per cent interest, that could not possibly exceed $500,000. Yet its total expenditures were over $5 million, of which $3.8 million was distributed through 1,600 grants and projects. Although the president's remarks noted recent grants from AID and the State Department's Bureau of Educational and Cultural Affairs (CU), no specific amounts were given. In 1969, the balance sheet of the foundation's security assets showed $3.6 million, which would yield an income of $295,000. When this amount was combined with other cash assets, the total available income amounted to $708,275, yet its financial outlay for grants and program support was $3.5 million, of which $2.9 million went for projects. This time however, a note in the fine print on another page revealed that Government funds from AID ($2.1 million) and CU ($400,000) had been received which amounted to over $2.5 million, or over two-thirds of the total expenditures of the Foundation. Additional sources of income were small grants from the National Science Foundation and private organizations. The degree of influences that AID and CU funds have on Foundation grant/project decisions is unclear, although AID has stipulated that its monies may be used only in those countries with which AID has a bilateral or regional program.[50]

While questions remain about foundation funding in these initial post-CIA years, whatever the amount of the CIA's final surge payment in 1967, these funds made it possible for the foundation to survive until it secured funds from the State Department and other sources.

ASIA FOUNDATION CONTACT WITH OTHER CIA ORPHANS

In the months following the *Times* story exposing CIA connections, foundation staff occasionally corresponded with staff at other CIA orphans. After *Ramparts* broke the news in April 1967 that American Friends of the Middle East (AFME) had received CIA funds, AFME director of programs Orin Parker sent the Asia Foundation's Mary Gray the public statement issued by AFME.[51] Parker claimed, "This statement should clarify any questions regarding AFME's integrity and effectiveness as a private organization," though there was little in the statement that could have reduced concerns about CIA links.[52] AFME's board statement followed the now formulaic and absurd claim that operations had not been influenced by any outside funding source.[53] This letter was sent to AFME's supporters and maintained the same sort of public line the CIA crafted for the Asia Foundation's board after its CIA links were exposed.

Foundation correspondence during this period records the foundation distancing itself from other CIA fronts, as one orphan starved another while struggling for its own survival. In late 1967, a National Student Association representative contacted the foundation seeking funds to cover financial shortfalls stemming from their loss of CIA funding. Martha Darling, NSA director of international programs, asked for financial assistance to help support the NSA's Asian program. In an internal memo, Calvin Scollon, head of the foundation's program services, summarized Darling's predicament and confirmed a general agreement that the foundation would no longer fund NSA programs. Still, Scollon wondered "if the Foundation does not have a 'moral' obligation to provide some minimal? short-term assistance to NSA this year, simply because we were largely responsible for the Asian Program in the past and because it is conceivable that we would want to reestablish program contacts with it in the future."[54] Even with such misgivings, the foundation could not afford to continue funding the NSA after both organizations' CIA links were exposed. Because the Asia Foundation had been founded and run by the CIA whereas the NSA originated as a legitimate organization that the agency predatorily co-opted during times of financial difficulty, the foundation's complete abandonment of the NSA while only fighting to save itself appears particularly unseemly.

USING THE CIA FUNDING LEGACY
AS AN INTERNAL FUND-RAISING TACTIC

In 1969, an impressive legion of influential cold warriors lobbied the State Department to fill the CIA funding gap threatening the foundation's survival. Asia Foundation trustee Lucian Pye privately pressed Henry Kissinger to lobby within the Nixon administration for financial support. Pye argued that America was being shortsighted and that the country needed to "think ahead to the 'post Vietnam period' in Asia."[55] He reminded Kissinger of the important roles the foundation had played, and CIA documents record Undersecretary of State for Political Affairs Alexis Johnson briefing Kissinger about the foundation's history. Johnson explained to Kissinger that Robert Murphy and other foundation trustees had made a similar request some months earlier. Johnson agreed that more government funds were needed, and he recommended the possibility of a meeting between "selected Trustees" and President Nixon. Still, Johnson did not feel it was "feasible or desirable to go much beyond what we have already done."[56] But by 1969 even Kissinger had distanced himself from the exposed foundation. Although Kissinger's Harvard programs had benefited from years of foundation financial support, he strategically stayed aloof during their time of need. A month later Kissinger responded politely to these requests, acknowledging the important roles played by the foundation but also reminding Pye that the government was providing $3 million a year in funds. He promised no additional assistance.[57]

Individuals once associated with the foundation experienced fallout from these CIA associations for years. Japanese jurists continued to feel pressure not to accept foundation funds into the late 1970s.[58] In a 1972 oral history interview, Douglas Ensminger, former Ford Foundation representative to India (1952–70), reflected on how the CIA's involvement in programs like the Asia Foundation negatively affected Ford's relationships in India. Ensminger noted that whenever accusations of CIA involvement with any program in India occurred, members of the Communist Party in India engaged in effective anti-West media campaigns that tainted the reputations of all Western foundations. He claimed that he could

> always predict when the Communists would let loose an anti-American propaganda campaign. They would find illustrations to highlight the manner and intensity of infiltration of the CIA in all foreign spon-

sored aid programs. The Communist outbursts were meant to throw a shadow of concern about motives; therefore causing the Government to move with greater caution in receiving foreign assistance, especially in areas where it could be assumed the aid would spread its influence over the minds of men.

Unfortunately, the U.S. Department of State and the Defense Department were not always discreet in contacting the U.S. universities and research institutions to carry out specific areas of research in a particular country. When specific cases of linkage with the CIA were revealed in such research programs, the communists made the most of it in warning the Government of India to be wary of all U.S. assistance programs. Because the Government did not want to fight the communists on all issues in Parliament, frequently the Government was silent in Parliament[,] implying they too suspected some truth in the communist charges.[59]

Whenever any CIA connections were revealed, damage to relationships between US and Indian institutions followed. After the Michigan State University–CIA story broke, all university relationships between the two countries suffered.[60] Given the Ford Foundation's funding of MIT-CENIS projects with elements in India, Indonesia, and elsewhere in Asia (which Ensminger only hesitantly mentioned), it is not surprising to find Indian suspicion of Ford.

Ensminger considered the Asia Foundation's CIA links unrelated to Ford Foundation work in India regardless of the overlap between the types of programs both organizations sponsored. While he was correct that these programs were not directly linked, he ignored larger patterns of directed American influence that connected outcomes and missions in remarkable ways. He maintained that Ford's programs were completely unrelated to the work of the Asia Foundation, though he complained that such distinctions separating these organizations were lost on most left-leaning Indians:

> When the Asia Foundation was exposed as receiving CIA funds the communists in India took advantage of the opportunity to imply all foundations were fronts for CIA. Fortunately, I had considerable knowledge the Asia Foundation had been and was receiving CIA funds when it entered India, and therefore, I took the position when the Asia Foundation came into India I would never go to any of their parties; I would not visit their office; that when anyone wanted to come and see

me I would be cordial to them. I also attempted to keep myself alert and informed of the areas where the Asia Foundation was carrying on discussion so I could avoid the [Ford] Foundation putting money in areas where the Asia Foundation was assisting, even though, in a very minor way. One has to recognize it is difficult if not impossible to get responsible people to discriminate between foundations. When the communists had an issue like the Asia Foundation they just simply talked about foundations in the plural. It is also clear because of the size of the Ford Foundation the communists liked nothing better than to be able to indict the Ford Foundation for having a relationship and linkage with CIA.[61]

Ensminger smugly declared that he had long known the Asia Foundation ran on CIA funds and that he and others at Ford took measures to not be associated with the Asia Foundation in India, yet he failed to reflect on the ways that Ford and the Asia Foundation's missions overlapped and that this overlap was one reason both foundations raised suspicions. He did not question what such mission overlap suggested about the functional overlap of Ford and CIA. Even without CIA funds, the rotating door of personnel between Ford and governmental national security personnel assured continuities of mission.[62]

To Ensminger, the funding source mattered more than the similarities in the projects both foundations funded. His complaint about MIT's economic projects in India was that CENIS had CIA ties, not that these economic projects fostered alignments and control by the Global North in ways similar to some of Ford's own projects. From his position within Ford, he was unable to even consider that he and the CIA-funded Asia Foundation's staff might functionally be different parts of the same neocolonial device.[63]

ON THE CIA'S LASTING IMPRINT

Historian Vijay Prashad observes that to accomplish the CIA's Cold War goals, private foundations as well as CIA front foundations "did not feel the need to finance right-wing and oligarchic intellectuals and social movements. These were already committed to the rule of the oligarchy and imperialism, and they got sufficient funds from private sources."[64] Both private liberal foundations and liberal CIA front organizations funded liberal anticommunist projects, not only to undermine communist movements abroad but also to stunt American intellectuals' critiques of imperialism or support for liberation movements around the globe. Prashad argues that the goal of these liberal anticommunist programs "was to produce an anti-Marxist and anti-communist mentality, even at the cost of rationality."[65] After the collapse of CIA funding for various fronts, it did not matter if this work was later openly funded by the Department of State or privately funded through Ford, Rockefeller, or other foundations. What mattered was that the general project continued.

In an effort to better understand what occurred when the CIA severed all ties to the foundation back in 1967, in January 2021 I wrote the then Asia Foundation president, David D. Arnold, asking him to clarify the amount of the CIA's final payout, in 1967, to the foundation. I also asked for the current foundation's response to now-released FOIA documents establishing significant pre-1968 CIA ties.[66] Amy Ovalle, Asia Foundation vice president of global communications, kindly responded to my inquiries, writing that there is no direct institutional memory of these now ancient events, as the longest serving current employees have only been with the foundation for three decades. In her efforts to answer my queries, Ovalle contacted the foundation's "last remaining alumni," but these individuals did not know the details of the arrangements made during this final CIA surge payment.[67]

I am not surprised that the foundation today has little institutional memory of its CIA roots. Such remembrances fade with retiring personnel, and there naturally are institutional pressures to leave this now embarrassing history in the past. Vice President Ovalle's response included an account of how the roots of the foundation are viewed institutionally:

> What we do know is that before there was The Asia Foundation there was the Committee for Free Asia. The Committee was comprised primarily of California businessmen who hoped to combat the expansive efforts of the Kremlin and push back the new communist regimes in China and North Korea through Radio Free Asia. In 1954, when it became apparent that a more long-term strategy to promote democratic development was needed, the Committee reorganized itself into a public charity called The Asia Foundation. The CIA remained the primary source of funds, but the anticommunist rhetoric diminished, and the programming began to focus on indigenous needs in Asia and initiatives on education, civil society, and international exchanges.

A commission authorized by President Johnson and led by Secretary of State Rusk determined that The Asia Foundation should be preserved. The Foundation began to restructure its programming, shifting away from its earlier goals of building democratic institutions and encouraging the development of democratic leadership, toward an emphasis on Asian development as a whole. All CIA funding ceased for the Foundation in 1967. In 1968, USAID and the State Department began to provide funding to sustain TAF's programming, but on a small scale. Thereafter the Foundation's annual budget was primarily from successful proposals for grants from international official development assistance agencies and multilateral organizations, and from private foundations, corporations, and individuals both in the United States and Asia.[68]

While vital elements of the CIA's relationships with the foundation are forgotten in this telling, the foundation now acknowledges that the CIA was "the primary source of funds" until 1967.

For decades after the foundation ceased receiving CIA funds, agency personnel continued to hold it in high esteem. In 1981, DCI William Casey sent memos to Alexander Haig and others in the Reagan White House urging them to fund the foundation.[69] Even after funding transitioned from covert to overt governmental support, during the Cold War the foundation's general mission and overt operations continued mostly unchanged, though some taint of scandal followed the foundation for years.

In 2010, WikiLeaks released an April 26, 1975, cable from Henry Kissinger, then serving as national security advisor, titled "'High Risk' Vietnamese Associated with the Asia Foundation." This cable expressed concerns that Asia Foundation employees in Vietnam faced "communist retaliation because of their close association with the Foundation and its programs through the years."[70] There were twenty-four Vietnamese individuals with past and current links to the foundation who fit this risk category. The cable designated eleven individuals as "most vulnerable" and thirteen others as "less vulnerable," and both groups included mostly government officials and academics, including current and former ministers and university administrators. This memo shows one dimension of the lasting damage of the CIA's use of an academic organization for covert activities. Years after breaking ties with the CIA, these twenty-four individuals' lives were still at risk from the CIA's past funding of the foundation.

Unfounded rumors of continuing covert connections between the Asia Foundation and CIA continued to circulate in Asia into the 1970s. In some foundation correspondence relating to a foundation program recipient affiliated with the International Rice Research Institute in the Philippines, the foundation representative for the Philippines advised that because there were claims that the foundation was an arm of "American academic imperialism and [of] alleged connections with the CIA," the foundation recommended that grant recipient Enche Tzauddin "not mention to his fellow students that he is a Foundation grantee."[71] Because the foundation had lied for so long about its CIA ties, it was natural that many would question whether they were now telling the truth about not receiving CIA funding, even though this was the truth.

Under FOIA, the CIA released a copy of some 1976 Asia Foundation correspondence—nine years after being exposed as a CIA front—between foundation president Haydn Williams and Senator Daniel Inouye (D-HI), in which Williams responded to inquiries about foundation funding sources. Acknowledging the foundation's past, Williams wrote that as with the foundation's former role, "to serve in appropriate ways our country's interests in Asia[,] . . . the Foundation's motivations have not changed and the desire on the part of its Trustees and staff to promote and further our country's interest in the development of stronger, more open and more just societies in Asia, and in stronger Asian and American understanding and cooperation remains as high today as when the Foundation was founded."[72] Skirting direct mention of the CIA, Williams noted that "over the years the Foundation has received support, financial and otherwise (contributions in kind and service) from a wide cross-section of America," noting private groups and state and federal government agencies but without specifying which agencies these might be. He clarified that at present most of the foundation's funding came from the Department of State. Williams expressed hopes that Asian donors would increasingly play an important funding role. At that time, the foundation's $66 million budget funding came half from private sources and half from the US government.

With nine years having passed since the revelations of CIA funding and no public acknowledgment of how extensive CIA funding had been, Williams appeared comfortable collapsing the decade and a half of extensive CIA funding into his gleeful assertion that "given its experience, its established presence in 12 Asian countries, its wide range of Asian contacts and associations built up over the past 25 years, and most importantly, its standing and acceptability in Asia—the Foundation is in a strong position to complement and support through its small grants our country's interest in Asia."[73]

Even though there is every indication that the CIA had completely severed its funding and oversight of the Asia Foundation by 1968, the copy of this document released by the CIA included a CIA internal routing slip with the handwritten remark, "given to me by TAF President Williams," indicating the CIA acquired this letter directly from Asia Foundation president Williams.[74] Notations indicating some communication with the CIA remained for almost a decade after the foundation indicated it would cease involvement with the agency, but of course all parents naturally have sustained interests in the lives of their children after they leave the nest as they apply the lessons of their upbringing as they venture out on their own into the world.

13 Conclusions, Implications, and Continuities during the Remaining Cold War Years

Whether the Asia Foundation still works with the CIA or not, it is performing the same functions as in the past: promoting corporate interests in Asia.

KONRAD EGE / Observation in "US Intervention in Afghanistan," 1980

After the world learned of the existence of CIA funding fronts, they became popular fixtures of Cold War novels, movies, and conspiracy theories. Mixing fact and fiction, Hollywood writers wove CIA fronts into films like *Three Days of the Condor*, *Air America*, and *The In-Laws* and even television shows like the comedy-satire *Get Smart*. Scholarly research later critically examined impacts of fronts on artistic and intellectual work, though this research minimally focused on the internal bureaucratic workings of these fronts, with more consideration focused on projects and people funded than the front institutions themselves.

When first confronted by the 1967 press revelations, the Asia Foundation publicly acknowledged receiving *some* CIA funds, but the foundation's lack of candor misrepresented the extent of this relationship. For years, the foundation nurtured the fiction that it had only received small amounts of CIA funding and that the agency had not shaped its activities. Because in 1967 there were only limited inquiries into the extent of CIA funding, there was no public accounting of the impacts of these fronts. The Katzenbach Committee was more interested in damage control than disclosure, so there was no meaningful external inquiry into the impacts or legalities of these operations following this public exposure. In the mid-1970s, following the Watergate scandal, some of this changed, and congressional hearings led by Senator Frank Church (D-ID) and Representative Otis Pike (D-NY) revealed numerous covert CIA operations—including secret CIA funding operations described in the Church Committee Report as having "massive" impacts on international research. Yet, these were limited inquiries, as Church and Pike refrained from identifying many of the organizations and individuals they uncovered working for the CIA.[1]

Researchers confront significant obstacles when analyzing unwitting scholars' past interactions with CIA fronts. Some obstacles were intentionally created, others are of the usual sort encountered in any historical research. Records have been lost, purged, or not deposited, knowledgeable informants are gone or choose silence, and institutional memories fade, but there are inherent difficulties encountered when studying secret, once classified activities. Today there is a general reticence by many to delve into such troublesome past events—especially since the foundation continued to exist as a non-CIA entity after 1968. These obstacles create difficulties for understanding exactly how the foundation once articulated with CIA dreamers, analysts, bureaucrats, and spies.

Despite these difficulties, we know a lot about how the CIA engaged with the Committee for Free Asia and Asia Foundation between 1951 and 1967. Declassified documents, archival records, published reports, congressional testimony, participant accounts, and raw ratiocination allow us to reconstruct elements of many of these incompletely understood engagements of scholars and others working, often unwittingly, in harness for the needs of the state. Records from funding fronts have generally been difficult to access, but the unusually large volume of archived Asia Foundation records and FOIA declassified CIA documents allows us to understand for what purposes the CIA used the foundation. These documents show DTPILLAR used the CFA and the Asia Foundation to support Asian political, cultural, religious, and intellectual movements aligned with US policies, as well as to undermine movements the CIA felt threatened US economic and political interests. DTPILLAR's support of these programs was part of larger CIA operations, including violent ones carried out in Asia that were designed to limit Asian political autonomy.

The Asia Foundation was only one of dozens of now known CIA fronts active in the 1950s and 1960s. It shared many traits with other fronts, funding a variety of scholars, students, and research projects producing knowledge of use to the agency and backing anticommunist and pro-American projects. What is most unusual about the Asia Foundation compared to other exposed fronts is that it remains in existence under the same name seven decades after being founded by the CIA. Equally unusual is that *some* records from the years it operated as a CIA front survive and are available to scholars. The existence of hundreds of feet of accessible foundation documents from the 1950s and 1960s provides far more detail of daily operations than is known of any other CIA front, and even though questions remain, these records reveal important information about what the CIA wanted from the foundation and what it got.

These documents establish how after a few years of operating as the clumsily propagandistic Committee for Free Asia, the CIA then reformed it into what appeared to be a normal educational and philanthropic foundation benevolently funding scholarships, libraries, book-buying funds, a tribal research center, conference sponsorships, Buddhist conferences, election support materials, international speakers programs, book translating and publishing, seminars and fellowships for promising Asian journalists, procapitalist filmmakers, union leadership programs, and many other programs associated with pro-Western or free market/free enterprise activity. These efforts became the foundation's generous public face, and CIA funding of these programs allowed DTPILLAR to establish contacts with thousands of Asians, many of whom the foundation hoped would later take on important leadership roles.

The foundation's public image was intentionally misleading. Foundation leaders went to great lengths to pretend it was a private organization, hiding that it was founded, funded, and directed by the CIA under its code name: DTPILLAR. These lies meant that sometimes even its most mundane activities had hidden meanings and hid abuses of governmental power. Until 1968, the foundation's scholarships, conferences, folk art programs, and seminars were part of CIA anticommunist soft-power operations, and reports from foundation staff stationed throughout Asia at times became valuable sources of intelligence for CIA analysts. The foundation's decades of silence about the extent of these past activities—even while partially acknowledging receipt of some CIA funds—amplifies rather than diminishes the significance of this past.

The committee and early foundation's dishonesty and then later the protracted silence about its CIA origins hid two significant features of its mission. First, this silence hid DTPILLAR's false claim of being a nongovernmental organization. Second, the foundation claimed not to be involved in politics, while the CIA used the committee and pre-1968 foundation to try and shape Asian nations' political self-determination in ways that aligned with CIA interpretations of US interests.

THE WEIGHT OF FOUNDATION MISREPRESENTATIONS AND PROLONGED SILENCE

The CIA's Cold War anticommunist strategy for Asia sought to eliminate regional political movements not aligned with US capitalism, and DTPILLAR was one of the agency's most significant soft-power weapons in this fight. It wasn't that the foundation was simply silent about its role in this political struggle; during this period, the foundation actively lied. It lied not only about its status as a government-founded and funded organization but about its involvement in political struggles, and it lied about its efforts to limit Asian political autonomy.

Between 1951 and 1967, committee and foundation employees in positions necessitating awareness of DTPILLAR lied daily through their misrepresentations of CIA links. They lied to unwitting foundation employees, the press, grant and fellowship applicants, foreign contacts, family members, colleagues, or anyone else with whom they worked. Even though these lies were easily rationalized under a certain Cold War logic, they accumulated and created their own weight—a weight that has not been fully discharged by the foundation's ongoing failure to fully address the details of its history. It's not that the foundation today lies about this past but that decades of silence helped it institutionally bury this past in ways that allow it to avoid grappling with its institutional roots.

President Blum's 1959 article "The Asia Foundation: Purpose and Program" exemplifies how the foundation pressed its two big lies—that it was not linked to the US government and that it was apolitical—on the public to strengthen its credibility. This was a typical foundation domestic propaganda piece spreading disinformation about the foundation's claimed apolitical orientation. As he often did, Blum falsely claimed that the foundation "does not promote any particular foreign policy in the Asian countries where it works," and he also falsely represented the foundation as not having ties to the US government.[2] Blum misled his audience, directing attention away from the ways this CIA-funded program supported a narrow spectrum of US-backed, politically linked programs in Asia, while at times undermining Asian movements challenging the inequalities of market capitalism. Blum claimed that

> to some extent private American aid efforts appear in a different light than do governmental programs. They are not so directly related to American foreign policy and do not imply involvement in the "cold war." Private organizations are better able to extend aid without "strings" which are resented by the recipients. Although such private organizations presumably would not deliberately work against the broad policies of their own government, they are under no responsibility to reflect fluctuating foreign policy considerations. In addition, they are also often able to establish friendly and cooperative relations with a broader range of groups and individuals than is possible for official governmental programs.[3]

Blum's descriptions of these differences between "private" and governmental foreign aid programs identified elements of why the CIA capitalized on the pretense that the foundation was a nongovernmental organization.

Pre-1968 foundation leadership routinely lied about foundation funding sources. When pressed by foreign representatives for information on foundation funding, Blum often claimed, as he told Pakistan's President Ayub Khan in 1959, that "funds were derived from corporations, charitable trusts, other Foundations and from individuals in the United States." In this instance, Blum added that President Khan "did not comment on this reply but remarked that he had great respect for such organizations as the Ford Foundation and the Asia Foundation which worked selflessly and impartially for the development of Pakistan."[4] This was just the sort of respect the CIA hoped to nurture with this lie.

The foundation's secret government ties shaped its activities in other ways. In several reports Blum made excuses for military dictators and hard-line rulers in ways that aligned with the sort of American political-economic interests backed by the CIA. In one 1959 report Blum downplayed the harmful impacts of General Ayub Khan declaring martial law in Pakistan, instead praising Khan's use of martial law to enact economic development programs in the name of progress.[5] Blum's position reflected the brutalities of the CIA's anticommunist Cold War line, and it illustrates one of the ways the foundation at times aligned with antidemocratic practices, and reveals how CIA soft power easily connected with CIA-backed violence. Blum's apologist rhetoric stressed that "the government [of Pakistan] is not organized along totalitarian lines and has not set about mobilizing social and pressure groups in an organized way, nor does one see any evidence of political slogans and ideological propaganda that normally accompany a regime set on establishing itself as a dictatorship. This is an interesting example of a government that has all power in its hands, is occasionally arbitrary and dictatorial in its decisions, but is not acting in an authoritarian way as a matter of principle, and is certainly not totalitarian."[6] Like the CIA itself, Blum's views on authoritarian leaders and human rights were flexibly linked to a leader's stance toward US Cold War interests.

Like other CIA assets, Blum publicly advocated the virtues of open society, open democracy, and free markets. In a 1962 introduction to a book published by the American Assembly, he wrote,

> The diversity within a democratic society does not permit the government to command the nation's cultural life. The communist countries

have no such difficulty in reconciling their cultural tradition with their political purposes or in devising international policies and procedures consistent with what is done domestically. The church's missionary work, one of the best established expressions of international cultural activity, has not had to contend with this dilemma, either. In America, the decentralized and highly diversified structure of educational and cultural life creates for the government the further problem of how most effectively to tap the resources—the artists, teachers, scientists and books that are needed for international cultural activities, but that are not normally subject to government control.[7]

Blum's sermonizing about the importance of government not interfering in democracy and the formation of free expression highlights a fundamental cynicism at DTPILLAR's core, as this operative in a covertly government-linked political operation preached the virtues of the government eschewing political interference. By its own actions, DTPILLAR betrayed its lack of faith in the democratic private enterprise dogma it espoused. Instead of supporting free thought and expression, DTPILLAR corralled these. It supported the subversion of Asian political developments not aligned with the US version of capitalism.

While the impacts on those unwittingly receiving CIA funds were not always obvious or dramatic, they were nonetheless real. As author and editor Jason Epstein observed over fifty years ago, such impacts were most often "nothing so simple as coercion, though coercion at some levels may have been involved, but something more like the inevitable relations between employer and employee in which the wishes of the former become implicit in the acts of the latter."[8] Whether they liked it or not, most everyone involved with the Asia Foundation during this period was in some way supporting DTPILLAR's CIA mission. For those few who were witting of or suspected these political aspects of the committee or the foundation's work, these engagements had different personal meanings than they did for those who were clueless. While, generally speaking, levels of guilt are calculated by levels of knowledge, there are other ways one might calculate guilt. In Don DeLillo's novel *The Names*, after a central character becomes aware that he has unwittingly been working for a CIA front, he wonders if "those who engaged knowingly were less guilty than the people who carried out their designs. The unwitting would be left to ponder the consequences, to work out the precise distinctions involved, the edges of culpability and regret."[9] If we follow this argument, then guilt reaches beyond witting complicity and extends to all involved in such endeavors, as those connected to such machinations may at times have their own guilt to contend with regardless of their knowledge at the time.

DID IT WORK?

In order to understand whether DTPILLAR succeeded in its efforts to undermine the spread of communism in Asia, DTPILLAR's operations must be placed within the context of the CIA's larger anticommunist Cold War operations of which it was but one part. The CIA used both "good cop" and "bad cop" operations to limit political and economic developments, and DTPILLAR at times played important "good cop" Cold War roles. Insofar as DTPILLAR was designed to establish contacts with Asian intellectuals and political figures, while supporting Western-linked political developments and spreading positive views of the United States, DTPILLAR was at times a successful CIA operation. These successes were why the CIA was so insistent that the foundation continue many of its activities after the agency terminated funding and connections to the foundation in 1967.

Attempts to completely separate these relatively friendly ("good cop") anticommunist operations from the CIA's more lethal ("bad cop") anticommunist operations during this period create illusions that DTPILLAR activities were minor transgressions unrelated to the agency's Cold War history of murders, coups, torture, kidnappings, election interference, and other efforts to destroy postcolonial movements choosing not to align with American-style capitalism. CIA soft-power operations like DTPILLAR were but one arm of the agency's lethal and nonlethal anticommunist operations, and it is important to understand these arms were linked to the same body of narrow anticommunist policy that crudely interpreted nonalignment as akin to Soviet control, and this body worked to eliminate any such threats. DTPILLAR's procapitalism mission was not just a pro-American propaganda mission; it was part of larger CIA operations rejecting Asians' rights to freely choose their own political and economic systems. DTPILLAR was the CIA's "nice ask," trying to win converts, while other CIA operations used more violent means to try and eliminate those not embracing Western capitalism. With all its aid and apparent kindness, DTPILLAR was designed to be a CIA operation limiting choices for Asia's developing nations. As Vincent Bevins has observed, "Washington's violent anticommunist crusade destroyed a number of alternative possibilities for world development. The Third

World movement fell apart partly because of its own internal failures. But it was also crushed. These countries were trying to do something very, very difficult. It doesn't help if the most powerful government in history is trying to stop you."[10] DTPILLAR tried to undermine independent political movements in ways that were linked to the CIA's larger anticommunist mission. This mission viewed violence and soft-power "gifts" as tools, both types of action being required in tandem, in strategically invisibly linked ways, for the CIA to successfully attack Asian sovereignty. Understanding this linkage between what might otherwise appear as vastly separate operations is vital.

It would be a mistake to think DTPILLAR's soft-power operations were somehow better than or preferable to the CIA's violent methods—beyond the obvious fact that it is better to not be killed or wounded than it is to be killed or wounded. Such a position asks the wrong questions and offers the wrong choices. CIA soft-power operations were not implemented *instead* of lethal CIA operations; they were linked parts of CIA strategies that used both unbridled violence and gifts to achieve American hegemony. Asking if CIA soft power was better than CIA violence is like asking someone if they would rather be beaten with soft power or hard power—when of course they would rather not be beaten at all. This false dichotomy only diverts attention from confronting how US Cold War policy in Asia opposed the self-determination of Asian nations during this crucial post–world war, postcolonial period.

It would be absurd to imagine there being something like "two CIAs"—one engaging in violent operations and the other kindly funding projects for humanitarian reasons. All anticommunist CIA operations were linked to parts of a larger Cold War scheme trying to force alignments with American political and economic interests.

While the CIA interfered in some early Cold War Western European elections (e.g., in 1948 in Italy and 1958 and 1961 in Greece), it also tolerated some occasional European socialistic social democracy developments in Nordic countries, France, and the United Kingdom, while Asian countries were not afforded the same post–World War II latitude for self-determination.[11] During the Cold War, many postcolonial nations were naturally anti-imperialist and wary of being placed under the control of the Soviet or US government, and those who tried to remain unaligned or develop a third path between communism and capitalism were suspect and targets of CIA interventions—often violent interventions, like Operation Ajax in 1953 Iran, Operation PBSUCCESS in 1954 Guatemala, and Operation FUBELT in 1973 Chile, or the violent events in

Indonesia between 1965 and 1967, when the United States played a role that was "the Cold War equivalent of aiding and abetting the Hutu genocide in Rwanda."[12]

Evaluating how well the CIA accomplished DTPILLAR's anticommunist, pro-American, procapitalism goals finds lots of successes, as well as some mixed results, in part because it threw a lot of money around, sometimes somewhat aimlessly, as it funded diverse programs seeking to make friends and influence people. While some of the small programs DTPILLAR funded appear to have had few tangible Cold War outcomes, many DTPILLAR programs did, as its secret charter mandated, successfully "assist non-Communist and non-totalitarian elements" in Asia.[13] DTPILLAR's secret funding successfully produced a recognizable body of academic and journalistic writing, films, radio broadcasts, and other materials championing pro-American, anticommunist principles. Scholarship and fellowship recipients generally had positive experiences and at times thought kindly of the sponsors and the United States, or they brought home anticommunist or pro-American messaging from seminars or DTPILLAR-sponsored events. Internal CIA memos also positively evaluated the intelligence functions occasionally performed by the foundation. The CIA's refusal to release documents showing which specific Asia Foundation reports produced what the CIA described as actionable intelligence makes it difficult to evaluate how significant the foundation's intelligence functions were to larger CIA operations. It also makes it impossible to know whether the foundation supplied intelligence that informed violent operations the CIA undertook in Asia during this period—we simply don't know what "actions" this actionable intelligence informed, but we do know it did. Unless the CIA releases this information, we cannot fully evaluate this dimension of DTPILLAR outcomes.

From outside the Pentagon and CIA it remains difficult to assess the value to intelligence agencies of many of these CIA-funded projects. But a 1963 CIA memo from Asia Foundation president Russell Smith (discussed in chapter 4) reporting on his first year as foundation president indicated that some CIA-funded programs that might have appeared disconnected from CIA matters often had agency uses that were not apparent to outsiders. After becoming president, Smith told the CIA, he learned that many of these apparently "window-dressing" programs that had seemed "frivolous, may have concealed edges [of] potential" to the CIA.[14]

With access to non-public data on various CIA orphan programs, the Katzenbach Committee concluded that DTPILLAR's operations made significant Cold War contributions. They found enough value in the foundation's operations that they decided to terminate all CIA connections immediately but continue most of its existing activities so as to preserve the foundation's contributions to US interests. Their calculus was based on the assumption (which proved correct for many years) that the public would not learn that until late 1967 the Asia Foundation had not just received some occasional CIA funding but was instead created by, funded by, and guided by the CIA. As long as this knowledge remained hidden, this calculus of value appeared solid. Had these truths been known in the late 1960s, it is unlikely that the Asia Foundation would have continued to exist even though it had severed all CIA ties.

The CIA's organizational structure separates operations and intelligence analysis. While there can be significant bureaucratic distinctions between the operations providing academic scholarships to Asian students and very different types of operations (such as the CIA's Vietnam counterinsurgency, or torture and assassination programs), many DTPILLAR-funded projects supporting regimes friendly to the United States broadly met the criteria of counterinsurgency operations by providing forms of stability that strengthened Asian host governments. It matters that apparently "neutral" educational projects were sometimes part of CIA soft-power operations designed to strengthen or weaken specific Asian political movements. While the CIA's soft-power campaigns, such as book-buying programs, supporting certain types of labor unions, or granting scholarships, might appear less controversial than CIA hard-power assassination programs, both these forms of CIA operations were part of the agency's larger strategy of shaping Asian countries in ways that limited self-determination.

DTPILLAR funding for various programs supporting counterinsurgency goals was a significant successful outcome for the foundation. These programs included projects stabilizing regimes aligned with the United States, funding scholars to study potentially troublesome local groups, programs supporting the growth of anticommunist labor unions, programs developing cadres of anti-Marxist Asian intellectuals, and various cultural programs generating goodwill toward Americans or toward regimes linked with the United States.

Some Cold War CIA supporters might downplay the damage of DTPILLAR's approach to anticommunism, arguing that these 1950s and 1960s programs were normal forms of American diplomacy whose only small sin was that they were unfortunately funded by an organization whose reputation raises suspicions. But suspicions of the CIA are not due to some misunderstanding; this is a well-earned distrust owing to the agency's history of brutal antidemocratic practices that include murder, treachery, torture, and coups. Some CIA apologists claim that Cold War global anticommunist movements required deceitful tactics, but these claims always gloss over the agency's damage to postcolonial democratic movements seeking independence and justice for nations of the Global South.[15] While this has long since become a sort of Cold War international relations catechism, the United States had other options during the Cold War. Such arguments ignore how many post–World War II newly decolonized nations first looked to the United States for help as a fellow postcolonial nation only to have the US back neocolonialism, leaving many recently independent nations to look toward Moscow or nonalignment.[16] The United States' choice to suppress rather than embrace post–World War II anticolonialist liberation movements narrowed the political developments that the United States supported in Asia, and this narrowing betrayed America's historical anticolonial roots and claims of valuing democracy and self-determination in favor of strengthening Western-dominated forms of market capitalism.

There is no distancing the foundation from DTPILLAR operations collecting names and dossiers of individuals who came into the foundation's orbit, its concerted interference in the development of elections, union organizing, academic critiques, newspapers, movies, school curriculum, and book publications from the CIA's larger mission of trying to control global political developments. One's judgments of the morality or wisdom of American capitalism's expansive Cold War projects shape interpretations of whether it matters that the CIA secretly funded and oversaw the running of the Asia Foundation for a decade and half. But this covert funding matters tremendously if one supports the rights of nations to determine their own political and economic destinies in the crucial postcolonial era.

COLD WAR CONTINUITIES OF MISSION

While the period of this book's inquiry ends in late 1967, the Cold War continued to rage for over twenty more years and the Asia Foundation continues to exist today, albeit in a very different form, with a different mission from the early organization described here. That the foundation, unlike so many other exposed CIA fronts, survived its CIA orphanhood to continue without CIA ties is remarkable, and while it did sever contact with and funding from the agency in late 1967, the fact that it continued to undertake some of the same types of programs and tasks during the remaining Cold War needs some consideration.

The foundation's silence about the extent of its CIA past, especially in areas of programmatic Cold War continuity connecting its mission and activities before and after 1968, complicates our interpretations of CIA impacts on the foundation during the remaining years of the Cold War. How this silence emerged seems understandable; initially, as the foundation was trying to remain intact after severing all CIA ties, it naturally wanted to avoid dredging through this history, much less to reveal that it had been *created* by the CIA and had been a CIA proprietary until late 1967. It simply avoided acknowledging all this. But as is often the case with the "return of the repressed," the longer this history has been unacknowledged and unconfronted, the more it festers.

While the CIA ended financial support of the Asia Foundation in 1967, the agency's liquidation agreement committed the foundation to continue the same Cold War mission and types of activities the CIA established for DTPILLAR. This meant the foundation ended the CIA's funding and managerial control without publicly confronting the existential issues of being an organization founded and charged by the agency, while *secretly* agreeing in the liquidation agreement to continue the CIA's established institutional mission. Because of the foundation's silence, questions about the contradictions inherent in this arrangement remain. Individual interpretations of the significance of the foundation secretly agreeing to continue the mission of its CIA creator after its 1967 break with the agency in part depend on one's approval of the Cold War CIA's role in undermining Asian countries' right to self-determination.

The final report from the 1975 Church Committee hearings concluded that the Katzenbach Committee's investigations led the CIA to reexamine seventy-seven secret projects and to identify "projects to be terminated, projects to be transferred to other sources of funding, projects to continue, and projects whose future required higher level decisions. The 303 Committee met frequently throughout 1967 and 1968 to deal with [these] difficult questions."[17] The Church Committee concluded that the CIA's termination of program funding did not mean these programs necessarily ended. In many instances the agency's decision to end funding only meant these programs were moved to other governmental agencies, with the understanding that those agencies would continue most of these same projects. The Katzenbach Report called for shutting down domestic (CL4 funded) programs by the end of 1967, though programs like Radio Free Europe and Radio Liberty continued much as before but under new governmental funding sources. The Church Committee described one CIA program that, while unidentified, must surely be the Asia Foundation. The committee determined that this program was provided with enough funds to sustain it for at least an additional year while it became a non-CIA-operated, public foundation. The report concluded that the committee's conclusion regarding this "one case suggests that even a clean termination of funding with a private organization did not necessarily end the CIA's support of the policies and programs of the organization. A CIA report on termination plans for a large project in the Far East indicated that, with surge funding, the organization could continue into fiscal year 1969, and that thereafter '[the organization's] Board of Trustees will assume full responsibility for the organization and has pledged to continue its policies and range of activities.'"[18] If this unnamed organization was the Asia Foundation, this statement that even after shifting oversight from the CIA to its board of trustees, this foundation pledged "to continue its policies and range of activities" (which was spelled out in the CIA's liquidation agreement with the Asia Foundation) highlights why simply tracing funding sources to intelligence agencies does not resolve what makes a program problematic. Clearly, the CIA's 1967 DTPILLAR liquidation agreement stipulates that the post-CIA Asia Foundation had committed itself to continuing the CIA's Cold War mission.

With the implementation of the CIA's secret Asia Foundation Liquidation Plan, the CIA lost direct access to reports and memos of interest to the agency. It lost direct input into selecting which programs or individuals were hired or sponsored. Routine meetings between CIA officers using embassy cover and the foundation's overseas country representatives ended, the use of foundation reports for intelligence purposes ended, and this ended the CIA's ability to use the foundation for stay-behind intelligence capabilities and other documented covert activities.[19] Yet even with these significant changes, the Church Committee found that former CIA funding fronts continued to follow the basic (overt) policies and ran most of the same sorts of programs they had operated as CIA appendages.

There have of course been many significant changes in the operation, mission, and programs of the Asia Foundation in the years since the end of the Cold War, and these changes show discernible breaks from its earliest practices. Yet, there are many questions about how, during the remaining post-1967 Cold War years, foundation programs were influenced by agreements to maintain a similar mission, even with all CIA contact broken off. Given what is known about some general continuity of the Asia Foundation's Cold War–era educational and cultural programs following the termination of CIA funding, there are two significantly different ways to interpret the impacts of this cessation of CIA funds during the remaining Cold War. Both interpretations accept that one significant change between the pre-1968 and post-1968 Cold War Asia Foundation was that the foundation stopped receiving CIA oversight and funding and stopped collecting intelligence later used by the CIA, but they differ in interpretations of other aspects of the foundation's continuity of operations.

One interpretation (we can call this the Pollyanna interpretation) could argue that because so many Asia Foundation–funded and operated programs continued during the Cold War essentially unchanged from the time of direct CIA funding and control, the CIA's pre-1968 involvement with the foundation was essentially insignificant. This position might argue that concerns over agency involvement show overblown concern and demonization of the CIA. The Pollyanna interpretation essentially finds nothing wrong with what the pre-1967 Asia Foundation did. The only problem was that the funding stream unfortunately came from the CIA (or, if you prefer, the only problem was they got caught); once CIA funds were replaced with State Department funds, all the problems related to CIA funding were resolved. Given DTPILLAR's Cold War commitment to undermining political and economic movements not closely aligned with US economic policies, the Pollyanna interpretation necessarily accepts such anti-self-determination activities as being nonproblematic.

The second interpretation (we can call this the hegemonic interpretation) also accepts that some significant elements of Asia Foundation Cold War–era programs changed after CIA funding and oversight ceased and things like occasional intelligence gathering, CIA clearing of individuals, and all covert activities ended. But this interpretation argues that the general continuity of types of programs and practices reveals a hegemonic dimension of the foundation's Cold War work, and this raises questions about the political nature of these foundation programs during the Cold War regardless of who funded them. Some critics of CIA funding have been less critical of the ways that normative "clean" funding programs align with state knowledge production, instead drawing lines around what are culturally seen as "good" (State Department, private foundations, private donations, etc.) or "bad" (CIA) funding sources, focusing less attention on the ways that funding projects are linked to larger political projects. Simply put, many academics would be willing to work on a specific project funded by the State Department yet would be unwilling to work on the same project if it were funded by the CIA.

The wealth of documents analyzed here supports a hegemonic interpretation over the Pollyanna alternative. The Pollyanna interpretation ignores the cozy relationship between foundation activities and CIA operations personnel during the pre-1968 formative period while downplaying what this relationship reveals about the foundation's political alignments. The Pollyanna interpretation also minimizes how DTPILLAR's goals supported Asian political developments aligned with the political and economic interests of US capitalism and opposed allowing Asian societies to develop as they saw fit.

The secret pipeline of funds, directives requiring CIA approval for the hirings, and information flowing between the foundation and CIA was severed in 1967, yet even without any agency ties the continuity of mission specified in the CIA's DTPILLAR liquidation agreement assured that basic features of the CIA-established Cold War mission for the foundation continued. After 1967 the foundation stopped taking orders from or providing intelligence to the CIA, its following the CIA's liquidation agreement meant that other continuities of mission remained even as the foundation operated independently.

This was not the only former CIA-funded organization that underwent such shifts from covert to public funds during the Cold War. Other once secret CIA-linked programs that later continued similar work with "cleaner" funding from other sources include operations like international labor union programs and "police training" programs that, once exposed, saw funding shifted from the CIA to AID and other agencies within the Department of State.[20] Such moves generally "normalized" these programs while changing little of the CIA's original intentions for them.

Some who would downplay the significance of DTPILLAR's covert nature might argue that one reason the CIA was used was because the executive branch was avoiding congressional funding battles and congressional oversight, and while this is correct, such interpretations are insufficient. Because DTPILLAR was a liberal anticommunist operation, the conservative, isolationist, anticommunist members of Congress would have opposed funding some of the soft-power projects it sponsored. But pretending to be a privately funded foundation also allowed the Asia Foundation to influence some Asian political developments in ways that would have been received very differently had they declared themselves to be a US governmental agency, much less a CIA asset.

The Pollyanna interpretation fails to interrogate the meaning of the foundation not replacing its president after CIA funding and oversight ended. Haydn Williams was foundation president for three years under DTPILLAR (1964–67), then continued as president for over two decades after the CIA link revelations (until 1989)—almost until the very end of the Cold War. His continued presidency meant the board and CIA didn't have to worry about someone internally digging into institutional history, and it would have allowed Williams to destroy any important remaining internal records from the CIA-linked period. Because the secret 1967 CIA liquidation agreement required "that the Foundation will continue its present policies and areas of interest and its normal functions and procedures" after the foundation's separation from the CIA, we know the board and president were committed to continuing the basic programming it had followed under the CIA aegis.[21] Had Williams resigned following the 1967 CIA funding revelations, it would have at least symbolically marked an institutional break with the past, and it would have created a significantly different interpretation of the foundation's post-CIA institutional continuity. This continuity declared the ongoing existence of DTPILLAR's Cold War–era pro-American, procapitalism, anticommunist, antisocialist, anti-third-way, antineutrality, pro-certain-types-of-democracy soft-power programs that the CIA instituted in the 1950s, even after all CIA ties were cut in 1967.

The history of how the CIA's DTPILLAR program shaped the work overtly funded by the Committee for Free Asia and the Asia Foundation between 1951 and the end of 1967 raises serious questions about what it would take to decolonize the funding institutions that shape the production and reproduction of knowledge. That the CIA established what appeared to be an independent *normal* foundation that colonized academic discourse for over a decade and half, then, once it was found out, shifted the funding stream to another branch of the US government while continuing many of the same programs with little notice or concern is one measure of how effective DTPILLAR's vision was. While offspring are not their parents, the parentage of the foundation matters. The liquidation agreement's extensions of mission from the earliest days of global covert activity to the post-CIA Cold War period align with Inderjeet Parmar's research documenting how the funding agendas of powerful private foundations overlap with US political economic interests. Perhaps the most unsettling element of DTPILLAR's story is that once this covert CIA operation was terminated and all foundation ties with the agency dissolved, during the remaining years of the Cold War the programs it birthed continued to influence, shape, and colonize academic, political, and cultural discourse at home and abroad with little notice, concern, or critique.

SCIENCE AS IDEOLOGY IMPACTED BY A MILITARIZED MODE OF PRODUCTION

DTPILLAR's efforts to shape the production and distribution of knowledge reveal links between America's militarized Cold War economy and the knowledge systems it produced. DTPILLAR funded a broad range of educational, cultural, and research projects, but as an organization existing to discredit communist ideology, projects adopting openly Marxist analysis were unwelcome, as were analyses of American militarism, colonialism, or neocolonialism that might undermine US-backed geopolitical developments in a region. The foundation's funding of projects like the Thai Tribal Research Centre was not a purely academic venture creating some sort of independent theorizing anthropological enterprise seeking knowledge for knowledge's sake; it was instead part of a regional counterinsurgency strategy designed to collect cultural knowledge for militarized uses. In similar ways, DTPILLAR nurtured certain political views at the academic conferences it sponsored, it funded the translation of certain books over others, and it sponsored certain types of speakers representing the United States abroad or sought out certain religious tendencies to support financially. Many of these choices are within the normal functions of private foundations, but when a US governmental agency secretly directs the funding for such activities, what might have been seen as selective editorial guidance becomes censorship and propaganda.

The knowledge generated as a result of DTPILLAR funding, whether it was projects connected to the Tribal Research Centre, sponsored conferences, studying Buddhist movements, or paying for Asian students and scholars to attend Harvard seminars, was never unlinked from the CIA's larger Asian mission, regardless of the interest or intentions of the individuals funded. It matters little that funded academics felt they were freely choosing their subjects of study; that their aligned views were selected by the foundation meant these views were supported over other views.

Some academics are offended by arguments that disciplinary discourse can be easily shaped by funding. There appear to be multiple reasons for their taking offense, ranging from epistemological aversions to metanarratives to more personal-biographical reasons. While postmodernism makes familiar the notion that power shapes regimes of knowledge, ontological commitments to disarticulating material forces, such as funding, from formations of cultural belief systems naturally create difficulties for such claims. Sometimes there appear to be more personal reasons for this resistance, as the individuals considering these claims are themselves, if not directly, then indirectly through their academic ancestors, enmeshed in the intellectual traditions and academic funding lines.

It strikes some as crude to suggest that intellectuals' heads can so easily be turned, as if intellectual curiosities, strands of interpretation, and integrity can simply be purchased or manipulated by funding agencies. Notions of agency have importance to most people, scholars included, and the individual desires that scholars experience as forces guiding decisions and shaping research and interpretations are real. Yet one's research desires can also be highly malleable when presented with funding opportunities that are roughly within the range of topics a scholar initially set out to pursue. As Harold Laski observed almost a century ago, "Foundations do not control, simply because, in the direct and simple sense of the word, there is no need for them to do so. They have only to indicate the immediate direction of their minds for the whole university world to discover that it always meant to gravitate swiftly to that angle of the intellectual compass."[22] Just because scholars view themselves as pursuing questions that appear to be of their own design and interest does not mean there are no other forces at work. Unless one pursues unpopular questions or challenges basic precepts of funders, there may be no reason for them to understand the force of the wind at their back.

This is not to argue that the Asia Foundation or those entities it funded during this period did not, at times, produce or disseminate intellectually useful or interesting knowledge or that it did not discover "truths" (temporarily setting aside arguments about exactly what this might be). Instead, this foundation established by the CIA helped shape the sort of questions asked and answered as DTPILLAR worked to mold political discourse in the Asian countries where it operated.

The CIA shaped elements of academic discourse on Asia by doing things like tracking and meeting with Asian scholars at various professional associations; steering agendas and shaping debates at academic conferences; influencing the intellectual contours of Asian journalists; producing what became soft-intelligence reports and dossiers on Asian leaders, current events, and Asian dissidents; shaping brain trusts; funding certain types of academic journals; and dozens of other things described in this book. Through such programs the foundation produced useful results. Furthermore, in some sense the extent to which any of these practices continued in more open ways after 1967 suggests a detectible functional continuity of purpose bridging the pre- and post-Cold War period of CIA funding in the years after these agency strings were cut.

Rewarding individuals whose work aligned with or informed larger projects of the American national security state helped some scholars "freely" choose topics or theoretical approaches of interest in ways that maintained certain illusions of academic free will. Most academics spend their lives agreeably working within the confines of their disciplines, departments, and universities, content enough with the parameters delimiting the boundaries of mainstream scholarship. For those who seldom question the directions of funded research, there is little to see that does not appear as a freely chosen area of study. To some degree, all people create illusions of agency and choice while reinforcing cultural norms. To argue that the dominant cultural milieu and political-economic forces did not shape academics' work would place the discipline of academics outside the sort of usual influences of culture that anthropologists normally take for granted when studying other cultures. From the post–World War II rush to follow the funding of area studies and thereafter, the Cold War brought recurrent episodes of scholars shifting their work to align with the era's funding opportunities, as well as recurrent instances of governmental agencies acquiring and consulting this work.[23] It remains troubling that this adaptive adjustment of research direction occurred, with so many unwitting individuals following tunes covertly called by the CIA.

Notes

ABBREVIATIONS

AAAP American Anthropological Association Papers, National Anthropological Archives, Smithsonian Institution
CIA DTPILLAR CIA declassified documents on the DTPILLAR program, released by the CIA
DB David Bell, Ford Foundation records, Office of the Vice President, Office Files of David Bell, Rockefeller Foundation Archive Center
EWA Education and World Affairs records, 1961–71, Hoover Institution Archives, Stanford University
FB Franklin Book Programs records, Princeton University Library Special Collections
FFR Ford Foundation records, Rockefeller Foundation Archive Center
JW Jules Weinberg Papers, Catholic University of America Archives
RB Robert Blum Papers, Manuscripts and Archives, Yale University
RFA Rockefeller Foundation Archives, Rockefeller Foundation Archive Center
SC Sol Chaneles Papers, National Security Archives, George Washington University
TAF The Asia Foundation Papers, Hoover Institution Archives, Stanford University

PREFACE

1. Wallace Turner, "Asia Foundation Got CIA Funds," *New York Times*, 3/22/67, 17.
2. Department of State, INR/IL Historical Files, Minutes of 303 Committee, "132. Memorandum from the Central Intelligence Agency to the 303 Committee," 6/22/66, https://history.state.gov/historicaldocuments/frus1964-68v10/d132 (hereafter cited as Department of State, Memorandum 132, 6/22/66).
3. Saunders, *Culture Cold War*; Wilford, *Mighty Wurlitzer*; Paget, *Patriotic Betrayal*; Whitney, *Finks*. Karen Paget's remarkable investigation of the CIA's infiltration of the National Student Association, *Patriotic Betrayal*, stands as the most detailed organizational account of CIA covert funding of an organization during this period.
4. My earliest analysis of these DTPILLAR documents was in an invited 2017 talk to the New York Academy of Sciences; see Price, "Reframing the Impacts."
5. See Ford, *Cold War Monks*; Emma Best, "Robert Blum, the Spy Who Shaped the World Part 1," *Muckrock*, 8/17/17, https://www.muckrock.com/news/archives/2017/aug/17/rober-blum-spy-who-shaped-world-part-1/; Emma Best, "Robert Blum, the Spy Who Shaped the World Part 2: How the 'Clever Clerk' Became 'the Most Dangerous Man in Indochina,'" *Muckrock*, 8/18/17, https://www.muckrock.com/news/archives/2017/aug/17/robert-blum-spy-who-shaped-world-part-2/; Klein, "Cold War Cosmopolitanism"; and S. Lee, "Creating an Anti-Communist."
6. RB MS 87, accessed 2/11/23, https://archives.yale.edu/repositories/12/resources/3023.
7. The large collection of records of the Committee for Free Asia and the Asia Foundation deposited at the Hoover Institution Library and Archives consists of at least 480 large boxes, but the precise number of boxes deposited with Hoover is unknown for two reasons.

First, there is not a comprehensive finding aid for the collection. There are sets of fragmented finding aids identifying box numbers by geographical areas covered, though these are little more than lists of identified areas. I constructed my own reverse index of boxes listed in Hoover's existing finding aids and determined that at least 168 of 481 boxes are not identified on the available finding aids. This means that, at a minimum, just over a third (34.9 percent) of the boxes are not listed in Hoover finding aids and thus may or may not be deposited there. Through experimental means (i.e., making requests for a dozen of these 168 nonlisted boxes), I learned that some of these boxes are indeed held at Hoover and several of them had never been opened before I requested them, as they still were sealed with shipping tape.

Second, there are boxes that should sequentially appear between 1 and 481 but were not deposited at the Hoover Institution. I learned this by requesting boxes appearing as gaps in the sequential list I made from the finding aids.

8. "Sukarno Warns World," *New York Times*, 6/2/55.

1   ROOTS OF COMMITTEE FOR FREE ASIA

1. Bevins, *Jakarta Method*; W. Blum, *Killing Hope*; McCoy, *Politics of Heroin*; Marks, *Search for the "Manchurian Candidate"*; Prashad, *Washington Bullets*; J. Dana Stuster, "Mapped: The 7 Governments the U.S. Has Overthrown," *Foreign Policy*, 8/20/13, http://foreignpolicy.com/2013/08/20/mapped-the-7-governments-the-u-s-has-overthrown/; Valentine, *Phoenix Program*.
2. Saunders, *Culture Cold War*; Wilford, *Mighty Wurlitzer*; Wilford, *America's Great Game*.
3. US Congress, "Tax-Exempt Foundations," 191; Foster Hailey, "Kaplan Fund, Cited as C.I.A. 'Conduit,' Lists Unexplained $395,000 Grant," *New York Times*, 9/3/64, 10.
4. "Misusing CIA Money," *New York Times*, 9/4/64, 28; US Congress, "Tax-Exempt Foundations," exhibit 48.
5. "Misusing CIA Money," 28.
6. Stern, "Short Account of International Student Politics and the Cold War."
7. Stern, "Short Account of International Student Politics and the Cold War," 31.
8. Paget, *Patriotic Betrayal*.
9. P. Richardson, *Bomb in Every Issue*, 74–81.
10. The groups were the Independence Foundation, National Student Association, International Student Conference, the World Assembly of Youth, US Youth and Students Council, Independent Research Service Educational Foundation, International Marketing Institute, J. Frederick Brown Foundation, American Friends of the Middle East, American Society of African Culture, Committee of Correspondence, American Fund for Free Jurists, Pan American Foundation, Foreign Policy Research Institute, National Education Association, International Development Foundation, Foundation for Youth and Student Affairs, National Student Association, International Union of Socialist Youth, Oficina Relacionadas Movimientos Estudiantiles Universitarias, Young Christian Workers, International Union of Young Christian Democrats, American Newspaper Guild, Inter-American Federation of Working Newspapermen (based in Panama), and the International Federation of Journalists (based in Brussels). Don Irwin and Vincent J. Burke, "21 Foundations, Union, Got Money from CIA," *Los Angeles Times*, 2/23/67, 3B.

11. Troy, *Donovan and the CIA*, 303, 313–14; Price, *Cold War Anthropology*, 3–5.
12. CIA, "CIA Organizational History in Brief," March 1975, 2–3, CIA Electronic Reading Room, https://www.cia.gov/readingroom/docs/CIA-RDP89B00552R000800090005-8.pdf.
13. Currey, *Edward Lansdale*, 63.
14. Currey, *Edward Lansdale*, 63.
15. Wisner oversaw Operation Mockingbird, a covert operation planting CIA propaganda stories in news outlets; he played significant roles in the CIA coups in Iran and Guatemala.
16. Stoner, *Cultural Cold War*, 106.
17. CIA, "CIA Organizational History in Brief," 3.
18. Currey, *Edward Lansdale*, 66.
19. CIA DTPILLAR 1, 1, 2. DTPILLAR, like other CIA code names, does not mean anything. The CIA has declassified (under FOIA) and released a cache of CIA documents relating to the CIA's code name DTPILLAR project. These documents are available on the CIA's "FOIA Electronic Reading Room" website, accessed 1/3/23, https://www.cia.gov/readingroom/search/site/dtpillar. The CIA has organized these documents by designating three volumes and then assigning numbers to the volumes. I have followed the CIA's designation of volume and document numbers in citations to these documents, and my citations of them identify this collection as "CIA DTPILLAR," then list the volume number, then the document number given by the CIA in this FOIA release. If date and/or page number are available or needed, these are then listed. Following this pattern, the citation "CIA DTPILLAR 1, 40, 2" designates an item from the CIA DTPILLAR FOIA document collection, volume 1, document 40, page 2. Because some PDFs combine multiple documents with different page numbers, when citations refer to page numbers, these numbers reference the PDF page number, not numbers that might be listed on original documents.
20. Between 1951 and 1953, CFA documents, including letterhead, sometimes referred to the Committee for Free Asia as the Committee for *a* Free Asia. For simplicity, I use Committee for Free Asia, and at times when there was continuity of practice stretching between CFA and the Asia Foundation, for simplicity I mention only the Asia Foundation.
21. "US Group Expands Its Aid to Asians," *New York Times*, 7/30/52, 3.
22. Matt Schudel, "F. Haydn Williams," *Washington Post*, 4/27/16.
23. CIA DTPILLAR 3, 14, 18.
24. Charles Burress, "James L. Stewart—Longtime Liaison to Asia," *San Francisco Chronicle*, 1/29/06.
25. CIA DTPILLAR 3, 14, 18 (original emphasis).
26. Brewster, *American Overseas Library*, 163.
27. Weissman and Shoch, "CIAsia Foundation," 3.
28. Weissman and Shoch, "CIAsia Foundation," 3–4. CFA's board included the presidents of the University of California and Stanford University, and of Standard Oil, and author James Michener; see Defty, *Britain, America, and Anticommunist Propaganda*, 207; and Cummings, *Radio Free Europe's "Crusade for Freedom,"* 48–49. A 1953 CIA memo discussing "DTPILLAR—Cover—Fund Raising" indicated that James Michener would be chairing a foundation committee that would "undertake a fund-raising effort on behalf of DTPILLAR." See CIA DTPILLAR 2, 40, 2, 9/25/53.
29. CIA DTPILLAR 1, 1, 2–3.
30. CIA DTPILLAR 2, 52, 6, 1951.

31. CIA DTPILLAR 2, 52, 8, 1/26/51.
32. CIA DTPILLAR 1, 40, 2, 9/28/51.
33. CIA DTPILLAR 2, 52, 5, 1951.
34. CIA DTPILLAR 1, 51, 2, 19, 7/19/51. Indications of the dual filing system appear in foundation records. For example, one 1963 memo on the Cambodia office's filing system mentions using colored filing tabs "for reasons of security," noting that "local employees do not have access to the files listed on the attached outline, mainly for reasons of security. However, the Vietnam bookkeeper keeps the accounting files and, upon request, is given a particular project folder if it is necessary to the performance of her duties. The files of the Phnom Penh office occupy six four-drawered metal file cabinets with full-length bar locks, plus a four-drawered combination safe. They are physically separated into four groups: accounting files, active program and administrative files, storage, and clipping files." TAF P-259, General Cambodia, Clare E. Humphrey to TAF President, 12/12/63, CAM-SX-557.
35. CIA DTPILLAR 1, 1, 3–5.
36. CIA DTPILLAR 1, 1, 5.
37. Chang, *Chinese Journals of L. K. Little*.
38. CIA DTPILLAR 1, 23, 3, 12/12/51.
39. CIA DTPILLAR 1, 32.
40. CIA DTPILLAR 1, 88, 3. Hugh Wilford's research on Harvard's International Summer School program records Henry Kissinger's important role in bringing the program to Harvard, with valuable connections established between students and the CIA. See Wilford, *Mighty Wurlitzer*, 123–28.
41. The estimated budget for this summer program operation was $61,000; see CIA DTPILLAR 1, 88, 3, 12/17/51.
42. Price, *Cold War Anthropology*, 102–14.
43. CIA DTPILLAR 1, 89, 12/14/51.
44. CIA DTPILLAR 1, 22, 9, 12/20/51.
45. CIA DTPILLAR 1, 90, 11/28/51.
46. See McGranahan, *Arrested Histories*; Jackson, "Life, Work, and Writings," 613.
47. These press releases are undated but appear to be from 1951 or 1952.
48. TAF P-13, RFA First Program Data, undated "Questions and Answers" sheet.
49. TAF P-13, RFA First Program Data, undated "Questions and Answers" sheet. This ban on US domestic propaganda appears to have come from the CIA charter's prohibition on targeting Americans in such campaigns.
50. "Members of the Committee for a Free Asia Work in San Francisco, California," October 1951, available at Critical Past, accessed 6/14/16, http://www.criticalpast.com/video/65675065079_American-people_men-stand_women-work_mails-on-table.
51. CIA DTPILLAR 1, 29.
52. CIA DTPILLAR 1, 25, 12/8/51.
53. CIA DTPILLAR 1, 21, 12/21/51.
54. CIA DTPILLAR 1, 3, 1–4.
55. CIA DTPILLAR 1, 16, 5.
56. CIA DTPILLAR 1, 3.
57. CIA DTPILLAR 1, 4, 7.

58. TAF P-13, RFA First Program Data, 9/4/51 (emphasis added).
59. TAF P-13, RFA First Program Data, 9/4/51.
60. CIA DTPILLAR 1, 31, 2, 11/20/51.
61. John Crewdson with Joseph B. Treaster, "Worldwide Propaganda Network Built by the CIA," *New York Times*, 12/26/77, A1, A37.
62. Defty, *Britain, America, and Anticommunist Propaganda*.
63. A decade later, the Asia Foundation purchased radios for remote peoples in Malaysian jungles as part of a new anticommunist program. "Malaysia Aiding Tribes in Jungle: Concern over Subversion Is Spurring Program," *New York Times*, 5/23/65, 28.
64. CIA DTPILLAR 1, 11, 2, 1/22/52.
65. CIA DTPILLAR 1, 14, 1, 1/5/52.
66. CIA DTPILLAR 1, 20, 12/21/51.
67. CIA DTPILLAR 1, 14, 1, 1/5/52.
68. J. B. Smith, *Portrait of a Cold Warrior*, 168–69.
69. J. B. Smith, *Portrait of a Cold Warrior*, 168.
70. Such assurances were supplied by James L. Stewart, CFA director of Asian operations, in December 1951; see Defty, *Britain, America, and Anticommunist Propaganda*, 207.
71. Defty, *Britain, America, and Anticommunist*, 208.
72. J. B. Smith, *Portrait of a Cold Warrior*, 168.
73. CIA DTPILLAR 1, 2, 1, 8/7/52.
74. CIA DTPILLAR 1, 3, 6.
75. CIA DTPILLAR 1, 16, 2, 1/3/52 (handwritten date).
76. CIA DTPILLAR 1, 16, 4.
77. CIA DTPILLAR 1, 16.
78. CIA DTPILLAR 1, 81, 3.
79. John F. Sullivan letter, 3/25/53, found tucked in a copy of Committee for Free Asia, *Land Reform*, that I received from interlibrary loan; copy of letter is with author.
80. CIA DTPILLAR 2, 43, 1, 5/22/53.
81. CIA DTPILLAR 2, 43, 2, 5/22/53.
82. CIA DTPILLAR 2, 43, 2, 5/22/53.
83. CIA DTPILLAR 2, 34, 7, 6/25/54.
84. TAF P-49, Project Proposal Discussion, 9/28/53.
85. The Committee on International Information Activities was chaired by William H. Jackson and comprised Robert Cutler, Gordon Gray, Barklie McKee Henry, John C. Hughes, C. D. Jackson, Roger M. Kyes, and Sigurd Larmon; see CIAA, "Report to the President by the President's Committee on International Information Activities," 6/30/53, https://history.state.gov/historicaldocuments/frus1952-54v02p2/d370.
86. CIAA, "Report to the President by the President's Committee on International Information Activities," 6/30/53.
87. Blum played a significant role on the Jackson Committee. Emma Best has identified a previously secret interview with Allen Dulles in which Dulles credits Blum with having done "most of the investigation and writing" of the report; another CIA source found by Best claimed Blum wrote the entire report, with Jackson later adding the summary. See Best, "Robert Blum, the Spy Who Shaped the World Part 1."

88. Finley, "Recommending Political Warfare."
89. CIAA, "Report to the President by the President's Committee on International Information Activities," 73.
90. CIAA, "Report to the President by the President's Committee on International Information Activities," 6, 125.
91. CIAA, "Report to the President by the President's Committee on International Information Activities," 44.
92. CIAA, "Report to the President by the President's Committee on International Information Activities," 60.
93. CIAA, "Report to the President by the President's Committee on International Information Activities," 63.
94. CIAA, "Report to the President by the President's Committee on International Information Activities," 86.
95. CIAA, "Report to the President by the President's Committee on International Information Activities," 121.
96. TAF P-23, JLS, 2/15/52.
97. TAF P-23, JLS, 2/15/52.
98. TAF P-23, JLS, 2/15/52.
99. TAF P-23, JLS, 2/15/52.

2 BIRTH OF THE ASIA FOUNDATION

1. Crewdson with Treaster, "Worldwide Propaganda Network Built by the CIA," 1.
2. The *New York Times* statement that Blum had moved from CIA to the foundation may be incorrect, though it is likely that Blum had worked cooperatively with the CIA.
3. Emma Best concludes that despite claims by the *New York Times* and counterinsurgency warfare expert William Corson that Blum worked for these CIA predecessors, there is no evidence that he was a CIA officer. See Best, "Robert Blum, the Spy Who Shaped the World Part 1."
4. "Robert Blum, 54, Asia Expert Dies," *New York Times*, 7/10/65.
5. Best, "Robert Blum, the Spy Who Shaped the World Part 2."
6. For example, Blum wrote his friend William Jackson, congratulating him on his appointment as deputy director of the CIA. RB 5, Blum to William H. Jackson, 8/30/50.
7. In June 1951, Blum wrote David Bruce, US ambassador to France, that he was unsure when he would leave Vietnam or what he would do next. He wrote that he had "decided to turn down the CIA job as Executive Assistant to Bedell-Smith, partly because I preferred not to return to Washington and also because I felt that such a job, however interesting, would make of me a kind of jack-of-all-trades without clear responsibility. Bill Foster and Milt Katz have spoken in general terms of various things they have in mind, but so far there has been nothing definite.," RB 5, Group 78, Blum to Bruce, 6/6/51.
8. "Robert Blum, 54, Asia Expert Dies."
9. Corson, *The Betrayal*, 36.
10. See Best, "Robert Blum, the Spy Who Shaped the World Part 2." Best found Blum "had the Director of Central intelligence fired" and that Blum was such a central player in American intelligence that he "redesigned a significant portion of the [American intelligence

community], including its mechanisms for covert action and propaganda." See Best, "Robert Blum, the Spy Who Shaped the World Part 1." Blum certainly had connections to the CIA and other intelligence agencies' inner circles before being appointed president of CFA, though while certainly possible, this may attribute too much power to him. While Blum's work on the Jackson Committee report placed him in a unique position to shape the CIA's use of funding fronts, he does not appear to have designed these intelligence agency shifts so much as supported emerging trends.
11. Best, "Robert Blum, the Spy Who Shaped the World Part 2."
12. TAF P-105, MIT, Blum to Millikan, 8/20/53. Blum then made inquiries about what must have been the Modjokuto Project, describing a Ford Foundation program doing sociological studies in Indonesia and India and asking for any available information on the project.
13. After the establishment of the Asia Foundation, the use of CFA's name continued, as is seen in the 4/6/54 letter from Allen Dulles to Vice President Richard Nixon, lobbying for support for the CFA's efforts to fund five hundred "overseas Chinese to attend the University of Taiwan." Dulles to Nixon, 4/6/65, in CIA Reading Room, https://www.cia.gov/readingroom/docs/DOC_0000481167.pdf.
14. CIA DTPILLAR 2, 34, 8, 6/25/54. The memo was labeled "SECRET."
15. CIA DTPILLAR 3, 22, 11–12.
16. During the war, Blum oversaw OSS operations in France (directing the OSS Paris branch, 1944–45), Germany, the Netherlands, and Switzerland. He later became deputy director of the OSS European counterintelligence clearinghouse. National Archives and Records Administration at College Park, MD, OSS Personnel Files, RG 226, Box 62, Location 230/86/27/05, Robert Blum's OSS files, 6/25/45.
17. CIA DTPILLAR 1, 3, 4.
18. Moorehouse, *American Institutions and Organizations Interested in Asia*, 52–53; CIA DTPILLAR 2, 29, 19. The foundation personnel and geographic assigned regions listed in the directory were as follows: President Robert Blum, Robert B. Hall (Japan), Laurence G. Thompson (Korea), Earl Swisher (Taiwan), James T. Ivy (Hong Kong), L. Albert Wilson (Philippines), Edgar N. Pike (Vietnam), Leonard C. Overton (Cambodia), Noel F. Busch (Thailand), Patrick Judge (Malaya), Raymond V. Johnson (Indonesia), John H. Tallman (Burma), William T. Fleming (Ceylon), Richard J. Miller (Pakistan), and Harold L. Amoss Jr. (Afghanistan).
19. Moorehouse, *American Institutions and Organizations Interested in Asia*: Association of Asian Studies, 56; Boy Scouts, 64; East Asia teacher training, 70; Burmese scholars, 56; Japanese scholars, 71; book buying, 83; citizen education, 86–87; business education, 143; summer study, 239; radio commentaries, 289; economic analysis, 395.
20. CIA DTPILLAR, 2, 27, 3.
21. RB 1, Summary, July 1954.
22. TAF P-135, Vacation Life Camp, 1960.
23. RB 1, Executive Committee Report, 6/9/54, 1.
24. CIA DTPILLAR 2, 29, 27, 1955.
25. CIA DTPILLAR 2, 29, 19.
26. CIA DTPILLAR 2, 29, 19.
27. CIA DTPILLAR 2, 33, 1954.
28. CIA DTPILLAR 2, 35, 2 and 5, 1955.

29. RB 1, Report of Recent Trip to N. Afghanistan, Harold L. Amoss, 2/16/55, 1.
30. RB 1, Report of Recent Trip to N. Afghanistan, Harold L. Amoss, 2/16/55, 2.
31. RB 1, Report of Recent Trip to N. Afghanistan, Harold L. Amoss, 2/16/55.
32. TAF P-242, *Survey*, 12/15/64.
33. TAF P-242, *Survey*, 6/3/64.
34. TAF P-242, *Survey*, 7/7/64.
35. TAF P-242, *Survey*, 4/1/64.
36. CIA DTPILLAR 3, 14, 18.
37. CIA DTPILLAR 3, 14, 18 (emphasis added).
38. CIA DTPILLAR 3, 14, 19.
39. CIA DTPILLAR 3, 22, 2–3, 1963.
40. This document mentions two other methods used by the CIA to provide funds to the foundation, referred to without explanation as "Category I funding mechanisms (as defined by HR 240-3)" and "Category IV funding mechanisms (as defined by HR 240-3)." I was unable to determine what these Category I and Category IV funding mechanisms referenced. See CIA DTPILLAR 3, 22, 8.
41. The CIA redacted the memo author's identity, but the title "Chief, International Operations Division" remains, suggesting Thomas Braden.
42. The memo added, "Consideration is being given to including some of the following in addition to a few of the present DTPILLAR committee members[:] James A. Michener, Chester Bowles, James W. Landis, Walter Mallory, Walter H. Judd, William Philipps, Henry F. Grady, Roger Lapham, Fowler McCormick, Paul Smith." CIA DTPILLAR 2, 40, 2. Michener offered to travel to Asia on behalf of CFA; see RB 1, November 1953 Monthly Report.
43. CIA DTPILLAR 2, 34, 8, 6/25/54.
44. Listed individuals were Manly Fleischmann, Chester Bowles, Murray D. Lincoln, John Farrar, Henry F. Grady, Eric Johnston, Charles W. Cole, Thomas S. Nichols, Charles E. Wilson, Joseph Grew, Harold Hoskins, Henry Wriston, Allen Griffin, Whitney Griswold, James Michener. CIA DTPILLAR 2, 34, 13–14, 6/25/54.
45. RB 1, Board of Trustees Monthly Report, 9/13/55, 3; see also Klein, "Cold War Cosmopolitanism," 287. Klein mistakenly claims that Michener became Asia Foundation president in 1953, likely confusing TAF with the Fund for Asia; see Klein, *Cold War Orientalism*, 124. After Michener's death in 1997, *The Economist* observed that he "was more than anything a political writer," describing him as "an American patriot" and "Anti-Soviet." "James Michener, Spurned by Many but Read by Millions," *The Economist*, October 1997, http://www.economist.com/node/104895.
46. See CIA DTPILLAR 2, 40, 3, 8/25/53.
47. RB 1, Monthly Board Report, 6/14/55, 1.
48. The CIA reported, "James Michener resigned from the Board of Trustees in January 1963. James D. Kellerbach and Eric Johnston passed away. No replacements have been elected pending installation of new president." CIA DTPILLAR 3, 21, 18.
49. CIA DTPILLAR 3, 17, 12, Attachment B, 4/14/64.
50. Ford Foundation, *Ford Foundation Annual Report*, 11. Ford spent $124,600,000 on overseas development projects during this period.

51. CIA DTPILLAR 3,18, 4, 9/30/64. According to one memo, "In Fiscal Year 1963 these funds totaled $15,296." CIA DTPILLAR 3, 18, 19, 9/30/64.
52. CIA DTPILLAR 3,18, 4, 9/30/64.
53. CIA DTPILLAR 3, 18, 10–11.
54. CIA DTPILLAR 3, 18, 10–11.
55. CIA DTPILLAR 3, 18, 10–11.
56. CIA DTPILLAR 3, 18, 11–13, 9/30/64.
57. See CIA DTPILLAR 3, 18, 15, 9/30/64. The report added, "While there are numerous other American private and government foundations and similar institutions in other Western nations . . . all have more restrictive charters than TAF. Communist efforts in the foundation field have been easily recognizable."
58. CIA DTPILLAR 3, 18, 4, 9/30/64.
59. CIA DTPILLAR 3, 22, 1–2. This 1963 plan revised protocols that had been in place since September 13, 1957.
60. CIA DTPILLAR 3, 22, 4.
61. CIA DTPILLAR 3, 22, 4.
62. CIA DTPILLAR 3, 22, 27, appendix C, point 3.
63. CIA DTPILLAR 3, 22, 8.
64. CIA DTPILLAR 3, 22, 11. This language raises the possibility that a board member could be unwitting of the foundation's CIA links. Given agency activities, however, any such instances must have been rare.
65. CIA DTPILLAR 3, 22, 11.
66. CIA DTPILLAR 3, 22, appendix A, point 4.
67. CIA DTPILLAR 3, 22, 28, appendix C, point 7c.
68. CIA DTPILLAR 3, 22, 29.
69. Having examined archival records of many foundations, I have never observed other foundations keeping correspondence and applications of all applicants, most of whom, by the nature of the process, fail to receive funding. The Asia Foundation's record keeping thus appears extraordinary in this regard.
70. CIA DTPILLAR 3, 22, 27.
71. CIA DTPILLAR 3, 22, 28.
72. CIA DTPILLAR 3, 22, 28.
73. CIA DTPILLAR 3, 22, 26.
74. CIA DTPILLAR 3, 22, 22.
75. CIA DTPILLAR 3, 22, 23.
76. CIA DTPILLAR 3, 22, 24.
77. RF 111, Box 10, 8/26/54.
78. RF 111, 2-D, Box 10, Blum to J. Rockefeller III, 9/10/54.
79. RF 111, 2, Jamison to J. Rockefeller III, 9/20/54.
80. RF 111, 2, Jamison to J. Rockefeller III, 9/20/54.
81. RF 111, 2-D, Box 10, J. Rockefeller III to Dulles, 7/28/54.
82. RF 111, 2-D, Box 10, telegram, 10/15/54.
83. Parmar, *Foundations of the American Century*, 3.
84. Parmar, *Foundations of the American Century*, 264.

85. Parmar, *Foundations of the American Century*, 5.
86. Parmar, *Foundations of the American Century*, 99.
87. CIA DTPILLAR 3, 6, 7, 6/6/67.
88. CIA DTPILLAR 3, 22, 15.
89. TAF P-290, John F. Sullivan to Fleming, 10/23/64.
90. TAF P-216, Graham J. Lucas to Louis Lazaroff, 3/26/62.

3 EXCHANGES, CULTURAL PROGRAMS, CONFERENCES, SCHOLARSHIPS

1. CIA, "Communist Cultural and Propaganda Activities, in the Less Developed Countries," Director of Intelligence, Office of Research and Reports, Secret, January 1966, 1, CIA Reading Room, https://www.cia.gov/readingroom/docs/DOC_0000313542.pdf.
2. CIA, "Communist Cultural and Propaganda Activities," 1–2.
3. CIA, "Communist Cultural and Propaganda Activities," 2.
4. CIA, "Communist Cultural and Propaganda Activities," 2.
5. CIA, "Communist Cultural and Propaganda Activities," 3.
6. CIA, "Communist Cultural and Propaganda Activities," 4.
7. CIA, "Communist Cultural and Propaganda Activities," 5.
8. CIA, "Communist Cultural and Propaganda Activities," 6.
9. CIA, "Communist Cultural and Propaganda Activities," 7.
10. CIA, "Communist Cultural and Propaganda Activities," 7.
11. CIA, "Communist Cultural and Propaganda Activities," 8.
12. CIA, "Communist Cultural and Propaganda Activities," 8.
13. The CIA observed that, "during 1964, Indonesia refused to sign a cultural agreement with East Germany because, Indonesia claimed, it could not afford the travel expenses of students and trainees to East Germany as provided under the proposed agreement." CIA, "Communist Cultural and Propaganda Activities," 8.
14. CIA, "Communist Cultural and Propaganda Activities," 9.
15. Wilford, *Mighty Wurlitzer*.
16. CIA, "Communist Cultural and Propaganda Activities," 10.
17. CIA, "Communist Cultural and Propaganda Activities," 10.
18. CIA, "Communist Cultural and Propaganda Activities," 13.
19. CIA, "Communist Cultural and Propaganda Activities," 13.
20. CIA, "Communist Cultural and Propaganda Activities," 13.
21. Price, "The CIA Book Publishing Operations: Fragments of Sol Chaneles' Lost Manuscript," *CounterPunch*, 9/13/20, https://www.counterpunch.org/2020/09/13/fragments-of-sol-chaneles-lost-manuscript-on-cia-book-publishing-operations.
22. Price, *Cold War Anthropology*, 241–45.
23. CIA, "Communist Cultural and Propaganda Activities," 15.
24. CIA, "Communist Cultural and Propaganda Activities," 15–16.
25. CIA, "Communist Cultural and Propaganda Activities," 21.
26. RB 1, Judd Remarks of 1/17/56 as reported at TAF Trustees Meeting, 2/8/56.
27. TAF P-111, Harvard Seminar I, Kissinger to Richard A. Gard, 10/22/54.
28. TAF P-320, Report, 1961 Harvard International Seminar.
29. TAF P-111, Harvard International Seminar, 1st session, 7/3/61.

30. TAF P-111, Harvard International Seminar, 1st session, 7/3/61.
31. TAF P-111, Harvard International Seminar V, Heggie to Mrs. Pollard, 12/19/56.
32. TAF P-111, Harvard International Seminar VII, Blum to Kissinger, 1/3/57.
33. TAF P-111, Harvard International Seminar VII, Kissinger to Robert V. Sedwick, 2/7/58.
34. TAF P-111, Harvard International Seminar VII, Sedwick to Kissinger, 2/14/58.
35. Coliver sent six paragraph-long descriptions of individuals recommended for the program; the six recommended individuals were Nissanka Wijeratne, Liyanage Sarath Perera, Dr. J. A. Wilson, Sivapragaan Mahaligan, I. M. Gamani Iriyagelle, and Mervyn de Silva. TAF P-188, Harvard International Seminar, Coliver to Kissinger, 3/20/62.
36. TAF P-188, Education Scholarship and Fellows Harvard International Seminar 1962, J. M. Gallagher to Kissinger, 4/23/62
37. Crewdson with Treaster, "Worldwide Propaganda Network Built by the CIA," 37.
38. "11 Selected Nieman Fellows," *New York Times*, 6/7/56.
39. The Asia Foundation also funded programs bringing Asian journalists to Columbia University. See "Japanese Newsmen Here for Seminar," *New York Times*, 4/19/59, 8; and "Grants at Columbia Won by 8 Newsmen," *New York Times*, 9/17/64, 38.
40. "Japanese Newsmen Here for Seminar," 8; Crewdson with Treaster, "Worldwide Propaganda Network Built by the CIA," 1.
41. Parmar, *Foundations of the American Century*, 5.
42. RB 2, "Blum Report, Visit to India, 5/29–6/5/56, appendix, 8.
43. RB 2, Blum, Notes on visit to India, 7/27–8/3/59, 5.
44. TAF P-88, Nguyen Thai to John Plate, 5/28/63.
45. TAF P-88, Edith S. Coliver notes for the record, 9/19/63
46. TAF P-88, Nguyen Thai to John Plate, 5/28/63.
47. TAF P-42, Ahmed to Hoover, 11/15/55.
48. TAF P-42, Nasim Ahmed, CDE Report, 12/14/55.
49. TAF P-42, Nasim Ahmed, CDE Report, 12/14/55.
50. Bass, "Spy Who Loved Us."
51. TAF P-145, Phan Xuan An, "Captain JD Horner, visit," 8/21/58; Berman, *Perfect Spy*, 74.
52. TAF P-145, Phan Xuan An, An to James C. Porterfield, 12/22/58.
53. TAF P-145, Phan Xuan An, An to Porterfield, 9/22/58.
54. TAF P-145, Phan Xuan An, 1/7/59.
55. TAF P-145, Phan Xuan An, TAF memo, 8/13/59.
56. TAF P-145, Phan Xuan An, Porterfield to An, 8/18/59.
57. TAF P-145, Phan Xuan An, cable, 8/18/59.
58. RB 2, Notes on Visit to Japan, 9/8/59 and 9/12–17/59, 5.
59. American Assembly gatherings were initiated at Columbia University in 1950 by Dwight Eisenhower, then serving as the school's president. The gatherings brought academic experts and politicians to campus to discuss topics with domestic or international policy implications.
60. Blum suggested the following individuals: Dr. John E. Fairbank (Harvard) ("Fairbank is a somewhat controversial figure, having been identified with the 'agrarian reformers,' interpreters of Chinese Communism"), Dr. Edwin O. Reischauer (Harvard), Dr. George Taylor (University of Washington), Dr. David N. Rowe (Yale), Dr. Walt W. Rostow (MIT), Dr. Shannon McCune (University of Massachusetts), Admiral Chester Nimitz, Admiral

Raymond A. Spruance, General Mark Clark (The Citadel), John McCone (no affiliation listed, but CIA links), William F. Davin (former mayor of Seattle, head of Japan Society), Joseph C. Grew (Seattle), Paul Nitze (former State Department official), Roger D. Lapham, Barry Bingham (president, *Louisville Courier-Journal*), Brayton Wilbur, Eric A. Johnston (president, Motion Picture Association of America), Robert Sherrod (*Saturday Evening Post*), Russell G. Smith (executive vice president, international banking, Bank of America; president, World Affairs Council), S. D. Bechtel (president, Bechtel Corporation), Burton Fahs (director, Humanities Division, Rockefeller Foundation), Dr. Henry C. Houghton (former director, Peking Union Medical College), and Paul G. Hoffman. TAF P-79, American Assembly, Blum to Henry M. Wriston, 8/23/56.

61. RB 1, Nelson to Blum, 2/7/57.
62. Wilbur was president of Wilbur-Ellis Company and an Asia Foundation board member; Smith was executive vice president, Bank of America; Anderson was a retired air force major general with NATO links; McCone was a former undersecretary for air; Condliffe was a professor of international economics, University of California, Berkeley; and Spruance, a retired admiral. RB 1, Blum to Nelson, 2/13/57.
63. See RB 1, Blum to Nelson, 2/13/57. A similar incident occurred when Lawrence Ebb (Stanford School of Law) sent him a draft of an upcoming conference; see RB 1, Ebb to Blum, 2/12/57. Blum critiqued Ebb's initial agenda; see RB 1, Blum to Ebb, 2/15/57. Ebb later sent Blum a revised agenda, thanking him for his suggestions, adding that he had incorporated "almost all of the points you raised," RB 1, Ebb to Blum, 2/20/57.
64. RB 1, American Assembly, Blum to Allen, 3/20/57.
65. Coleman, *Liberal Conspiracy*; Rubin, *Archives of Authority*.
66. TAF P-123, CCF 2nd General Conference, Berlin, 6/16–22/60, Blum report, 7/11/60.
67. TAF P-254, Blum to Hook, 12/9/55; TAF P-254, Hook to Blum, 1/24/56.
68. RB 1, Monthly Report of Board of Trustees, Confidential, 4/1/57, appendix, 1.
69. TAF P-93, CCF Islamic Seminar at Karachi, Aslam.
70. TAF P-93, CCF Islamic Seminar at Karachi, Aslam.
71. For example, while attending the 1961 Asian Studies Association conference in Chicago, a foundation representative collected copies of papers such as "Ramification of Sino-Indian Rivalry in the Himalayan Border States (Nepak, Sikkim and Bhutan)" by L. Rose, University of California. TAF P-167, Asian Studies Association Conference, 1961.
72. TAF P-322, George Lerski reflections on Hoover Inst. Conference on Revolutionary Internationals, Cot 5-6-7, 11/10/64; compare Price, *American Surveillance State*, 224–37.
73. TAF P-325, Murray report, 9/17/65.
74. Funded projects include Afghanistan museum studies, Burmese publishing projects, Cambodian bookmobiles, book publishing in Ceylon, scholarly research facilities in Hong Kong, academic lecture series in India, Japanese publishing, Korean museum education, museum display cases in Laos, Malayan museum support, furniture for a Pakistan arts council, subsidies for archaeology and art projects in the Philippines, a new hall to display Taiwanese art treasures, funds for a museum in Thailand and for the study of hill tribes, and Vietnamese art and archaeology projects. RB, 1, Program Plastic Performing & Literary Arts, no. 14, 5/18/62, Arts Programming appendix.
75. RB 1, Program Plastic Performing & Literary Arts, no. 14, 5/18/62, Arts Programming appendix A, 6.

76. RB 1, Program Plastic Performing & Literary Arts, no. 14, 5/18/62, Arts Programming appendix, 10.
77. TAF P-271, Institute for the Study of Japanese Social Thought.
78. TAF P-271, Institute for the Study of Japanese Social Thought, "Revised Project for Approval."
79. US Ambassador to Japan Douglas MacArthur II told Blum that Hook's speaking tour had confronted "the Japanese intellectuals with their weakness." RB 2, "Notes on Visit to Japan 9/8/59 and 9/12–17/59," 8–9.
80. TAF P-185, PEN, Sedwick to Farrar, 10/9/59.
81. CIA interest in supporting Lerski's work is clear. There is, for example, a 5/24/56 CIA memo for DCI Dulles approving a list of projects: "Lectures on European Affairs (Lerski—for two-year period, attached to a Japanese University)." CIA DTPILLAR 2, 20, 7.
82. Lerski, *Origins of Trotskyism in Ceylon*.
83. TAF P-127, Social & Economic, Communism General, Contemporary Communist Strategy-Tactics, 8/25 [no year].
84. TAF P-127, Social & Economic, Communism General, Contemporary Communist Strategy-Tactics, 8/25 [no year]. Lerski represented the foundation at the Congress for Cultural Freedom seminar in Pakistan in April 1960; see TAF P-320, Jamis Talim-i-Mill Seminar; Lerski report, PAK-335, 5/10/60.
85. See TAF P-127 Social & Economic, Communism General, Contemporary Communist Strategy and Tactics, 8/25 [no year]. Although the year of this document is unknown, its identifying Lerski as "formerly associated with the Committee for Free Europe" suggests it may have been written relatively early during his association with the foundation.
86. Wolfe, *Freedom's Laboratory*, 146.
87. Sutton quoted in Simpson, *Economists with Guns*, 227. See also Frank, "Underdevelopment of Development."

4 MAKE FRIENDS AND INFLUENCE PEOPLE

1. The consultants were Professors Shannon McCune (Colgate University), Richard Park (UC Berkeley), and George Taylor (University of Washington).
2. RB 1, Monthly report to Board of Trustees, 5/11/55, 1.
3. In 1951–52, DTPILLAR considered hiring Levin Gale Shreve from the Baltimore public relations firm Counsel Services, Inc., as a consultant to develop a culturally appropriate publicity campaign for CFA in the Philippines; see TAF P-260, 1/31/52. Counsel Services was later described by a 1955 *Saturday Evening Post* article as a "private OSS"; see Kobler, "He Runs a Private OSS." Shreve was with the CIA for two decades, suggesting the likelihood that Counsel Services was an agency asset or an outsourced business running CIA operations; see Erskine, "Frank W. Price," 568–62.
4. For Taylor, see Price, *Anthropological Intelligence*, 171–73; for McCune, see Korff, "Shannon McCune," 460; for Park, see Dimock, "Obituary: Richard L. Park (1920–1980)."
5. RB 2, Report to Board of Trustees, 9/61, 3.
6. RB 2, Report to Board of Trustees, 9/61, 3.
7. RB 3, 1957–58 Speeches, "Peasants, Students, and Communism," 1.
8. Tania Long, "Boy Scouts Face World Problems," *New York Times*, 11/2/61.

9. TAF P-80, Boy Scouts of America, L. K. Little to J. L. Stewart, 8/24/51.
10. TAF P-335, Sheeks to TAF reps, SX-AR-1298, 10/20/60.
11. TAF P-335, Sheeks to TAF reps, SX-AR-1298, 10/20/60.
12. TAF P-335, Louis Connick memo, Visit of Major General D. C. Spry, 1/23/62.
13. TAF P-65, Program Development.
14. Long, "Boy Scouts Face World Problems."
15. TAF-P-335, Comparative statement, 11/15/62.
16. TAF P-175, Cambodian Royal Socialist Youth Movement, Overton to Blum, 3/15/58.
17. TAF P-175, Cambodian Royal Socialist Youth Movement, Overton to Blum, 3/15/58.
18. TAF P-175, Cambodian Royal Socialist Youth Movement, Overton to Blum, 3/15/58.
19. TAF P-175, SIVANNARY, TAF rep Cambodia to TAF president, re: Youth Leader Training Grant to US, 6/16/58.
20. TAF P-177, Cambodia, H. Bradley's 1958 foundation report on Cambodia, 8/11/58.
21. A handwritten note next to this suggestion to bring leaders of the socialist youth group to the United States reads, "cancelled by Bud [likely Bud Overton]." TAF P-177, Cambodia, Bradley 1958, Report on Cambodia, 8/11/58.
22. TAF P-175, SIVANNARY, note affixed to 3/15/58 Cambodian Royal Socialist Movement report, from [Cambodia Desk] to "Mr. Bradley and Mr. Sullivan," 5/25/58, commenting on Overton's 3/15/58 report.
23. TAF P-175, SIVANNARY, note affixed to 3/15/58 Cambodian Royal Socialist Movement report.
24. TAF P-185, Peace Corps, Sheeks to Blum, Peace Corps and TAF, 3/30/61.
25. TAF P-185, Peace Corps, Sheeks to Blum, Peace Corps and TAF, 3/30/61.
26. TAF P-185, Peace Corps, Pierson to Blum, TH-264, 5/15/61.
27. The Peace Corps manual, section 611, forbids individuals conducting intelligence from working for the Peace Corps and declares "automatic disqualification" for "any previous employment with the Central Intelligence Agency." Peace Corps, accessed 7/3/18, https://www.peacecorps.gov/stories/who-can-and-who-cannot-apply-to-be-a-peace-corps-volunteer/.
28. TAF P-185, Peace Corps, Pierson to Blum, TH-264, 5/15/61.
29. TAF P-185, Peace Corps, Howard C. Thomas to Blum, 5/15/61
30. TAF P-185, Peace Corps, Stewart to Blum, J-352, 5/11/61.
31. TAF P-185, W. Mallory Browne to Blum, SX-AR-1399, 4/25/61; Yang, "Cultural Cold War," 154–59.
32. Not all these countries launched Peace Corps programs.
33. TAF P-185, Peace Corps, James to Sullivan, 3/22/61.
34. TAF P-185, Graham J. Lucas to Blum and Sullivan, 1/5/62.
35. TAP P-185, Afghanistan Representative to Blum, 2/6/62: "The Asia Foundation's name was left out of final discussions, as a result of my request to Mr. Shook, based on your guidance."
36. RB 2, Monthly report to Board of Trustees, 3/61, 5–6.
37. TAF P-185, Peace Corps, Raymond V. Johnson to TAF president, 12/22/61. The meaning of Johnson's remark that Shook was "an old friend of the Foundation's" is unclear, but others claimed Shook was an old CIA hand. Dene McGriff, who worked for Shook in the late 1970s, claimed Shook originally went to Afghanistan as a missionary in the 1950s but that

later "he became the CIA eyes and ears in Afghanistan and later Iran, started the Peace Corps with Sargent Shriver, and though a wonderful Christian, was an emissary for the empire." See Dene McGriff, "Building of the American Global Empire," *World-Mysteries Blog*, 5/10/13, http://blog.world-mysteries.com/modern-world/building-of-the-american-global-empire/. A 1978 article claimed to identify Shook as a CIA asset, a charge Shook denied, claiming that "charges of CIA connections had been 'trumped up from the opposition (by) anthropological scholars who say 'don't disturb the natives.'" Jeff Stein, "A Ticket to Bolivia—One Way," *Michigan Daily*, 12/6/78, 4. The accuracy of claims Shook was a CIA asset remains uncertain.

38. CIA DTPILLAR 3, 18, 16.
39. TA P-340, Peace Corps, Thangathurai to Williams, 4/21/67.
40. One effort by CIA-linked personnel to influence the early Peace Corps was made by Max Millikan, a former CIA assistant director of the Office of Research and Reports. While considering establishing the Peace Corps, in January 1961, President Kennedy requested Millikan write a white paper on the formation of "An International Youth Service," which later became the Peace Corps. Millikan wrote this memo while working at the CIA-funded Center for International Studies (CENIS) at MIT. This memo later became appendix D in *Final Report: The Peace Corps*. In this memo, Millikan recommended sending young Americans to underdeveloped nations as cultural ambassadors bringing technological, health, and economic development projects. Millikan envisioned a youth service "governed by a board of directors on which should sit representatives from ICA, USIA, the State Department, the major foundations, representatives of the principal professions in which the Service is active (education, health, agriculture, etc.) and at least one senior social scientist distinguished for his work on underdeveloped areas." Millikan, "Memorandum on an International Youth Service," D-11.
41. TAF P-127, Social & Economic, Communist World Youth gathering, Bucharest, 7/25–30, 8/2–16/53, 10/53.
42. TAF P-127, Social & Economic, Communist World Youth gathering, Bucharest, 7/25–30, 8/2–16/53, 10/53.
43. TAF P-127, Social & Economic, Communist World Youth gathering, Bucharest, 7/25–30, 8/2–16/53, 10/53.
44. TAF P-127, Social & Economic, Communism, Harry Pierson to all reps, 2/11/54.
45. WAY was revealed in 1967 to have received CIA funds; see Roy Reed, "President Orders C.I.A. to Halt Aid to Private Groups," *New York Times*, 3/30/67, 1.
46. TAF P-166 Report on 3rd Gen Assembly and 7th WAY Council, Judge to Blum, 9/15/58, 1–2.
47. TAF P-166 Report on 3rd Gen Assembly and 7th WAY Council, Judge to Blum, 9/15/58, 6–7.
48. TAF P-166 Report on 3rd Gen Assembly and 7th WAY Council, Judge to Blum, 9/15/58, 5.
49. Ford, *Cold War Monks*.
50. Ford, *Cold War Monks*, 48. Patrice Ladwig has argued that Asia Foundation efforts to cultivate anticommunist Buddhist movements recognized that in Asian cultures "Buddhism has been crucial for political legitimacy, and alliances and tensions between state ruling elites and the monastic order form a crucial part of conceptions of statecraft of the region." Ladwig, "'Special Operation Pagoda,'" 85.

51. TAF P-130, CFA stimulation of Asian religions, 1/53.
52. TAF P-130, Klausner's comments on conference paper, 9/28/60.
53. There were other Buddhism-linked projects DTPILLAR chose not to fund. In a particularly strange example, recently fired Harvard psychologist Richard Alpert approached the foundation's New York representative, James R. Basche Jr., in 1963 and inquired if the foundation could help fund the establishment of a Tibetan lamasery in rural Freewood Acres, New Jersey, for students wishing to become Buddhist monks. Basche reported that "Dr. Alpert maintained that these men would have a good influence on the future of America when they were prepared to go out and teach Buddhism throughout this country." Alpert needed $30,000 for the venture. Basche reported, "Dr. Alpert was vague about his antecedents and was rather arrogant in his demands that we assist the lamasery. I explained the Foundation's general program objectives in Asia and our limitations in assisting a program of this kind. Alpert requested that we send him a copy of our brochure which we did." Basche included two articles from the previous day's *New York Times* mentioning Alpert and his interests and noted that "one of the other articles points out that Dr. Alpert was dismissed from Harvard University earlier this year because of his experiments with hallucinogenic drugs. He and his colleague have taken up residence on an estate in Millbrook, New York[,] where they are apparently continuing their unusual experiments in psychological phenomena." Basche advised the San Francisco office to be aware of this history should Alpert approach them with a funding request. TAF P-253, File A, Basche to TAF director, South Asia Division, 12/16/63. The *New York Times* articles in this file told of Timothy Leary and Alpert's efforts to establish their Buddhist enclave and included details of the professors' firing from Harvard for using LSD. See Murray Illson, "Ex-Ivy Leaguers Aim to Be Monks," *New York Times*, 12/15/63; "Psychic-Drug Tests Living in Retreat," *New York Times*, 12/15/63; M. Lee and Shlain, *Acid Dreams*.
54. TAF P-130, Social & Economic, Spencer report on observations, 1/15/55. Spencer was funded by CFA, but by the time of his travel CFA had become TAF.
55. The reason for sending a non-CFA affiliated scholar to Rangoon to report on the third World Buddhist Conference was to gain an outside view on the proceedings. Harry Pierson and Cora DuBois provided names of several possible academics, a list that did not initially include Spencer. See TAF P-14, World Buddhist 3rd Conference, Rangoon, Pierson to R. P. Conlon, 11/19/5
56. TAF P-130, Social & Economic, Spencer report on observations, 1/15/55, 3.
57. TAF P-130, Social & Economic, Spencer report on observations, 1/15/55, 45.
58. TAF P-130, Social & Economic, Spencer report on observations, 1/15/55, 68.
59. TAF P-130, Social & Economic, Spencer report on observations, 1/15/55, 69.
60. TAF P-130, Social & Economic, Spencer report on observations, 1/15/55, 108.
61. TAF P-130, Social & Economic, Spencer report on observations, 1/15/55, 109.
62. Swanger, "World Fellowship of Buddhists."
63. TAF P-16, Gard report on 4th WFB Conference, Kathmandu, 12/28/56.
64. TAF P-164, Gard to the record, 12/26/56, 3.
65. TAF P-164, Gard to the record, 12/26/56.
66. TAF P-130, G-32, Gard to Blum, Report on 5th WFB, 1/6/59.
67. The foundation was concerned that Gard viewed Japan as the center of Buddhism and resisted accepting any foundation assignments that would refocus his field efforts toward

Southeast Asia or Ceylon. Gard wanted to attend the conference with members of the Buddhist delegation from Japan, and John Sullivan insisted he remain a neutral observer. He was cautioned not to go as a delegate—no matter how concerned he might be that "communists not be permitted to maneuver the Conference." TAF P-130, Sullivan to Gard, 8/14/58.
68. TAF P-324 report, undated.
69. Foundation program officer Stephen Uhalley wrote, "We found that Holmes Welch was an especially well-informed adviser and extremely cooperative. We would certainly encourage consideration being given to future use by the Foundation of him." TAF P-324, WFB Gen Conf, Uhalley memo, 12/31/64. Ritzinger's excellent scholarship documents Welch's work with the foundation and concludes he likely knew it had CIA ties; see Ritzinger, "Tinker, Tailor, Scholar, Spy," 436–37.
70. TAF P-324, WFB report to S. Uhalley, undated, 5.
71. TAF P-324, Welch WFB report, undated, 5.
72. TAF P-324, Welch WFB report, undated, 5.
73. RB 2, Monthly report to Board of Trustees, 9/60, 1.
74. RB 2, Blum memo for the record, Visit to Ceylon, 11/23–27/60, 5.
75. TAF P-326, Kunstadter to Pierson, 7/29/65.
76. TAF P-326, Pierson to Kunstadter, 8/13/65.
77. TAF P-326, Pierson to Humphr[e]y, 8/16/65.
78. TAF P-326, Pierson to Kunstadter, 9/2/65.
79. TAF P-326, Pierson to Kunstadter, 9/2/65.
80. CIA DTPILLAR 3, 24, 1, 1/28/63. Board member Russell Gordon Smith was executive vice president in charge of international banking at Bank of America. "Russell Gordon Smith," Asia Foundation, accessed 1/20/2020, https://asiafoundation.org/people/russell-gordon-smith/.
81. CIA DTPILLAR 3, 24, 1, 1/28/63.
82. CIA DTPILLAR 3, 24, 2, 1/28/63.
83. Smith argued that the foundation being forced out of Burma made it easier to absorb these lost funds; see CIA DTPILLAR 3, 18, 9/30/64.
84. CIA DTPILLAR 3, 24, 2.
85. RB 2, Monthly report to Board of Trustees, 11/3/58, suppl., 2.
86. TAF Monthly report to Board of Trustees, 2/3/58, 5–6.
87. RB 2, TAF Monthly report to Board of Trustees, 8/1/58, 4.
88. RB 2, TAF Monthly report to Board of Trustees, 8/1/58, suppl., 1–3.
89. RB 2, Monthly report to Board of Trustees, 9/3/58, 4.
90. RB 1, Board of Trustees meeting minutes, TAF, 2/11/55, 2.
91. "Doing a Touchy Job," *Newsweek*, 9/12/55, 106.
92. RB 1, Board of Trustees meeting minutes, TAF, 2/11/55, 1.

5 COLLECTING INTELLIGENCE

1. CIA DTPILLAR 3, 21, 18.
2. CIA DTPILLAR 3, 21, 19.
3. CIA DTPILLAR 3, 21, 19.
4. CIA DTPILLAR 3, 21, 20.

5. CIA DTPILLAR 3, 21, 20.
6. CIA DTPILLAR 3, 21, 20
7. CIA DTPILLAR 3, 14, 34.
8. CIA DTPILLAR 3, 14, 34.
9. CIA DTPILLAR 3, 12, 27.
10. Robert Trumbull, "Burma Banning Fulbright Men, Ford and Asia Fund Advisers," *New York Times*, 4/20/62; "Ford Group Moves to Halt Burma Aid," *New York Times*, 6/17/62; "Asia Foundation Nears End of Work in Burma," *New York Times*, 6/27/62.
11. RB 2, Monthly report to Board of Trustees, 6/20/58, 1–2.
12. TAF CFA-1, Information and Reference Section, Radio Free Asia, 10/30/52.
13. TAF CFA-1, Information and Reference Section, Strangulating Security Controls in China, 10/9/52.
14. TAF CFA-1, Chungking paper admits endless meetings seriously affecting production, 7/31/52.
15. CIA DTPILLAR 3, 18, 14. For current definitions of an operations officer's duties, see the CIA Careers page, accessed 5/9/23, https://www.cia.gov/careers/jobs/?keywords=Staff%20Operations%20Officer&page=1.
16. TAF P-120, Wittfogel to Blum, 9/5/58.
17. TAF P-120, Blum to Wittfogel, 9/18/58. In December 1957 and January 1958, the foundation assisted Wittfogel and his wife, Esther Goldfrank, in a research trip to examine documents on Chinese communism in Taipei. TAF P-120, Wittfogel.
18. TAF P-230, Communism, Research on Chinese Communism, Taiwan, L. Z. Yuan to EP, 12/13/61
19. TAF P-230, Communism, Research on Chinese Communism, Sources in Taiwan for Research on Chinese Communism, 3.
20. TAF P-230, Communism, Research on Chinese Communism, Sources in Taiwan for Research on Chinese Communism, 4.
21. TAF P-230, Communism, Research on Chinese Communism, Sources in Taiwan for Research on Chinese Communism, 6.
22. TAF P-230, Communism, Research on Chinese Communism, Sources in Taiwan for Research on Chinese Communism, 6.
23. TAF P-230, Communism, Research on Chinese Communism, Sources in Taiwan for Research on Chinese Communism, 9. In 1962, a foundation staffer named Yuan called Guy Pauker at RAND asking if RAND might want to purchase a clipping collection of Chinese communist press materials, referred to as the "Freedom Press Collection." TAF P-230, Yuan to the record, 1/26/62. See also Alex Visser, "Celebrating Eugene Wu and the Crown Jewel of UW Libraries" *The Daily* (University of Washington, Seattle), 11/9/17, http://www.dailyuw.com/news/article_55a932d0-c4ff-11e7-bc9a-ff03465d1b2c.html.
24. TAF P-230, Communism, Research on Chinese Communism, Sources in Taiwan for Research on Chinese Communism, 9.
25. TAF P-230, Communism, Research on Chinese Communism, Sources in Taiwan for Research on Chinese Communism, 11.
26. TAF P-65, Draft: CFA Afghanistan Plan, 12/21/53.
27. Another reason for these gaps is that it appears that the Asia Foundation did not deposit at Hoover a complete set of records from the period of its CIA ties (1951–67).

28. TAF P-65, Amoss to Stewart, 3/26/53 (emphasis added).
29. TAF P-65, General, Afghanistan, Amoss, Report on recent trip to northwestern Afghanistan, 2/16/55.
30. TAF P-65, TAF interim report, Afghanistan, 10/1/57.
31. TAF P-65, Afghanistan, 1955–58.
32. TAF P-178, Laos, Rural-border tribes, undated, 9.
33. TAF P-178, Laos, Rural-border tribes, undated, 12.
34. TAF P-178, Laos, Rural-border tribes, undated, 13.
35. TAF P-178, Laos, Rural-border tribes, undated, 13.
36. TAF P-178, Laos, Rural-border tribes, Gordon H. Messegee's report on Haut Mekong Province, 2/26–29 [year missing], 6.
37. TAF P-178, Laos, Rural-border tribes, Messegee's report on Haut Mekong Province, 2/26–29, 6–7 (emphasis added).
38. TAF P-318, Hill Tribes of Thailand, Anthropologist, Pierson to Blum, 12/2/60.
39. TAF P-318, Social and Economic, Hill Tribes of Thailand–Anthropologist II, undated.
40. TAF P-318, Hill Tribes of Thailand, Anthropologist reports, Manual for field workers among Hill Tribes, 2.
41. TAF P-318, Hill Tribes of Thailand, Anthropologist reports, Manual for field workers among Hill Tribes, 2.
42. TAF P-318, Hill Tribes of Thailand, Anthropologist reports, Manual for field workers among Hill Tribes, 3.
43. TAF P-318, Hill Tribes of Thailand, Opium production, 1/22/62, 1.
44. TAF P-318, Hill Tribes of Thailand, Opium production, 1/22/62, 2. During this period, Klausner was in high demand. In 1962, RAND political scientist Guy Pauker approached President Blum to ask if the foundation "might lend to RAND the services of Bill Klausner for a three months' period to conduct certain investigations in Northern Thailand." TAF P-254, Blum to Pierson, 4/4/62. Blum expressed concerns about Klausner's research being linked with RAND's military-intelligence work, which "might reflect adversely on the Foundation," but Blum forwarded the request to TAF's Thailand office; see TAF P-254.
45. TAF P-318, Hill Tribes of Thailand, Anthropologist, Klausner report on opium, 1/22/62, 3. Given DTPILLARS's funding of Manndorff's early Tribal Research Centre work, claims that "Manndorff was not involved with the CIA in any way" misdirect attention from ways that many Cold War scholars unwittingly engaged with intelligence agencies; see Jonsson, "Phantom Scandal," 272.
46. TAF P-318, Hill Tribes of Thailand, Anthropologist, Klausner report on opium, 1/22/62, 3.
47. TAF P-318, Hill Tribes of Thailand, Anthropologist, Klausner report on opium, 1/22/62, 3.
48. TAF P-318, Hill Tribes of Thailand, Anthropologist, Klausner report on opium, 1/22/62, 5.
49. Thai anthropologist Acharn Pataya Saihoo helped the foundation develop elements of the early Hill Tribe Project and later the Tribal Research Centre. TAF P-318, Social and Economic, Hill Tribes of Thailand–Anthropologist II, William Klausner to the record, 10/12/62.
50. TAF P-318, Social and Economic, Graham Lucas to TAF president, re: Tribal Research Centre, 2/27/63.
51. TAF P-318, Social and Economic, Hill Tribes of Thailand–Anthropologist II, Proposed plan for the establishment of a tribal research center in Thailand.

52. For several months prior to this Cornell academic's visit, foundation memos mentioned Sharp as an important scholar to recruit for the Hill Tribes Project; see TAF P-318, Social and Economic, Hill Tribes of Thailand–Anthropologist II, Proposed plan for the establishment of a tribal research center in Thailand, G. J. Lucas to TAF president, 1/2/63.
53. TAF P-318, Social and Economic, Hill Tribes of Thailand–Anthropologist II, Klausner to TAF president, 4/18/63.
54. Cover letter is dated 1/23/65, TAF P-318, Hill tribes of Thailand, Anthropologist Reports. Frederick Mote, a Princeton history professor, was an OSS officer in World War II. Ruth Stevens, "Frederick Mote, Key Figure in Advancing the Study of China, Dies at Age 82," Princeton University, 3/10/2005, https://www.princeton.edu/news/2005/03/10/frederick-mote-key-figure-advancing-study-china-dies-age-82.
55. TAF P-318, Hill Tribes of Thailand, Anthropologist reports, Mote report, Preliminary survey of the Haw villages in Amphur Fang, Chiengma, 6; compare Manndorff, "Report on the Establishment"; and Manndorff, "Hill Tribe Program."
56. TAF P-318, 318, Hill Tribes of Thailand, Anthropologist reports, Mote Report, Manndorff, 10/23/64. For more on Manndorff's ethnographic methods, see Trupp and Butratana, "Images of Hans Manndorff's Anthropological Research on the 'Hill Tribes.'"
57. TAF P-318, Hill Tribes of Thailand, Anthropologist reports, Visit to Mae Sod border station, 12/17/63, 3–4.
58. TAF P-318, Social and Economic Hill Tribes of Thailand–Anthropologist III, Lucas to TAF president, 5/10/65.
59. Buadaeng, "Rise and Fall of the Tribal Research Institute."
60. TAF P-318, Social and Economic, Hill Tribes of Thailand–Anthropologist III, Lucas to TAF president, 5/10/65.
61. See TAF P-318, Social and Economic, Hill Tribes of Thailand–Anthropologist III, Sutter to Manndorff, 11/3/66.
62. This list was later reduced by Jane Wilson, of the foundation's library staff, to twenty-nine books, including many structural functional anthropological classics. TAF P-318, Social and Economic, Hill Tribes of Thailand–Anthropologist III, Wilson to "Willie" [TAF representative, Malaysia], 11/18/66.
63. See TAF P-245, W. J. Klausner to Calvin Scollon, JS-TH-5, 5/24/66.
64. TAF P-245, Social and Economic, Hill-Tribe Cultural Minority Programming, Klausner to TAF president, 5/17/66.
65. See TAF P-245, Klausner to TAF Scollon, JS-TH-5, 5/24/66.
66. TAF P-245, Social and Economic, Hill-Tribe Cultural Minority Programming, Klausner to TAF president, 4/11/66.
67. Jones, "Reply to Jorgensen and Wolf"; Jones, "Social Responsibility and the Belief in Basic Research"; Wolf, and Jorgensen, "Anthropology on the Warpath"; Price, Cold War Anthropology, 314–21; Wakin, Anthropology Goes to War.
68. After the October 1966 coup in Laos, Asia Foundation headquarters cautioned Connick to keep his distance from AID village projects because US government programs brought more suspicions than those of supposedly private nongovernmental organizations. TAF-P-282, 10/21/66.
69. TAF-P-282, 7/62, Connick to TAF president, 11/1/66.
70. Several detailed Connick reports from Laos survive in Hoover Institution archives, TAF P-417.

71. Oakley Brooks, "One Reporter's Odyssey Tracking His Uncle's Legacy in Laos," *Christian Science Monitor*, 4/22/08.
72. Brooks, "One Reporter's Odyssey."
73. One example of such information that could be gathered is in July 1955 correspondence between Asia Foundation president Blum and DCI Allen Dulles. Blum wrote Dulles a two-page letter after his meeting with Prime Minister U Nu of Burma. Blum privately shared "full reports" of his conversations with the prime minister and apprised DCI Dulles of shortcomings in the State Department's hosting duties during the prime minister's recent visit. CIA FOIA, Blum to Dulles, 7/22/55, in CIA Reading Room, https://www.cia.gov/readingroom/docs/CIA-RDP80B01676R004200020082-6.pdf.
74. US Senate, Committee on Foreign Relations, *Asia Foundation*, 1–2.
75. RB 2, Monthly report to Board of Trustees, 12/3/59, 5.
76. See Corson, *The Betrayal*; "How the CIA Turns Foreign Students into Traitors," *Ramparts*, April 1967, 22–24. In 1962, the foundation provided a grant of $6,500 for the US-run Foreign Student Advisers Workshop, run in cooperation with Human Relations Area Files. RB 2, Monthly board report, May 1962, suppl., 6.
77. Charles Stuart Kennedy, "James L. Woods, Research Analysis Division (1964–67), DOD, Advisor ARPA (1969–73)," 222, Association for Diplomatic Studies and Training Foreign Affairs Oral History Project, 2001, https://www.adst.org/Readers/Thailand.pdf.
78. Kennedy, "James L. Woods," 222.

6 ANTICOMMUNISM AND COUNTERINSURGENCY

1. TAF P-66, "Indonesia," 11/25/53–12/3/53.
2. Currey, *Edward Lansdale*.
3. CIA DTPILLAR 1, 82, 3/3/52.
4. Satoshi, "Gabriel L. Kaplan and U.S. Involvement," 154.
5. Satoshi, "Gabriel L. Kaplan and U.S. Involvement," 154–55.
6. J. B. Smith, *Portrait of a Cold Warrior*, 258–59; Satoshi, "Gabriel L. Kaplan and U.S. Involvement," 155.
7. CIA DTPILLAR 1, 82, 3, 3/3/52.
8. Currey, *Edward Lansdale*, 106. According to another source, "A different group with a very similar name, the National Movement for Free Elections, that was formed before the 1953 elections, also used the nickname NAMFREL. Some observers charged that this earlier NAMFREL funneled CIA funds to the presidential campaign of Ramon Magsaysay, who was elected president in 1953." Bjornlund, *Beyond Free and Fair*, 355n2. See also Byinton, *Bantay ng Bayan*, 69; Bonner, *Waltzing with a Dictator*, 40; and Wurfel, *Filipino Politics*, 285.
9. See Headman, "Global Civil Society in One Country?" Evan Thomas observed that NAMFREL was "supposedly organized by various civic groups but actually run by Kaplan and funded by the CIA. NAMFREL pushed for clean elections while making sure that Magsaysay would be the one elected." Thomas, *Very Best Men*, 58.
10. Currey, *Edward Lansdale*, 106–8.
11. Currey, *Edward Lansdale*, 107.
12. TAF P-36, Dalton to Schuckman, 11/25/52.

13. TAF P-36, Dalton to Schuckman, 11/25/52.
14. TAF P-36, William Fleming to Maddocks, 4/14/53.
15. See TAF P-36, Memo, Meeting with CARE, 3/11/53. News of Quirino's opposition to the centers was covered by the Associated Press in "President [Elpidio] Quirino said Tuesday there is no need for the Committee for Free Asia (CAP, C.F.A.) to teach Democracy in the Philippines." TAF P-36, AP story, 3/11/53.
16. TAF P-36, Maddocks to Andres, 3/26/53.
17. TAF P-26, W. Fleming to CFA president, 5/27/53.
18. Attached to a 5/13/53 memo from Helen Hackley to James L. Stewart, reporting on a phone conversation she had recently had with Ed Flynn, of CARE, is a handwritten note on an interoffice routing sheet, from an unknown individual asking, "Mr. Stewart—are we 'out of the frying pan & in the fire?" to which Stewart replied, "Time will tell." TAF P-36, Hackley to Stewart, 5/13/53.
19. Satoshi, "Gabriel L. Kaplan and U.S. Involvement," 165.
20. Satoshi, "Gabriel L. Kaplan and U.S. Involvement," 166.
21. Satoshi, "Gabriel L. Kaplan and U.S. Involvement," 163.
22. Satoshi, "Gabriel L. Kaplan and U.S. Involvement," 154.
23. Kerkvliet, "Contested Meanings," 154–55.
24. RB 2, Monthly report to Board of Trustees, 5/5/60, 2–3. Candidates traveling with the military took some risks, as there was widely held hostility toward the Lao army, and Messegee speculated that "if it ever comes to war, the Lao army officers will receive nothing but a slit throat from the people they are supposed to protect." RB 2, Monthly Report to Board of Trustees, 5/5/60, 3.
25. TAF P-310, Cooperative Research and Training Center.
26. TAF P-79, Pike Report, Luncheon-AFV, 10/13/56.
27. RB 2, Notes on visit to Vietnam, Blum 11/12–19/56, 8; compare Darrell Berrigan, "Operation Brotherhood," *Saturday Evening Post*, 11/12/55, 146–48.
28. RB 2, Monthly report to Board of Trustees, 9/61, 4–5.
29. RB 2, Monthly report to Board of Trustees, 12/61, suppl., 3.
30. RB 2, Monthly report to Board of Trustees, 8/61, suppl., 3.
31. TAF P-147, Vietnam Program Office, V-SX-407, 9/7/61.
32. TAF P-147, Rural Montagnard Resettlement Program, 9/18/61.
33. TAF P-147, Project Proposal: Montagnard Resettlement, Porterfield to Blum, 8/30/61.
34. TAF P-147, Project Proposal: Montagnard Resettlement, Porterfield to Blum, 8/30/61.
35. TAF P-147, Project Proposal: Montagnard Resettlement, Porterfield to Blum, 8/30/61.
36. TAF P-147, Rural Montagnard Resettlement Program, undated note.
37. TAF P-147, Rural Montagnard Resettlement Program, CE Humphrey to Vietnam rep, 10/5/61.
38. TAF P-309, Strategic Hamlet, E. M. Howell to Bui Yuong Nuan, 7/3/64.
39. CIA DTPILLAR 3, 26, 1/26/63.
40. CIA DTPILLAR 3, 26, 1/23/63.
41. CIA DTPILLAR 3, 26, 12/14/62.
42. TAF P-416, Koontz to TAF president, 8/12/66.
43. TAF P-416, Evans [WDE] note on memo, 8/22/66.
44. TAF P-416, Evans [WDE] note on memo, 8/22/66.

45. TAF P-326, Tribal and Minority Peoples in SE Asia, Conference, 5/24/65; Kunstadter, *Southeast Asian Tribes*, ix; compare the citation for Kunstadter's 2021 American Anthropological Association Executive Director Award, stating "Dr. Kunstadter actively resisted the Defense Department overtures." "2021 Executive Director's Award Presented to Dr. Peter Kunstadter," American Anthropological Association, accessed 2/2/23, https://www.americananthro.org/ConnectWithAAA/Content.aspx?ItemNumber=28199.
46. Kunstadter edited a collection of papers from the conference, published by Princeton University Press; see Kunstadter, *Southeast Asian Tribes*.
47. TAF P-326, Tribal and Minority Peoples in SE Asia, Graham J. Lucas [TAF Thailand rep] to TAF president, 12/9/64.
48. TAF P-326, Tribal and Minority Peoples in SE Asia, Kunstadter to Dalton, 12/11/64.
49. TAF P-326, Tribal and Minority Peoples in SE Asia, Dalton to Kunstadter, 12/31/64.
50. The initial list of invitees identified the following individuals: for Thailand, Don Mickelwait, Hans Manndorff, William Geddes, Michael Moerman; for Laos, Gordon Donner, Miles Osborne, AID; for Vietnam, "Jerry" Hickman, George Tannam, Georges Condominas; for Burma, F. K. Lehman and Maran LaRaw; and for Malaysia, Tom Harrisson. Pierson later published his conference paper; see Pierson, "Asia Foundation's Programming for Tribal and Minority Peoples."
51. TAF P-326, Tribal and Minority Peoples in SE Asia, Pierson to the record, 1/26/65.
52. TAF P-326, Tribal and Minority Peoples in SE Asia, Director R&D to TAF president, 1/29/65.
53. Geddes, "Tribal Research Centre."
54. Geddes, "Tribal Research Centre," 559–62.
55. Geddes, "Tribal Research Centre," 559. The draft of the original paper presented at the conference is located in TAF P-168, Wlf/Civic/Recr. Tribal Minority Peoples in SE Asia, Conference papers, 5/24/65.
56. Geddes, "Tribal Research Centre," 559.
57. Geddes, "Tribal Research Centre," 560.
58. TAF P-326, Pierson to Kunstadter, 4/2/65; Pierson, "Asia Foundation's Programming for Tribal and Minority Peoples."
59. TAF P-326, Williams to Kunstadter, 5/5/65.
60. TAF P-326, Basche to Haydn Williams, 5/18/65. Kunstadter later queried Pierson, asking him, "Who is the American anthropologist in Thailand referred to on p. 15—was this John Brohm? Was the article ever published?" TAF P-326, Kunstadter to Pierson, 7/29/65. Pierson replied that it was Brohm, adding, "But I do not want his name mentioned as the information was taken from a paper he gave me in confidence. I don't know whether the article was ever published, although I can't remember having seen it." TAF P-326, Pierson to Kunstadter, 8/13/65.
61. TAF P-326, Basche to Williams, 5/18/65.
62. TAF P-326, Dalton to the record, Re: Hill Tribes Research Center, Discussions with Prof Geddes, 5/24/65, 5/26/65.
63. TAF P-326, Dalton to the record, Re: Hill Tribes Research Center, Discussions with Prof Geddes, 5/24/65, 5/26/65.
64. TAF P-326, Kunstadter to Williams, 5/18/65.
65. TAF P-326, handwritten note on back of J. F. Sullivan note, 5/20/65.

66. RB 2, Monthly Board of Trustees report, 9/3/59, 4.
67. RB 2, Monthly Board of Trustees report, 11/4/59, 3.
68. RB 2, Monthly Board of Trustees report, 11/4/59, 3.
69. TAF P-128, Social and Economic, Military General 1959–60, Gange to all Asia Foundation representatives, SX-AR-895, 1/6/59.
70. A November 1958 report from an Asia Foundation conference in Hong Kong includes a draft operational guidance report on "Assistance to Asian Military Police," which identified several positive outcomes for supporting military education programs. TAF P-128, Social and Economic, Military General 1959–60, Assistance to Asian Military and Police, 11/9–15/58.
71. Hinckle et al., "University on the Make"; TAF P-305, Assistance to Asian Military and Police, 11/9–15/58.
72. TAF P-305, Assistance to Asian Military and Police, 11/9–15/58.
73. See TAF P-128, Social and Economic, Military General 1959–60, Sola Pool to R. Heggie, 6/13/60. Sheeks wrote, "Guy Pauker has commented that the civil-military relations program at Harvard is unsuitable, be[ing], as it is, in the Western context and aimed at limiting the role of the military. (Is the latter an objective or cure?)." TAF P-128, Social and Economic, Military General 1959–60, Sheeks to John F. Sullivan and Heggie, 8/22/60.
74. TAF P-128, Social and Economic, Military General 1959–60, Blum to Speier, 2/29/60.
75. TAF P-128, Social and Economic, Military General 1959–60, Heggie to the record, 5/5/60.
76. TAF P-128, Social and Economic, Military General 1959–60, Sola Pool to Heggie, 6/1/60.
77. TAF P-128, Social and Economic, Military General 1959–60, Sheeks to John F. Sullivan and Heggie, 8/22/60.
78. TAF P-128, Social and Economic, Military General 1959–60, Sheeks to Sullivan and Heggie, 8/22/60.
79. TAF P-128, Social and Economic, Military General 1959–60, Sullivan to Heggie, 9/14/60.
80. TAF P-128, Social and Economic, Military General 1959–60, Sullivan to Heggie, 9/14/60.
81. TAF P-320, E. Pakistan Police Training College, 11/30/59.
82. TAF P-198, Military Army Psych Warfare Training Program, 11/30/59.
83. TAF P-198, Military Army Psych Warfare Training Program, telegram, 11/23/59.
84. TAF P-206, Japan, Military General, 11/30/60.
85. RB 2, Monthly report to Board of Trustees, 5/5/60, suppl., 1.
86. Sahlins, *Confucius Institutes*; Carroll Doherty, "Fast Facts about Americans' Views on Russia amid Allegations of 2020 Election Interference," Pew Research Center, 2/21/20, https://www.pewresearch.org/fact-tank/2020/02/21/fast-facts-about-americans-views-on-russia-amid-allegations-of-2020-election-interference/.
87. Bevins, *Jakarta Method*, 197.
88. CIA 1966 DTPILLAR 3, 14, 21.
89. CIA 1966 DTPILLAR 3, 14, 22. See also Wakin, *Anthropology Goes to War*.

7 INTERACTIONS WITH OTHER ORGANIZATIONS AND FOUNDATIONS

1. TAF P-127, Social and Economic, Communism General, R. D. Grey to Conlon, 1/15/54.
2. TAF P-127, Social and Economic, Communism General, Colin D. Edwards, 1/54.
3. JW 3, TAF, Policy Guidance No. 2, Labor Policy, 1/25/55.

4. Morgan, *Covert Life*; compare Jacobs, "How the CIA Makes Liars Out of Union Leaders"; and Harry Kelber, "AFL-CIO's Dark Past: U.S. Labor Secretly Intervened in Europe, Funded to Fight Pro-Communist Unions," *Labor Educator*, 11/22/04, http://www.labor educator.org/darkpast3.htm.
5. Shorrock, "Labor's Cold War."
6. Shorrock, "Labor's Cold War."
7. Gerteis, "Labor's Cold Warriors."
8. RB 1, General Committee Quarterly Report, 4/9/54, 4.
9. TAF P-183, ICFTU, Foreign Service dispatch of the American embassy, Karachi, 8/26/59.
10. TAF P-21, Katsumata report, Study of Katsumata visit, 10/19–11/19/55.
11. TAF P-71, F. Robertson's visit to Indonesia, Part II, 6/3/54.
12. JW 3, Weinberg report on Lovestone meeting, NYC, 3/14/56.
13. JW 3, Weinberg report, 3/12/56.
14. JW 3, Weinberg report on Reuther meeting, 3/12/56.
15. Reuther's minor error was in assuming this labor union influence strategy was part of "the State Department's game in Pakistan" rather than considering this was the CIA's game.
16. TAF P-38, Weinberg to Pakistan TAF rep, Memo: Pakistan labor personalities, 9/6/57.
17. RB 2, Notes on visit to Malaya and Singapore, 9/14–19/57, 4.
18. RB 2, TAF monthly report to Board of Trustees, 8/1/58, 2–3.
19. TAF P-38, Lazaroff to Sullivan, Jules Weinberg's report, 11/27/57.
20. JW 3, TAF RB, 1956–1958, Weinberg to Blum.
21. RB 2, TAF monthly report to Board of Trustees, 8/4/60.
22. RB 2, TAF monthly report to Board of Trustees, 8/61, suppl., 10; TAF P-183, James Greene to TAF president, 6/23/63.
23. TAF P-218, Budget, 1/25/60.
24. TAF P-15, Sullivan to Hoover, 5/27/55.
25. The Reece Committee was the Select Committee to Investigate Tax-Exempt Foundations and Comparable Organizations, chaired by Representative B. Carroll Reece (R-TN) from 1952 to 1954 and established to investigate both tax fraud and American nonprofit organizations searching for communists.
26. TAF P-15, Sullivan to Hoover, 5/27/55, note.
27. TAF P-15, Meeting of foundations' reps, NY, 1955, Hoover to Blum, 9/29/55.
28. TAF P-15, Meeting of foundations' reps, NY, 1955, Hoover to Blum, 9/29/55.
29. TAF P-15, Folder: Meeting of foundations' reps, NY, 1955. Hoover reported that the following foundations attended this August 1955 meeting: Association for the Aid of Crippled Children, the Vincent Astor Foundation, Asia Foundation*, Doris Duke Foundation, Thomas Alva Edison Foundation, Thomas Hofheimer Foundation, James Foundation of New York, J. M. Kaplan Fund*, Madeline M. Low Foundation, Josiah Macy Jr. Foundation*, Ray and Charles Newman Memorial Foundation, Inc., New York Fund for Children, Inc., New York Heart Association, Inc., Jessie Smith Noyes Foundation*, Gustavus and Louise Pfeiffer Research Foundation, James Picker Foundation, Richardson Foundation, Fannie E. Rippel Foundation, Rockefeller Brothers Fund, Benjamin Rosenthal Foundation, Inc.*, Russell Sage Foundation, Helen Hay Whitney Foundation. TAF P-15, Meeting of foundations' reps, NY, 1955, Hoover to Blum, 9/29/55. Foundations marked with an asterisk were later revealed to have CIA connections.

30. CIA DTPILLAR 3, 22, appendix A, point 7.
31. "Noel Fairchild Busch," *Gale Literature: Contemporary Authors* (online, with paywall), 2007.
32. John Crewdson, "C.I.A. Established Many Links to Journalists in U.S. and Abroad," *New York Times*, 12/27/77, A1. Busch's *Times* article chronology is problematic, stating that he conducted this CIA interview in the mid-1950s while working for *Time*, before working for the Asia Foundation, yet Busch first worked for CFA in 1952.
33. For example, a 9/10/59 meeting between Busch and former State Department officer Kenneth T. Young, then an advisor for Standard Vacuum Oil Company on its operations in Asia, discussed establishing "community service programs in Asian countries" or an Asian institute to train managers. TAF P-121, Busch memo, 10/5/59.
34. TAF P-121, Busch memo, 3/23/59.
35. "Foundations, Private Organizations Linked to CIA," *Congressional Quarterly*, 2/24/67, 2.
36. TAF P-121, Busch memo, 3/23/59. In early 1957 Edmund Rosenthal undertook a seven-week Asian trip, visiting foundation offices in Burma, Ceylon, Hong Kong, Indonesia, Japan, Pakistan, the Philippines, Singapore, and Thailand. Rosenthal met regularly with Lyman Hoover. TAF P-39, "R" folder, Harry Pierson to foundation representatives, 1/11/57.
37. TAF P-121, Busch, Noel Busch memo on meeting with Edmund Rosenthal, 9/10/59.
38. TAF P-121, Busch record of Noyes meeting, 3/17/59.
39. See Robert Mcg. Thomas, "Raymond S. Rubinow, 91," *New York Times*, 4/7/96, S1, 28.
40. TAF P-121, Conversation with Rubinow, Princeton Club, 3/26/59. Adlai Stevenson became a trustee in 1959. "Foundation Elects Stevenson," *New York Times*, 4/17/59, 10.
41. Price, "Anthropology *Sub Rosa*."
42. RB 2, Monthly report to Board of Trustees, 2/3/60, 4–5.
43. On the AAA, see Price, *Cold War Anthropology*, 176–91; AEA, see RB 2, Board of Trustees Report, 2/3/60, 4–5; AMS, see TAF P-179, AMS, Mrs. Norman Colliver to Gordon L. Walker, 5/26/62; APGA, APA, APSA, see RB 2, Board of Trustees report, 2/3/60, 4–5; ASA, see TAF P-179, Kingsley Davis to J. F. Sullivan 1/18/60; ASA, see TAF P-179, ASA, R. V. Sedwick to Benning Cohen, 3/20/59.
44. See RB 2, Board of Trustees report, 2/3/60, 4–5. Foundation staff also interfaced with US professional associations in other ways. For example, the foundation in 1959 offered through the American Political Science Association a $29,500 Congressional Fellowship Program that brought students from Thailand, Japan, the Philippines, Pakistan, and Hong Kong to Washington, DC. TAF P-179, Blum to Evron Kirkpatrick, 12/8/59.
45. AAAP Series 13, Box 14, correspondence of association president Sol Tax, 7/29/59.
46. AAAP 49, Mandelbaum memo, 1/8/58.
47. The 413 figure includes individuals participating for multiple years. Gaps in AAA records suggest the total number of recipients was likely higher than this number. See AAAP 73.
48. TAF P-180, AAA, Stephen Boggs to Blum, 1/27/61
49. In 1959, President Blum sent AAA president Sol Tax a $2,500 grant check, requesting "brief reports describing the utilization of funds transmitted to the Association under this grant." AAAP 13, 14, Blum to Tax, 4/22/59.
50. TAF P-79, Heggie to Pollard, Assistance to Asian anthropologists in the US, 12/18/56.
51. Price, *Cold War Anthropology*, 176–93.
52. TAF P-455, Flanagan to Frantz, 5/21/68.

53. TAF P-455, Flanagan to Frantz, 5/21/68.
54. For APA, see TAF P-447, Lawrence T. Forman to Sherman Ross, 7/27/67; for ASA, see TAF P-447, Edith S. Coliver to All TAF reps, 7/5/72.
55. TAF P-455, SfAA file.
56. See TAF P-112, NSA, R. G. Schwantes to Blum, 7/5/60. As a National Student Association representative, James Scott corresponded with Blum about a South Korean student's trip to the United States. TAF P-112, USNSA Scholarships & Fellowships, Scott to Blum, 10/11/60. While studying in Burma and representing the USNSA, Scott worked with the local foundation representative, who, according to an internal memo, "advised Mr. Scott on how to proceed to secure Burmese governmental approval, but I should caution you, as this is a most delicate matter." The foundation maintained a low profile while advising Scott on how to navigate the governmental bureaucracy to secure permission for exchanges that were frequently looked at with suspicion by foreign governments. TAF P-112, USNSA Scholarships & Fellowships, Foreign Student Leadership, John Reed to Harold C. Bakken, 4/27/59.
57. TAF P-112, USNSA Scholarships & Fellowships, Malay rep to Blum, 2/11/59.
58. TAF P-112, USNSA Scholarships & Fellowships, Foreign Student Leadership, J. Dalton, 12/23/58, Conversation with James Scott, Memo to the record, 12/29/58.
59. TAF P-112, USNSA Scholarships & Fellowships, Foreign Student Leadership, J. Dalton, 12/23/58, conversation with James Scott, Memo to the record, 12/29/58.
60. TAF P-112, USNSA Scholarships & Fellowships, Foreign Student Leadership, J. Dalton, 12/23/58, Conversation with James Scott, Memo to the record, 12/29/58.
61. James Scott, email to author, 12/8/20.
62. James Scott, email to author, 12/10/20.
63. Quote from Scott email to author, 12/10/20. In a 2009 interview, Scott reflected on being approached by intelligence personnel during this period, saying that even while he "was very much involved with anthropologists against the War," when he was the NSA international vice president and visiting Washington, DC, he was "asked to go to a meeting with someone who turned out to be a CIA agent, who wanted me to write reports for them; at the time I don't think I was ideologically opposed to that, but I refused; it turned out that during my period working for the National Student Association, all my reports were sent by the president, who had been recruited by the CIA, to them; I wasn't paid, but I was in effect a CIA agent; I had some sense of being a little cog in a machine I didn't much care for." Alan Macfarlane, "James Scott interviewed by Alan Macfarlane, 26th March 2009," 9:51:20 time mark, http://www.alanmacfarlane.com/DO/filmshow/scott1_fast.htm.
64. TAF P-181, Lerski ASA report, 9/14/61.
65. TAF P-335, McGinnis ASA report, 9/12/66.
66. The immediate source of this rumor was the (CIA-funded) NSA's director of Asian programs, Greg Delin, who had written Norman Coliver, director of the TAF's Program Services Division, passing along rumors he had heard about Assifi. Ironically, one of the sources of Delin's information was personnel at the American Friends of the Middle East. This means that this information originated in an echo chamber of messages exchanged among three CIA assets talking to each other in ways that generated so much distorted blowback it becomes difficult to know what truth may have been within this claim. TAF P-335, Delin to Coliver, 6/27/66.
67. TAF P-335, McGinnis ASA report, 9/12/66.

68. TAF P-335, Shahryar to Jerry Joldersma, 4/13/67.
69. TAF P-335, John A. Bannigan to Shahryar, 5/9/67. An internal document itemized each foundation grant provided to the ASA; all were for specific individual requests such as travel to conferences, subscriptions, etc. TAF P-335, 4/6/67.
70. Ramparts Editors, "How the CIA Turns Foreign Students into Spies," 22.
71. At the time of the *Ramparts* article in April 1967, Noorzay had returned to Afghanistan, where he was president of the Afghanistan State Treasury. Hotaki claimed Noorzay's career path fit an ongoing pattern in which individuals who established CIA links as students later took important government jobs back in Afghanistan, including at cabinet levels. Ramparts Editors, "How the CIA Turns Foreign Students into Spies," 24.
72. Ramparts Editors, "How the CIA Turns Foreign Students into Spies," 24.
73. Ramparts Editors, "How the CIA Turns Foreign Students into Spies," 24.
74. Ramparts Editors, "How the CIA Turns Foreign Students into Spies," 24. *Ramparts* identified AFME's funding as coming from five CIA fronts: the San Jacinto Foundation, Chesapeake Foundation, Andrew Hamilton Fund, Broad-High Foundation, and Granary Fund.
75. Ramparts Editors, "How the CIA Turns Foreign Students into Spies," 24.
76. Ramparts Editors, "How the CIA Turns Foreign Students into Spies," 24.
77. Kamrany, "Open Letter," 10.
78. "Questions and Answers at the National Press Club of Washington," *Afghan Student News*, March–April 1967, 4–5.
79. DB 35, 803.
80. DB 35, 803.
81. RB 1, Board of Trustees monthly report, 2/1/57, 3.
82. The American Committee for Cultural Freedom's CIA backing was not publicly known until 1966.
83. RB 1, Monthly report to Board of Trustees, 8/1/57, appendix, 2.
84. CIA DTPILLAR 3, 12, 2.
85. Ramparts Editors, "How the CIA Turns Foreign Students into Spies"; Corson, *The Betrayal*.

8 CIA-FUNDED PROPAGANDA

1. US Senate, "Foreign and Military Intelligence, Book I, Final Report of the Select Committee," 193 (hereafter cited as US Senate, Church Committee Report).
2. Saunders, *Cultural Cold War*; Whitney, *Finks*; Wilford, *Mighty Wurlitzer*.
3. It appears Chaneles completed his "CIA and Books" manuscript, but the only known surviving document is incomplete, containing only portions of the first chapters, then skipping to pages 256–94, and then including 50 pages of detailed endnotes. After reading this partial manuscript in 2016, I undertook a significant effort to locate a complete manuscript but failed to find one. See my online *CounterPunch* article, Price, "CIA Book Publishing Operations."
4. SC, "CIA and the Books" manuscript, 8.
5. SC, "CIA and the Books" manuscript, 8, 267, 268.
6. US Senate, Church Committee Report, 193.
7. "Communist penetration into the industry was carried on under the control of the Propaganda Department of the Chinese Communist South China Bureau. Before 1948, this

control was exercised in Hong Kong through the *Hwa Shang Pao.*" TAF P-55, Quarterly activity report, October–December 1956.
8. Lombardo, "Mission of Espionage," 66.
9. See J. B. Smith, *Portrait of a Cold Warrior*, 168–69.
10. TAF P-55, Quarterly activity report, October–December 1956.
11. TAF P-55, Quarterly activity report, October–December 1956.
12. TAF P-55, Quarterly activity report, October–December 1956.
13. Lombardo, "Mission of Espionage," 71.
14. TAF P-58, Operation Broomstick, Brown to R. T. Maddocks, 2/19/53.
15. TAF P-58, Operation Broomstick, Brown to Maddocks, 2/19/53.
16. TAF P-58, Operation Broomstick, Brown to Maddocks, 2/19/53.
17. TAF P-58, MEDIA Fiction Enterprise, undated.
18. John F. Sullivan was less worried about these matters than Delmer Brown. TAF P-58, MEDIA Fiction Enterprise, Sullivan to Brayton Wilbur, 6/30/53.
19. TAF P-57, Trips and Reports, J. L. Stewart, 9/2/54, 18.
20. TAF P-58, Fiction, Miller to rep, Hong Kong, TKY-HK-29, 7/13/54.
21. TAF P-58, Fiction, Miller to rep, Hong Kong, TKY-HK-29, 7/13/54.
22. Leary, "Most Careful Arrangements for a Careful Fiction," 550–51.
23. CFA records include backchannel correspondence between the Ford Foundation's Jonathan King and CFA's James Ivy. In it, King informs Ivy that Ford won't fund Lifton's proposed brainwashing research. There is also internal CFA correspondence alerting Blum that Ford would not fund Lifton, which led CFA to fund Lifton. TAF P-55, Dr. R. J. Lifton, King to Ivy, 6/28/54; TAF P-55, Dr. R. J. Lifton, Stewart to Blum, 7/6/54.
24. TAF P-55, Lifton to Blum, 12/29/55; TAF P-55, Lifton, routing slip, 1/3/56; TAF P-55, Stewart to Lifton, 1/5/56.
25. TAF P-55, Lifton, Rowe to Richard Conlon, 4/13/54.
26. CFA funded Lifton's research to be conducted in Hong Kong. TAF P-55, Stewart to Blum, 3/8/54 & telegram 3/19/54.
27. Price, *Cold War Anthropology*, 195–220.
28. TAF P-12, Byington to Stewart, 4/2/53.
29. TAF P-12, Dick Taplinger to C. Lowenberg, 4/22/55. Dick Taplinger was an occasional TAF consultant, and he was "in charge of the CIA's Asia Book Club which distributed anti-communist books through funds provided by the Asia Foundation." SC, "CIA and the Books" manuscript, 274.
30. An unauthorized or "bootleg" abridged Burmese translation of *1984* had already been published. In 1954 the pirated print run of twenty thousand copies of *1984* sold out, and CFA calculated they could sell copies for five cents (US) and cover the costs. TAF P-11, Orwell's *1984*; Rubin, *Archives of Authority*, 37–46.
31. TAF P-33, Media, Cartoons & Comics, Malaya, Sheeks to CFA president, 9/28/53.
32. TAF P-30, M. G. McAlister to Blum, 7/24/53.
33. TAF P-30, M. G. McAlister to B. Wilbur, 7/17/53.
34. RB 1, Executive Committee report, 11/53, 3.
35. See, e.g., RB 2, Notes on visit to Korea, 10/29–11/2/56.
36. RB 2, Memo for the record, Blum conversation in Singapore with Noel Busch, 7/2/56. For more on Franklin Publications, see Robbins, "Publishing American Values."

37. Crewdson with Treaster, "Worldwide Propaganda Network Built by the CIA," 37.
38. TAF P-115, Media, Publishers: Franklin, Darius Smith to Blum, 10/27/58. "Mutual friends" was a phrase sometimes used to reference agency contacts, but this may simply have referred to some mutual friends.
39. TAF P-45, Media, Publishers: Franklin, Banning to the record, 6/7/56.
40. TAF P-12, Ken Yasuda to TAF president, 2/17/55.
41. TAF P-12, Stewart memo on Rostow, SX-B-450, 1/17/55; compare Price, *American Surveillance State*, 224–37; and Rostow, *Prospects for Communist China*.
42. TAF P-12, Stewart memo on Rostow, SX-B-450, 1/17/55.
43. SC 2, Minutes, 17th Meeting of the Advisory Committee Books Abroad, 12/9/55, 1/16/56.
44. SC 2, Minutes, 17th Meeting of the Advisory Committee Books Abroad, 12/9/55, 1/16/56. May claimed that Nazi Germany had developed a ploy of teaching elements of proprietary knowledge with textbooks that would require those following the techniques to buy German manufactured goods. See SC 2.
45. TAF P-55, Aw Boon Haw, "A Report on Aw Boon-Haw's Newspapers" ca. 1954, undated.
46. Central Intelligence Group Report, Political Information: Newspapers published by Aw Boon Haw, 6/3/47, CIA Reading Room, https://www.cia.gov/readingroom/docs/CIA-RDP82-00457R000600440007-4.pdf.
47. TAF-P-55, Aw Boon Haw, "Report on Aw Boon Haw's Newspapers," undated.
48. TAF P-55, Aw Boon Haw, Nobel to George Greene Jr., 9/19/51.
49. TAF P-55, Aw Boon Haw, Blum to Erwin D. Canham, 8/5/54.
50. TAF P-55, Aw Boon Haw, L. Z. Yuan to Mr. James, 8/26/54.
51. TAF P-57, unsigned draft memo on Aw Boon Haw, undated.
52. TAF P-57, unsigned draft memo on Aw Boon Haw, undated (original emphasis).
53. TAF P-57, unsigned draft memo on Aw Boon Haw, undated.
54. See, e.g., the CIA-collected *New York Daily News*, 9/8/71, article on Aw Sian, at the CIA Reading Room, accessed 1/13/22, https://www.cia.gov/readingroom/docs/CIA-RDP88-01314R000300010031-8.pdf.
55. On the CFA taking title to the newspaper, see TAF P-30, Stewart to McAlister, 12/30/53.
56. TAF P-30, Edwards to Amoss, 1/29/54.
57. TAF P-30, Edwards to Amoss, 1/29/54.
58. TAF P-30, McAlister to Blum, 1/16/54.
59. Rodriguez, "Organizational Hegemony," 112.
60. TAF P-30, 9/19/54.
61. TAF P-30, McAlister to Blum, 3/10/54.
62. Harrington, "Greatest Movie Never Made," 397.
63. S. Lee, "Asia Foundation's Motion-Picture Project," 110.
64. RB 1, Executive Committee report, Blum, 5/5/54, 2. See also Eldridge, "'Dear Owen.'"
65. CIA DTPILLAR, 3, 32, 10.
66. CIA DTPILLAR, 3, 32, 12.
67. S. Lee, "Asia Foundation's Motion-Picture Project," 108. See also S. Lee, "Creating an Anti-Communist Motion Picture Producers' Network."
68. TAF P-9, Tanner to Alsop, 11/3/53.
69. TAF P-9.
70. TAF P-9, Blum to DeMille, 1/16/54.

71. TAF P-33, Media, Stewart to Tanner, 10/22/53.
72. TAF P-33, Sheeks to J. Stewart, 11/14/53.
73. RB 2, Visit to Pakistan, Blum, 8/22/57–9/2/57, 10.
74. TAF P-45, S. H. Rickard to Blum, 1/17/55.
75. Caroline Davis wrote that "according to Jack Thompson [one-time executive director of the Farfield Foundation], the CIA's main purpose in funding African literary publishing was not so much to produce political propaganda as to exert American imperialism in a broader sense." This broader sense included efforts to weaken the regional grip of British book publishers. See Davis, *African Literature and the CIA*, 21.
76. Davis, *African Literature and the CIA*.
77. US Senate, Church Committee Report, 197–98; Neil Sheehan, "News Guild Aided by Groups Linked to CIA Conduits," *New York Times*, 2/17/67; Neil Sheehan, "News Guild Cuts Ties with Funds; Act on Groups Believed to Be Conduits for CIA," *New York Times*, 3/14/67, A13.
78. In August 1951, CFA provided the Indonesian Ministry of Education with free American textbooks. These books were shipped though Jakarta's Pacific Book and Supply Company, an offshore company run by one-time CIA officer Lloyd Millegan. TAF P-71, Indonesia, General, 1951–53, program, 3/26/51–4/1/51; Price, *Cold War Anthropology*, 238–45; *Indira Selects* (Pacific Book and Supply Catalogue, 1951).
79. Leary, "Most Careful Arrangements for a Careful Fiction," 555.

9 REPORTS AS ACTIVE AND PASSIVE INTELLIGENCE

1. TAF P-137, Carroll, Borneo trip, 8/10/59.
2. TAF P-61, Stewart, Korea trip, 9/28/[52]. No year is indicated, but "Sunday September 28th" suggests 1952.
3. TAF P-254, Laswell, Importance of studying corruption, Laswell to Walter Mallory-Browne, 5/62.
4. Mallory later became executive director of the Council on Foreign Relations.
5. TAF P-71, Mallory trip, 1952–53, Mallory to Slocum, 1/16/53, #13.
6. TAF P-71, Mallory trip, 1952–53, 9/16/52, #4. "Point IV" was an economic aid technical assistance program for developing nations announced by President Truman during this 1949 inauguration address.
7. TAF P-71, Mallory trip, 1952–53, 10/31/52, #7.
8. TAF P-71, Mallory trip, 1952–53, 10/11/52, #6.
9. TAF P-45, Folder: "General A–Z, Pakistan."
10. TAF P-45, Folder: General A–Z, Pakistan.
11. TAF P-45, Folder: General A–Z, Pakistan.
12. TAF P-45, Folder: General A–Z, Pakistan.
13. TAF P-45, Folder: General A–Z, Pakistan.
14. TAF P-62, Stewart to Maddocks, 9/3/52.
15. TAF P-62, Stewart to Maddocks, 9/3/52.
16. TAF P-62, Stewart to Maddocks, 9/3/52.
17. TAF P-284, Klausner to Laos rep, 5/14/60, 3–4.
18. TAF P-284, Klausner to Laos rep, 5/14/60, 3–4.

19. TAF P-284, Rural-Klausner, Klausner to Laos rep, 5/14/60, 6.
20. TAF P-284, Klausner to Laos rep, 5/14/60, 13.
21. TAF P-284, Klausner to Laos rep, 5/14/60, 15.
22. TAF P-284, Klausner to Laos rep, 5/14/60, 26.
23. CIA DTPILLAR 2, 34, 7–8, 6/25/54.
24. CIA DTPILLAR 2, 28, 1954.
25. RB 2, Visit to India, 11/12–23/55.
26. RB 2, Visit to Hong Kong, 9/29/61–10/8/61.
27. RB, TAF monthly report, 11/57.
28. TAF P-39, US Visitors to Asia, Lists of nonfoundation grantees, McCune to Blum, #10.
29. RB 2, Visit to India, 11/12–23/55, 1.
30. RB 2, Visit to India, 11/12–23/55, 1, appendix, 1.
31. RB 2, Visit to India, 11/12–23/55.
32. RB 2, Visit to India, 11/12–23/55, 4.
33. TAF P-144, Blum folder, Blum Visit to India, 11/1–11/58, 12/17/58.
34. RB 2, Monthly report to Board of Trustees, 9/3/59, 3.
35. RB 2, Conversation with Ali Sastroamidjojo, 11/25/56, 1.
36. RB 2, Conversation with Ali Sastroamidjojo, 11/25/56, 2.
37. RB 1, Monthly report to board, confidential, 8/1/57, 1.
38. RB 1, Monthly report to board, confidential, 11/1/57.
39. RB 2, Notes on visit to Afghanistan, 9/3–9/57, 1.
40. RB 2, Notes on visit to Thailand, 9/10–14/57, 5.
41. RB 2, Notes on visit to Burma, 8/16–22/57.
42. RB 2, Memorandum for the record, Visit to Vietnam, 11/10–15/60, 12/21/60.
43. RB 2, Visit to the Philippines, 10/20–24/60, 11/10/60, 2.
44. RB 2, Visit to Singapore, 11/18–23/60.
45. RB 2, Report on visit to Laos, 9/26–29/61, 3.
46. RB 2, Report on visit to Laos, 9/26–29/61, 3. Robert Blum continued: "We should not overlook that there is a continued state of insecurity in Laos. Travel outside of Vientiane is hazardous, especially for Americans. I was told that any person who is thought by the Pathet Lao to be American is immediately questioned to determine whether he is an American and if this is the case he is arrested. Otherwise, he is released. At the present time, about 15 Americans are being detained by the Pathet Lao. If the present negotiations fail it is likely that hostilities will resume in a month or six weeks at the end of the rains. Gordon Messegee and I discussed under what conditions he should remain or evacuate[,] but we agreed that it is impossible to define precisely in advance such a situation" (4).
47. TAF P-177, Cambodia, Visit to Cambodia, 11/16–18/60, 12/23/60.
48. TAF P-177, Cambodia, Visit to Cambodia, 11/16–18/60, 12/23/60.
49. RB 2, Visit to Burma, 10/9–13/61, 2.
50. McCoy, *Politics of Heroin*, 168–70.
51. RB 2, Memorandum for the record, Visit to Burma, 10/9–13/61.
52. RB 2, Visit to Cambodia 1 through 4, 12/23/58.
53. RB 2, Visit to Indonesia, 11/26–29/58, 1.
54. RB 2, Visit to Vietnam, 11/22–26/58, 11/29/58–12/1/58.
55. RB 2, Visit to Vietnam, 11/22–26/58, 11/29/58–12/1/58.

56. RB 2, Report on visit to certain Asian countries, 3/17/63–4/20/63, 2.
57. RB 2, Report on visit to certain Asian countries, 3/17/63–4/20/63, 10.
58. TAF P-190, Raymond V. Johnson to TAF president, 5/4/60
59. RB 2, Notes on visit to Afghanistan, 7/24–27/59, 1.
60. RB 2, Notes on visit to Afghanistan, 7/24–27/59, 2.
61. RB 2, Memorandum for the record, Visit to Afghanistan, 9/6–10/61, 6.
62. RB 2, Monthly report to Board of Trustees, 2/61, 8.
63. RB 2, Visit to Nepal, 9/1–4/61, 2.
64. US Department of State, *Foreign Service List, 1960*, 56.
65. Charles Stuart Kennedy and Thomas Stern, "Interview with John M. Steeves," March 27, 1991, 23, Association for Diplomatic Studies and Training, https://tile.loc.gov/storage-services/service/mss/mfdip/2004/2004ste04/2004ste04.pdf; "Ralph H. Redford, Foreign Service Officer" (obituary), *Washington Post*, 5/22/13, 28.
66. RB 2, Memo for the record, Visit to Nepal, 9/1–4/61, 2.
67. This appears to refer to Eric Himsworth but could also be Norman Himsworth, who was with MI5. Security Service file release, August 2010, National Archives (UK), https://media.nationalarchives.gov.uk/index.php/mi5-file-release-august-2010/.
68. RB 2, Report on visit to Nepal, 9/1–4/61, 10–11.
69. RB 2, Report on visit to Nepal, 9/1–4/61, 11.
70. TAF P-258, Trip Notes, Kandahar/Bost, John E. James, 3/13–15/66.
71. James's postscript noted, "The ride home was a nightmare. Two blowouts, the additional flat tires. All of which had to be fixed on the road, plus a punctured gas tank. No car should go out on a long trip like this one without a full set of tire tools and a wider variety of patches than we had." TAF P-258, Trip Notes, Kandahar/Bost, John E. James, 3/13–15/66.

10 SUSPICIONS

1. Natarajan, *American Shadow over India*, 212.
2. Natarajan, *American Shadow over India*, 212–13.
3. Natarajan also correctly raised questions about now verified intelligence operations such as S. Dillon Ripley's ornithological expedition to the Himalayas. See Natarajan, *American Shadow over India*, 241; and Lewis, "Scientists or Spies?," 2326.
4. TAF P-13, Asian Student, Fernandes to *Asian Student* editor, 12/26/52.
5. TAF P-13, Asian Student, *Asian Student* editor to Fernandes, 1/14/53.
6. TAF P-13, Asian Student, draft signed "GMK," undated.
7. TAF P-13, Asian Student, Fernandes to Bradley, 2/9/53. A 1952 memo noted that Malcolm Sabhan, a "young Indian" studying at Berkeley, belonged to a campus "Indian group" and had "become so vocal here last week on the subject of the paper—the Committee and the United States in general." TAF P-13, Asian Student, Bradley to John Grover, 12/22/52.
8. TAF P-13, Asian Student, Fernandes to Bradley, 2/9/53.
9. In a telegram reporting to the San Francisco office, Stewart wrote that this mix-up had occurred due to "totally mistaken identification of myself with some unsavory character STOP Feel it essential to clear up this misconception before my return so that our cooperative program can move forward in perfect understanding." TAF P-31, Mr. Stewart's Trips, telegram, 10/50/52.

10. TAF P-31, Mr. Stewart's Trips, M. McAlister to J. Stewart, 12/21/52.
11. TAF P-31, Mr. Stewart's Trips, Political comments by Burmese journalist Satpyemaung, 11/4/52.
12. In 1960 Burmese bandits killed Carl R. Herczeg, an Austrian who worked as an economist for the Asia Foundation. Herczeg was shot during a holdup while conducting a rural survey; later investigations concluded the foundation had not been targeted. TAF P-165, Herczeg, Cable, 10/30/60; "Bandits Slay Fund Official," *New York Times*, 11/1/60, A17. The bandits were soon arrested. TAF P-165, Herczeg, Cable, 11/4/60.
13. TAF P-62, Principal Allegations by the Government of India, DRAFT, 4/4/55.
14. TAF P-62, Principal Allegations by the Government of India, DRAFT, 4/4/55.
15. TAF P-62, A Review of Indian Attitudes toward the Asia Foundation, DRAFT, 4/4/55.
16. TAF P-62, Background and summary of Mr. Blum's visit to India, 5/29/56–6/5/56.
17. TAF P-66, Registration and Status, Indonesia, Blum to Abdulgani, 12/4/56.
18. TFA P-144, Lazaroff and Rusch memo, 8/29/57.
19. TAF P-212, Trip Files, Chester Roberts, 8/26/56–9/11/56.
20. TAF P-212, Trip Files, Chester Roberts, 8/26/56–9/11/56.
21. TAF P-212, Trip Files, Chester Roberts, 8/26/56–9/11/56.
22. TAF P-212, Trip Files, Chester Roberts, 8/26/56–9/11/56.
23. TAF P-212, Trip Files, Chester Roberts, 8/26/56–9/11/56.
24. TAF P-212, Trip Files, Chester Roberts, 8/26/56–9/11/56.
25. TAF P-212, Trip Files, Chester Roberts, 8/26/56–9/11/56.
26. TAF P-212, Trip Files, Chester Roberts, 8/26/56–9/11/56.
27. TAF P-212, Trip Files, Chester Roberts, 8/26/56–9/11/56.
28. TAF P-13, Asian Student, General, Pierson to Conlon, 10/28/53, 11/1/53.
29. TAF P-13, Asian Student, General, Pierson to RP Conlon, 10/28/53, 11/1/53; Kahin, *Southeast Asia*.
30. See CIA DTPILLAR 2, 8, 1.
31. TAF P-66, Extract from personal letter from James Stewart regarding discussion with Subandrio, foreign minister, 8/857.
32. TAF P-66, Memorandum for the record, 8/1/57.
33. TAF P-488, Proposed budget, 1958–59.
34. CIA DTPILLAR 2, 8, 2.
35. CIA DTPILLAR 2, 8, 3.
36. CIA DTPILLAR 2, 8, 2.
37. Tillman Durdin, "Indonesia Ousts Private US Unit," *New York Times*, 6/12/58.
38. RB, TAF Monthly report to Board of Trustees, 5/12/58, 1.
39. RB, TAF Monthly report to Board of Trustees, 5/12/58, 1.
40. RB, TAF Monthly report to Board of Trustees, 5/12/58, 1.
41. TAF P-66, Budget Correspondence 1958/59, Undated 1958 memo labeled "Indonesia."
42. In 1972, former Czechoslovakian intelligence officer and defector Ladislav Bittman published *The Deception Game*, detailing Czech and Soviet-backed intelligence operations against the United States. In one 1965 operation, William Palmer, the American Motion Picture Association of Indonesia (AMPAI) president and a film importer, was falsely accused in the Indonesian press of being a CIA agent. While Bittman concocted bogus evidence claiming to link Palmer to the CIA, the truth was that since 1956 the Asia Foun-

dation *had* supported Palmer's efforts to bring films to Indonesian audiences. These sorts of CIA-funded "lite" propaganda operations were far removed from Bittman's invented mastermind CIA co-op–running agent. Bittman, *Deception Game*; TAF P-66, Finance and Accounting, Currency, MPEA blocked funds, Indonesia, Administration, Holbrook Bradley to Jusuf Wibisono, 11/23/56.
43. RB 2, Report on visit to Indonesia, 9/16–24/61, 4.
44. Blum reported discussions with Sukarno's secretary, Maria Ulfah Santoso, who had a good relationship with the foundation. Santoso discussed the "the circumstances under which the Foundation had left Indonesia," saying she understood the "true situation" and that James Stewart's travels to Sumatra, while "completely proper and . . . sponsored by the Ministry of Education," had added to suspicions raised by activities of the American Field Service, which increased suspicions about foundation activities. RB 2, Memorandum, Report on visit to Indonesia, Blum, 9/16–24/61, 4.
45. RB 2, Report on visit to Indonesia, Blum, 9/16–24/61, 4.
46. TAF P-52, Holbrook Bradley to CFA president, 11/3/53, C-119. Early in discussions of purchasing NATC, CFA considered leveraging a hostile takeover of NATC, observing that the committee could purchase 140 shares of the available 260 shares, then use its voting rights to enact whatever policies DTPILLAR desired. TAF P-52, Bradley to TAF president, 1/6/54.
47. TAF P-52, Bradley to CFA president, 11/3/53, C-119.
48. TAF P-52, Stewart to N. D. Grey, 4/27/54.
49. TAF P-52, Stewart to N. D. Grey, 4/27/54.
50. Chernyavsky, "U.S. Intelligence and the Monopolies," 60.
51. Several writers since Chernyavsky repeated this claim with no further information. For example, in 2017 Tatah Mentan claimed the CIA used the New Asia Trading Company to "camouflage U.S. intelligence agents operating in South-east Asia." Mentan, *Africa in the Colonial Ages of Empire*, 247.
52. Nkrumah, *Neo-Colonialism*, 251. Chernyavsky also claimed that "the Rockefeller Foundation, the Ford Foundation, the Asia Foundation, the Carnegie Foundation and many other 'charity' institutions set up by the monopolies also have a big role to play in Big Business intelligence operations. They possess huge sums of money." Chernyavsky, "U.S. Intelligence and the Monopolies," 60. See the CIA's review of Nkrumah, *Neo-Colonialism*, at the CIA Reading Room, accessed 2/3/23, https://www.cia.gov/readingroom/docs/CIA-RDP75-00149R000600010011-6.pdf.
53. For Pacific Books, see Price, *Cold War Anthropology*, 242–45.
54. RB 1, Board of Trustees report, 4/12/55, 1.
55. TAF P-177, Cambodia, 12/8/55.
56. TAF P-177, Cambodia, 12/8/55.
57. TAF P-177, Socio-Anthropological Study of Cambodia, Overton to Blum, 6/28/55.
58. TAF P-177, Socio-Anthropological Study of Cambodia, Overton to Blum, CAM-5X-74, 3/22/57.
59. TAF P-177, Socio-Anthropological Study of Cambodia, TAF Cambodia rep to Joel W. Scarborough, 4/18/57.
60. TAF P-261, Overton to TAF president, 12/3/63.
61. TAF P-261, Overton to TAF president, 12/15/63.
62. TAF P-261, Overton to TAF president, 12/15/63.

63. TAF P-261, telegram, 3/2/64.
64. TAF P-261, Overton to TAF president, 3/23/64.
65. TAF P-261, Political Situation in Cambodia, Overton to TAF president, 4/1/64.
66. TAF P-261, Political Situation in Cambodia, Overton to TAF president, 4/2/64.
67. TAF P-261, Political Situation in Cambodia, Overton to TAF president, 5/14/64.
68. TAF P-259, Undated 1965 report, Cambodia, 1.
69. TAF P-259, Undated 1965 report, Cambodia, 1.
70. TAF P-259, Undated 1965 report, Cambodia, 6.
71. TAF P-259, Undated 1965 report, Cambodia, 6.
72. TAF P-259, TAF president to all reps, Personal and confidential, SX-AR-2501, 2/24/66.
73. TAF P-259, undated news story headlined "Cambodia Closing Asia Foundation."
74. TAF P-259, General Cambodia, Williams to Harris, Personal, 2/17/66.
75. TAF P-259, General Cambodia, President to all reps, Re: closing Cambodian office, 2/17/66.
76. TAF P-259, General Cambodia, President to all reps, Re: closing Cambodian office, 2/17/66.
77. TAF P-245, Communism General, quoted in Yuan to TAF president, 6/26/65.
78. TAF P-245, Communism General, Yuan to TAF president, 6/25/65.
79. "Ambassador Princeton Lyman Interviewed by Charles Stuart Kennedy, Initial interview, May 12, 1999," 23, Association for Diplomatic Studies and Training Foreign Affairs Oral History Project (2006), https://www.adst.org/OH%20TOCs/Lyman,%20Princeton.toc.pdf.
80. McGarr, "'Quiet Americans in India,'" 1053–54.
81. These ongoing suspicions about foundation staff left them sometimes worried they might be accused of CIA activities in which they had no involvement. There was an odd incident in that regard in 1960, in which Harry Pierson notified the San Francisco office that he had just encountered a Blanche Y. Belitz teaching in Thailand. While using open channels, Pierson's correspondence appears to have indicated Belitz was with the CIA, as he inquired if anyone in the foundation knew what she was doing in Thailand, while the foundation reacted with some concern over her appearance in the midst of foundation business. TAF P-162, Pierson to Blum, 2/23/60; "Blanche Y. Belitz, 1914–2008," *The Interpreter* (University of Colorado at Boulder Libraries), no. 170, 4/1/2012, 4; Bryan Batty, "Comment on Blanche Y. Belitz," *The Interpreter*, no. 106A, 12/15/2006; Blanche Belitz, "JLS WAVE in the CIA," *The Interpreter*, no. 87A, 5/15/2005.
82. Anthony Lukas, "CIA Disclosures May Damage Project for India Foundation," *New York Times*, 5/6/66, A5.
83. See "CIA Maker of Policy or Tool?," *New York Times*, 4/25/66, A1. See also E. W. Kenworthy, "CIA Denies Using a Student 'Cover,'" *New York Times*, 7/30/66, A4.
84. CIA DTPILLAR 3, 12, 3.
85. CIA DTPILLAR 3, 12, 21, 11/14/66.

11 EXPOSED FRONTS AND THE FATE OF CIA ORPHANS

1. Paget, *Patriotic Betrayal*.
2. Paget, *Patriotic Betrayal*, 359.
3. Stern, "Short Account of International Student Politics and the Cold War," 34.
4. Emanuel Perlmutter, "Guild Denies Knowing of CIA Links," *New York Times*, 2/9/1967.

5. Many scholars mistakenly claim Stern's *Ramparts* article disclosed the foundation's CIA links (e.g., Ford, *Cold War Monks*, 225), but Stern's article on the NSA's CIA ties had only one mention of the Asia Foundation: the statement that, like the Ford and Rockefeller Foundations, its support of the NSA appeared to *not* be directly linked to the CIA. Stern, "Short Account of International Student Politics and the Cold War," 34.
6. CIA DTPILLAR 3, 7, 2, 3/19/67.
7. CIA DTPILLAR 3, 7, 2, 3/19/67.
8. Wallace Turner was a Pulitzer Prize–winning journalist, working as the *Times*'s San Francisco correspondent.
9. Wallace Turner, "Asia Foundation Got CIA Funds," *New York Times*, 3/22/1967, 17. For the board's full statement, see SC 2, TAF trustees' statement, 3/21/67.
10. Turner, "Asia Foundation Got CIA Funds," 17.
11. Turner listed the following foundation board members and affiliations: Robert B. Anderson, former US treasury secretary; Barry Bingham, publisher of the *Louisville Courier-Journal*; Ellsworth Bunker, ambassador to South Vietnam; Arthur H. Dean, State Department; Mortimer Fleishhacker Jr., San Francisco businessman and philanthropist; R. Allen Griffin, publisher of the *Monterey (CA) Peninsula Herald*; Caryl P. Haskins, president of the Carnegie Institution of Washington; Charles J. Hitch, vice president of the University of California and formerly a fiscal officer in the Pentagon; Grayson L. Kirk, president of Columbia University; Walter H. Mallory, former executive director of the Council on Foreign Relations; Turner H. McBaine, San Francisco lawyer; Robbins Milbank, a retired New York advertising executive; Mrs. Maurice T. Moore, chair of the Institute of International Education; Lucian W. Pye, professor of political science, Massachusetts Institute of Technology; Edwin O. Reischauer, former ambassador to Japan; board chair Russell G. Smith, Bank of America vice president; J. E. Wallace Sterling, president of Stanford University; and Haydn Williams, foundation president and former assistant secretary of defense. Turner also identified former board members: Adlai E. Stevenson, US representative to the United Nations; Paul Hoffman, Ford Foundation president; and J. D. Zellerbach, US ambassador to Italy. Turner, "Asia Foundation Got CIA Funds," 17.
12. Turner, "Asia Foundation Got CIA Funds," 17.
13. Anthony J. Lukas, "India to Conduct Inquiry on CIA," *New York Times*, 3/23/1967.
14. TAF P-310, Closing of India Office, Heggie to TAF president, 8/30/67.
15. TAF P-310, Closing of India Office, Heggie to TAF president, 8/30/67.
16. "India Curbs Groups for Its Tie to CIA," *New York Times*, 9/29/1967.
17. An internal memo announced, "The Government of India has asked The Asia Foundation to *suspend* its activities in India but will permit existing projects to be completed. We have been informed that this decision was made because of the Foundation's having accepted in the past some support from foundations and trusts backed by the CIA." TAF P-310, Registration and Status India, E. S. Colvier to TAF staff distribution list, 2/19/68.
18. Joseph Lelyveld, "Asia Foundation Banned by India," *New York Times*, 2/16/1968.
19. There are several pages of lists of files held by the Indian office, including files on individuals and conferences; see TAF P-310.
20. TAF P-310, Closing of India Office, Heggie to TAF president, 1/4/68.
21. TAF P-310, Closing of India Office; "Historians Oppose Outside Finance," *Hindustan Times*, 1/2/68.

22. TAF P-310, Closing of India Office, Heggie to TAF president, 4/20/68.
23. TAF P-313, Area Studies in India, Jannuzi to TAF president, 8/26/67.
24. DB, Box 35, 803; Emanuel Phadnis, "Guild Denies Knowing of CIA Links," *Hindustan Times*, 6/8/67.
25. DB, Box 35, 803, Warning against CIA-fed authors.
26. DB, Box 35, 803.
27. David Steinberg interview, 2014, https://soundcloud.com/the-asia-foundation/covertfunding.
28. Steinberg interview, 2014.
29. TAF P-392, Betsy Donley to Joel Scarborough, 7/27/66.
30. TAF P-392, John F. Sullivan to Datus C. Smith, 7/8/66.
31. TAF P-392, Lindley S. Sloan to TAF president, 6/20/67.
32. A handwritten note by an Asia Foundation staff member at the bottom of a 3/17/66 letter from Atiquallah Pazhwak, president of Franklin Books programs, Kabul, to John James suggests the foundation "avoid meaningless bookkeeping" work and consider forgiving the loan, arguing that "if we trusted them enough to make a loan of $100,000 we can trust them to properly use the funds resulting from TAF forgiveness of the loan." TAF P-392, note written on Pazhwak to James, 3/17/66; see also Franklin Book Programs records, Princeton University Library Special Collections, 161.
33. TAF P-392, Lindsey S. Sloan to TAF president, 4/12/67. In 1967 there were seventy-five afghanis to one US dollar, so the loan would take less than a decade to pay off. "Treasury Reporting Rates of Exchange as of March 31, 1967," https://www.govinfo.gov/content/pkg/GOVPUB-T63_100-0f6bf56c53116165b41c6ac230f1d518/pdf/GOVPUB-T63_100-0f6bf56c53116165b41c6ac230f1d518.pdf.
34. Katzenbach, *Some of It Was Fun*, 238.
35. DB, RFA Office files of DB, Folder 803, CIA Orphans, Report of Katzenbach Committee, 1.
36. "No federal agency shall provide any covert financial assistance or support[,] direct or indirect, to any of the nation's educational or private voluntary organizations. This policy specifically applies to all foreign activities of such organizations and it reaffirms present policy with respect to their domestic activities. Where such support has been given, it will be terminated as quickly as possible without destroying valuable private organizations before they can seek new means of support." DB 35, Folder 802, CIA Orphans, Report of Katzenbach Committee, 3.
37. US Senate, Church Committee Report, 182–83; Price, *Cold War Anthropology*, 21–22.
38. Members of the Rusk Committee CIA-Funding Panel were Ramsey Clark, Charles Schultze, Sen. Carl Hayden, Sen. Richard B. Russell, Sen. J. W. Fulbright, Sen. Milton R. Young, Rep. George Mahon, Rep. L. Mendel River, Rep. Thomas Morgan, Rep. Frank Bow, Dr. Milton S. Eisenhower, Thomas S. Gates Jr., Dr. James H. McCrocklin, Paul R. Porter, Frank A. Rose, Henry S. Rowen, Robert M. Travis, and Dr. Herman B. Wells.
39. Robert Phelps, "Panel on CIA Subsidies Divided over Alternatives," *New York Times*, 12/18/1967.
40. Phelps, "Panel on CIA Subsidies Divided over Alternatives."
41. DB 35, 802, CIA Orphans, Cuninggim to Danforth Foundation trustees, 4/16/67. Education and World Affairs (1961–71) in 1971 became the International Council for Educational Development.
42. DB 35, 802, CIA Orphans, Cuninggim to Danforth Foundation trustees, 4/16/67.

43. DB 35, 802, CIA Orphans, Interim report etc., 4/26/67, 3.
44. EWA 8, Report on a New Instrumentality, 3/21/67.
45. Herman B. Wells (chair, EWA) and William W. Marvel (president, EWA) signed off on the confidential draft report. EWA 8, Report on a New Instrumentality, 3/21/67, 5.
46. EWA 8, Report on a New Instrumentality, 3/21/67, 5.
47. DB 35, 802, CIA Orphans, Education and World Affairs, 1967. "Report on a New Instrumentality for Government Financing of Private International Activities in Education and Related Areas," 3/21/67, 6–7.
48. EWA 8, Situation report of private bills before Congress in re CIA affair.
49. DB 35, 802, CIA Orphans, Education and World Affairs, 1967. "Report on a New Instrumentality for Government Financing of Private International Activities in Education and Related Areas," 3/21/67.
50. DB 35, 802, CIA Orphans, Education and World Affairs, 1967. "Report on a New Instrumentality for Government Financing of Private International Activities in Education and Related Areas," 3/21/67. 7
51. EWA 8, 28, see William W. Marvel, 5/31/67.
52. DB 35, 802, CIA Orphans, Bell to Bundy, 5/1/67.
53. DB 35, 802, CIA Orphans, Bell to Bundy, 5/1/67.
54. DB 35, 802, CIA Orphans, Bell to Bundy, 5/1/67.
55. DB 35, 802, CIA Orphans, Bell to Bundy, 5/1/67.
56. "CU" appears to have been the Department of State's Bureau of Educational and Cultural Relations (CU). See "History and Mission of ECA," Bureau of Educational and Cultural Relations, accessed 5/25/20, https://eca.state.gov/about-bureau/history-and-mission-eca.
57. DB 35, 802, CIA Orphans, Bell to Bundy, 5/1/67.
58. DB 35, 802, CIA Orphans, Bell to Bundy, 5/1/67.
59. DB 35, 802, CIA Orphans, Bundy to Bell, 5/1/67. Bundy was referring to John James Rooney (D-NY).
60. DB 35, 802, CIA Orphans, Staples to Bell, 5/3/67.
61. DB 35, 802, CIA Orphans, Ward to Bell, 5/1/67.
62. DB 35, 802, CIA Orphans, Sutton to Bell, 5/9/67.
63. DB 35, 802, CIA Orphans, Sutton to Bell, 5/9/67.
64. DB 35, 802, CIA Orphans, Sutton to Bell, 5/9/67.
65. The 1974 report prepared for Congress on the Rockefellers, *Probing the Rockefeller Fortune*, described Lockwood as the "personal and legal adviser to the Rockefeller brothers." *Probing the Rockefeller Fortune*, available from the University of California, Berkeley, accessed 4/8/22, https://www.ocf.berkeley.edu/~schwrtz/Rockefeller.html.
66. RF JRD3, 5, 42, Lockwood to Rockefeller III, 3/4/67.
67. RF 245, Philanthropy and Public Interests, 3/6/67 draft.
68. RF 245, Philanthropy and Public Interests: CIA 1967, 3/20/67 draft.
69. RF 245, Philanthropy and Public Interests: CIA 1967, 3/20/67 draft.
70. Katzenbach, *Some of It Was Fun*, 239.
71. TAF P-480.
72. Charles Burress, "James L. Stewart—Longtime Liaison to Asia," *San Francisco Chronicle*, 1/29/2006.
73. Phelps, "Panel on CIA Subsidies Divided over Alternatives."

74. Phelps, "Panel on CIA Subsidies Divided over Alternatives."
75. "$3-Million Sought for Asia Program," *New York Times*, 2/27/68, 53.
76. "Panel on CIA Aid Has a Stopgap Plan to Help Some Groups," *New York Times*, 5/27/68, A16.

12 TERMINATION AND LIQUIDATION OF DTPILLAR

1. CIA DTPILLAR 3, 6, 1, 6/6/67.
2. JAMFR memo 180, from 5/27/67, does not clarify which agency would supply funds directly. Johnson Administration, *Foreign Relations of the United States, 1964–1968*, accessed 1/30/23, https://history.state.gov/historicaldocuments/frus1964-68v10/d180.
3. CIA DTPILLAR 3, 5, 1, 6/5/67.
4. CIA DTPILLAR 3, 5, 1, 6/5/67.
5. CIA DTPILLAR 3, 5, 1, 6/5/67.
6. CIA DTPILLAR 3, 6, 1, 6/6/67.
7. CIA DTPILLAR 3, 6, 1, 6/6/67.
8. CIA DTPILLAR 3, 6, 1, 6/6/67. The dollar amounts in the passage were redacted by the CIA.
9. In 1954 the CIA established the "DTPILLAR Liquidation Reserve Fund . . . by authority of the Director of Central Intelligence to provide sufficient funds to meet 'all actual or contingent liabilities which would exist in the event unforeseen circumstance necessitated the abrupt termination of CIA's underwriting of the DTPILLAR program." CIA DTPILLAR 2, 5, 12. It is unclear whether these funds remained available several years later or what the size of this fund was.
10. CIA DTPILLAR 3, 6, 2, 6/6/67.
11. CIA DTPILLAR 3, 6, 2, 6/6/67.
12. CIA DTPILLAR 3, 6, 2–3, 6/6/67.
13. The online *Encyclopedia Britannica* entry for Cambodia shows Leonard C. Overton as an author/contributor and states that he was "Country Representative, Asia Foundation, Phnom Penh, Cambodia, 1955–59, 1961–64; Saigon, South Vietnam, 1965–67." *Britannica*, accessed 5/26/20, https://www.britannica.com/contributor/Leonard-C-Overton/2222.
14. CIA DTPILLAR 3, 6, 5, 6/6/67.
15. CIA DTPILLAR 3, 6, 6, 6/6/67.
16. CIA DTPILLAR 3, 6, 6, 6/6/67.
17. CIA DTPILLAR 3, 6, 3, 6/6/67 (emphasis added).
18. CIA DTPILLAR 3, 6, 3, 6/6/67.
19. CIA DTPILLAR 3, 6, 4, 6/6/67.
20. CIA DTPILLAR 3, 1, 1968; Warren Unna, "State Dept. to Ask Congress for Asia Foundation Funds," *Washington Post*, 2/26/68, A4.
21. Unna, "State Dept. to Ask Congress for Asia Foundation Funds."
22. Unna, "State Dept. to Ask Congress for Asia Foundation Funds."
23. CIA DTPILLAR 3, 1, 1968; Unna, "State Dept. to Ask Congress for Asia Foundation Funds,"A4.
24. US Congress, "Foreign Assistance and Related Agencies Appropriations for 1969," 5/9/68, 997.
25. US Congress, "Foreign Assistance and Related Agencies Appropriations for 1969," 5/9/68, 1017, testimony of Bullitt.

26. US Congress, "Foreign Assistance and Related Agencies Appropriations for 1969," 5/9/68, 1017, testimony of Bullitt.
27. US Congress, "Foreign Assistance and Related Agencies Appropriations for 1969," 5/9/68, 1017, comments by Conte.
28. US Congress, "Foreign Assistance and Related Agencies Appropriations for 1969," 5/9/68, 1018, comments by Conte.
29. US Congress, "Foreign Assistance and Related Agencies Appropriations for 1969," 5/9/68, 1018.
30. US Congress, "Foreign Assistance and Related Agencies Appropriations for 1969," 5/9/68, 1018, testimony of Bullitt.
31. US Congress, "Foreign Assistance and Related Agencies Appropriations for 1969," 5/9/68, 1018.
32. US Congress, "Foreign Assistance and Related Agencies Appropriations for 1969," 5/9/68, 1018.
33. US Congress, "Foreign Assistance and Related Agencies Appropriations for 1969," 5/14/68, 1198.
34. US Congress, "Foreign Assistance and Related Agencies Appropriations for 1969," 5/14/68, 1198, testimony of Bundy. This financial independence from the federal government did not occur.
35. US Congress, "Foreign Assistance and Related Agencies Appropriations for 1969," 5/14/68, 1199–1200, testimony of Bundy.
36. Department of State, Memorandum 132, 6/22/66. Copies of Memorandum 132 were sent to US ambassador to Japan Ural Alexis Johnson, Vance, and Richard Helms, who would become director of central intelligence the following week.
37. Department of State, Memorandum 132, 6/22/66.
38. Department of State, Memorandum 132, 6/22/66.
39. Department of State, Memorandum 132, 6/22/66 (emphasis added).
40. Department of State, INR/IL Historical Files, Minutes of 303 Committee, 7/8/66, "Secret; Eyes Only," 134. Memorandum for the Record," prepared by Jessup on July 9, accessed 2/11/23, https://history.state.gov/historicaldocuments/frus1964-68v10/d134. Copies were sent to U. Alexis Johnson, Vance, and Helms.
41. Department of State, INR/IL Historical Files, 303 Committee, "Secret; Eyes Only," 176. Memorandum From the Central Intelligence Agency to the 303 Committee 4/12/67, https://history.state.gov/historicaldocuments/frus1964-68v10/d176.
42. Department of State, Memorandum 176, 5/27/67.
43. Department of State, Memorandum 176, 176, 5/27/67.
44. Department of State, Memorandum 176, 5/27/67.
45. Department of State, Memorandum 176, 5/27/67.
46. Department of State, INR/IL Historical Files, re. Minutes of 303 Committee meeting 6/21/68, Memorandum 209, Trueheart to Bundy, 6/27/68, https://history.state.gov/historicaldocuments/frus1964-68v10/d209.
47. CIA DTPILLAR 3, 3.
48. CIA DTPILLAR 3, 3.
49. CIA DTPILLAR 3, 3.
50. Brewster, *American Overseas Library Technical Assistance*, 165–66.

51. Ramparts Editors, "How the CIA Turns Foreign Students into Traitors."
52. TAF P-446, Parker to Gray, 5/22/67.
53. TAF P-446, Earl Bunting, Statement for AFME board of trustees, 4/26/67.
54. TAF P-456, US NSA, Scollon to Patricia Flanagan, 12/14/67. Scollon was willing to reject this request, but he wanted everyone at the foundation involved in this decision to agree on the course of action. TAF P-456, Darling to Scollon, 11/27/67.
55. CIA-LOC-HAK-1-5-33-8, Pye to Kissinger, 5/20/69, CIA FOIA Electronic Reading Room, https://www.cia.gov/readingroom/docs/LOC-HAK-1-5-33-8.pdf (second document).
56. CIA-LOC-HAK-1-5-33-8, U. Johnson, 6/7/69, CIA FOIA Electronic Reading Room, https://www.cia.gov/readingroom/docs/LOC-HAK-1-5-33-8.pdf (first document).
57. CIA-LOC-HAK-1-5-33-8, Kissinger to Pye, 6/23/69, CIA FOIA Electronic Reading Room, https://www.cia.gov/readingroom/docs/LOC-HAK-1-5-33-8.pdf (third document).
58. "Grants to Japanese Judges by Asia Foundation Assailed," *New York Times*, 5/12/76, 87.
59. RFA, FFR, Douglas Ensminger Oral History, Series A: Topics Related to Non-Project Areas, Box 1.
60. Hinckle et al., "University on the Make."
61. RFA, FFR, Douglas Ensminger Oral History.
62. For more on CIA and Ford Foundation alignment, see Ross, *Malthus Factor*, 144–54.
63. Vonnegut, *Cat's Cradle*, 3.
64. Prashad, *Washington Bullets*, 92.
65. Prashad, *Washington Bullets*, 92.
66. Price to Arnold, 1/22/21.
67. Ovalle to Price, 9/22/21.
68. Ovalle to Price, 9/22/21.
69. Casey notes to administration officials, 4/2/81, CIA FOIA Electronic Reading Room, https://www.cia.gov/readingroom/docs/CIA-RDP83M00914R002300060009-6.pdf.
70. WikiLeaks, accessed 1/22/2015, https://www.wikileaks.org/plusd/cables/1975STATE097649_b.html (no longer available).
71. TAF P-434, William D. Evans to Malaysia rep, 1/19/70.
72. CIA FOIA Doc, Williams to Inouye, 7/16/76, https://www.cia.gov/readingroom/docs/CIA-RDP79M00983A002200050056-9.pdf.
73. CIA FOIA Doc, Williams to Inouye, 7/16/76.
74. CIA FOIA Doc, handwritten notation on Williams to Inouye, 7/16/76.

13 CONCLUSIONS, IMPLICATIONS, AND CONTINUITIES

1. US Senate, Church Committee Report, 182.
2. R. Blum, "Asia Foundation," 5.
3. R. Blum, "Asia Foundation," 3.
4. RB 2, Luncheon with President Ayub Khan, 8/8/59. Blum complained on this occasion that India's President Nehru was a "communist who took his orders directly from Moscow."
5. RB 2, Notes on visit to Pakistan, 8/3–12/59.
6. RB 2, Notes on visit to Pakistan, 8/3–12/59, 4.
7. R. Blum, "Flow of People and Ideas," 5.
8. Epstein, "CIA and the Intellectuals."

9. DeLillo, *The Names*, 317.
10. Bevins, *Jakarta Method*, 241.
11. J. Richardson, *My Father the Spy*, 122–23; Miller, "Taking Off the Gloves"; Bevins, *Jakarta Method*, 184.
12. Simpson, *Economists with Guns*, 194.
13. CIA DTPILLAR 1, 1, 2.
14. Smith memo in DTPILLAR 3, 24, 2, 1/28/63.
15. Kessler, *Inside the CIA*.
16. Bevins, *Jakarta Method*, 19.
17. US Senate, Church Committee Report, 187.
18. US Senate, Church Committee Report, 188.
19. With TAF's post-1967 State Department sponsorship, as well as State Department personnel's presence on the 303 Committee, possibilities for the foundation's continuing role in intelligence activities remained.
20. See Carew, "American Labor Movement," 40; Hills, "Trojan Horses?"; Langguth, *Hidden Terrors*.
21. CIA DTPILLAR 3, 6, 1, 6/6/67.
22. Laski, "Foundations, Universities, and Research," 174.
23. Perhaps scholars' best hope of not accidentally supporting the CIA with our scholarship lies in the agency's ongoing incompetence. Many decades ago the chief of staff for Senator Fred Harris (D-OK) described to anthropologist Ralph Beals the existence of warehouses in Washington with "great piles" of unread research reports by American scholars, which offers some consolation in the promise of intelligence agencies' inability to use our work. Price, *Cold War Anthropology*, 288.

Bibliography

ARCHIVAL COLLECTIONS

American Anthropological Association Papers. National Anthropological Archives, Smithsonian Institution, Washington, DC.

Asia Foundation Papers. Hoover Institution Archives, Stanford University, Stanford, CA.

Bell, David. Office files, Office of the Vice President. Ford Foundation records, Rockefeller Foundation Archive Center, Sleepy Hollow, NY.

Blum, Robert. Papers. Manuscripts and Archives, Yale University, New Haven, CT.

Chaneles, Sol. Papers. National Security Archives, George Washington University, Washington, DC.

CIA DTPILLAR. CIA declassified documents on the DTPILLAR Program, released by the CIA. Available at the CIA's Freedom of Information Electronic Reading Room, https://www.cia.gov/readingroom/home.

Conde, David W. Papers. University of British Columbia Archives, Vancouver, BC.

Education and World Affairs. Records, 1961–71. Hoover Institution Archives, Stanford University, Stanford, CA.

Ford Foundation. Records. Rockefeller Foundation Archive Center, Sleepy Hollow, NY.

Franklin Book Programs. Records. Princeton University Library, Special Collections, Princeton, NJ.

National Anthropological Archives. Smithsonian Institution, Washington, DC.

National Archives, College Park, MD.

Rockefeller Foundation Archives. Rockefeller Foundation Archive Center, Sleepy Hollow, NY.

Weinberg, Jules. Papers. Catholic University of America Archives, Washington, DC.

PUBLISHED SOURCES

Bass, Thomas A. "The Spy Who Loved Us: The Double Life of *Time*'s Saigon Correspondent during the Vietnam War." *New Yorker*, May 23, 2005, 56–67. http://www.newyorker.com/magazine/2005/05/23/the-spy-who-loved-us.

Benson, Peter. *Black Orpheus, Transition, and Modern Cultural Awakening in Africa*. Berkeley: University of California Press, 1986.

Berman, Larry. *Perfect Spy: The Incredible Double Life of Pham Xuan An*. New York: HarperCollins, 2007.

Bevins, Vincent. *The Jakarta Method: Washington's Anticommunist Crusade and the Mass Murder Program That Shaped Our World*. New York: PublicAffairs Books, 2020.

Bittman, Ladislav. *The Deception Game: Czechoslovak Intelligence in Soviet Political Warfare*. Syracuse, NY: Syracuse University Research Corporation, 1972.

Bjornlund, Eric. *Beyond Free and Fair: Monitoring Elections and Building Democracy*. Baltimore, MD: Johns Hopkins University Press, 2004.

Blum, Robert. "The Asia Foundation: Purposes and Program." *United Asia* 11, no. 5 (1959): 3–7.

———. "The Flow of People and Ideas." In *Cultural Affairs and Foreign Relations*. Englewood Cliffs, NJ: Prentice-Hall, 1963.

———. "The Work of the Asia Foundation." *Pacific Affairs* 29, no. 1 (1956): 46–56.
Blum, William. *Killing Hope: U.S. Military and CIA Interventions since World War II*. Monroe, ME: Common Courage, 1995.
Bonner, Raymond. *Waltzing with a Dictator: The Marcoses and the Making of American Policy*. New York: Random House, 1987.
Brewster, Beverly J. *American Overseas Library Technical Assistance, 1940–1970*. Metuchen, NJ: Scarecrow, 1976.
Buadaeng, K. "The Rise and Fall of the Tribal Research Institute." *Southeast Asian Studies* 44, no. 3 (2006): 359–84.
Byinton, Kaa. *Bantay ng Bayan: Stories from the NAMFREL Crusade*. Manila: Bookmark, 1988.
Carew, Anthony. "The American Labor Movement in Fizzland: The Free Trade Union Committee and the CIA." *Labor History* 39, no. 1 (1998): 25–42.
Chang, Chihyun. *The Chinese Journals of L. K. Little, 1943–54: An Eyewitness Account of War and Revolution*. 3 vols. Oxfordshire: Routledge, 2017.
Chernyavsky, V. "U.S. Intelligence and the Monopolies." *International Affairs* (Moscow) 11, no. 1 (1965): 55–60.
Clark, William. 2007. "Philanthropic Imperialism." *Lobster*, no. 53 (Summer 2007).
Coleman, Peter. *The Liberal Conspiracy: The Congress for Cultural Freedom and the Struggle for the Mind of Postwar Europe*. New York: Free Press, 1989.
Committee for Free Asia. *Land Reform: Communist China, Nationalist China, Taiwan, India, Pakistan*. San Francisco: Committee for Free Asia, 1953.
Conde, David W. *CIA—Core of the Cancer*. New Delhi: Entente Private, 1970.
Congressional Quarterly Report. "Foundations, Private Organizations Linked to CIA." *Congressional Quarterly*, February 24, 1967, 1–2.
Corson, William R. *The Betrayal*. New York: Norton, 1968.
Cumings, Bruce. *Parallax Visions: Making Sense of American-East Asian Relations*. Durham, NC: Duke University Press, 1999.
Cummings, Richard H. *Radio Free Europe's "Crusade for Freedom": Rallying Americans behind Cold War Broadcasting, 1950–1960*. Jefferson, NC: McFarland, 2010.
Currey, Cecil B. *Edward Lansdale: The Unquiet American*. Boston: Houghton Mifflin, 1988.
Davis, Caroline. *African Literature and the CIA: Networks of Authorship and Publishing*. Cambridge: Cambridge University Press, 2020.
Defty, Andrew. *Britain, America, and Anticommunist Propaganda, 1945–53: The Information Research Department*. New York: Routledge, 2004.
DeLillo, Don. *The Names*. New York: Knopf, 1982.
Dick, Philp K. *Through a Scanner Darkly*. New York: Doubleday, 1977.
Dimock, Edward C., Jr. "Obituary: Richard L. Park (1920–1980)." *Journal of Asian Studies* 40, no. 3 (1981): 659–60.
Ege, Konrad. "US Intervention in Afghanistan." *Counterspy* 4, no. 1 (1980): 8–19.
Eldridge, David N. "'Dear Owen': The CIA, Luigi Luraschi and Hollywood, 1953." *Historical Journal of Film, Radio and Television* 20, no. 2 (2000): 149–96.
Epstein, Jason. "The CIA and the Intellectuals." *New York Review of Books*, April 20, 1967, 16–21. https://www.nybooks.com/articles/1967/04/20/the-cia-and-the-intellectuals/.
Erskine, Kristopher C. "Frank W. Price, 1895–1974: The Role of an American Missionary in Sino-U.S. Relations." Doctoral diss., University of Hong Kong, 2013.

Finley, Sonya Lynn. "Recommending Political Warfare—The Role of Eisenhower's Presidential Committee on International Information Activities in the United States' Approach to the Cold War." Doctoral diss., Virginia Polytechnic Institute and State University, 2016.

Ford, Eugene. *Cold War Monks: Buddhism and America's Secret Strategy in Southeast Asia*. New Haven: Yale University Press, 2017.

Ford Foundation. *Ford Foundation Annual Report*. New York: Ford Foundation, 1960.

Frank, Andre Gunder. "The Underdevelopment of Development." In *The Promise of Development: Theories of Change in Latin America*, edited by Peter F. Klarén and Thomas J. Bossert. New York: Routledge, 1986.

Geddes, William R. "The Tribal Research Centre: An Account of Plans and Activities." In *Southeast Asian Tribes, Minorities, and Nations, Volume 2*, edited by Peter Kunstadter, 553–81. Princeton: Princeton University Press, 1967.

Gerteis, Christopher. "Labor's Cold Warriors: The American Federation of Labor and 'Free Trade Unionism' in Cold War Japan." *Journal of American-East Asian Relations* 12, no. 3–4 (Fall 2003): 207–24.

Harrington, Laura. "The Greatest Movie Never Made: The Life of the Buddha as Cold War Politics." *Religion and American Culture* 30, no. 3 (2021): 1–29.

Headman, Eva-Lotta E. "Global Civil Society in One Country? Class Formation and Business Activism in the Philippines." In *Southeast Asian Responses to Globalization*, edited by Francis Loh Kok Wah and Joakim Öjendal, 138–72. Copenhagen: Nordic Institute of Asian Studies, 2005.

Hills, Alice. "Trojan Horses? USAID, Counterterrorism and Africa's Police." *Third World Quarterly* 27, no. 4 (2006): 629–43.

Hinckle, Warren, Robert Scheer, Sol Stern, and Stanley K. Sheinbaum. "The University on the Make." *Ramparts* 4 (April 1966): 11–22.

Jackson, David P. "The Life, Work and Writings of Robert Brainerd Ekval (1893–1983)." In *Three Mountains and Seven Rivers*, edited by Shoun Hino and Toshiro Wada, 609–35. Delhi: Motilal Banarsidass, 2004.

Jacobs, Paul. "How the CIA Makes Liars Out of Union Leaders." *Ramparts* 5 (April 1967): 25–28.

Johnson Administration. *Foreign Relations of the United States, 1964–1968: Volume X, National Security Policy*, edited by David S. Patterson. 1968. Washington, DC: United States Government Printing Office, 2002. https://history.state.gov/historicaldocuments/frus1964-68v10.

Jeans, Roger B. *The CIA and Third Force Movements in China during the Early Cold War*. Lanham, MD: Rowman & Littlefield, 2017.

Jones, Delmos. "Reply to Jorgensen and Wolf." *New York Review of Books*, July 22, 1971.

———. "Social Responsibility and the Belief in Basic Research." *Current Anthropology* 12, no. 3 (1971): 347–50.

Jonsson, Hjorleifur. "Phantom Scandal: On the National Uses of the 'Thailand Controversy.'" *SOJOURN: Journal of Social Issues in Southeast Asia* 29, no. 2 (2014): 263–99.

Kahin, George McT. *Southeast Asia: A Testament*. London: Routledge, 2003.

Kamrany, Nake M. "An Open Letter to the Editors of *Ramparts*." *Afghan Student News* 3, no. 3 (1967): 10–11.

Katzenbach, Nicholas. *Some of It Was Fun*. New York: Norton, 2008.

Kerkvliet, Benedict J. Tria. "Contested Meanings of Elections in The Philippines." In *The Politics of Elections in Southeast Asia*, edited by R. H. Taylor, 147–63. Cambridge: Cambridge University Press, 1996.

Kessler, Ronald. *Inside the CIA*. New York: Pocket Books, 1994.

Klein, Christina. "Cold War Cosmopolitanism: The Asia Foundation and 1950s Korean Cinema." *Journal of Korean Studies* 22, no. 2 (2017): 281–316.

———. *Cold War Orientalism: Asia in the Middlebrow Imagination, 1945–1961*. Berkeley: University of California Press, 2003.

Kobler, John. "He Runs a Private OSS." *Saturday Evening Post*, May 21, 1955, 31, 141–44.

Korff, Serge A. "Shannon McCune, Director of the American Geographical Society." *Geographical Review* 57, no. 4 (1967): 460–62.

Kunstadter, Peter, ed. *Southeast Asian Tribes, Minorities, and Nations*. 2 vols. Princeton: Princeton University Press, 1967.

Ladwig, Patrice. "'Special Operation Pagoda': Buddhism Covert Operations and the Politics of Religious Subversion in Cold-War Laos (1957–1960)." In *Changing Lives in Laos: Society, Politics and Culture in a Post-Socialist State*, edited by Vanina Bouté and Vatthan Pholsena, 81–108. Singapore: National University of Singapore Press, 2017.

Langguth, A. J. *Hidden Terrors: The Truth about U.S. Police Operations in Latin America*. New York: Pantheon, 1978.

Laski, Harold Joseph. "Foundations, Universities, and Research." In *The Dangers of Obedience and Other Essays*, 150–77. London: Harper Brothers, 1930.

Leary, Charles. "The Most Careful Arrangements for a Careful Fiction: A Short History of Asia Pictures." *Inter-Asia Culture Studies* 13, no. 4 (2012): 548–58.

Lee, Martin, and Bruce Shlain. *Acid Dreams: The Complete Social History of LSD, the CIA, the Sixties, and Beyond*. New York: Grove, 1992.

Lee, Sangjoon. "The Asia Foundation's Motion-Picture Project and the Cultural Cold War in Asia." *Film History* 29, no. 2 (2017): 108–37.

———. "Creating an Anti-Communist Motion Picture Producers' Network in Asia: The Asia Foundation, Asia Pictures, and the Korean Motion Picture Cultural Association." *Historical Journal of Film, Radio and Television* 37, no. 3 (2017): 517–38.

Lerski, Jerzy Jan. *Origins of Trotskyism in Ceylon: A Documentary History of the Lanka Sama Samaja Party, 1935–1942*. Stanford, CA: Hoover Institution, 1968.

Lewis, Michael. 2002. "Scientist or Spies? Ecology in a Climate of Cold War Suspicion." *Economic and Political Weekly* 37, no. 24 (2002): 2322–32.

Lifton, Robert Jay. *Thought Reform and the Psychology of Totalism: A Study of "Brainwashing" in China*. New York: Norton, 1961.

Lombardo, Johannes R. "A Mission of Espionage, Intelligence and Psychological Operations: The American Consulate in Hong Kong, 1949–64." In *The Clandestine Cold War in Asia, 1945–65: Western Intelligence, Propaganda, and Special Operations*, edited by Richard Aldrich, Gary D. Rawnsley, and Ming-Yeh T. Rawnsley, 64–81. New York: Frank Cass, 2000.

Mailer, Norman. *Harlot's Ghost*. New York: Ballantine, 1991.

Manndorff, H. "The Hill Tribe Program of the Public Welfare Department, Ministry of Interior, Thailand: Research and Socio-economic Development." In *Southeast Asian Tribes, Minorities and Nations*, vol. 2, edited by Peter Kunstadter, 525–52. Princeton: Princeton University Press, 1967.

———. "A Report on the Establishment of a Tribal Research Center in Northern Thailand." *Bulletin of the International Committee on Urgent Anthropological and Ethnological Research* 7 (1965): 34–38.

Marchetti, Victor, and John D. Marks. *The CIA and the Cult of Intelligence.* New York: Knopf, 1974.

Marks, John. *The Search for the "Manchurian Candidate."* New York: New York Times Books, 1979.

McCoy, Alfred. *The Politics of Heroin.* New York: Lawrence Hill, 1991.

McGarr, Paul Michael. "'Quiet Americans in India': The CIA and the Politics of Intelligence in Cold War South Asia." *Diplomatic History* 38, no. 5 (2014): 1046–82.

McGranahan, Carole. *Arrested Histories: Tibet, the CIA, and Memories of a Forgotten War.* Durham, NC: Duke University Press, 2010.

Mentan, Tatah. *Africa in the Colonial Ages of Empire: Slavery, Capitalism, Racism, Decolonization, Independence as Recolonization, and Beyond.* Bamenda, Cameroon: African Books Collective, 2017.

Miller, James. "Taking Off the Gloves: The United States and the Italian Elections of 1948." *Diplomatic History* 7, no. 1 (1983): 35–56.

Millikan, Max F. "Memorandum on an International Youth Service." Appendix D in *Final Report: The Peace Corps.* A Study by the Colorado State University Research Foundation, Fort Collins, Colorado. Washington, DC: International Cooperation Administration, 1961.

Moorehouse, Ward. *American Institutions and Organizations Interested in Asia: A Reference Directory.* Marlboro, NJ: Taplinger, 1957.

Morgan, Ted. *A Covert Life: Jay Lovestone, Communist, Anti-Communist, and Spymaster.* New York: Random House, 1999.

Natarajan, L. *American Shadow over India.* Bombay: People's Publishing House, 1952.

Nkrumah, Kwame. *Neo-Colonialism: The Last Stage of Imperialism.* London: Thomas Nelson & Sons, 1965.

Orwell, George. "The Frontiers of Art and Propaganda." In *The Collected Essays, Journalism, and Letters of George Orwell.* 1941. Boston: Godine, 2019.

———. *1984.* New York: Penguin. 1949.

Paget, Karen M. *Patriotic Betrayal: The Inside Story of the CIA's Secret Campaign to Enroll American Students in the Crusade against Communism.* New Haven: Yale University Press, 2015.

Parmar, Inderjeet. *Foundations of the American Century: The Ford, Carnegie, and Rockefeller Foundations in the Rise of American Power.* New York: Columbia University Press, 2012.

Pierson, Harry H. "The Asia Foundation's Programming for Tribal and Minority Peoples in Southeast Asia." In *Southeast Asian Tribes, Minorities, and Nations, Volume 2,* ed. Peter Kunstadter, 847–64. Princeton: Princeton University Press, 1967.

Prashad, Vijay. *Washington Bullets: A History of the CIA, Coups, and Assassinations.* New York: Monthly Review Press, 2020.

Price, David H. *American Surveillance State: How the U.S. Spies on Dissent.* London: Pluto Press, 2022.

———. *Anthropological Intelligence.* Durham, NC: Duke University Press, 2008.

———. "Anthropology *Sub Rosa*: The AAA, the CIA and Ethical Problems Inherent in Secret Research." In *Ethics and the Profession of Anthropology,* edited by Carolyn Fluehr-Lobban, 29–49. Walnut Creek, CA: Alta Mira, 2003.

———. "The CIA, the Asia Foundation, and the AAA: How the AAA Linked Asian Anthropologists to a CIA Funding Front." Paper presented at the Annual Meeting of the American Anthropological Association, Montreal, Canada, November 19, 2011.

———. *Cold War Anthropology: The CIA, the Pentagon and the Growth of Dual Use Anthropology*. Durham, NC: Duke University Press, 2016.

———. "David W. Conde: Lost CIA Critic and Cold War Seer." *CounterPunch* 26, no. 1 (2019): 21–26.

———. "Reframing the Impacts of Cold War Fronts: How the CIA Shaped Social Science at the Pre-1968 Asia Foundation." Paper presented at New York Academy of Sciences Anthropology Lecture Series, Wenner-Gren Foundation, New York, NY, January 30, 2017.

———. *Weaponizing Anthropology: Social Science in Service of the Militarized State*. Petrolia, CA: CounterPunch Books, 2011.

Richardson, John H. *My Father the Spy*. New York: HarperCollins, 2006.

Richardson, Peter. *A Bomb in Every Issue: How the Short, Unruly Life of "Ramparts" Magazine Changed America*. New York: New Press, 2009.

Ritzinger, Justin. "Tinker, Tailor, Scholar, Spy: Holmes Welch, Buddhism, and the Cold War." *Journal of Global Buddhism* 22, no. 2 (2021): 421–41.

Robbins, Louise S. "Publishing American Values: The Franklin Book Programs as Cold War Cultural Diplomacy." *Library Trends* 55, no. 3 (2007): 638–50.

Rodriguez, Hector. "Organizational Hegemony in the Hong Kong Cinema." *Post Script* 19, no. 1 (1919): 107–19.

Ross, Eric B. *The Malthus Factor: Poverty, Politics and Population in Capitalist Development*. London: Zed, 1998.

Rostow, Walt. *The Prospects for Communist China*. Cambridge, MA: MIT Press, 1954.

Rubin, Andrew N. *Archives of Authority: Empire, Culture, and the Cold War*. Princeton: Princeton University Press, 2012.

Saberwal, Satish. "The Problem." In *To See Ourselves: Anthropology and Modern Social Issues*, edited by Thomas Weaver, 174–77. Glenview, IL: Scott, Foresman 1973.

Sahlins, Marshall. *Confucius Institutes: Academic Malware*. Chicago: Prickly Paradigm, 2015.

Satoshi, Nakano. "Gabriel L. Kaplan and U.S. Involvement in Philippine Electoral Democracy: Tale of Two Democracies." *Philippine Studies* 52, no. 2 (2004): 149–78.

Saunders, Frances Stoner. *The Cultural Cold War: The CIA and the World of Arts and Letters*. New York: New Press, 1999.

Shorrock, Tim. "Labor's Cold War." *The Nation*, May 1, 2003, 276.

Sihanouk, Norodom, with Wilfred Burchett. *My War with the CIA*. London: Penguin, 1973.

Simpson, Bradley R. *Economists with Guns: Authoritarian Development and U.S.-Indonesian Relations, 1960–1968*. Stanford, CA: Stanford University Press, 2008.

Smith, John D. *I Was a CIA Agent in India*. 1967. Bombay: Communist Party of India, 2015.

Smith, Joseph Burkholder. *Portrait of a Cold Warrior*. Quezon City, Philippines: Plaridel, 1976.

Stern, Sol. "A Short Account of International Student Politics and the Cold War with Particular Reference to the NSA, CIA, etc." *Ramparts* 5 (March 1967): 29–38.

Swanger, Eugene Rodgers. "The World Fellowship of Buddhists 1950 to 1966 C.E.: Unitive and Divergency Factors in the Buddhist Quest for Unity." PhD diss., University of Iowa, 1971.

Thomas, Evan. *The Very Best Men, Four Who Dared: The Early Years of the CIA*. New York: Touchstone, 1995.

Troy, Thomas F. *Donovan and the CIA*. Frederick, MD: University Publications of America, 1981.
Trupp, Alexander, and Kosita Butratana. "Images of Hans Manndorff's Anthropological Research on the 'Hill Tribes' of Northern Thailand (1961–1965)." *Austrian Journal of South-East Asian Studies* 2, no. 2 (2009): 153–61.
Ulam, Adam. *The Unfinished Revolution: An Essay on the Sources and Influence of Marxism and Communism*. New York: Random House, 1960.
US Congress. "Foreign Assistance and Related Agencies Appropriations for 1969 [Part two, Economic Assistance]." *Hearings before a Subcommittee of the Committee on Appropriations, House of Representatives*. 90th Congress, 2nd session (1968). Washington, DC: US Government Printing Office, 1968.
———. "Tax-Exempt Foundations." *Hearings before Subcommittee No. 1 on Foundations, Select Committee on Small Business, House of Representatives*. 88th Congress, 2nd session (1964). Washington, DC: US Government Printing Office, 1964.
US Department of State. *Foreign Service List*. Washington, DC: US Government Printing Office, 1960.
US Senate. "Foreign and Military Intelligence, Book I, Final Report of the Select Committee to Study Government Operations with Respect to Intelligence Activities [Church Committee Report]." Senate Report No. 94-755. Washington, DC, 1976.
———. Committee on Foreign Relations. *The Asia Foundation: Past, Present, and Future*. Washington, DC: US Government Printing Office, 1983.
Valentine, Douglas. *The Phoenix Program*. New York: Avon, 1990.
Vonnegut, Kurt. *Cat's Cradle*. New York: Dial, 1963.
Wakin, Eric. *Anthropology Goes to War: Professional Ethics and Counterinsurgency in Thailand*. Madison: Center for Southeast Asian Studies, University of Wisconsin, 1991.
Weissman, Steve, and John Shoch. "CIAsia Foundation." *Pacific Research and World Empire Telegram*, September–October 1972, 3–4.
Whitney, Joel. *Finks: How the CIA Tricked the World's Best Writers*. New York: OR Books, 2017.
Wilford, Hugh. *America's Great Game: The CIA's Secret Arabists and the Shaping of the Modern Middle East*. New York: Basic Books, 2013.
———. *The Mighty Wurlitzer: How the CIA Played America*. Cambridge, MA: Harvard University Press, 2008.
Wolf, Eric R., and Joseph G. Jorgensen. "Anthropology on the Warpath in Thailand." *New York Review of Books*, November 19, 1970, 27.
Wolfe, Audra J. *Freedom's Laboratory: The Cold War Struggles for the Soul of Science*. Baltimore, MD: Johns Hopkins University Press, 2018.
Wurfel, David. *Filipino Politics: Development and Decay*. Ithaca: Cornell University Press, 1988.
Yang, Zhang. "Cultural Cold War: The American Role in Establishing the Chinese University of Hong Kong (CUHK)." In *The Power of Culture: Encounters between China and the United States*, edited by Priscilla Roberts, 148–69. Newcastle upon Tyne, UK: Cambridge Scholars, 2016.

Index

academic conferences, 57–60, 117–20, 135–37, 193–98, 271–72, 286n63, 286n71, 302n69, 331n19
Advanced Research Projects Agency (ARPA), 102, 106, 117–20
Afghanistan, 30–31, 74–75, 93–94, 139–43, 185–86, 188–90, 288n37, 302n71; Soviet influence in, 30–31, 93–94, 185. *See also* Maiwandwal, Mohammad Hashim
Africa, 46, 48, 76, 77, 127, 131, 143, 154, 164, 228
Agency for International Development (AID), 66–67, 104, 125, 210, 225–26, 231, 246, 294n68, 297n50; as replacement for CIA funds, 235–39, 242, 252, 269
Ahmed, Nasim, 54–55
Ahn Ho Sang, 170–71
Air America, 255
Alpert, Richard, 290n53
Alsop, Carlton, 162
American Anthropological Association, 103, 134–36, 198, 300n47, 300n49. *See also* Frantz, Charles; Tax, Sol
American Anthropologist, 134, 135
American Assembly, 58, 259–60, 285n59
American Institute for Free Labor Development (AIFLD), 127
American Federation of Labor (AFL), 127, 129–30, 219
American Federation of Labor-Congress of Industrial Organizations (AFL-CIO), 127, 219
American Friends of the Middle East (AFME). *See* Central Intelligence Agency fronts; Parker, Orin
American Friends of Vietnam, 113–14
American Newspaper Guild, 213, 214, 276n10
American Philosophical Association, 134
American Political Science Association, 134, 198, 300n44
American Psychological Association, 134, 136

American Sociological Association, 134, 136
Amoss, Harold, Jr., 30–31, 93–94, 97, 160, 281n18
An, Pham Xuan, 56–57
Andrew Hamilton Fund. *See* Central Intelligence Agency fronts
Anthropological and Ethnological Sciences, 5th International Congress, 195–98
anthropologists, 79, 97, 103, 106, 119–20, 134–36, 195–98, 204–5, 297n60, 301n63; Ralph Beals, 317n23; Richard Beardsley, 97; John Brohn, 297n60; John Donahue, 196; Ted Dongras, 97; Raymond Firth, 196–97; Charles Frantz, 136; David Ingersoll, 97; Delmos Jones, 103; Joseph Jorgenson, 103; Robert Kickert, 102; Jean M. Laur, 59; David Plath, 97; Acharn Pataya Saihoo, 293n49; George William Skinner, 97; Soviet, 197–98; Mel Spector, 97; Mysore Narasimhachar Srinivas, 195; Eric Wolf, 103. *See also* American Anthropological Association; Amoss, Harold, Jr.; Geddes, William; Harrisson, Tom; Klausner, William; Kunstadter, Peter; Manndorff, Hans; Moerman, Michael; Oka, Masao; Scott, James C.; Sharp, Lauriston; Spencer, Robert
anti-Marxism, 127, 264
archaeology, 59, 197, 286n74
Arnold, David D., 251
Asch, Moe, 195
Asia Foundation: board of trustees, 34–35, 39, 41–42, 86, 191, 198, 214–15, 232–34, 267, 270; board reports, xi–xii, 18, 68, 82, 86, 89, 181; book burning, 151, 164; CIA chiefs of station and, 40, 41, 87, 187; CIA funding of, ix–xiv, 1–14, 27–28, 33–40, 42–45, 83–86, 212–54, 255–73, 275n3, 281n10; CIA funding revelations of, ix–x, 4–5, 75, 105, 141, 190, 214–31, 241; CIA liquidation plan

Asia Foundation (*continued*)
and, 232–54, 266–67, 269–70, 314n9; CIA orphans and, x, 212–31, 232, 245, 247, 263, 265; CIA relationships and, ix–x, 1–2, 33, 37, 39–40, 145, 160, 217–18, 255–56, 260–61; CIA surge payment to, 236, 243, 245–46, 251; Committee for Free Asia roots, 1–26; and conferences, 12, 57–60, 63–64, 77–82, 117–20, 135–37, 179–80, 193–98, 257, 271–72; covert mail system, 11; cultural programs, 2–3, 46–65, 67, 76–77, 102–3, 208, 221–27, 235, 238, 259–60; "DTPILLAR-Cover-Fund-Raising," 34–35, 277n28; dual filing system, 11, 93, 146, 278n34; and exchange programs, 3, 11–12, 20, 23, 58, 63–65, 145, 225, 251, 301n56; expulsions of, 88, 199–201, 206–8, 216–17, 239, 311n17, 309n44; and Harvard seminars, 50–55; intelligence collection, 13, 18, 33, 87–107, 149, 167–90, 203, 229, 263–64, 267–69; leveraging debt, 159–61; lies, 23, 37, 79, 83, 86, 136, 189, 241, 253, 257–59; military engagements, 19, 56, 95–99, 102–3, 106, 113, 120–24, 154, 168, 204; Office of Special Operations, 7; professional association funding, 133–36; publishing ventures, 17, 61–62, 85, 108, 147–60, 164–66, 202–5, 238, 286n74; scholarships 8, 16, 55, 113–14, 142, 196, 237, 257, 263–64; suspicions of CIA connections, 53, 114, 135, 181, 191–211, 222, 239, 264, 301n56, 310n81. *See also* book programs: buying and distribution; bookstores and libraries; Buddhism; counterinsurgency; DTPILLAR codename; educational programs; election interference; Franklin Books; McCone, John; Orwell, George; propaganda; Radio Free Asia; students

Asia Foundation and Committee for Free Asia staff: John Bannigan, 206–7, 215; John A. Banning, 155; James Basche, 119–20, 290n53; Holbrook Bradley, 192, 202; Noel Busch, 9, 131–33, 281n18; Ann Byington, 154; John Carroll, 167–68; Pat Casey, 55; Edith Coliver, 52, 285n35; Norman Coliver, 52, 285n35, 301n66; Louis Connick, 9, 103–5, 294n68, 294n70; Colin D. Edwards, 55, 160–61; Bill Evans, 117; Patricia Flanagan, 136; William T. Fleming, 45, 110–11, 281n18; John Gange, 122; Richard Gard, 81, 290n67; Robert B. Hall, 197, 281n18; James T. Ivy, 91, 281n18, 303n23; John James, 74, 307n71, 312n32; Raymond V. Johnson, 281n18, 288n37; Walter Judd, 50, 281n18, 282n42; Patrick Judge, 16, 76–77, 123, 281n18; George M. Keller, 192; Richard Koontz, 116–17; Louis Lazaroff, 45, 129, 195; Graham Lucas, 101–2; Gordon Messegee, 112, 296n24, 306n46; John W. Miller, 152; Richard J. Miller, 281n18; Douglas P. Murray, 60; Harold Nobel, 157; George Noronha, 79; Amy Ovalle, 251–52; Edgar Pike, 9, 281n18; James C. Porterfield, 115; Chester Roberts, 195–98; Donald Riegle, 238–39; Frank Robertson, 128; Robert Schwantes, 122; Calvin Scollon, 247, 316n54; David Steinberg, 9–10, 219; John F. Sullivan, 123, 130, 291n67; John Sutter, 102; Earl Swisher, 281n18; John H. Tallman, 281n18; Charles Tanner, 162–63; Howard C. Thomas Jr., 116; Laurence G. Thompson, 281n18; Stephen Uhalley, 291n69; L. E. Yuan, 196, 208, 209, 292n23. *See also* Amoss, Harold, Jr.; Dalton, James J.; Heggie, Richard; Klausner, William; Lerski, Jerzy "George"; Overton, Leonard; Pierson, Harry; Sheeks, Robert; Stewart, James L.

Asian Pictures, 165
Asian Student, 191–92, 307n7
Aslam, Q. M., 59
Associated Students of Afghanistan, 139–43, 145, 302n69
Association of Asian Studies, 28, 286n71
Aw Boon Haw, 156–59

Bell, David, 221, 225–27
Best, Emma, 24–26, 279n87, 280n3
Bevins, Vincent, ix, 65, 66, 261–62
Bhashani, Abdul Hamid Khan, 173–75

Bittman, Ladislav, 308n42-43
Blum, Robert, 8, 24-30, 53-55, 67-68, 130-31, 177-89, 258-60, 280n2, 280n3, 280n10; board reports, 89, 177-89, 194, 201, 306n46, 309n44, 316n4; Buddhist strategy, 82-83; at conferences, 57-58; fundraising of, 34; and the Jackson Committee, 19-21, 279n87; papers of, xi-xii; and Rockefeller, 42, 145; transforming TAF into CFA, 26-29, 86. *See also* Committee for Free Asia
Blyth, Charles R., 10-11
book burning, 151, 164
book programs, 147-56; buying and distributing, 48-50, 122-26, 147-56, 151-56, 174-75, 200-203, 219, 257, 264; publishing, 17, 19, 46, 62, 85, 153-55; translation programs, 14, 28, 60-61, 70, 108, 153-55, 170, 202, 257, 271. *See also* Franklin Books; New Asia Trading Company; Operation Broomstick; Pacific Book and Supply
bookstores and libraries, 14, 85, 144, 150-53, 164, 170, 305n78
Borneo, 38, 44-45, 87, 167-68
Bowles, Chester, 282n42, 282n44
Bowles, Paul, 154
Boy Scouts, 14, 28, 69-72, 108
brainwashing, 14, 153, 303n23
Brewster, Beverly J., 167, 246
British Council, 222, 223, 239
British intelligence, 16, 307n67; MI5, 307n67; MI6, 149
Broad-High Foundation, 302n74
Brooks, Oakley, 104-5
Brown, Delmer, 97, 151-53, 303n18
Buddhism, 32, 37, 73, 77-85, 132, 161, 176, 257, 290n55, 290n67; conferences 257, 290n54, 290n55; movements xi, 271, 289n50; World Fellowship of Buddhists, 79, 81-83. *See also* Leary, Timothy
Bullitt, John, 236-38
Bundy, McGeorge, 222, 225-26
Bundy, William, 238-40
Burma, 30, 79-80, 88, 121-24, 137-39, 156-61, 177, 179, 180-82, 194; U Nu, 295n73. *See also* Rangoon University

Cambodia, 25, 70-72, 89, 150, 177, 182-83, 203-8, 239, 281n18, 286n74
Capra, Frank, 162
CARE, 111, 208, 296n18
Carnegie Endowment for International Peace, 28
Carnegie Foundation, 42-43, 143, 145, 178, 220, 221, 222, 309n52, 311n11
Catholics, 114, 176, 183, 199
Center for International Studies (CENIS), 26, 249, 250, 289n40
Central Intelligence Agency (CIA): actionable intelligence, 30, 87-89, 105, 167, 263; Blanche Y. Belitz, 310n81; Richard Bissell, 6; Marshall Carter, 116; William Casey, 252; chief of station, 40, 41, 87, 187; Jim Clark, 232; John M. Clarke, 232-34; Committee for Cultural Freedom, 145, 302n82; "Communist Cultural and Propaganda Activities in Less Developed Countries" report, 46-50; conduits, x, 2, 132, 142, 213, 216, 218, 235; Congress for Cultural Freedom, 59, 287n84; contact with foundation staff, 38-41; coups, 1, 109, 261, 264, 277n15; covert action staff, 6, 33, 35, 38-39, 147, 210, 233-35, 244-45; covert mail system, 11; directorate of plans, 4, 7, 28; "DTPILLAR-Cover-Fund-Raising," 34-35, 277n28; dual filing system, 11, 93, 146, 278n34; family jewels, xiv; fronts, x-xi, 1-4, 104, 153, 212-31, 250-51, 255-56, 265-67; funding, 1-8, 33-45, 62-64, 83-85, 145-66, 212-31, 232-54, 255-57, 263-64, 267-71; funding termination, 220-31, 232-36, 240-50; Roscoe H. Hillenkoetter, 25; intelligence collection, 18, 33, 87-107, 134, 144-45, 167-90, 207, 217, 229-30, 263-64, 267-69; "mutual friend," 75, 155, 288n37, 304n38; Office of Special Operations, 7; open source intelligence, 18, 90-93; Operation Ajax, 262; Operation FUBELT, 262; Operation PB-Success, 262; "orphans," x, 212-31,

Central Intelligence Agency (*continued*) 232, 245, 247, 263, 265; pass-throughs, x, 2–3, 34, 52, 132, 213–14; stay-behind operations, 17, 88–89, 267; surge payment, 236, 243, 245–46, 251; violence, xiii, 1, 65, 66, 256, 259, 261–64. *See also* congressional hearings; DTPILLAR codename; Dulles, Allen; election interference; Freedom of Information Act; Helms, Richard; Office of Policy Coordination (OPC); publishing programs; Smith, Walter Bedell; 303 Committee; Wisner, Frank

Central Intelligence Agency fronts, x–xi, 1–4, 104, 132, 148, 153, 211–31, 255–56, 265–67, 302n75; American Friends of the Middle East (AFME), 49, 139, 142, 247, 276n10, 301n66, 302n74; Andrew Hamilton Fund, 3, 302n74; Beacon Fund, 3; Borden Trust, 3; Catherwood Foundation, 110; Chesapeake Foundation, 302n74; Edsel Fund, 3; Farfield Foundation, 305n75; Gotham Foundation, 3; Kaplan Fund, 3, 131, 133, 299; Kentfield Fund, 3; Michigan Fund, 3; New Asia Trading Company, 202–3, 309n46, 309n51; Pacific Book and Supply, 49, 165, 203, 305n78; Wright Patman, 2–3; Price Fund, 3; San Jacinto Foundation, 213, 302n74. *See also* Asia Foundation

Central Intelligence Agency pass-throughs and conduits, x, 2–3, 34, 52, 132, 142, 213–14, 216, 218, 235; Foundation for Youth and Student Affairs, 213, 276n10; Granary Fund, 302n74; Independent Foundation, 213; J. Frederick Brown Foundation, 213, 276n10; Rabb Foundation, 213; Rosenthal Foundation, 131, 132, 299n29; San Jacinto Foundation, 213, 302n74

Ceylon, 30, 45, 80, 82, 126, 127, 180, 202–3, 208, 281n18, 300n36

Chaneles, Sol, 148–49, 302n3

Chang Kuo-Sin, 151–53, 165

Chernyavsky, V., 202–3, 309n51, 309n52

Chiang Kai-Shek, 156, 175

Chile, 1, 127, 225, 226, 262; Salvador Allende, 127; Operation FUBELT, 262

China, 8, 14–18, 38, 48–49, 90–91, 152–53, 157, 163, 207–8, 302n7

Chinese ethnographers, 97

Church, Frank, 255, 266–67

Church Committee, 127, 147, 149, 165, 221, 255, 266–67

Circus, The, 161

Clark, Ramsey, 312n38

Columbia University, 58, 61, 218, 285n59, 311n11

Committee for Cultural Freedom, 145, 302n82

Committee for Free Asia: xi, xiv, 1–34, 41–45, 75–79, 93–94, 149–62, 191–98, 277n20; Robert Blum, xi–xii, 8, 19, 24–28, 86; intelligence gathering, 16–19, 90, 108, 175–77; lies, 15, 23; propaganda, 26, 42, 45, 53; suspicions of, 191–99, 202–3; transition to Asia Foundation, 19–23, 24–31, 33–34, 86, 124–25, 166, 193–97, 251–52, 281n13, 290n54; youth festivals, 75–76. *See also* Asia Foundation; Aw Boon Haw; Greene, George H., Jr.; Maddocks, Ray; National Movement for Free Elections (NAMFREL); Operation Broomstick; Radio Free Asia; Seeds for Democracy; Valentine, Allen; Wilbur, Brayton

Committee on Books Abroad, 148; George Brett and, 148; Cass Canfield and, 148; Robert Crowell and, 148

Committee on International Information Activities, 279n85

Communist Party, 31, 47, 49, 76, 90, 94, 161, 183, 216, 248; American Communist Party, 92

Communist Youth Festival, 76

Community Development Counseling Service, 111–12

Conde, David, 126

conferences, 57–64, 79–81, 135–39, 179–80, 239, 271–72; Sinocentric World Order Conference, 60; Tribal and Minority Peoples in Southeast Asia Conference, 117–120. *See also* American Assembly; American Political Science Association; Congress for Cultural Freedom;

330 INDEX

International Congress of Anthropological and Ethnological Science
Congress for Cultural Freedom, 59, 287n84
congressional hearings, 1, 2, 105, 127, 236–40, 255, 266
Conte, Silvio, 237–38
Cooperative Research and Training Center, 113–14
Cornell University, 97, 100, 178, 198, 204, 294n52
Corson, William, 25, 280n3
Counsel Services, Inc., 287n3
counterinsurgency, 60–61, 95–96, 99, 102–3, 106–108, 113–18, 122–25, 213, 264, 271; aid and, 124–25; Roger Hilsman and, 115; Strategic Hamlet Program, 114–17, 124; Tribal and Minority Peoples in Southeast Asia Conference, 117–20. *See also* Lansdale, Edward; National Movement for Free Elections (NAMFREL); Tribal Research Centre, Chiang Mai
Crusade for Freedom, 13, 191

Dalton, James J., 31–32, 63, 118, 120, 123–24, 137–39
Davis, Caroline, 164, 305n75
Diem, Ngo Dinh, 54, 113, 181, 183
Disney, Walt, 162
Donovan, William, 25
DTPILLAR codename, x–xii, 1–2, 7–9, 16–19, 23–28, 277n19; continuity between CFA and TAF, 19–30; creation of, x–xii, 2, 7–9; funding of ix–xiv, 1–14, 27–28, 33–40, 42–45, 83–86, 212–54, 255–73, 275n3, 277n28, 281n10, 295n8; liquidation of, 232–54, 266–67, 269–70, 314n9; mission of, xiv, 13, 17, 26–28, 33–44, 84, 144, 243–45, 249–50, 260–62, 265–72; plans, 7–14; radio broadcasts, 10, 11, 14–16, 86, 251. *See also* Asia Foundation; Central Intelligence Agency; Committee for Free Asia
Dulles, Allen, 25, 42, 51, 279n87, 281n13, 287n81, 295n73

East Pakistan, 18, 74, 123, 135, 173–75
Economic Cooperation Administration, 6, 24
Economic Stabilization Agency, 8
economists. *See* Herczeg, Carl R.; Millikan, Max; Rostow, Walt
educational programs, 11–12, 14–16, 50–56, 63–65, 93–94, 113–14, 124–28, 154–55, 257–58, 264; military, 31, 122–24, 154, 298n70; student leadership, 85, 136–43
Education and World Affairs, 222–24, 312n41, 313n45
Eight Months behind the Bamboo Curtain, 151
Eisenhower, Dwight, 19, 25–26, 285n59
Eisenhower, Milton, 230, 312n38
Ekvall, Robert, 13
election interference, 1, 109–12, 124–25, 180, 257, 261, 262, 265, 295n8, 295n9
Ensminger, Douglas, 248–50
exchange programs, 3, 20, 23, 48–50, 58, 63–65, 145, 301n56

Fairbanks, John King, 12–13, 285n60
Federal Bureau of Investigation, xi, 5, 20, 92, 232
Fernandes, B. G., 191–92
Ferrer, Jaime, 109–11
"Fiction" codename, 151–53
Fishel, Wesley, 114
Fitzgerald, Desmond, 109
Fleishhacker, Mortimer, Jr., 245, 356n11
Ford, Eugene, 77–79
Ford Foundation, 35, 42–43, 143–46, 153, 213, 220–22, 225–28, 248–51, 259, 309n52; attacks on, 33, 208–9; Modjokuto Project, 281n12; projects monitored by the Asia Foundation, 32, 88, 175, 178, 204; suspicions of, 121, 208–9, 215, 239
Foreign Student Advisors Workshop, 295n76
Foreign Student Leadership Program, 85, 136–39
Forrestal, James, 24–25
Foundation for Youth and Student Affairs, 213, 276n10
Franklin Books, 37, 49, 155, 219, 303n36, 304n38 312n32
Franklin Press. *See* Franklin Books
Frantz, Charles, 136

INDEX   331

Freedom of Information Act, xi, xii, 18, 87, 133, 177, 251, 253, 256, 277n19
Fulbright, William, 230, 312n38
Fulbright fellowships, 9, 88, 97, 178

Gallup, George, 19
Geddes, William, 118–20, 297n50
Georgetown University, 10, 62
Greene, George H., Jr., 8, 10, 14
Greene, Graham, 187, 189
Guatemala, 1, 66, 109, 262, 277n15; Operation PBSuccess, 262

Harrisson, Tom, 120, 297n50
Harvard University, 12, 50–55, 85, 122–23, 142, 271, 278n40, 285n60, 290n53, 298n73; James Conant, 52; International Seminar Program, 14, 37, 50–52, 248; Nieman Fellowships, 52–55, 85. *See also* Kissinger, Henry
Heggie, Richard, 9, 51–52, 122–23, 216–18
Helms, Richard, 7, 220–21, 233, 241, 315n36, 315n40
Herczeg, Carl R., 308n12
Himsworth, Mr., 187–88, 307n67
historians: George Kennan, 19; Wallace Stirling, 61. *See also* Brown, Delmer; Fairbanks, John King; Lerski, Jerzy "George"; Mote, Frederick W.; Taylor, George; Wittfogel, Karl
Hoffer, Eric, 127–28
Hong Kong, 9, 91, 130, 149–59, 161–63, 172, 281n18, 298n70, 300n36, 300n44; intelligence operations in, 16, 91; movies, 161–65; publishing operations in, 14, 149–54; Tiger Balm in, 156–57
Hook, Sydney, 59, 61, 287n76
Hoover, Lyman, 55, 130–31, 300n36
Hoover Institution, xii–xiii, 60, 62, 92, 132, 275n7, 292n27, 294n70
Hotaki, Abdul Latif, 141–43, 302n71
Human Relations Area Files, 98, 156, 295n76

India, 14, 53–54, 144, 175–80, 183–84, 188, 193–97, 216–19, 248–50, 281n12; book programs in, 59, 170; neutrality 77, 175; Soviet influence in 48, 76, 177–78; suspicions of the foundation, 30, 38, 42, 72, 179, 193–97, 209, 216–19, 239, 249, 311n17. *See also* Nehru, Jawaharlal
Indonesia, 14, 85, 108, 123, 172–73, 177–78, 180, 183, 187, 198–203; book and publishing programs in, 49, 128, 150, 152, 165; communists, 108, 183; expulsion of foundation, 199–202, 239, 309n44; Djuanda Kartawidjaja, 201; suspicions of the foundation, 42, 194, 198–202, 208, 239, 308–9n42. *See also* Sukarno
In-laws, The, 255
Inouye, Daniel, 253–54
International Confederation of the Free Trade Unions (ICFTU), 127–29
International Congress of Anthropological and Ethnological Science, 195–98
International Cooperation Administration, 67
Iran, 1, 66, 109, 142, 262, 277n15; Operation Ajax, 262

Jackson, William H., 19–21, 25, 279n87, 280n6
Jackson Committee, 19–21, 24–26, 279n85, 280n10
Jain, G. L., 53–54
Jamison, Francis A., 42
Japan, 9–10, 18–19, 28–30, 85, 124, 157, 184–85, 196–97, 248, 290n67; labor unions in, 127, 129–30; publishing in, 37, 61, 154–55
Japan Society, 28, 85, 197, 230, 286n60
J. Frederick Brown Foundation. *See* Central Intelligence Agency pass-throughs and conduits
John Simon Guggenheim Memorial Foundation, 178
Johnson, Lyndon B., 2, 68, 213, 220–23, 231, 240, 251–52
Johnson, U. Alexis, 248, 315n36, 315n40
Josiah Macy Jr. Foundation, 131, 299n29
journalists, 9, 25, 49, 58, 131, 156–61, 167, 168, 177, 179, 192, 209, 257; investigative, ix–xi, 3–4, 141–43, 210, 212–16, 236, 240, 247, 302n7; Nguyen Thai, 54; supported by

DTPILLAR, 17, 52–57, 85, 146, 151, 157, 165, 263, 272, 276n10. *See also* An, Pham Xuan; Aw Boon Haw; Conde, David; Nguyen Thai; Stern, Sol; Turner, Wallace

Kahin, George McT., 178, 198–99
Kamrany, Nake M., 142–43
Kaplan, Gabriel, 109–11, 295n9
Kaplan Fund: Raymund Rubinow, 133. *See also* Central Intelligence Agency fronts
Karen tribe, 101, 138
Katsumata, Seiichi, 127–28
Katzenbach, Nicholas, 213, 220–23, 230
Katzenbach Committee, 220–23, 230–31, 233, 241, 255, 263–64, 266, 312n36
Kauffman, Howard, 113
Kennedy, John F., 68, 72, 289n40
Khan, Ayub, 259, 316n4
Khrushchev, Nikita, 57, 68, 178–79
King Hu, 152–53
Kirk, Grayson, 61, 311n11
Kissinger, Henry, 50–52, 122–23, 248, 252, 278n40, 285n35
Klausner, William, 32, 79, 98–100, 118, 176–77, 293n44
Korea, 9–10, 209; Conflict, 9, 10, 126, 168–72; Democratic People's Republic of Korea, 76, 90, 251; language of, 28, 168, 209; Republic of Korea, 14, 81–82, 85, 127, 130, 135, 162, 177, 219, 231
Kunstadter, Peter, 82–83, 117–20, 138, 162, 297n45, 297n46, 297n60
Kurosawa, Akira, 163

labor unions, 45, 108, 126–30, 144, 221, 225, 257, 265, 269, 299n15
land reform, 17, 68, 285n60
Lansdale, Edward, 56, 110, 114
Laos, 25, 89, 95–97, 103–4, 112, 176–78, 181–82, 294n68, 297n50, 306n46; elections in, 99
Laski, Harold, 24, 272
Laswell, Harold, 172, 305n3
Leary, Timothy, 290n53
Lerski, Jerzy "George," 60, 62–63, 78, 139, 287n81, 287n84, 287n85

libraries, xiii, 17, 55, 73, 85, 91–93, 154, 170, 195; military, 123–24, 154; sponsoring, 50, 59, 110, 122, 144, 164, 185, 219, 238, 257
Lifton, Robert J., 153, 303n23, 303n26
Linebarger, Paul, 11
Lippman, Walter, 19, 52
Little, L. K., 11
Lockwood, John E., 228–29, 313n65
Lovestone, Jay, 127–28

MacArthur, Douglas, 6–7, 287n79
MacLeish, Archibald, 52
Maddocks, Ray, 8, 110–11
Magsaysay, Ramon, 111–12, 124, 295n8, 295n9
Maiwandwal, Mohammad Hashim, 143
Malaya, 14, 70, 74, 76, 154, 163, 180, 281n18, 279n63
Mallory, Walter H., 172–73, 282n42, 305n4, 311n11
Manndorff, Hans, 97, 99, 101–2, 118, 293n45, 294n55, 297n50
Mao Zedong, 12, 152
Marshall Plan, 6, 9, 24
Marxism, 29, 51, 60, 80, 184, 195, 251, 271
Marvel, William W., 222–23
Massachusetts Institute of Technology, 26, 122, 249–50, 311n11. *See also* Center for International Studies (CENIS)
McBaine, Turner H., 245, 311n11
McCarthyism, 44, 219
McCone, John, 58, 83–84, 116, 286n60, 286n62
McCune, Shannon, 67, 285n60, 287n1
McGinnis, J. Michael, 139–40
McNarney Report (NSC 50), 25–26
Meyer, Cord, 116, 240–41
Michener, James, 34, 277n28, 282n42, 282n44, 282n45, 282n48
Michigan State University, 114, 122, 196, 249
microfilm, 85, 92–93
Middle East, 46, 49, 115, 276n10, 301n66
Milbank, Robbins, 41–42, 311n11
Millegan, Lloyd, 49, 165, 305n78
Millikan, Max, 26, 122–23, 289n40
Modjokuto Project, 281n12

Moerman, Michael, 120, 297n50
Montagnard Resettlement Program, 114–17
Mote, Frederick W., 100–101, 294n54
movies, 20, 46–49, 61, 110, 112, 151–56, 161–66, 203, 255, 308n42
Moyers, Bill, 240–41
Mutual Security Agency, 19, 24–25

National Academy of Sciences, 225
National Association of Foreign Student Advisors, 28, 295
National Committee for a Free Europe, 10, 13, 20
National Movement for Free Elections (NAMFREL), 109–12, 124, 125, 295n8, 295n9. *See also* Thomas, Evan
National Research Council, 100, 204, 225
National Science Foundation, 224, 225, 246
National Security Agency, 25
National Student Association (NSA), 9, 85, 136–39, 220, 245, 247, 301n56, 301n63, 301n66, 311n5; and Martha Darling, 247; *Ramparts* report of CIA funding, x, 3–4, 212–13, 215–16, 220. *See also* Foreign Student Leadership Program
Nehru, Jawaharlal, 77, 175–76, 179, 184, 194, 316n4
Nepal, 48–49, 81–82, 113, 177, 187–88
New Asia Trading Company. *See* Central Intelligence Agency fronts
Nguyen Thai, 54
Nieman Fellowships, 28, 37, 52–54, 85, 194
Nimitz, Chester, 58, 285–86n60
Nitze, Paul, 19, 285–86n60
Nixon, Richard, 79, 248, 281n13
nonalignment, 44, 66, 69, 77, 193, 261, 265; Bandung Conference, 77
Noorzay, Zia H., 141–42, 302n71
Noyes, Charles, 133
Noyes Foundation, 131, 299n29

Office of Policy Coordination (OPC), 1, 4–7, 11, 13–14, 24–25, 100, 109, 212, 214. *See also* Fitzgerald, Desmond; Wisner, Frank
Office of Strategic Services (OSS), 3, 4–6, 10, 24, 28, 191, 281n16, 294n54. *See also* Donovan, William
Office of War Information (OWI), 67, 148
Oka, Masao, 196–97
Operation Ajax, 262
Operation Broomstick, 151–53, 312n32
Operation Brotherhood, 114
Operation Mockingbird, 277n15
opium, 96, 98–100, 293n44, 293n45
Oram, Harold L., 34
Orwell, George, 147, 154, 303n30; *Animal Farm*, 154; *1984*, 154, 303n30
Overton, Leonard, 72, 89, 204–6, 234, 281n18, 288n21, 314n13

Pacific Book and Supply. *See* Central Intelligence Agency fronts
Paget, Karen M., x, 212, 275n3
Paik, George, 168, 170
Pakistan, 54–55, 123, 127–30, 139, 185–86, 259, 286n74, 287n84, 299n15, 300n44; labor unions in, 127–30; Pakistan Society, 55; Pakistan Student Federation, 55; radio broadcasts, 15. *See also* East Pakistan; West Pakistan
Palmer, William, 308–9n42
Parasuram, T. V., 53–54
Paris Review, 148
Park, Richard, 67, 195, 287n1
Parker, Orin, 247
Parmar, Inderjeet, 42–43, 46, 53, 270
Patman, Wright. *See* Central Intelligence Agency fronts
Pauker, Guy, 292n23, 293n44, 298n73
Peace Corps, 72–75, 288n27, 288n32, 288n37, 289n40
Peale, Norman Vincent, 154
PEN American writers tour, 61, 62, 219
Philippines, 13–15, 102–3, 109–12, 124–25, 146, 162, 253, 287n3, 300n44; International Rice Research Institute, 253. *See also* National Movement for Free Elections (NAMFREL)
Pierson, Harry, 63, 73, 82–83, 118–19, 198–99, 290n55, 293n44, 297n50, 297n60, 310n81

Pike, Otis, 255
Point Four Program, 67, 172, 305n6
political scientists, 9, 60, 84, 134, 137–39, 172, 178, 195, 198, 293n44, 300n44, 311n11. *See also* Blum, Robert; Laswell, Harold; Linebarger, Paul; Kahin, George McT.; Kissinger, Henry; Park, Richard; Pauker, Guy; Pool, Ithiel de Sola; Pye, Lucian; Scott, James C.; Whiting, Allen
Pool, Ithiel de Sola, 122–23
Praeger Press, 49
Prashad, Vijay, 66, 250–51
Princeton University, 58, 100, 117–20, 122, 131, 133, 294n54
Princeton University Press, 297n46
propaganda, 11–26, 42–47, 63–65, 86, 147–66, 179–80, 193–94, 230–31, 256–59, 277n15; anti-communist, 7–8, 19, 30, 42, 59, 61, 75–77, 181, 194, 231; communist, 15, 19, 22, 30, 46–47, 61, 80, 83, 248–49. *See also* movies; Operation Broomstick; Operation Mockingbird
psychological warfare, 19, 22, 26, 56, 123–24, 148, 189, 278n49
psychologists, 136, 153–54, 290n53. *See also* American Psychological Association
publishing programs, 17, 38, 49, 61, 64–65, 85, 125, 147–66, 202–3, 205; book buying and distribution, 28–29, 48–50, 64, 122–26, 147–56, 174–75, 200–203, 235–39; book, 17, 19, 46, 62, 85, 153–55; translation, 14, 28, 60–61, 64, 70, 108, 153–55, 170, 202, 257, 271; and ventures, 1, 7, 21, 37, 61, 65, 147–60, 164–66, 202–5, 238. *See also* bookstores and libraries; Franklin Books; Praeger Press; Princeton University Press
Pye, Lucian, 139, 248, 311n11

Quirino, Elpidio, 110–11, 296n15

Radio Free Asia, 10, 11, 14–16, 86, 251
Radio Free Europe, 6, 10, 14–15, 228, 266
Ramparts magazine, x, 3–4, 141–43, 210, 212–13, 215–16, 220, 236, 247, 302n71

RAND Corporation, 122, 292n23, 293n44. *See also* Speier, Hans
Rangoon University, 76, 137, 138
Reddy, Gunupati Keshava, 53–54, 184
Redford, Ralph, 187–88
Reece Committee, 130, 299n25
Reuther, Victor, 128–29, 299n15
Rockefeller, John D., III, 41–42, 145, 313n65
Rockefeller Foundation, 42–43, 133, 145, 178, 213, 221–22, 228–29, 251, 286n60, 309n52; and CIA orphans, 221–22, 228–29; suspicions concerning, 33, 143, 192, 208. *See also* Jamison, Francis A.
Rostow, Walt, 60, 64, 122–23, 155–56, 165, 241–42, 285n60
Rosenthal, A. M., 177–78, 209
Rosenthal, Edmund, 132, 300n36
Rosenthal Foundation. *See* Central Intelligence Agency pass-throughs and conduits
Rotary Fellowship, 137–38, 145
Rowe, David N., 153, 285n60, 312n38
Rusk, Dean, 192, 221, 252
Rusk Committee, 221, 223, 225, 227, 230–43, 312n38
Russia, 30, 55, 59, 82, 92, 94, 125, 161, 182, 188, 197, 199, 202

Salim, Hadji Agus, 172–73
Salzburg Seminars, 12
Satoshi, Nakano, 111
Saunders, Frances Stoner, x, 162, 163
Scott, James C., 137–39, 145, 301n56, 301n63
Second World War, 4–5, 8–9, 24, 78, 143, 172, 262, 265, 273, 294n54. *See also* Office of Strategic Services (OSS); Office of War Information (OWI)
Seeds for Democracy, 10, 13–14, 28, 110, 174
Sen, S. P., 217–18
Shahryar, Ishaq, 140–41
Sharp, Lauriston, 100, 198, 294n52
Sheeks, Robert, 9, 72–73, 123, 154, 163, 298n73
Shook, Cleo, 74–75, 288n35, 288n37
Shriver, Garner E., 236–37
Shriver, Sargent, 288–89n37

Sihanouk, Norodom, 66, 71–72, 182–83, 206, 208
Simpson, Bradley R., 66
Singapore, 16, 29, 74, 86, 149, 152, 157, 158, 168, 180–82
Singh, Raghunath, 218–19
Sloan Foundation, 222
Smith, Darius C., 155, 304n38
Smith, Paul, 11, 282n42
Smith, Russell G., 8, 58, 83–84, 116, 245, 263, 286n60, 291n80, 291n83, 311n11
Smith, Walter Bedell, 7, 79, 280n7
Social Science Research Council, 58
sociologists, xiii, 73–74, 113–14, 136, 281n12. *See also* American Sociological Association; Chaneles, Sol; Kauffman, Howard
Soviet Union, 46–50, 62, 66–67, 76–77, 143–44, 164, 197, 202–3, 261–62, 308n42; advisors, 30–31; aid programs, 29–31, 66–68, 93–94 177–78, 185; Americans monitoring activities of, 6, 46–50; exchange programs, 20–21, 46–50; propaganda, 161, 164, 165, 199
Spector, Mel, 97
Speier, Hans, 122
Spencer, Robert, 79–80, 86, 290n55
Spiller, Robert, 43
Stanford Research Institute, 28
Stanford University, 58, 61, 142, 277n28, 286n63, 311n11. *See also* Stirling, Wallace
Stern, Sol, 3–4, 212–13, 311n5
Stevenson, Adlai, 133, 311n11
Stewart, James, L., 9, 19, 21–23, 121, 163, 168–72, 175–76, 192–93, 199, 230
Stirling, Wallace, 61
Strategic Hamlet Program, 114–17, 124
Stuart, J. Leighton, 11
students, 11–12, 28–29, 50–57, 75–77, 85–86, 105–14, 135–46, 191–92, 212–13, 220–24. *See also* *Asian Student*; Associated Students of Afghanistan; Foreign Student Advisors Workshop; Foreign Student Leadership Program; Foundation for Youth and Student Affairs; National Association of Foreign Student Advisors; National Student Association (NSA)
Sukarno, xiii, 70, 173, 178, 183, 201, 239, 309n44
Survey: Program Information Service Bulletin, 31–33
Sutton, Francis X., 64, 227–28

Taiwan, 14, 15, 18, 85, 92, 117, 135, 163, 281n18, 286n74
Tax, Sol, 300n49
Taylor, George, 67, 285n60, 287n1
Thailand, 14, 84–85, 97–104, 106–7, 118–20, 123–25, 158, 180–81, 293n44, 293n45; Buddhism in, 32, 78, 82; folk art of, 61; hill tribes of, 31, 61, 97–103, 125, 286n74; Peace Corps in, 73–74. *See also* Tribal Research Centre, Chiang Mai
Thomas, Evan, 295n9
Three Days of the Condor, 255
303 Committee, 210, 232–33, 235, 240–43, 266, 317n19
Tibet, 13, 290n53; Thubten Jigme Norbu, 13
Tribal Research Centre, Chiang Mai, 97–103, 107, 118–19, 120, 124, 261, 271, 293n45
Trotskyism, 62–63
Truman, Harry, 2, 4–7, 67, 305n6
Turner, Wallace, 214–16, 311n8, 311n11

Ulam, Adam, 51
Union of Journalists, 47
Union Press, 29, 150
Union Research Institute, 120, 130
unions. *See* labor unions
United Nations, 55, 57, 97, 100, 169, 171, 187, 188, 204
University of Michigan, 28, 97
US Agency for International Development (USAID). *See* Agency for International Development (AID)
US Department of Defense, 5–6, 9, 24, 25, 106, 117, 141, 249, 297n45, 311n11. *See also* Advanced Research Projects Agency (ARPA); Woods, James L.

US Department of State, 16–18, 115–16, 150–51, 156–57, 170, 227–28, 235–36, 242–46, 251–53; funding of, 53, 105, 231, 233, 238, 248, 268. *See also* Agency for International Development (AID); Economic Stabilization Agency; International Cooperation Administration; US Information Agency; Voice of America

US embassies, xii, 175, 184, 185, 187, 203, 205, 206, 216, 267; and CIA use of embassy pouch, 13, 177; and CIA personnel, 18, 40–41, 138

US Immigration and Naturalization Service, 40, 142

US Information Agency, 67, 225, 226, 236, 289n40

US Information Service, 14, 94, 112, 150–51, 225, 236

Valentine, Allen, 8, 14

Vietnam, 24–25, 54, 56–57, 82–83, 113–17, 124–25, 183, 205–6, 234, 252

Voice of America, 17, 20

Watergate, 4, 255

Weinberg, Jules, 128–30

Welch, Holmes, 81–82, 291n69

West Pakistan, 127, 128, 173–74

Whiting, Allen, 60

Wilbur, Brayton, 8, 10–11, 13, 14, 58, 286n60, 286n62

Williams, (Franklin) Haydn, 8–9, 38, 75, 102, 119–20, 206–9, 242–43, 245, 253–54, 269–70

Wilford, Hugh, x, 163, 278n40

Wisner, Frank, 6–7, 14, 28, 43, 212, 277n15

Wittfogel, Karl, 91, 292n17

Woods, James L., 106

World Affairs Council, xiii, 10, 286n60

World Assembly of Youth, 75–77, 276n10

World Fellowship of Buddhists, 79, 81–83. *See also* Spencer, Robert

World War II. *See* Second World War

Yale University, xi–xii, 9, 24, 153, 177, 285n60

Zellerbach, James, D., 10–11, 311n11

www.ingramcontent.com/pod-product-compliance
Lightning Source LLC
Chambersburg PA
CBHW030605230426
43661CB00053B/1845